FAMILY
LAW

Other books in *Essentials of Canadian Law* Series

Criminal Law

The Law of Evidence

Statutory Interpretation

Media Law

The Law of Trusts

Intellectual Property Law

Income Tax Law

The Law of Partnerships and Corporations

Constitutional Law

Immigration Law

Environmental Law

Young Offenders Law

International Trade Law

Computer Law

The Charter of Rights and Freedoms

ESSENTIALS OF
CANADIAN LAW

FAMILY LAW

SIMON R. FODDEN

Professor of Law
Osgoode Hall Law School, York University

FAMILY LAW

Published in 1999 by
Irwin Law
325 Humber College Blvd.
Toronto, Ontario
M9W 7C3

ISBN: 1-55221-031-6

Canadian Cataloguing in Publication Data

Fodden, Simon
  Family law

(Essentials of Canadian law)
Includes bibliographical references and index.
ISBN 1-55221-031-6

1. Domestic relations – Canada.
I. Title.   II. Series.

KE539.S62 1998   346.7101'5   C98-930584-8
KF505.ZA2F62 1998

Printed and bound in Canada.

1   2   3   4   5   03   02   01   00   99

To Christine Hawkes with love

SUMMARY
TABLE OF CONTENTS

DETAILED
TABLE OF CONTENTS

CHAPTER 13:
SEPARATION AGREEMENTS   293

PREFACE

This small book about family law is written for students of the subject and for practitioners who need a convenient means of refreshing their knowledge. It aims to guide without dictating or giving the false impression of completeness and is a useful starting point.

Family law is a large topic—essentially any and all intersections of the family and the law—and much must be left out in order for a book to remain small. The fact that something such as young offenders or surrogate motherhood or tort actions by dependants is not discussed within these pages does not mean it is unimportant, merely that limited aims must be reflected in omission. And, because family law is divided between federal and provincial jurisdictions, it is only sensible in a book such as this to focus on one province, which is Ontario in this case, but the issues will be very much the same throughout the country.

There must also be compression: as do most textbooks, this one uses a shorthand that speaks as if cases can be reduced to phrases and social context to a line here and there or, worse, to an evocative absence. Texts may mislead the beginner into imagining that there is "law" out there, like some mineral ore, which requires only to be dug up (by drudgery) and refined (by more drudgery) to become useful. This is not true, of course. The truth is there is no escape, thank goodness, from the messy, political—*real*—world, despite any neatness (or drudgery) there may be in these pages. Everything in this work, then, even the one-line ratio, belongs to the realm of power applied, power sought, power considered and rationalized.

Judicial decisions come and sometimes go. Statutes are amended, repealed, replaced. The roil continues. How may a book stay useful? Only by turning out to have been right about which issues will endure in spite of this or that solution. It may be easier to do this in family law than in other areas because of the felt sense that family problems come very close to the basic problems of human nature. There will always be issues of personal loyalty, betrayal, anger and revenge, of loving attachment to children or another adult—in short, issues of self and other. However, while this may be so, the persistence of the broad issues in family law owes as much to the slowness of our current realization that matters of love and its relations are not apolitical, something apart, but are in fact elements of the whole. To give effect to this awareness, language must be redeployed and fundamental linkages built and tested. This procedure takes time.

This book is organized with what is perhaps a lawyer's attraction for pathology, proceeding as it does from union to break-up and eventual settlement, a structure based on function that I have used in my teaching materials since I began some thirty years ago. Part One begins—as many people begin their adult years—with the creation of intimate relations with others, and the law's response to this conduct. (Another book might well begin with the laws touching on conception, abortion, pregnancy, and birth; no more of this springing full-grown from the brow of Zeus—the myth of Athena's birth and the patriarch's reproduction envy.) In Part Two there is a small sampling of the law's involvement in the ongoing family when it fails to serve a member well. It is believed that the law leaves the healthy well enough alone; and while that is a misconception, it is certainly true that lawyers have little business with the smoothly functioning family. Finally, Part Three examines the break-up of the family and the reorganization of relations. Here, traditionally, the practice of law comes into its own.

There are many people to thank. I owe a great deal to my students generally, who teach me far more than they like. Particularly, I gladly acknowledge the help of my research assistants, especially Marie Maron, who was especially helpful with chapter 8 on spousal violence, and also Meghan McCreary, Ravi Jain, and Lauren Shapera. Latterly I have taught family law from a casebook (*Family Law: Cases and Materials*, Osgoode Hall Law School) originally developed by my colleagues Mary Jane Mossman and Brenda Cossman, and revised over the last while by the former; these materials have helped me in many ways, and I recommend them to anyone wishing to pursue an issue in more depth. All the mistakes and infelicities in this book are, of course, of my own making.

February 1999

CHAPTER 1

INTRODUCTION

It is perhaps sensible at the outset to offer an overview of the major issues that recur throughout the subject of family law and throughout this book. These issues do not form the basis for the book's organization and are not always examined elsewhere in it. It may be that, in the chapters that follow, an issue raised here is addressed only in a fractional form, piece by piece in particular contexts, while another is treated more directly and more abstractly. In still other cases, the reader is bound to see portions of the text as dealing with these issues, whether or not that aim was consciously intended.

A. UNDERSTANDING THE FAMILY

The traditional—what some have called "monolithic"[1]—Western understanding of the family is changing. This understanding, which was probably never really an accurate picture of even this part of the world, has a family consisting of a man and a woman, married to each other, and their children, all cohabiting. Change is needed not so much because this no longer describes any family, for clearly it still does, but because this description no longer is adequate or exclusive.

---

1   M. Eichler, *Families in Canada Today: Recent Changes and Their Policy Consequences,* 2d ed. (Toronto: Gage, 1988).

This book does not directly ask: What is a family? The question, put that way certainly, provokes a great deal of hand waving but not much that is useful, since the law does not now, and has rarely ever, used the word "family" as a term of art. But it matters a great deal how clients, lawyers, courts, and other officials understand that institution and its scope, for out of this sense of what is "normal" or, at least, within the range of acceptable human behaviour, will come the permissions and prohibitions that allocate power.

The relatively high divorce rate over the last few decades has compelled us to acknowledge that it is possible, and may be desirable, for children to have more than two parents. The increased interest in children has begun to shift our understanding of what it means to be a parent away from "blood" ties towards a social and psychological relationship. As serial monogamy becomes widespread, we acknowledge, but do not yet adequately grapple with, the fact that spouses accumulate. So, fractioning and recombination do their work. Relations multiply.

Mores change. Sex and sexuality are more openly discussed today than they were even decades ago, with the consequence that we come to accept that normality is simply whatever people do, and people do a wider variety of things than it was permitted once to know. Particularly, homosexuality is acknowledged; and many (but not all[2]) gays and lesbians are knocking on the doors of marriage and other closed rooms in the family mansion. As settled institutions change or are repositioned to respond to demands from same-sex couples, other basic questions arise and invite answers.[3]

As well, longer lives mean that larger and extended families will become more common than they have been of late. Old parents may need to be supported and may have to sue for it. Grandparents want rights to see their grandchildren. And others will likely discover a need for stronger links to the centre, wherever that is conceived to be. If the nuclear family is not being split, it is being re-bonded to the rest.

---

2   D. Herman, "Are We Family? Lesbian Rights and Women's Liberation" (1990) 28 O.H.L.J. 789; but see also W. Rubenstein, "We Are Family: A Reflection on the Search for Legal Recognition of Lesbian and Gay Relationships" (1991) 8 J. L. & Pol. 89.

3   Speaking of sex, some commentators question our basing of "family" on the erotic adult pair-bond and suggest instead the nurturer-dependant relationship (literally and metaphorically: mother and child) as the core around which other persons should be grouped. See, for example, M. Fineman, *The Neutered Mother, The Sexual Family, and Other Twentieth Century Tragedies* (New York: Routledge, 1995).

Finally, this country has yet to take recent immigration fully into account. The cities, at least, continue to become increasingly cosmopolitan and are home to a wide variety of customs and practices respecting the family. Some of these customs and practices will come to be reflected in law, and many will doubtless play a role in the reformulation of our understanding of family.

B. WOMEN CLAIMING POWER

For many decades now families and family law have been sites for the battle between the sexes. The struggle by women to obtain their rightful share of economic and political power goes on and continues to mark the nature of family law in almost every respect. Despite gender-neutral rules, inequality persists; courts and legislatures learn that one set of phrases does not fit all, and that true law reform requires language that explicitly takes gender into account. But the way is still not certain—or certainly not agreed upon.

We learn, too, although it has yet to be reflected widely in judicial decisions or statutes, that our conceptual separation of the family and the marketplace is misleading.[4] Public and private interrelate—are mutually constituting—and the apparent distinction serves the interests of the powerful.

Thus, for example, the issues of "who must and who may not work" and "what is the proper pay for work done" become married to issues of "who must and who may care for children" and "how will caregivers be paid."

C. CITIZEN CHILD

The role of children is undergoing re-examination and change. Children are now the largest group in our society that does not participate immediately in the political process or in employment. As "non-market" beings, in theory at least, children have an uncertain position before the law. Where once it was clear that parents spoke for children, it is now sometimes declared that parents have no rights to their children,[5] and all

---

4   See F.E. Olsen, "The Family and the Market: A Study of Ideology and Legal Reform" (1983) 96 Harv. L. Rev. 1497.

5   See, for example, *Racine* v. *Woods*, [1983] 2 S.C.R. 173 at 174.

is to be child-centred. Children were "property," we are told (never true, but never mind),[6] and now they are not. But what are they, then?

Some would accord children the full set of legal rights, or as full a set as each child can manage. Others argue that our protracted childhood is valuable and important and ought to be protected. In law this means we are uncertain about whether and when children ought to be involved in processes that concern them, and when involved, what procedures are necessary to accommodate their special needs.

We have increasingly chosen to examine ourselves through our children, with the consequence that they are at times constructed as "other" and "different." Thus, child development specialists become ever more important in our legal and other dealings with children. And laws continue to incorporate the results of experts' studies and practical insight.

At the same time, we leave children in poverty and abuse them physically and sexually, and we present them with large unemployment rates as they depart the special land of childhood for the privileges of full citizenship: we are ambivalent about children, as perhaps about ourselves, but do not always show that we understand the fact of our ambivalence.

D.   BELONGING

It is possible to see much of family law as about belonging. But families are not the only groups to which we belong. Races, religions, nations, tribes, cultures, and communities all may claim us for their own. And when, in the course of exploring an issue in family law, questions of belonging and relation emerge, it becomes possible—or necessary—to ask what role should be given to these "suprafamilial" groups, what account should be taken of their interests. When a child is adopted and changes families, is the child also deracinated? When does a child have a religion—or a religion have the child? May a person from a different land or culture be permitted to continue cultural practices that are at odds with mainstream local values?

Family law is a good occasion to examine the law's difficulty with groups. Rights are held by individuals; this is the basic structure. But how then should the law respect the reality of family (and other group) life, in which ties to others—relationships—are complex and intersecting? (Law is arithmetic: add one person to a family of five and there will

---

6   See P. Aries, *Centuries of Childhood: A Social History of Family Life*, trans. R. Baldick (New York: Vintage Books, 1962).

be one more individual; family is geometric: add that one person to a family of five and there will be five new relationships.) What would a true law of families look like?

E. LEGAL STRUCTURE

Finally, it is worth noting that the very structure of law—at least as classically imagined—is often felt to be inappropriate to the solution of family problems, that there is something almost oxymoronic about the phrase "family law": family is all about subjectivity, emotional expression, privacy, treating each person differently, continuing relationship; law is all about objectivity, reason, public debate, rules of general application, and strangers, or perhaps neighbours. Neither caricature is true, of course; however, there is a strong sense in which the form of the law has had to be changed in order to deal with families. Thus, discretion rather than rule is the order of the day in most areas; special family courts are created; social science and health professionals are routinely consulted; mediation and conciliation are encouraged; and the proper role of counsel is debated, especially where representation of children is concerned.

PART ONE

FORMATION OF LEGAL RELATIONS

This part examines the various ways in which the law does and does not accord legal consequences to family relationships. It is true that to a degree social relations between people are chosen or avoided on the basis of whether or not the law recognizes them. But it is more true to say that the law lags and does not usually lead in this area: people tend to live together or have children for reasons that in the first instance have little to do with the law. However, it can be important to know whether or not a relationship once formed—or merely contemplated—in fact gives rise to legal consequences. If only as a secondary matter, then, the law can have a serious impact on family relationships.

Chapter 2 looks at formal marriage. Here, with some significant exceptions, the law does not set up obstacles or strictures that bind uncomfortably, but rather provides for a loose regime of rituals to mark a change of legal status. Law is seen in its now rare ceremonial function, and the important questions may be directed more to social practice than to any necessary legal hurdles. As far as legal rights are concerned, marriage accomplishes little that could not be arranged in other ways: strictly speaking, legal marriage is unneccessary.

Chapter 3 deals with the role of contract as a means of establishing legal family relations between adults. Once restricted to ante-nuptial agreements among the rich, contracts are now available as well to unmarried couples who wish to live together outside marriage.

Chapter 4 explains how cohabitation leads to legal relation. The chapter examines the ways in which conduct alone, unsanctified by ceremony and unordered by contract, can give rise to legal rights and obligations between adults. That critical modern term "spouse" is introduced and its difficulties explored.

Chapter 5 brings us to the initiation of relations between adults and children, the most important of which is parentage. Conduct leads to parentage in law, both the act of reproduction and the treatment of another's child as a child of your family.

Chapter 6 continues to examine the establishment of legal relations between adults and children by focusing on adoption. Not an institution native to the common law, this statutory and relatively modern process is the formal (half ceremonial, half contractual) way in which an adult and child may establish a legal relationship. Once important, perhaps, to rescue children from orphanages and to provide children for adults unable to procreate, it may no longer serve the same functions.

CHAPTER 2

MARRIAGE

A. INTRODUCTION

This chapter might be entitled "Marriage and Annulment" because the law of marriage and the law of annulment are, for the most part, two sides of the same coin. From the legal point of view at least, a valid marriage is one that cannot be annulled; and so the requirements for a valid marriage, when slightly restated, become the grounds for nullity. In the material that follows, the "positive" view is generally taken, and rules are expressed as requirements for validity of marriage. It is sensible to give primacy to the law of marriage because there are some legal requirements that touch marriage but are directory only and do not affect validity or annulment, and also because a great many people get married but very few obtain annulments.

The law of marriage is the only aspect of family law that has not been thoroughly reformed in recent times. As a consequence, aspects of its policy make an ill-fitting garment for society, and the intellectual armature on which it hangs strikes the modern lawyer as quaint, if not downright archaic. This structure sports a number of dichotomies, or pairs of categories, three of which will be relevant here and require some treatment in this introduction: a political pair, a theoretical pair, and a consequential pair.

1) The Division of Powers

The political dichotomy is a function of the division of legislative powers between the federal and provincial governments. Section 91(26) of the *Constitution Act, 1867,* gives the federal Parliament power to make laws respecting "marriage and divorce"; section 92(12) gives the provinces power over "the solemnization of marriage."[1] Judicial attempts to make sense of this distinction adopted a "form" and "substance" interpretation, such that provinces are said to have power to make laws respecting the formal requirements of marriage, while matters of substance belong to Parliament.[2]

Parliament and the provincial legislatures have used their powers in very different ways. The provinces have kept their Marriage Acts more or less in touch with societal needs for the sensible reason that the public has most contact with the formal or ceremonial aspects of marriage law. The federal law of marriage, however, is, with the exception of one area, seriously out of date.

There is no federal legislation that sets out nationwide laws. Each province derives its federal marriage law, that is, those aspects concerning matters of "substance," as a result of the historical reception of base law into the jurisdiction. This original received law is nowhere spelled out, of course, and (except for Quebec) must be constructed from the English common law and statutes obtaining at the time of reception. Thus, federal marriage law is old, foreign, and uncertain.

2) Ontario's Federal Law

An examination of the slightly unusual circumstance of Ontario makes this situation clear. What is now Ontario received English base law as of 1792.[3] Properly understood, this statute ought to have imported the same ability to deal with marriage as existed in England. However, it

---

1   *Constitution Act, 1867* (U.K.), 30 & 31 Vict., c. 3.
2   Be aware, however, that it is not always possible to rely on one's intuitive sense of "form" and "substance" to determine which matters belong to which jurisdiction, as we shall see below. And it is important not to imagine that "substance" is necessarily more important to the law than "form": the courts have decided that it is within the power of the province to pass laws that invalidate marriages for want of form. As we shall see, however, it is a vexed question whether any aspect of Ontario's statute ought to be interpreted as making actual use of that power.
3   The first parliament of Upper Canada passed 32 Geo. III (1792), c. 1. In its current manifestation, the reception statute is the *Property and Civil Rights Act*, R.S.O. 1990, c. P.29, s. 1.

was repeatedly held by the Ontario Supreme Court that, not being the equivalent of the English Ecclesiastical Court, it lacked the jurisdiction to entertain suits to annul marriages for "substantial" failures. It had power, it declared, to decide on the validity of a marriage when that question was raised incidentally in another matter (whether in respect of property or civil rights or in a criminal matter) and a power to declare a marriage void for want of form, since that power was at the time specifically conferred upon it by valid provincial legislation. But it could not annul a marriage with respect to any matter over which the federal Parliament had power to legislate.[4] As a result, Ontarians lacked a fully functioning annulment law.

This odd situation continued for well over a hundred years, until, in 1930, Parliament passed the *Divorce Act (Ontario) 1930*,[5] now the *Annulment of Marriages Act (Ontario)*.[6] This statute did two things that concern us here: it made clear that the Supreme Court of Ontario did indeed have the jurisdiction which it had always denied itself, and it changed the marriage law that applied (in Ontario alone), importing the law of England as it existed on 15 July 1870. So, in Ontario, to discover the actual content of the federal law respecting marriage, it is necessary to research English law that is more than a century and a quarter old.

Moreover, this reception statute truly fixes the law at 15 July 1870:

> The law of England as to the annulment of marriage, as that law existed on the 15th day of July 1870, in so far as it can be made to apply in the Province of Ontario, and *in so far as it has not been repealed, as to the Province, by any Act of . . . the Parliament of Canada . . ., and as altered, varied, modified or affected, as to the Province, by any such Act,* is in force in the Province of Ontario.[7] [Emphasis added.]

Thus, Ontario courts cannot pursue the changes in English law since 1870; and neither, it seems, can they make the received English law their own to develop judicially because the power to cause the law to be "altered, varied, modified or affected" appears to be within the sole purview of Parliament.

---

4   See *Ranger v. Ranger* (1920), 18 O.W.N. 66 (C.A.); and *Vamvakidis v. Kirkoff*, [1930] 2 D.L.R. 877 (Ont. C.A.).
5   S.C. 1930, c. 14.
6   R.S.C. 1970, c. A-14. This Act continues in force as "unconsolidated [in the 1985 consolidation] but not repealed."
7   *Ibid.*, s. 2.

Because of this federal failure to produce explicit, modern rules, the provinces, including Ontario, exercised their power over "solemnization of marriage" by legislating Marriage Acts that attempt to fill the void; and, so, many of the provisions of the Ontario *Marriage Act*[8] are arguably *ultra vires* the province,[9] dealing as they essentially do with matters of substance rather than form.

3) Essence and Form

In addition to the dichotomy that describes the division of powers, there is a theoretical dichotomy that classically separates the rules governing validity of marriage into those going to "essential" validity and those going to "formal" validity. Matters of essential validity address the legal and personal capacity of the persons marrying, whereas those relating to formal validity, as might be supposed, deal by and large with ritual and bureaucratic requirements. A discussion of these matters forms the major content of this chapter.

4) Void and Voidable

Failure to meet the requirements of a valid marriage may render that marriage void *ab initio* or voidable only. This distinction, once of importance in old English law, remains with us to some degree, even though it serves no clearly discernible modern social purpose. Briefly put, a marriage that is void *ab initio* is one that never existed; that is, it is no marriage at all and gives rise to no legal consequences. Such "non-marriages" strictly speaking need no court decision to annul them or to declare them void; even so, those caught in such a situation may well be reluctant to proceed to another marriage without the sanction of a court judgment. Marriages that are voidable only give rise to legal consequences and are valid, subsisting marriages unless and until a court pronounces them null and void.

The fuller discussion that occurs below[10] addresses the matter of which defects render marriages void *ab initio* and which voidable only, and goes into the different consequences in more detail.

---

8   R.S.O. 1990, c. M.3, as amended by S.O. 1994, c. 27, s. 89(2).

9   See section B(2)(a)(iv), "Shadow Sections," in this chapter.

10   See section C(1), "The Void-Voidable Distinction," in this chapter.

B. THE REQUIREMENTS OF A VALID MARRIAGE

1) Essential Validity

a) Sexual Capacity

The parties to a marriage must have the capacity to consummate it;[11] that is, they must be able to engage in sexual intercourse, and the lack of this power may render a marriage voidable. The capacity must exist at the time of the marriage.[12] Typically, a plaintiff will rely on the inability of the marriage partner, but it is possible to plead one's own inability to consummate.[13] It may be important to note that although the law's original concern here was likely with the ability of the parties to procreate, sterility *per se* is not a ground for annulment.[14]

Inability to consummate a marriage renders it voidable only.[15] Although the void/voidable dichotomy is examined below, it is important to touch on certain aspects of that distinction here because of their application in the context of consummation. A marriage that is merely voidable may be challenged only by the parties to it, and only during their joint lives. This restriction is appropriate in the sexual context and permits parties to a marriage to decide for themselves whether or not they are aggrieved by the inability of one of them to have sexual intercourse. As well, the defence of insincerity is available where a challenged marriage is voidable only. This defence permits the argument that a plaintiff is not truly aggrieved by the partner's lack of sexual capacity but is merely using it to achieve an ulterior aim, that of obtaining

---

11   There is a common misconception that "non-consummation" is a ground for annulment: the law requires merely that sexual capacity be present, not that it be used. See, generally, J. David Fine, "Annulment of Marriage for Impotence in the Common Law of Canada" (1973) 8 R.F.L. 129.

12   *Napier* v. *Napier*, [1915] P. 184 at 190. Obviously, the capacity is not in actual fact demonstrated until some time after the moment the ceremony is performed; but the subsequent consummation or failure of consummation is taken as evidence of the capacity or its lack at the earlier, legally critical time. Thus, the fact that a party did or did not have the capacity prior to marriage is relevant only insofar as it goes to capacity at the time of ceremony.

13   See, for example, *D.* v. *D.*, [1973] 3 O.R. 82 (H.C.); *Gajamugan* v. *Gajamugan* (1979), 10 R.F.L. (2d) 280 (Ont. H.C.).

14   *Tice* v. *Tice* (1936), [1937] O.R. 233, aff'd [1937] 2 D.L.R. 591 (C.A.).

15   *D.* v. *D.*, above note 13. It is, indeed, the sole ground for annulment that indisputably renders a marriage voidable only. Although there are others that likely do, cases can be found in each instance that say the other grounds render the marriage void *ab initio*.

freedom from the marriage.[16] Proof that a plaintiff knew of the sexual incapacity at the time of marriage but went ahead with the ceremony even so might be the clearest evidence of insincerity.[17] Thus, it becomes possible, in spite of the requirement of sexual capacity, for persons to contract companionate marriages that are beyond challenge.[18]

Perhaps the commonest physical expressions of sexual incapacity are, for men, the inability to obtain a penile erection or to sustain an erection long enough to permit penetration, and, for women, a septum or an obstruction of the vagina through vaginismus such that the admission of the penis is impossible or painful.[19]

The law does not care about the cause of the incapacity. It may be the result of organic illness, congenital condition, or psychological disturbance. Moreover, the psychologically based impotence may exist with respect to the marriage partner but not with respect to other persons,[20] and yet may form the basis for a nullity action.

There is scant interest in developing any aspect of nullity law today, given the ease with which judicial divorce is available as a means of becoming free of the bonds of marriage.[21] It might seem necessary, however, to retain some law of annulment if only as the logical consequence of having rules governing valid marriage; even then, it would be hard to justify keeping the requirement that parties be able to consummate the marriage as part of any reformed law of annulment. For one thing, it is no longer necessary to get at the matter of fertility through the proxy of the functioning of the external sexual organs. If a law was wanted enabling parties to obtain an annulment upon discovering that their spouses were sterile, which seems highly unlikely, it could now be framed far more directly. Otherwise it is likely the case that citizens do

---

16 See *Norman v. Norman* (1979), 9 R.F.L. (2d) 345 (Ont. U.F.C.).

17 See *H. v. H.,* [1927] 3 D.L.R. 481 (Alta. C.A.).

18 See *Foster* v. *Foster,* [1953] 2 D.L.R. 318 (B.C.). Otherwise, it might not be possible for some old or disabled people to marry without anxiety about possible nullity actions.

19 Intercourse need not be "impossible" but only "impractical": *D.* v. *A.* (1845), 1 Rob. Ecc. 279, 163 E.R. 1039. In earlier times, especially before judicial divorce became commonly available, this ground was much relied upon by those seeking the ability to remarry, probably because it turned on private acts that might depend for proof almost entirely on the evidence of the parties themselves. There was some anxious concern in the jurisprudence as to exactly what might amount to consummation.

20 See *Gajamugan,* above note 13. In men this condition is known as impotence *quoad hanc,* and in women, impotence *quoad hunc.*

21 See section A(1), "A Brief History," in chapter 9, "Divorce."

not wish this form of state interference with respect to sexual practices within marriage.

b) Sexual Difference

It *is* currently a matter of debate whether the law does or ought to require that parties to a marriage be of different sexes. There is no such traditional requirement; that is, the law of England as of 1870[22] had never confronted the question,[23] and so there is no explicit requirement as a part of our law that parties to marriage must be of opposite sexes. Any rule on the point must, then, be derived as a matter of historical and social analysis.

The leading case in Ontario at the time of writing is *Layland v. Beaulne and Ontario (Minister of Consumer & Commercial Relations)*.[24] This was an application by two men for judicial review of a clerk's refusal to issue them a marriage licence.[25] The majority of the Divisional Court bench examined the two (trial court level) Canadian cases[26] and

---

22 See *Annulment of Marriages Act (Ontario)*, above note 6.

23 But see "Nullity of Marriage," 10 *Encyclopaedia of the Laws of England*, 2d ed., at 90: "To put the most extreme case, a ceremony of marriage performed between two persons of the same sex would, by the law of nature, and by all laws human and divine, be nothing but a mockery and absolute nullity" quoted, *obiter*, in *Barnet (otherwise MacKay) v. Barnet*, [1934] O.R. 155 (H.C.).

24 (1993), 14 O.R. (3d) 658 (Div. Ct.) [*Layland*].

25 Section 8(4) of the *Marriage Act*, above note 8, provides for judicial review of a refusal to issue a licence. Note that the basic issue of substance in *Layland*, above note 24, has to do with the parties' capacity to marry, which is *ultra vires* the province; and, so, it would seem that no clerk could properly refuse a licence on grounds that lie within federal legislative jurisdiction. However, the majority judgment simply proceeded to address the question of whether two men have the capacity to marry. (The judgment makes clear that the Minister of Community and Social Services took no position on an alleged *Charter* violation, "because capacity to marry is a matter within the exclusive legislative authority of the Parliament of Canada," above note 24 at 660.) Indeed, both the majority and the dissent fail to deal competently with the nature of the law under review, treating it as if it were simply "the common law of Canada" instead of statute-based law having a peculiar character. (See section A(2), "Ontario's Federal Law," in this chapter.) Greer J., in dissent, observes correctly that Ontario's *Marriage Act* "makes no reference to sexual orientation," but fails to address the issue of law-making jurisdiction; and she then goes on to say that, "[t]he *other* statute which affects marriages is the Marriage (Prohibited Degrees) Act . . ." (emphasis added). No mention whatever is made in the judgment of the central federal statute, the *Annulment of Marriages Act (Ontario)* (above note 6).

26 *North v. Matheson* (1974), 20 R.F.L. 112 (Man. Co. Ct.); *C.(L.) v. C.(C.)* (1992), 10 O.R. (3d) 254 (Gen. Div.).

the major English case[27] on the point, and concluded that "under the common law of Canada applicable to Ontario . . . persons of the same sex do not have the capacity to marry one another."[28] There was more discovery involved in this finding than there was reasoning, the court essentially deciding that what was apparently the case (i.e., an absence of approved homosexual marriages) was therefore right.

This essentialist view was not shaken by scrutiny of the *Charter*.[29] Southey J., for the majority, held that "the common law limitation of marriage to persons of the opposite sex does not constitute discrimination against the applicants contrary to s. 15."[30] He decided that "[u]nions of persons of the same sex are not 'marriages', because of the definition of marriage."[31] Any success under section 15 would "bring about a change in the definition of marriage. I do not think the *Charter* has that effect."[32] And in a pronouncement that would be worthy of Anatole France[33] if one could be certain of any irony, Southey J. said: "The law does not prohibit marriage by homosexuals provided it takes place between persons of the opposite sex."[34]

Greer J., in dissent, was of the view that the refusal to issue a marriage licence violated the applicants' section 15 *Charter* rights and that this violation could not be justified under section 1.[35] She also decided that "there is no common law prohibition against same-sex marriages in Canada."[36] This latter conclusion seems based on her view that "the common law must grow to meet society's expanding needs,"[37] with the *Charter* as a fac-

---

27   *Corbett v. Corbett (Ashley) (No. 2)*, [1970] 2 All E.R. 33 (P.D. & A. Div.).

28   *Layland*, above note 24 at 663.

29   *Canadian Charter of Rights and Freedoms*, Part I of the *Constitution Act, 1982*, being Schedule B to the *Canada Act 1982* (U.K.), 1982, c. 11 [*Charter*].

30   *Layland*, above note 24 at 667. The characteristic of sexual preference is "not irrelevant" to the restriction of marriage because of a principal purpose of that institution to produce and care for children, unable to be achieved "as a general rule" in a homosexual union: at 666.

31   *Ibid*. at 667.

32   *Ibid*.

33   Who observed that the law forbids rich and poor alike from sleeping under bridges: *Le Lys Rouge*, chapter 7.

34   *Layland*, above note 24 at 666.

35   *Ibid*. at 681. She finds the applicants to be members of a group that has been seriously disadvantaged by society, and within that broader context the denial of a marriage licence is burdensome discriminatory treatment; and this discrimination cannot be justified because "it is surely in the interest of the state to foster all family relationships, be they heterosexual or same-sex relationships."

36   *Ibid*. at 668.

37   *Ibid*. at 678.

tor affecting that growth.[38] She says, too, that if it were found that it did prohibit same-sex marriage, it could not withstand *Charter* scrutiny.[39]

c) Capacity to Consent

At the time of the ceremony the parties must possess the mental capacity to consent to marriage. Mental capacity may be affected by mental illness,[40] developmental disability,[41] age,[42] or intoxication.[43] It has been said that marriage does not require a high level of understanding, and indeed there is a case in which a man was first found (by a jury) not to possess the mental capacity to make a will, but subsequently found (by a judge) to have sufficient mental capacity to marry.[44]

Lack of mental capacity renders a marriage void *ab initio*;[45] however, some courts adopted the curious notion that a person who recovered mental capacity could affirm the void marriage and make it valid.[46] And it would appear that this unusual doctrine has been confused with the defence of insincerity, which has led some courts to say lack of mental capacity renders a marriage voidable only.[47]

The rule about mental capacity is a manifestation of the basic requirement in contract law, and indeed in civil law generally, that a person must have an appropriate degree of mental functioning in order to be held accountable for an act. As in other areas, courts have little difficulty stating this requirement but find it nearly impossible to elaborate on it in any way that will be generally useful.

---

38 *Ibid.* at 674. The "growth" of this "common law" may not be possible in quite the way Greer J. seems to assume; an argument can be made that it is not true common law, which is capable of modification by judges over time. It is rather statute law that, instead of spelling out its provisions in so many words, enacts a "snapshot" of English common law taken at one moment, and then reserves the power of change to Parliament: see above note 25. The more accurate approach would be to determine what the law of England was in 1870, and if it was found to prohibit homosexual marriage, to declare that law in violation of the *Charter*.

39 *Layland, ibid.* at 680.

40 *Chertkow v. Feinstein*, [1929] 3 D.L.R. 339 (Alta. C.A.), aff'd [1930] 1 D.L.R. 137 (S.C.C.).

41 *Durham v. Durham* (1885), 10 P.D. 80.

42 *Re McElroy* (1978), [1979] 22 O.R. (2d) 381 (Surr. Ct.).

43 *Roblin v. Roblin* (1881), 28 Gr. 439 (Ont. Ct. Chanc.); *Meilen v. Andersson* (1977), 6 A.R. 427 (T.D.).

44 *Estate of Park; Park v. Park*, [1953] 2 All E.R. 408, aff'd [1953] 2 All E.R. 1411.

45 *Capon v. McLay*, [1965] 2 O.R. 83 (C.A.).

46 See H.R. Hahlo, *Nullity of Marriage in Canada* (Toronto: Butterworths, 1979) at 38.

47 See C. Davies, *Family Law in Canada: Fourth Edition of Power on Divorce and Other Matrimonial Causes* (Toronto: Carswell, 1984) at 65.

In an oft-cited judgment, it is said that the capacity to marry is "[a] capacity to understand the nature of the contract, and the duties and responsibilities which it creates."[48] What is not so often quoted is what follows in the case as to the content of understanding concerning marriage:

> It is an engagement between a man and woman to live together, and love one another as husband and wife, to the exclusion of all others. This is expanded in the promises of the marriage ceremony by words having reference to the natural relations which spring from that engagement, such as protection on the part of the man, and submission on the part of the woman.[49]

The point here is not that views about marriage have changed—they clearly have—but rather that mental capacity can be judged by views as to what marriage is, and that content is not as clear today as it once may have been.

The typical legal concept of understanding (and, thus, mental capacity) employed here is a highly rationalist one that gives little scope to emotional or feeling-based understanding. On the one hand, the capacity to have an intellectual understanding of marriage is appropriate as the standard, given that the parties will not, in theory at least, have had any experience with marriage;[50] they are seeking to marry, after all. On the other hand, marriage is now seen as a forum for the expression of the emotional sides of our being, and a merely rational understanding is evidently no guide to the true or full nature of the institution.

d) Freedom of Consent

Consent to marry must be given freely at the time of the ceremony. Thus, duress is a ground for annulment.[51] The essence of duress is that a party's will is overborne as a result of fear or oppression.[52] As with mental incapacity, lack of consent because of duress should render the

---

48   *Durham v. Durham* (1885), 10 P.D. 80 at 82.

49   *Ibid.*

50   Today, however, it is far more common than it was in the England of 1870, say, that people who marry for the first time will have some experience with intimate relationships with others: in 1991, for example, nearly 1.5 million people were living together outside marriage; a quarter of all these unions were in Ontario, while over 40 percent were in Quebec. (Statistics Canada, Demography Division)

51   *Pascuzzi v. Pascuzzi*, [1955] O.W.N. 853 (H.C.); *Truong v. Malia* (1975), 25 R.F.L. 256 (Ont. H.C.).

52   *S.(A.) v. S.(A.)* (1988), 65 O.R. (2d) 174 (U.F.C.).

marriage void *ab initio*;[53] however, some courts have recently ruled that it makes marriages voidable only.[54]

In assessing whether the consenting party exercised a sufficiently free will, the court must consider the particular circumstances, character, and age of the party:[55] the question is not whether a particular act or course of conduct would have deprived the reasonable person of the ability to consent freely, but whether it so deprived this person. That said, it must be noted that an element of "objective" judgment is always present in such cases, whether as a matter of credibility or otherwise; and it is not easy to know whether a particular set of pressures brought to bear on a person will be thought to justify a finding of duress.

This tension between the "subjective" and "objective" aspects of this issue reflects a more fundamental tension between policies that might underlie marriage law generally. It is sometimes said that the aim of the requirements for marriage, or some of them at least, is the protection of the institution of marriage. Thus, courts once said that these requirements ought to be interpreted strictly, so marriage could not be too easily dissolved.[56] The notion is that if the institution of marriage is clearly defined and not easily attacked, the public good will be advanced because of the resulting stability of unions and because of the peace of mind of the parties to such strong marriages generally. Another view of the aim of marriage law—the more modern view—has it that what these rules are about is the protection of the particular individuals within a marriage. In this view, the requirements should be interpreted in a given case so as to minimize the harm to the parties to the suit. Both approaches sketched here aim ultimately at the good of citizens, of course; but the former conceives that this goal is best achieved through the instrument of an institution, whereas the latter goes more directly to the personal circumstances of the litigants in a case at bar.[57]

---

53   See section B(1)(c), "Capacity to Consent," in this chapter.
54   See, for example, *S.(A.)* v. *S.(A.)*, above note 52.
55   *Ibid.* And see *Pascuzzi* v. *Pascuzzi*, above note 51.
56   See, for example, *Scott* v. *Sebright* (1886), 12 P.D. 21.
57   This tension is itself evidently a manifestation of that central tension in law between "order" and "justice"; and, less grandly, it is a part of the movement identified by Maine from "status" to "contract": Sir H.S. Maine, *Ancient Law* (London & Toronto: J.M. Dent & Sons, Ltd.; New York: E.P. Dutton & Co., 1917). More concretely, this tension may be seen in the issue of whether a particular defect ought to render a marriage void *ab initio* or merely voidable: see section C(1), "The Void-Voidable Distinction," in this chapter.

e) Requisite Age

Persons below a certain age lack the capacity to marry. Although a concern about youth might have been subsumed under the more general (and flexible) requirement of capacity to consent, the law has always chosen to set precise age limits.[58] Astonishingly, the present law is that girls of twelve and boys of fourteen have the capacity to marry.[59] The law of England as of 1870, and so the law in Ontario today, holds that the marriage of a child under seven is void *ab initio*, but that the marriage of a girl between the ages of seven and twelve or a boy between the ages of seven and fourteen is voidable only.[60] A marriage that is voidable for nonage may be ratified when the child becomes of age—that is, twelve or fourteen.[61]

It is perhaps worth spelling out the consequences of this law in a bit of detail, so that its true impact can be appreciated. Not only does it mean that a fourteen-year-old may marry, but it means further that if a child under twelve (but older than seven) were to marry, because the marriage would be voidable only, it could not be challenged by anyone (parents, for example) other than the parties to it themselves. It must be said that the likelihood of children of this age marrying is small indeed; even so, the state of this law is deplorable and reflects no aspect of current social policy.

This unsatisfactory state of affairs is complicated in three respects. First, it seems unlikely that the blatantly unequal treatment of girls and boys in this rule could withstand a challenge under the *Charter*. One would be hard-pressed to argue that this different treatment is justifiable under section 1, given that the whole discussion would take place in the context of a law that permits marriages between children who are simply too young, whether the age of twelve or the age of fourteen were to be picked as applicable to both sexes.

Second, the province of Ontario has exercised its legislative power to require parental consent before children of sixteen and seventeen

---

58   This is an illustration of a rule going to the protection of the institution of marriage rather than to the protection of the individuals within a particular marriage. A rule requiring maturity would concern itself with the safety or happiness of the individuals, but would make it difficult to determine with any degree of certainty whether a marriage was legally valid or not, and thus would make parties' status unclear, with attendant insecurity.

59   *Kerr v. Kerr*, [1934] S.C.R. 72 at 77.

60   *Legebokoff v. Legebokoff* (1982), 28 R.F.L. (2d) 212 at 215 (B.C.S.C.).

61   *Ibid.*; and *Kerr v. Kerr*, above note 59.

years of age may marry.[62] This may prevent some children who are too young from marrying, where parents withhold consent; however, it is also possible that parents may give consent and thus facilitate the marriage of youthful parties.

The third, and related, complication is that Ontario has also provided that a marriage licence may simply not be issued to a child under sixteen.[63] It is probably beyond the power of the province to fail to provide for the marriage of a person who has the capacity to marry, which is a determination proper to federal law. A province may regulate the marriage of children, by providing that parental consent is required,[64] but to regulate is to contemplate permission; and Ontario has decided that this would be too irresponsible a stand for a modern government to take, with respect to the marriage of children younger than sixteen.

The provincial rules that apparently prevent youthful marriage are effective, even if unconstitutional, because the public, unlikely to know of the existence of an "unwritten" federal law of marriage, let alone the contents of such a law, will typically take the more readily accessible provincial law for the whole legal truth. Even were a young person to learn of his or her capacity to marry, a costly, time-consuming legal challenge would be unlikely to ensue.[65]

f) Lack of Close Relationship

One may not marry a person who has too close a genetic relationship. Originally, the law proscribed marriage within what were known as the prohibited degrees of consanguinity and affinity, essentially a long list of persons related by "blood" or marriage.[66] But in 1990 Parliament passed legislation[67] replacing this old set of proscriptions based in religion

---

62 *Marriage Act*, above note 8, s. 5(2). See section B(2)(a), "The Ontario *Marriage Act*," in this chapter, for a discussion of provincial requirements generally. Perhaps counter-intuitively, parental consent was regarded in England as a matter of form rather than substance; and consequently, it has been held *intra vires* the province to make laws respecting it, under the provincial power to legislate respecting "solemnization of marriage."

63 *Marriage Act*, above note 8, s. 5(2).

64 Above note 62.

65 Simply lying about age might still be possible, of course. See *Clause* v. *Clause*, [1956] 5 D.L.R. (2d) 286 (H.C.), where the parties lied under oath on the application for a licence concerning the need for parental consent, and yet the marriage was held valid because they had the capacity to marry.

66 This was derived from Archbishop Parker's Table of 1563, which in turn was printed in the Book of Common Prayer of the Church of England. See *Seidler* v. *Mackie*, [1929] 4 D.L.R. 478 (Alta. S.C.).

67 *Marriage (Prohibited Degrees) Act*, S.C. 1990, c. 46.

with a simple scheme constructed almost entirely upon close genetic relationship. The main change effected by the legislation is the repeal of all prohibitions based on affinity, that is, relationship through marriage.[68] Now only a marriage between persons who are related

(a) lineally by consanguinity or adoption;
(b) as brother and sister by consanguinity, whether by the whole blood or by the half-blood; or
(c) as brother and sister by adoption[69]

is void.[70]

The "lineal" relationship, although not defined in the legislation, must describe the link between a person and his or her direct genetic forebears (parents, grandparents, great-grandparents, etc.) and direct genetic descendants (children, grandchildren, great-grandchildren, etc.).[71] Thus, for example, it is now permissible for a step-parent and step-child to marry. Note that this law clarifies the status of adopted persons in this respect, treating them exactly the same as persons born into the relevant family relationships.

Our concern about closeness of relationship in marriage partners most likely has in part to do with the incest taboo.[72] There is also a modern public health concern about inbreeding that seems to explain most of the content of the new law, with marriage here acting as a surrogate for procreation. There can, of course, be no real genetic concerns about adopted persons, and their inclusion should be seen as assisting provin-

---

68   *Ibid.*, s. 3(1).

69   *Ibid.*, s. 2(2). It is unfortunate that in a modern statute the ancient and emotive metaphor was used in which blood ("consanguinity" and "whole or half blood") represents the biological relationship that can exist between family members.

70   *Ibid.*, s. 3(2). It seems that this means the purported marriage would be void *ab initio* and not merely voidable.

71   See the Form (O.Reg. 726/91, s. 1) attendant to the Ontario *Marriage Act*, above note 8, s. 19, which helpfully, though without any constitutional authority, spells out in named relationships what the federal legislation describes functionally: "A man may not marry his 1. Grandmother 2. Mother 3. Daughter 4. Sister 5. Granddaughter . . ."

72   To say this is perhaps to explain nothing, because the taboo itself has an uncertain, much-debated purpose: see, for example, J. Teevan, *Introduction to Sociology: A Canadian Focus*, 4th ed. (Scarborough, Ont.: Prentice-Hall, 1992) at 293. The clearest legal manifestation of the taboo is, of course, found in the *Criminal Code* (R.S.C. 1985, c. C-46) restrictions in s. 155, forbidding sexual intercourse with parent, child, sibling, grandparent, or grandchild.

cial policies that aim to treat adopted children the same in law as children genetically related to their parents.[73]

g) Unmarried Status

One may have but a single marriage partner at a time. Put more positively, a person must be unmarried at the time of the marriage ceremony. A bigamous[74] marriage is void *ab initio* and, so, is not cured by the subsequent death of the first spouse.

In its focus on the simple "on/off" choice of states—one is either married/unmarried—this is perhaps the most basic of the requirements for a valid marriage. But this apparent simplicity can be deceptive because marital status is a compound fact, involving complex questions of law and factual proof.[75] A sense of the scope of possible difficulty here might be conveyed by the observation that there is no central registry of marriages or of deaths in Canada (let alone in the world as a whole), which means that there is no simple way to prove that as of a certain date—the date of the impugned marriage, typically—the person in question was or was not already married.

h) A Note on Mistake and Fraud

Mistake as to the nature of the ceremony or the identity of the other person may vitiate a marriage. Thus, for instance, if a person, owing to language difficulties perhaps, is under the mistaken belief that what is

---

73   See section C, "Cutting Ties with the Birth Family," in chapter 6, "Adoption." Note, however, that the *Child and Family Services Act*, R.S.O. 1990, c. C.11, s. 158(6) is careful *not* to obscure the genetic backgrounds of adopted persons; despite adoption, people who are in fact too closely related may not marry. The provision under examination here *also* eliminates persons related through adoption. Thus, an adopted person is precluded from marrying two sets of family members.

74   Some other jurisdictions permit polygamy, typically allowing a man to have more than one wife, rather than a woman to have many husbands. Historically, parties to such marriages, contracted validly, were denied any relief in our courts. See, for example, *Lim v. Lim*, [1948] 2 D.L.R. 353 (B.C.S.C.). Currently, the *Family Law Act*, R.S.O. 1990, c. F.3, s. 1(2) defines "spouse" to include a party to a polygamous marriage valid in the jurisdiction where it was contracted. See J.-G. Castel, *Canadian Conflict of Laws*, 4th ed. (Toronto: Butterworths, 1997) at 362ff, for a discussion of which laws govern the validity of polygamous marriages generally.

75   Indeed, in this one rule, all the other requirements for a valid marriage are involved: validity (on any count) of a former possible marriage is important to the validity (on account of bigamy) of a second possible marriage. See section D, "A Note on Proof of Marriage," in this chapter.

taking place is a mortgage transaction, when in fact it is a marriage ceremony, the marriage will not be valid.[76]

However, no amount of mistake as to the qualities or attributes of a partner will affect the validity of a marriage.[77] A person who marries "person A" under the mistaken belief that "person A" is wealthy, or kind, or titled, or not pregnant, for instance, is nevertheless validly married.

It sometimes happens that a marriage is contracted by one or both of the parties solely with the aim of achieving some purpose ulterior to the marriage and the life together it typically precedes. This may happen most frequently with respect to immigration into Canada, when the immigration rules give an advantage to a foreigner married to a Canadian citizen.[78] It has been argued in cases like this that there is such a lack of genuine intention to marry or be married that no legal marriage ought to result. However, the Ontario Court of Appeal has ruled that no amount of mental reservation as to the content of marriage or married life can invalidate a marriage; all that is required is that the parties intend to go through the ceremony and intend the legal status of marriage.[79] The merit of such a position is that it allows the state to evade the vexed question of what should be the proper or minimum "content" of marriage; there are more or less clear legal consequences to marriage, but there is no official view of marriage as a way of life.[80]

---

76 See, for example, *Nane (Sykiotis)* v. *Sykiotis*, [1966] 2 O.R. 428 (H.C.). The plaintiff believed the ceremony was "a permission to marry" ceremony.

77 *Moss* v. *Moss*, [1897] P. 263; see also: *Said* v. *Said* (1986), 33 D.L.R. (4th) 382 (B.C.C.A.).

78 See C. Wydrzynski, *Canadian Immigration Law and Procedure* (Aurora, Ont.: Canada Law Book, 1983) at 101.

79 *Iantsis* v. *Papatheodoru*, [1971] 1 O.R. 245 (C.A.). Some few cases have tried to distinguish this case on the basis that in *Iantsis* only one of the parties lacked the critical intention, and have held that where both parties intend to marry for no purpose other than to represent themselves, or one of them, to immigration authorities as married, the marriage is invalid: see *Asser* v. *Peermohamed* (1984), 46 O.R. (2d) 664 (H.C.). The distinction, however, does not seem sound. See also *United States* v. *Rubenstein*, 151 F.(2d) 915 (U.S.S.C. 1945), in which the U.S. Supreme Court takes the opposite view and holds that marriage has a minimum content that the state ought to require citizens to intend; that is, that marriage is not simply a status but a way of life, to some degree at least.

80 At least not one that courts are willing to declare in a clear, full fashion. As the examination of other areas will show, laws and courts operate on the basis of presumptions that do indeed adumbrate a "normal," if not minimum, content to married life. See section B(2)(b), "Persons Who Cohabit," in chapter 4, "Cohabitation," and section B(3), "By Reason of Living Separate and Apart," in chapter 9, "Divorce."

2) Formal Validity

a) The Ontario *Marriage Act*

i) *Form of Cermony*
Empowered by section 92(12) of the *Constitution Act, 1867,* to make laws respecting "solemnization of marriage,"[81] Ontario has provided an exhaustive statement of formal requirements in its *Marriage Act.*[82] Essentially, the Act provides for persons to become "authorized to solemnize marriage."[83] The solemnizer may be a person registered pursuant to the request of a religious body[84] or a person, such as a judge, designated by the state as capable of performing "civil" marriages.[85] The Act provides a form for civil marriage in the following language:

> 24 (3) No particular form of ceremony is required except that in some part of the ceremony, in the presence of the person solemnizing the marriage and witnesses, each of the parties shall declare:
>
> > *I do solemnly declare that I do not know of any lawful impediment why I, AB, may not be joined in matrimony to CD,*
>
> and each of the parties shall say to the other:
>
> > *I call upon these persons here present to witness that I, AB, do take you, CD, to be my lawful wedded wife (or husband),*
>
> after which the person solemnizing the marriage shall say:
>
> > *I, EF, by virtue of the powers vested in me by the Marriage Act, do hereby pronounce you AB and CD to be husband and wife . . .*

With respect to religious marriages, the Act is silent as to the particulars of form and requires only that "the religious body . . . [be] permanently established . . . as to its rites and ceremonies."[86]

---

81   See section A(1), "The Division of Powers," in this chapter.
82   Above note 8.
83   *Marriage Act,* above note 8, s. 20(1).
84   *Ibid.,* s. 20(3).
85   *Ibid.,* s. 24(1).
86   *Ibid.,* s. 20(3)(c).

ii) Licence

No marriage may be solemnized unless a licence permitting the marriage has been issued or religious banns have been published.[87] Issuers of licences (but not solemnizers) are given powers to require evidence from applicants as to "any matter pertaining to the issue of a licence."[88] The "matters" referred to are those raised in a number of sections that parallel federal law respecting capacity to marry and will be dealt with in section B(2)(a)(iv), "Shadow Sections," in this chapter.

When a marriage has been solemnized, whether pursuant to a licence or banns, the solemnizer must record the particulars in a register[89] and may give the parties a certificate of marriage if they request it.[90]

iii) Parental Consent

According to the terms of section 5(2), a licence may not be issued to a minor who is sixteen or seventeen unless the minor has the consent in writing of both parents.[91] Perhaps curiously, the requirement of parental consent has been found to be a matter of formal validity, and thus within the legislative competence of the province over "solemnization of marriage."[92]

Section 6 provides that where a required consent is "unreasonably or arbitrarily" withheld, the minor[93] may apply to a judge for an order that a licence issue.

As already mentioned,[94] parental consent is related to the requirement of particular age, a matter within federal jurisdiction. This intersection of jurisdictions will also be addressed immediately below.

---

87   *Ibid.*, s. 4. Parties may not proceed by way of publication of banns but must obtain a licence, only where, according to s. 18, either of the parties "has been married and the marriage has been dissolved or annulled."

88   *Ibid.*, s. 12.

89   *Ibid.*, s. 28(1).

90   *Ibid.*, s. 28(2).

91   *Ibid.*, s. 28, subs. 4 to 6, provide for cases where both parents are not available.

92   *Kerr* v. *Kerr*, above note 59; *Clause* v. *Clause*, above note 65. See section A(1), "The Division of Powers," in this chapter.

93   *Marriage Act*, above note 8, s. 6: "[T]he person in respect of whose marriage the consent is required may apply . . ." Although the permission is defined in relation to the marriage (and so there are two affected persons), the minor child of the refusing parents is the intended applicant because the definite article is used (instead of "*a* person . . .", and *the* person ". . . may apply to a judge without the intervention of a litigation guardian."

94   See section B(1)(e), "Requisite Age," in this chapter.

iv) *Shadow Sections*

It is exclusively within the federal power to make laws respecting capacity to marry, yet Ontario addresses matters of capacity in the *Marriage Act*,[95] typically forbidding the issuance of a licence to persons who lack capacity according to the terms of the various sections. This encroachment is understandable, given the unwillingness of the federal government to legislate precise rules respecting capacity to marry, in spite of the public's need to know about constraints on entering this basic social institution.

Age is treated in section 5(2), where it is forbidden to issue a licence to a minor under the age of sixteen years, although the federal law concerning capacity to marry permits girls of twelve and boys of fourteen to marry.[96] Here there is a clear conflict in the provisions, rather than an overlap in requirements. There would seem to be little doubt that the Ontario provision has in "pith and substance" to do with capacity to marry, with the result that this provision would be found *ultra vires*. There is small likelihood of a legal challenge, however, given that it would have to be maintained by a child. If a marriage were contracted pursuant to a licence obtained by lying about age, it would almost certainly be valid, because the Ontario legislation does not provide for its invalidity, but merely establishes an offence, punishable by fine, of providing a false statement.[97]

Section 7 contains a prohibition on issuing a licence to

> any person whom he or she knows or has reasonable grounds to believe lacks capacity to marry by reason of being mentally ill or mentally defective or under the influence of intoxicating liquor or drugs.[98]

This section, too, seems clearly to be "in pith and substance" about capacity to marry and so *ultra vires*, but because there is no necessity of conflict between the federal law concerning mental capacity to marry[99] and the provisions of this section, it may be that a successful challenge would be harder to structure; there would always be the likelihood that the challenge would be resolved by a court on the issue of substance, that is, mental capacity, in a way that left unclear the answer to the

---

95 Above note 8. Section 5(1) permits persons to obtain a licence "provided no lawful cause exists to hinder the solemnization." The phrase "lawful cause" begs the question of whether any cause related to capacity to marry can be "lawful" as a pretext on which Ontario can prevent a marriage.

96 See also section B(1)(e), "Requisite Age," in this chapter.

97 See *Clause* v. *Clause*, above note 65. But see section B(2)(b), "The Base Law of Form," in this chapter.

98 The terms "mentally defective" and "mentally ill" are defined in the *Interpretation Act*, R.S.O. 1990, c. I.11, s. 29.

99 See section B(1)(c), "Capacity to Consent," in this chapter.

constitutional question. As well, it is perhaps worth noting the practical matter that any challenge would in many cases have to be mounted by a person whose mental capacity is unclear at least; and such persons are perhaps unlikely to initiate a constitutional challenge, unless advocacy groups are involved.

The requirement that one be unmarried at the time of marriage[100] is shadowed in the Ontario Act by a set of provisions directed at those who have been previously married. Section 8 makes the issuance of a licence to such a person dependent on there having been an annulment or dissolution of the marriage that is "recognized under the law of Ontario."[101] Once again, this provision would seem to fall afoul of the division of powers. But because there is no conflict whatever between federal law and the terms of the Ontario requirement, it is highly unlikely that this section would ever be successfully challenged on constitutional grounds.

In a related matter, section 9 provides that "a married person whose spouse is missing" and has not been heard of for seven years may apply to a judge for an order declaring the spouse presumed dead. Section 4(4) makes clear that any order so obtained "has no effect for any purpose other than the issuance of a licence." Thus, no one should remarry in reliance on an order under section 9 because the order cannot affect one's capacity to marry: the person either is or is not married at the time of the application for the licence, and this fact cannot be altered by an order under section 9.[102]

Finally, in section 19, the least intrusive of shadow sections, the Ontario Act makes reference to the "prohibited degrees of consanguinity and affinity," another matter of capacity and so a federal legislative responsibility,[103] merely requiring that these be endorsed on the licence or on the proof of publication of banns.

---

100   See section B(1)(g), "Unmarried Status," in this chapter.

101   The section goes on to provide ways in which persons previously married may file proof of divorce or annulment. Canadian decrees or judgments may be filed with the issuer: *Marriage Act*, above note 8, s. 8(2); but for foreign judgments ministerial approval is required (s. 8(3)), which can routinely be obtained with an opinion from a solicitor that the judgment in question is recognized here.

102   The only safe course for a person whose spouse is missing is to assume that the spouse is alive and to obtain a divorce on that assumption. If it later turns out that the first spouse was in fact alive at the critical time, the divorce will have been effective in making the person free to marry again; and if it is later discovered that the first spouse was dead at the critical time, the second marriage will be valid, even though the divorce will be invalid.

103   See section B(1)(f), "Lack of Close Relationship," in this chapter. In fact, the federal law no longer involves "affinity," but this change is recognized clearly in the Form to the Ontario *Marriage Act* where the current federal law is explicitly referred to and, indeed, spelled out in detail.

b) The Base Law of Form

Although provinces may do so,[104] it is not clear that Ontario has in fact imposed the sanction of invalidity for breach of any of the formality requirements set out in the *Marriage Act*.[105] No section explicitly so provides, and courts have said that if provinces wish to invalidate marriages for want of form, they must do so explicitly or by necessary intendment.[106] The only section that even mentions validity is section 31:

> If the parties to a marriage solemnized in good faith and intended to be in compliance with this Act are not under a legal disqualification to contract such marriage and after such solemnization have lived together and cohabited as man and wife, such marriage shall be deemed a valid marriage, although the person who solemnized the marriage was not authorized to solemnize marriage, and despite the absence of or any irregularity or insufficiency in the publication of banns or the issue of the licence.

The Ontario Court of Appeal was of the opinion that this section "legislated the conditional invalidity of marriages."[107] There is no reported case, however, of a marriage having been invalidated under this section;[108] and it might well be argued that the language of this section

---

104 *Alberta (A.G.)* v. *Underwood*, [1934] S.C.R. 635.

105 Ontario once had a statute that acted as a companion piece to the federal *Annulment of Marriages Act (Ontario)*, and that imported English law as of 1870 insofar as it was in the legislative power of the province to do so, and provided that it might be altered by legislation (*Marriage Act*, S.O. 1933, c. 29; subsequently *Matrimonial Causes Act*, R.S.O. 1970, c. 265, s. 11). This may have furnished a base law of form by importing English laws that made marriage without a licence or banns void. But the Act was repealed by consolidation in R.S.O. 1980, and so now the only law is that explicitly contained in the *Marriage Act*, above note 8.

106 *Alspector* v. *Alspector*, [1957] O.R. 454 (C.A.). See also *Colvin* v. *Colvin*, [1952] 3 D.L.R. 510 (B.C.S.C.).

107 *Alspector* v. *Alspector*, *ibid*. It is likely that an invalidating formal defect would render the marriage void *ab initio*, rather than voidable. This is so because the requirement breached is not of personal interest to the parties, that is, a matter about which they might feel a sense of grievance. It was evidently treated this way in *Alspector* v. *Alspector* because the challenge to the marriage was allowed to proceed even though Mr. Alspector was dead. A marriage that is voidable only may not be attacked after the death of one of the parties.

108 But see *Harris* v. *Godkewitsch* (1983), 41 O.R. (2d) 779 (Prov. Ct.). A woman sought to be found a "spouse" under s. 1 of the *Family Law Reform Act*, R.S.O. 1980, c. 152, which was defined in part so as to include married persons (see section B(2), "The *Family Law Act*," in chapter 4, "Cohabitation"). The court held that "[s]he was, by design, never legally married to the respondent . . . although they participated in a Jewish wedding ceremony." There was, the court said, no need to explore the principle set out in *Alspector*, above note 106, touching on "good faith" because the marriage in question was "never intended to conform to the Ontario Marriage Act."

does not meet the test of explicitness that other courts have required. Were it to operate in the way the Court of Appeal has suggested, it would make a base law of form out of the requirements that (a) the person who solemnized the marriage be authorized, and (b) there be no irregularity or insufficiency in the publication of banns or the issue of a licence. In which case, it is arguable that a breach of nearly any section—even a minor breach—could at least raise the issue of invalidity because most sections set out constraints on the issue of licences and so could give rise to concerns about "irregularity or insufficiency." Of course, all marriages that were intended to be in compliance with the Act would be saved, where there was cohabitation subsequently. The question remains, however, whether this lack of perfect clarity is desirable.

An alternative view is that section 31 does not affect validity of marriage in this uncertain (or, indeed, any) way, but serves only to reassure nervous married persons who later discover that some detail in the solemnization of their marriage was irregular. If such a view were adopted it would assist most persons, who follow well-trodden paths of ritual and deviate from state rules only by accident or out of religious conviction; but it would also mean that there is no clear base law of form for marriage in Ontario, such that any ceremony might arguably suffice to produce marriage and no amount of deviation from the Act's requirements would be of serious legal import.

c) Common Law Marriage

A word should be said about common law marriage. Although misused by lawyer and layperson alike to mean cohabitation outside marriage, the term in fact describes a marriage that was indeed formerly valid—valid at the common law, if not by statute law. Its essence was—and may still be—a simple exchange of vows by the spouses, in which each agrees to take the other as wife or husband. It seems that in England, prior to the introduction of statutes governing formalities of marriage, one of the ways a valid (but perhaps limited) union could be made was through the exchange of vows just referred to.[109] And even after statutes came to require certain formalities, some marriages contracted in this old way were recognized as valid, particularly if they took place outside England.

Currently it would seem there are two narrow circumstances under which common law marriages, in England at least, may be recognized:

---

109   On this complicated and arcane history, see the helpful judgments in *Keddie* v. *Currie* (1991), [1992] 85 D.L.R. (4th) 342 (B.C.C.A.), and *Louis* v. *Esslinger*, [1981] 121 D.L.R. (3d) 17 (B.C.S.C.).

where it is impossible to comply with local law; and where the parties have not submitted to local law. The latter involves unusual and highly restricted circumstances, having essentially to do with the dislocations of war.[110] The former addresses physical impossibility in the main, though it could also include instances of moral or legal impossibility.[111]

Are common law marriages possible today? It would appear that in some jurisdictions in the United States, an exchange of vows—even conduct bespeaking such an exchange—might result in a valid common law marriage.[112] And in Canada, in the case of *Re Noah Estate*,[113] the court recognized as valid a marriage between Aboriginal persons that took place according to Inuit custom. In so doing, the court appeared to accord it validity as a common law marriage. However, in *Dutch v. Dutch*,[114] the court held that common law marriages are not possible under Ontario law.[115]

Whether or not this abstruse form continues to be legally possible, it would make sense to reserve phrases such as "common law marriage" or "common law husband" for discussions of quaint forms, and to develop new, more apt language to describe cohabitation without marriage.[116]

C. CONSEQUENCES OF INVALIDITY

1) The Void-Voidable Distinction

Having origins in English ecclesiastical law and its relationship with old secular law, the void-voidable distinction serves no clear purpose today. There would, however, seem to be two sorts of circumstances onto which the notions of void *ab initio* and voidable might sensibly be mapped—always presuming, of course, that legal marriage is retained

---

110   See *Dukov v. Dukov*, [1970] A.L.R. 650 (Queensland S.C.).

111   See C. Davies, *op. cit.*, above note 47 at 17.

112   See G. Blumberg, "Cohabitation without Marriage: A Different Perspective" (1981) 28 U.C.L.A. L. Rev. 1125.

113   (1961), 32 D.L.R. (2d) 185 (N.W.T. Terr. Ct.)

114   (1977), 1 R.F.L. (2d) 177 (Ont. Co. Ct.).

115   They may never have been legally possible for the reason that when English law as to form was received (see above note 105), it applied in Ontario as if Ontario were England; thus, because common law marriages could no longer be contracted in England (but only "abroad"), they could not be contracted in the new England that was Ontario.

116   See section A(1), "A Note on Common Law Relationship," in chapter 4, "Cohabitation."

and is freighted with some legal consequence such that challenging the validity of marriage continues to make sense. As explained above,[117] some requirements seem aimed more at protecting the institution of marriage *per se*, or carrying out broad social policies, rather than at protecting the very individuals involved in a particular union. Thus, for example, the requirement that parties must not be too closely related makes sense as a social policy about the dangers of inbreeding or society's incest taboo. This broad social purpose obtains whether or not it has any particular impact on the actual two individuals who have gone through the ceremony. In such cases, marriages ought to be void.

Where, however, the rule can appropriately be seen as a protection for the very individuals involved in the marriage—where matters such as consent and sexual capacity are involved, for example—breach of the rule ought to make marriages voidable only, leaving it up to the individuals to take steps to avoid it or affirm it as the case may be.

2) Effect of a Nullity Decree

a) Void *ab initio*

A marriage that is void *ab initio* simply does not exist in law and is of no legal effect, whether or not a court has ruled on its validity. A court judgment in such a case is merely declaratory. Consequently, relationships that never amounted to marriage in any sense will have none of the legal effects that automatically follow valid marriage.

However, statute law may allow rights and obligations to flow from certain of these relationships. The most important instance, perhaps, is the *Family Law Act*, under which a person who enters into "a marriage that is voidable or void, in good faith" may assert the rights of a "spouse" under the statute, entitling her or him to the same rights respecting property and support that a married person would have.[118]

It should be noted, too, that children born as a result of a void marriage are in no different legal position from children born to married persons, as the ancient concept of illegitimacy has been abolished.[119]

b) Voidable Only

Where a marriage is voidable, it may be challenged only by one of the parties to it, and only during their joint lives. The spouse who attacks

---

117   Section B(1)(d), "Freedom of Consent," in this chapter.

118   R.S.O. 1990, c. F.3, s. 1(1).

119   See section B(3), "Statutory Presumptions," para. 1, in chapter 5, "Parentage."

its validity must be "sincere," in that he or she must be acting out of a real grievance at the ground for nullity complained of, and may not plead the ground for ulterior purposes. Put positively, where the marriage is voidable only, the aggrieved party may approve of the marriage and validate it permanently.

Such a marriage is good until nullified by a court, and actions taken by the parties or others on the assumption that the marriage is good will be supported by the courts. When invalidated by a court, the decree will "relate back" to the time of the marriage and declare the marriage never to have existed.[120]

D. A NOTE ON PROOF OF MARRIAGE

It is sometimes necessary for a person to prove in court his or her status as a married person, which is not always an easy thing to do. Various factors may make proof of marriage difficult. For one thing, the status of being married results, obviously, from valid marriages; and these, in turn, are a function of the correct combination of personal capacities and of formalities at a particular moment in history. It may not be possible—many years later and in a different jurisdiction, for example—to prove by undeniable evidence all the essential components that are necessary for the court to form its own conclusions as to the validity of the marriage. Presumptions must therefore be relied upon.

To take the easiest case first, a person married in Ontario need simply introduce into evidence a certificate of marriage; according to the *Vital Statistics Act*, this will be proof of the facts (i.e., the marriage ceremony) so certified.[121] Like all presumptions relating to marriage, this one is rebuttable, and the provision qualifies the proof statement by the words "in the absence of evidence to the contrary." Even assuming no such contrary evidence, the proof does not take us far enough without more. The fact of the *status* of marriage cannot be certified under a provincial statute, at least not when based on a certificate produced under the *Marriage Act*; only the fact of the ceremony. Thus, for convenience, we require another presumption, which is, that upon the adducing of evidence of the *event* of the marriage ceremony, the *validity* of the resultant marriage will be presumed.[122]

---

120   See C. Davies, *op. cit.*, above note 47 at 46.
121   R.S.O. 1990, c. V.4, s. 46(1).
122   *Bate v. Bate* (1978), 1 R.F.L. (2d) 298 (Ont. H.C.).

It is not strictly necessary to use a marriage certificate in proving marriage. Oral evidence as to the event may suffice.[123] And from that evidence, validity of marriage may be presumed.

Indeed, it is possible to call into play a presumption *of* marriage, not simply a presumption of the *validity* of a marriage. Where there is evidence that a couple has lived together as man and wife for a sufficient length of time and under such circumstances as to have a reputation locally as being married, then a presumption of marriage arises "which can only be displaced by cogent evidence to the contrary."[124] Such a presumption might be most useful when the parties to the marriage in question are dead or otherwise unable to testify themselves.

Matters may be complicated in at least two ways, each of which invites more examination than is possible here. Repetition or "nesting" can produce difficulty; and conflict of laws imports a good deal of complexity.[125]

People often marry more than once, and the involvement of prior marriages and divorces can multiply the problems and presumptions at play when considering the validity of a current marriage. Burdens can shift back and forth as evidence is introduced, first for a marriage, and then for a prior marriage, and then for a divorce.[126] Of course, any issue in question, whether the validity of a first or second marriage or the divorce in between, may fall to be decided simply on the evidence submitted if the presumptions have been sufficiently rebutted and cease to play a role.[127]

Where jurisdictions other than Ontario are involved, which is common in today's world of mobility, it may be necessary for our courts confronted with a question of the validity of a marriage to make a "choice of law"—that is, to decide whether local Ontario laws or those of a foreign jurisdiction will govern the question. Essentially, the law that governs the formal validity of a person's marriage is the law of the place where the marriage was celebrated (the *lex loci celebrationis*). Thus, from the point of view of an Ontario court considering the validity of a marriage, if a couple from Ontario get married on a visit to Kuala Lumpur, it is Malaysian law that determines what the proper formalities must be. But capacity to marry—essential, not formal validity—is determined by the law of a party's domicile. And so, again from the point of

---

123 *Re Karnenas* (1978), 3 R.F.L. (2d) 213 (Ont. Surr. Ct.).

124 *Porteous v. Dorn*, [1975] 2 S.C.R. 37 at 40–41.

125 See C. Davies, *op. cit.*, above note 47 at 9–16, for an overview; and see J.-G. Castel, *Canadian Conflict of Laws*, above note 74.

126 A Canadian divorce may be conclusively proved in Canada by introduction into evidence of a certificate of divorce: *Divorce Act*, S.C. 1986, c. 4, s. 12(8).

127 See, for example, *Bate v. Bate*, above note 122.

view of an Ontario court considering the validity of a marriage, if a couple visiting from (and domiciled in) Malaysia marry in Ontario, our courts would look to the law of Malaysia to decide whether both had the capacity to marry here.

In a similar way, courts in Ontario may have to make judgments about whether or not to recognize the actions of foreign tribunals. The validity of a marriage here may depend upon whether Ontario courts are prepared to recognize and give effect to a divorce decree from Hungary, for example. The *Divorce Act* provides that a foreign divorce granted after 1 July 1986 will be recognized here if either former spouse was ordinarily resident in the jurisdiction granting the decree for at least one year immediately preceding the commencement of the divorce proceedings there.[128] The old common law rules are preserved as well and will most likely be used principally if not exclusively to govern marriages taking place before 1 July 1986.[129] The applicable common law rules are a matter of some difficulty, but

> [i]n recent years, Canadian courts have been committed to the view that they will recognize foreign decrees of divorce where there existed some real and substantial connection between the petitioner or the respondent and the granting jurisdiction at the time of the commencement of the proceedings.[130]

FURTHER READINGS

CASTEL, J.-G., *Canadian Conflict of Laws*, 4th ed. (Toronto: Butterworths, 1997) c. 17

DAVIES, C., *Family Law in Canada: Fourth Edition of Power on Divorce and Other Matrimonial Causes* (Toronto: Carswell, 1984) cc. 1–3

EEKELAAR, J.M., S.N. KATZ, eds., *Marriage and Cohabitation in Contemporary Societies: Areas of Legal, Social and Ethical Change: An International and Interdisciplinary Study* (Toronto: Butterworths, 1980)

HAHLO, H.R., *Nullity of Marriage in Canada* (Toronto: Butterworths, 1979)

ONTARIO LAW REFORM COMMISSION, *Report on Family Law*, Part II, "Marriage" (Toronto: Dept. of Justice, 1970)

---

128 Above note 126, s. 22(1).
129 *Ibid.*, s. 22(3). See J.-G. Castel, *Canadian Conflict of Laws*, above note 74 at 373.
130 J.-G. Castel, *Canadian Conflict of Laws*, above note 74 at 374.

CHAPTER 3

COHABITATION AGREEMENTS

A. INTRODUCTION

1) The Novelty of Cohabitation Agreements

Lawful cohabitation agreements are a relatively recent phenomenon. Prior to 1978,[1] the courts took the position that any contract envisaging the cohabitation of a man and a woman[2] outside marriage was void as against the public policy that held sexual intercourse between unmarried persons to be wrong. Those so cohabiting were said to be in a "meretricious union"[3] out of which few, if any, legal rights could flow.

With the liberalization of sexual mores and the rising rate of separation and divorce[4] in the second half of the century, cohabitation out-

---

1   The *Family Law Reform Act, 1978*, S.O. 1978, c. 2, s. 52, introduced cohabitation agreements.

2   Although the issue of cohabitation agreements between gay or lesbian partners is an important one today, no cases clearly involving such arrangements came before the courts; there is little doubt that had they done so, they would have met with even more disapproval than heterosexual "fornicators."

3   See, for example, *Barnet (otherwise MacKay) v. Barnet*, [1934] O.R. 155 at 160 (H.C.), Armour J.

4   See P. La Novara, *A Portrait of Families in Canada*, Statistics Canada, Catalogue 89-523E (Ottawa: Statistics Canada, 1993) at 17: in 1968, prior to the passage of the first modern divorce statute, the divorce rate (per 100,000 population) was 54.8; in 1987, the high point, it had risen to 355.1; by 1990 that had calmed to 294. See also J. Gentleman & E. Park, "Divorce in the 1990s" in *Health Reports*, vol. 9, no. 2 (Autumn 1997), Statistics Canada, Catalogue 82-003-XPB (Ottawa: Minister of Industry, 1997) at 55.

side of marriage became increasingly common[5] and acceptable. Consequently, cohabitation agreements came to be regarded as sensible tools that could provide rational solutions to realistically anticipated future problems. The turn to contract was assisted, perhaps, by a changed view of marriage itself that saw it less as a lifelong affair and more as a practical and profitable union—if not primarily a business arrangement in fact, then certainly one with a clear set of business-like issues, and consequently fit meat for the commercial practice of contract.[6]

Recently the "family-as-business" view has declined in importance, but there has been an increasing emphasis in legal practice and commentary on the importance of resolving disputes in family law matters through non-litigious and, ideally, non-adversarial means; and this desideratum has to some degree at least replaced the business approach as the source of support for contractual solutions generally.[7]

2) An Overview of the Legislative Provisions

a) Domestic Contracts

Ontario's *Family Law Act* provides for three kinds of "domestic contracts": cohabitation agreements, marriage contracts, and separation agreements.[8] This chapter concerns itself with family formation, and so it will focus on the cohabitation agreement, the novel means of establishing legal family relations between adults;[9] however, because the Act treats all domestic contracts very much alike, a great deal of what is discussed here will be of relevance to marriage and separation agreements as well.

---

5   The number of people living in informal unions in Canada tripled to over one million between 1981 and 1995: J. Gentleman & E. Park, "Divorce in the 1990s," *ibid.* at 53.

6   For example, according to the preamble of the *Family Law Act* (R.S.O. 1990, c. F.3, as amended by S.O. 1992, c. 32, s. 12; S.O. 1993, c. 27, Sched. [*FLA* or the Act]): "[I]t is necessary to recognize . . . marriage as a form of partnership." The legislation gives pride of place to contractual solutions.

7   See *FLA*, s. 3 (introduced in S.O. 1986, c. 4, s. 3), which permits the court to appoint a mediator. And see B. Landau *et al.*, *Family Mediation Handbook*, 2d ed. (Toronto: Butterworths, 1997) at 2.

8   The generic term, "domestic contract," is defined in *FLA*, above note 6, s. 51, to include these kinds of contracts, which are in turn defined in ss. 53, 52, and 54 respectively.

9   Marriage contracts are important for their ability to modify that package of rights and obligations that attends marriage, and so they are referred to throughout the book in the contexts of the rights and obligations they attempt to modify. Separation agreements are discussed in detail in chapter 13.

b) Cohabitation and Marriage

A cohabitation agreement permits parties to construct for themselves many of the rights and obligations that would automatically follow upon formal marriage, and in particular enables them to deal with title to any property, support during or upon the break-up of the union, and some aspects of their children's upbringing. Indeed, from a purely legal point of view, there is little difference remaining between marriage and cohabitation under a well-drafted cohabitation agreement. Put simply, marriage is a regime of rights and obligations that may be modified or largely eliminated by contract,[10] whereas cohabitation is a generally unregulated[11] relationship that may be "built up" by contract.

Section 53(1) of the *FLA* provides that a man and woman, not married to each other, who are already cohabiting[12] or who intend to cohabit in the future may enter into a cohabitation agreement.

c) Scope of Cohabitation Agreements

The scope permitted cohabitation agreements is both generous and open-ended. Parties may agree on their "respective rights and obligations" during cohabitation and upon the end of cohabitation through separation or death.[13] There are some limitations imposed by the Act, both on the scope of the agreements and on aspects of contract formation. These are considered in some detail below.[14] Essentially, they aim at protecting the rights of children and at ensuring that the party with the stronger position not be able to force a one-sided bargain on the other.

B. WHO MAY CONTRACT

1) A Man and a Woman

The legislation does not provide for cohabitation agreements between persons of the same sex. Unlike marriage law, where the discrimination

---

10   See *FLA*, above note 6, s. 52, (defining and setting out the permissible scope of marriage contracts) and s. 2(10) which gives general precedence to contract over statute.

11   Cohabitation can itself give rise to rights and obligations, but these do not arise immediately upon initiation of the relationship: see chapter 4, "Cohabitation."

12   See section B(2), "Persons Who Cohabit," in this chapter.

13   *FLA*, above note 6, s. 53(1). Until these reforms were enacted, it was illegal as against public policy for cohabiting (married) persons to make an agreement that provided for rights upon their separation, for fear that this ability would act as an inducement to the evil of separation. As to marriages that end by death, see *FLA*, s. 6. Matters of succession or estates generally will not be considered in this book.

14   Section C(3), "Restrictions," in this chapter.

results from judicial interpretation of history and policy,[15] the law governing cohabitation agreements is explicit in extending the benefits of the legislation only to heterosexual couples. As was seen in the prior chapter when same-sex marriage was considered, the objection to homosexual unions remains grounded upon a morality rather than upon any set of persuasive rational, utilitarian arguments.

It seems clear that the cohabitation agreement was conceived of by its creators as providing an approximation of or an approach to marriage, rather than as inaugurating a wholly new form of union between persons. For one thing, it is dependent upon "cohabitation," defined, as we shall see in the next section, by reference to marriage; for another, provision is made for conversion of the agreement into a "marriage contract" if the parties marry;[16] and, less explicitly, it is contemplated that only two persons[17] could be privy to the agreement because the model of monogamy so strongly dominates.

As with marriage, the failure to extend the benefits of the law to same-sex couples renders it vulnerable to challenge under the *Charter*.[18] Indeed, it would seem that the exclusion here is even less supportable than it might be in respect of marriage, given that there can be no reference

---

15 See section B(1)(b), "Sexual Difference," in chapter 2, "Marriage."

16 *FLA*, above note 6, s. 53(2).

17 ". . . a man and a woman . . ."

18 *Canadian Charter of Rights and Freedoms*, Part I of the *Constitution Act, 1982*, being Schedule B to the *Canada Act 1982* (U.K.), 1982, c. 11 [*Charter*]. No case has yet directed a challenge at this restriction on *Charter* grounds. However, in *M. v. H.* (1996), 31 O.R. (3d) 417 (C.A.) (application for leave to appeal granted (24 April 1997) S.C.C. Bulletin, 1997, p. 1106) the challenge to heterosexual limitations on the extended definition of "spouse" in Part II (s. 29) of the same Act was successful, and so it would seem that this restriction has fallen, too, by necessary implication. The dissenting judge in that case, Finlayson J.A., makes this point, (at 435, 436) albeit with a different aim in mind:

> [P]artners to any cohabitation agreement as provided for in Part IV must be "a man and woman". This means that homosexuals who are unhappy with the prospect of being drafted into this new regime [as "spouses"] do not have the option of making their own mutual support arrangements. Thus a significant burden is cast upon persons such as H without the opportunity to "opt out" available to their heterosexual counterparts.

The majority made reference to the same anomaly at 463:

> While it may still be open to same-sex couples to enter into agreements to regulate their affairs outside the purview of the FLA, it is beyond the purview of this litigation to determine whether such alternative would be adequate to resolve the anomaly. The legislature may wish to consider this.

to a long, exclusively heterosexual history[19] of the institution of cohabitation contracts. Simply put: a new legal relationship has been denied to same-sex couples.[20]

The situation is different from that of marriage in another way as well. Marriage is the only formal, ceremonial institution available that would result in a legal and social uniting of two people, with a consequent change of legal status; marriage is unique, not generic. This often prompts the argument that part of its uniqueness has to do with heterosexuality, and so it is "nonsensical" to open it to homosexuality. Quite apart from whether any such "essentialist" argument is supportable, nothing like this obtains with respect to the cohabitation agreement, which is simply one sort of contract. And the argument might be made for same-sex couples that their agreements are not "cohabitation agreements" as defined in the *FLA*, but contracts of another kind, or, simply, contracts. To withhold the benefit of the general law of contract from same-sex couples ought arguably to be harder to justify than withholding the benefit of historically determined marriage or marriage-approximating arrangements.

This is a stronger argument today than it might have been a number of years ago because of the change in social and sexual mores that has made homosexuality far more acceptable; and it would be difficult to maintain that any contract envisaging or depending on cohabitation of a same-sex couple is so repugnant to society that it ought to be illegal or void.

The Ontario Law Reform Commission has recommended that Part IV of the *FLA* be amended so as to permit same-sex couples to enter into cohabitation agreements (and, therefore, separation agreements as well).[21]

---

19 But as to the history of marriage and its exclusively heterosexual nature, see J. Boswell, *The Marriage of Likeness: Same-Sex Unions in Pre-Modern Europe* (London: Fontana Press, 1996).

20 See also the comments of Charron J.A., speaking for the majority in *M. v. H.*, above note 18 at 440, to the effect that, when considering whether or not the Act's restriction of "spouse" to heterosexual couples violates the *Charter*'s s. 15 right to equality, the proper comparators are not married persons but unmarried heterosexual couples.

21 Ontario Law Reform Commission, *Report on the Rights and Responsibilities of Cohabitants under the Family Law Act* (Toronto: The Commission, 1993) at 52. This is described as a "modest reform option" and is only one of a number of reforms recommended in respect of same-sex couples.

2) Persons Who Cohabit

Contracting parties must be "cohabiting" or intending to "cohabit" if they wish to create a "cohabitation agreement" and so take advantage of the *FLA*. "Cohabit" is defined in section 1 of the Act as meaning "to live together in a conjugal relationship, whether within or outside marriage." This definition will be analysed in chapter 4, which deals with rights and obligations based on the act of cohabitation itself rather than on contract. In the current context, it will suffice to provide a brief outline of how the courts have approached the interpretation of this definition. A cursory treatment is appropriate here because it is unlikely to be much of a practical problem: contracting parties are always actively seeking to conform to the requirements of the law in order to obtain its benefits, and so there will be little likelihood of their failing to meet the test of cohabitation whatever it may be.[22]

The courts have typically focused on "conjugal relationship" as being the phrase of difficulty requiring interpretation. In ordinary usage a conjugal relationship means a marriage relationship, or that of a husband and wife. Courts commonly, therefore, will proceed to compare the relationship in question with some idealized or "normal" marriage relationship along a set of arbitrarily derived coordinates,[23] and if a sufficient (but unspecified) number of similarities is found declare that there is cohabitation.[24]

Occasionally, a court has attempted to ground its interpretation in the context of the particular issue.[25] Such an approach might ask what the purpose was of the statutory provision in question: Why is it important to make this distinction; what turns on it? A court taking such an

---

22 A search of the QL database failed to reveal any case in which a cohabitation agreement was challenged on the basis that the parties were not cohabiting, or any case involving a cohabitation agreement in which the meaning of "cohabit" was relevant.

23 For example, in *Armstrong* v. *Thompson* (1979), 23 O.R. (2d) 421 (H.C.) the court compared the relationship in question with "the traditional married couple." The court took no evidence concerning the characteristics of this exemplar and gave no rationale for its selection of the characteristics chosen.

24 See, for example, *Molodowich* v. *Penttinen* (1980), 17 R.F.L. (2d) 376 (Ont. Dist. Ct.), where the court constructed seven categories of questions to be asked. See section B(2)(b), "Persons Who Cohabit," in chapter 4, "Cohabitation," for a criticism of this approach.

25 See, for example, *Stoikiewicz* v. *Filas* (1978), 21 O.R. (2d) 717 (Ont. U.F.C.), where, because the central issue was whether an obligation to provide financial support existed, the court emphasized the importance of those aspects of the relationship that had economic implications.

approach in this context of family formation, and, more particularly, of Part IV of the *Family Law Act*, would presumably consider the desirability of permitting parties to regulate their own affairs in a timely and reasoned fashion; the relative paucity of social harm that would likely result from a liberal, inclusive interpretation of "cohabit"; and the likelihood that failure to permit the parties to contract would not prevent the proposed behaviour but merely cause it to be unregulated.

C. SCOPE OF THE AGREEMENT

1) Parties' Pre-Contractual Position

Persons who are in fact cohabiting may by their conduct incur obligations to each other under the *FLA* and common law. These obligations will be explored in more detail in chapter 4. Here it will suffice to point out that support obligations may arise after three years continuous cohabitation or upon cohabitation "in a relationship of some permanence" where the parties are the parents of a child.[26]

The Act does not affect the property rights of unmarried couples. The courts, however, have developed the doctrines of unjust enrichment and constructive trust in such a way that cohabiting persons may develop financial obligations one to the other, or become tenants in common in equity of property that is held in the name of one of them.[27]

With respect to children, the *Children's Law Reform Act* provides generally that children of unmarried couples are in no different position than those born to married couples.[28] In either case, mother and father are equally entitled to custody of and access to their children, and this remains so until altered by court order or a separation agreement.[29] If cohabiting persons are the parents of a child, they may have support obligations towards the child, and in this context "parent" is given a legislatively extended definition.[30]

Persons making a cohabitation agreement will probably, then, have these potential rights and obligations in mind.

---

26   *FLA*, above note 6, ss. 29(a), (b), & 30.
27   See section E, "The Role of Common Law Remedies," in chapter 11, "Family Property."
28   R.S.O. 1990, c. C.12, Part I.
29   *Ibid.*, s. 20.
30   *FLA*, above note 6, s. 1: an adult who "has demonstrated a settled intention to treat a child as a child of his or her family" is included in the definition of "parent." See section D, "Parent of Intention," in chapter 5, "Parentage."

2) General Scope

The *FLA* permits contracting parties a wide and open-ended scope concerning the content of the agreement. They may

agree on their respective rights and obligations during cohabitation, or on ceasing to cohabit or on death, including,

(a) ownership in or division of property;

(b) support obligations;

(c) the right to direct the education and moral training of their children, but not the right to custody of or access to their children; and

(d) any other matter in the settlement of their affairs.[31]

Because a properly formed "cohabitation agreement" is a "domestic contract," its provisions will prevail over those of the Act, "unless [the] Act provides otherwise."[32]

Parties may wish to establish a contractual regime to govern their property rights, during cohabitation, upon the end of the relationship, or in both situations. The regime may be of their own devising, but three possibilities suggest themselves; and a brief discussion of these will illustrate the degrees of freedom possessed by the parties.

They might, for example, elect to institute a regime of separate property and to regard each other as strangers in respect of title to property. This is essentially the common law position for cohabiting couples absent any contract; but an explicit statement of their intention to hold property separately would go a long way towards forestalling the later applicability of restitutionary principles typically aimed at remedying unjust enrichment.[33] The parties might, in contrast, elect to fashion a regime of community of property, in which they hold everything as co-tenants—a more thorough sharing than that imposed by the Act on

---

31 *Ibid.*, s. 53(1).

32 *Ibid.*, s. 2(10).

33 The cohabitation agreement that explicitly adopts a regime of separate property might well be the "juristic reason" for any enrichment of one to the detriment of the other. See section E, "The Role of Common Law Remedies," in chapter 11, "Family Property." There will be limits, of course, on the reach of an agreement made at the very beginning of a relationship: equity may regard it as having been modified by tacit agreement and the conduct of the parties. It must be noted that s. 2(10) of the *FLA*, above note 6, gives domestic contracts clear precedence only with respect to "matters . . . dealt with in this Act"; and it is restitutionary principles in the common law, rather than any provisions of the Act, that affect property rights between cohabiting couples.

married persons. Or they might simply adopt by reference the regime under the Act for married persons, which is a regime of deferred sharing of wealth acquired during cohabitation.

Parties may contract about financial support, and could provide for support to be paid during cohabitation[34] or upon separation, or in both situations. The *FLA*, it was just seen, will impose support obligations on cohabiters under certain circumstances, and parties who go to the trouble of making a cohabitation agreement may want to address this likelihood explicitly and provide for support according to their own wishes rather than those of the legislation.

From the portion of the legislation quoted above, it is clear that parties have a limited ability to contract concerning the care and upbringing of their children. This will be addressed in the following section, when restrictions on the scope of contract are discussed.

The legislation provides that parties may address "any other matter." It is sometimes suggested that cohabiters might contract concerning aspects of daily life together that could become sources of friction and dispute.[35] It might be important to decide who will take out the garbage, or that the couple will share financial information, or that one of them will assume the primary responsibility for birth control. There is nothing impossible in parties' contracting about duties in detail—indeed, it may in fact be helpful to discuss before cohabitation the quotidian realities of life together and to record agreement as to these—but it seems unrealistic to imagine that the courts would be eager to enforce terms concerning such matters, even if a case could be made as to damages.

3) Restrictions

Some limitations are imposed by the *FLA* both on the scope of contracts and also concerning procedures whereby domestic contracts come into being. The majority of these will be explored in detail in chapter 13,

---

34   It will be a relatively rare case, one supposes, where support is contracted for during a relationship, if only because it seems unlikely that the parties would continue to cohabit and yet engage in litigation to enforce this term. More likely, support will become an issue only for separated couples, and so provision for support upon separation will typically be adequate.

35   See, for example, J. Keene, "Domestic Contracts between Cohabiting Couples" (1978) 1 Can. J. Fam. L. 477; L. Weitzman, "Legal Regulation of Marriage: Tradition and Change" (1974) 62 Calif. L. Rev. 1169. Cf. J. MacDonald *et al.*, *Law and Practice under the Family Law Reform Act of Ontario* (Toronto: Carswell, 1986) looseleaf service.

"Separation Agreements," because it is in that context that these legislative constraints have most commonly been considered by courts.

As has already been noted, section 2(10) of the Act provides that contracts are determinative of rights "unless this Act provides otherwise." What follows is a brief catalogue of those relevant instances where the legislation does indeed provide otherwise.

a) Children

It is only when cohabitation is at an end and the parties separated that they may deal with child custody and access by agreement. Prior to separation, all that may be affected by contract is the "right to direct the education and moral training" of the parties' children. The basic position is that children's interests, which govern, are best served by having their relations with both parents remain as full as possible and open to change on a day-to-day basis; disputes concerning the upbringing of children during an ongoing relationship ought not be resolved by resort to a fixed schedule or arrangement that likely must become out of date as children grow and develop. Only as a last resort—that is, when the adults simply cannot get along, and will, therefore, separate—may contract be used.

The exception for education and moral training reflects the importance of these aspects of child rearing for some members of society. Particularly, where unions are mixed as to religious affiliation, one of the parties may feel strongly about raising the children in his or her religion or according to his or her moral precepts. The legislation permits this practical social matter to be resolved before or at entry into the union.

More generally, section 56(1) provides that "the court may disregard any provision of a domestic contract pertaining to [the support, education, moral training, or custody of or access to a child] where . . . to do so is in the best interests of the child."[36] Essentially, then, adults do not have complete power to bargain away a child's rights or compromise a child's interests.

Courts do not have a general supervisory jurisdiction over contracts affecting children in the sense that they must approve of all arrangements, and they will become involved only when there is litigation.

---

36   "Best interests" is not defined in the *FLA*, but see definitions in the *Children's Law Reform Act*, above note 28, s. 24(2), and the *Child and Family Services Act*, R.S.O. 1990, c. C.11, s. 37(3), each of which is said to be for the purposes of the part of the Act in which it appears, and so would be helpful only by analogy.

b) Spouses[37]

In Part III of the *FLA*, dealing with obligations of financial support between spouses, section 33(4) provides:

> The court may set aside a provision for support or a waiver of the right to support in a domestic contract . . . and may determine and order support in an application under subsection (1) although the contract or agreement contains an express provision excluding the application of this section,
>
> (a) if the provision for support or the waiver of the right to support results in unconscionable circumstances;
>
> (b) if the provision for support is in favour of or the waiver is by or on behalf of a dependant who qualifies for an allowance for support out of public money . . .

Essentially, this provision aims at getting the wealthier or more powerful party to take care that any agreement is minimally fair concerning support obligations; and by working with the outcome of the deal—"results in circumstances that are unconscionable"—rather than process whereby the deal was struck, it seeks to withhold certainty from those contracting parties who drive too hard a deal, that is, one that might, therefore, produce unconscionable results later on and so turn out to be no deal at all.

Since this provision was enacted, other portions of the legislation have been amended with the incidental effect that this section may have been made less useful or necessary. It is now possible for a party to a domestic contract to file a domestic contract with the court, whereupon any provision for support in it may be enforced and varied as if it were a court order.[38] Variation by the court, it ought to be noted, will not be possible if

---

37   Note that the restrictions on freedom to contract that are under discussion in this section pertain only to those parties to a cohabitation agreement who meet the Act's definition of "spouse" and so would be under a statutory obligation to support each other. (See section B(2), "The *Family Law Act*," in chapter 4, "Cohabitation.") Thus, for instance, a childless couple who had cohabited for less than three years would not be affected by s. 33 of the *FLA*, above note 6, because they would not be spouses and so would not be entitled to a support order under the Act even if the agreement were set aside.

38   *FLA*, above note 6, s. 35(1) & (2). Note that any "person who is a party to a domestic contract" may file the agreement with the court. The significance of this is that the filing person does not need to be a "spouse" as defined in the Act; and, so, if there is a cohabitation agreement that provides for support, parties to it may have access to the courts even though they have cohabited for a very brief period, for instance.

there is "an agreement to the contrary."[39] Even where an agreement has been filed with the court, a party is still permitted to argue that the provision respecting support ought to be set aside under section 33(4).[40]

The Act also prevents contracting parties from making any right depend on one of them remaining chaste.[41]

c) Contract Formation

Domestic contracts are unenforceable unless "made in writing, signed by the parties and witnessed."[42] The requirement of this high degree of formality has created problems respecting minutes of settlement of litigation between separated parties,[43] but there will rarely be difficulty attending the creation of a cohabitation agreement, which is, after all, a deliberate planning exercise that does not depend for its success on a brisk capturing of the sense of a moment, as might be true of minutes of settlement. However, where lawyers or other knowledgeable advisers are not involved in the contracting process, parties may simply not know of these high formality requirements and may wind up relying upon an agreement that is "unenforceable." Perhaps surprisingly,[44] there has not developed a judge-made practice like that which allows circumvention of the *Statute of Frauds* formality requirements.

Of greater significance to cohabitation agreements is section 56(4) of the *FLA*, which describes the reasons why a court may later set aside the contract or any of its terms. These are:

(a) if a party failed to disclose to the other significant assets, or significant debts or other liabilities, existing when the domestic contract was made;

(b) if a party did not understand the nature or consequences of the domestic contract; or

(c) otherwise in accordance with the law of contract.

---

39   *Ibid.*, s. 35(4). The filed contract may be enforced as if it were a court order despite any agreement to the contrary, however.

40   *Ibid.*, s. 35(3).

41   *Ibid.*, s. 56(2). A right can be hinged upon one of the parties' remaining unmarried or not cohabiting with another person.

42   *Ibid.*, s. 55(1).

43   See *Geropoulos* v. *Geropoulos* (1982), 35 O.R. (2d) 763 (C.A.); and *Harris* v. *Harris*, [1996] O.J. No. 2430 (Gen. Div.); but see also: *Thornton* v. *Thornton* (1983), 33 R.F.L. (2d) 266 (C.A.). See section B, "Limits on Contract," in chapter 13, "Separation Agreements."

44   One likely, but undocumented, reason is that there are so few cohabitation and marriage agreements that the incidence of failure for lack of formality is insignificant.

It will be seen that these stipulations intend to guard against misuses of power by one of the contracting parties, and in that way to assist in the creation of fair deals. Although these provisions and the issues they raise will be dealt with more thoroughly later in the book, it is sensible to pay some attention to them here.

The disclosure requirement distinguishes domestic from general commercial contracts, where, in theory at least, knowledge (i.e., information) is power, and power may be used to drive as hard a bargain as possible. There are to be fewer, if any, advantages permitted in a domestic contract from this source of power. However, domestic contracts have not yet achieved the status of contracts *uberrimae fidei*, such as are found in the insurance industry, and in which *all* (and not merely "significant") relevant information must be disclosed.[45]

Clearly, some individuals may be reluctant to make full disclosure when contemplating cohabiting with another, and they may wish to "trade off" full disclosure against other benefits—the transfer of title to assets, perhaps. In such an arrangement, the secretive party might wish the other to be debarred from subsequently challenging the contract on the basis of lack of full disclosure, whether by an acknowledgment (counter-factual) in the agreement that there has been disclosure, or on the basis of a term in the contract waiving the right to disclosure. However, the latter course is clearly impossible, as the *FLA* provides in section 56(7) that all of the section 56 bases for setting aside contracts apply "despite any agreement to the contrary."

In theory, of course, this would prevent any reliance on a "constructed" acknowledgment, which would be merely an indirect way of arriving at the forbidden end. But in practice it may be difficult for a party to renege on a statement that there was full disclosure. The only satisfactory way to be clear subsequently about what was and what was not disclosed is to have the agreement contain an appendix listing the assets, etc., so that disclosure is confined to just what was set out in writing and that writing is preserved as part of the agreement.

An agreement may also be set aside, as was seen in the excerpt from the Act quoted above, if a party did not understand the "nature or consequences" of the contract. This difficulty is most effectively avoided if each party has adequate, independent legal advice, and one likely

---

45   See, for example, *S.(F.)* v. *H.(C.)* (1994), 120 D.L.R. (4th) 432 (Ont. Gen. Div.).

obstacle[46] to this solution is the desire of the parties contemplating cohabitation to act non-adversarially, and so to rely wholly or principally on a single adviser. A lawyer who acts for both parties in such a situation runs the risk of transgressing Rule 5 of the Rules of Professional Conduct:[47]

> The lawyer must not advise or represent both sides of a dispute and, save after adequate disclosure to and with the consent of the client or prospective client concerned, should not act or continue to act in a matter when there is or there is likely to be a conflicting interest.

And it would seem only sensible that parties who do in fact draft a contract with the help of a single lawyer should each then be sent to obtain independent legal advice as to the meaning and consequences of the contract.

The third basis for setting aside a contract contained in the excerpt above simply refers us to the (largely) common law of contract, where we find familiar wrongs such as duress, fraud, and the various species of equitable fraud, which will receive no more than this mention here.[48]

---

46 Other possible, but perhaps less likely, difficulties, would be a refusal by one party to get legal advice, or an attempt by one party to dominate the process and to minimize the other's access to legal advice. These behaviours are more common in the context of making separation agreements.

47 *Professional Conduct Handbook* (Toronto: Law Society of Upper Canada, 1996). Comment 5 to Rule 5 states:

> Before the lawyer accepts employment for more than one client in a matter or transaction, the lawyer must advise the clients concerned that the lawyer has been asked to act for both or all of them, that no information received in connection with the matter from one can be treated as confidential so far as any of the others are concerned and that, if a conflict develops which cannot be resolved, the lawyer cannot continue to act for both or all of them and may have to withdraw completely.

48 See section B(1), "Validity," in chapter 13, "Separation Agreements."

FURTHER READINGS

COSSMAN, B., & B. RYDER, *Gay, Lesbian and Unmarried Heterosexual Couples and the Family Law Act: Accommodating a Diversity of Family Forms, A research paper prepared for the Ontario Law Reform Commission* (Toronto: Ontario Law Reform Commission, 1993)

HOLLAND, W., & B. STALBECKER-POUNTNEY, eds., *Cohabitation: The Law in Canada* (Toronto: Carswell, 1990) looseleaf service

HUBBARD, P., & M. JOHNSON-LARSEN, "Contract Cohabitation: A Jurisprudential Perspective on Common-Law Judging" (1980–81) 19 J. Fam. L. 651

KEENE, J., "Domestic Contracts between Cohabiting Couples" (1978) 1 Can. J. Fam. L. 477

MACDONALD, J.C., *et al.*, *Law and Practice under the* Family Law Act *of Ontario*, rev. ed. (Toronto: Carswell, 1994) looseleaf service, Part IV

ONTARIO LAW REFORM COMMISSION, *Report on the Rights and Responsibilities of Cohabitants under the* Family Law Act (Toronto: The Commission, 1993)

CHAPTER 4

COHABITATION

A. INTRODUCTION

It is possible for adult[1] family members to create legal relations between themselves without explicitly intending to do so. Most everyone who marries understands and intends that the ceremony will have legal consequences, and all who enter cohabitation agreements do so for the express purpose of creating legal rights and obligations; but some people who simply live together, without benefit of ceremony or contract, may find themselves subject to legal relations they did not wish to incur or did not even know about.

The Ontario legislature determined in 1978 that in certain circumstances, heterosexual cohabiters should be deemed "spouses,"[2] and, so, liable to support each other. The purpose of such an extension has been stated by Charron J.A. in *M. v. H.*:[3]

---

1   Concerning informal creation of adult-child legal relations, see the extended definition of "parent" in the *Family Law Act*, R.S.O. 1990, c. F.3, s. 1(1) [*FLA* or the Act], and the equivalent provision in the *Divorce Act*, S.C. 1986, c. 4, s. 2(1), & (2) (as amended), defining "child of the marriage," discussed in section D(2), "Under the *Divorce Act*," in chapter 5, "Parentage."

2   Originally the *Family Law Reform Act, 1978*, S.O. 1978, c. 2, s. 14; now *FLA, ibid.,* s. 29.

3   (1996) 31 O.R. (3d) 417 at 451 (C.A.), application for leave to appeal granted (24 April 1997) S.C.C. Bulletin, 1997, p. 1106.

> [T]he legislature must simply be taken to have recognized that, in so far as spousal support obligations were concerned, it was neither fair nor effective to choose marriage as the exclusive marker for the identification of intimate relationships giving rise to economic interdependence which might require, upon breakdown, some access to the equitable dispute-resolution scheme created by the legislation. Nor was it fair or effective to use marriage as an exclusive marker for the identification of persons who, upon breakdown of a relationship, should bear the burden of providing support for the other party to that relationship based upon their capacity to pay.

Those who want to avoid the consequences of their conduct in cohabiting with another must now take the advertent step of contracting out of liability for support.[4]

There are two sorts of deemed or statutory spouses: those who have cohabited for a minimum of three years[5] (called here "three-year spouses") and those who have cohabited "in a relationship of some permanence" and are the parents of a child[6] (here "parent spouses").

No property rights arise under the current legislation simply as a result of cohabitation—cohabiting couples have no "matrimonial home," and no "net family property": these rights are reserved to married persons.[7] The privileging of marriage over informal cohabitation has been challenged successfully in the Supreme Court in a case in which a man was denied the benefits of his spouse's insurance policy; the denial was held to be an unjustified breach of section 15(1) of the *Charter*.[8] Apart from *Charter* rights, the courts may apply principles of the common law of restitution to remedy the unjust enrichment of one cohabiter at the expense of the other, and in so doing may require property sharing, typically through the device of a constructive trust.[9]

---

4   See an analysis of the limits on the ability to contract out of liability for support in section C(3)(b), "Spouses," in chapter 3, "Cohabitation Agreements."

5   *FLA*, above note 1, s. 29(a). The requisite length of time was five years in the original legislation; this was changed to the shorter period by S.O. 1986, c. 4.

6   *FLA*, above note 1, s. 29(b).

7   One must be a "spouse" under s. 1 of the *FLA*, above note 1, to have property rights; this includes both married persons and those claimants who entered marriage in good faith where it was void or voidable.

8   *Canadian Charter of Rights and Freedoms*, Part 1 of the *Constitution Act, 1982*, being Schedule B to the *Canada Act 1982* (U.K.), 1982, c. 11 [*Charter*]; *Miron v. Trudel*, [1995] 2 S.C.R. 418 (S.C.C.).

9   See section C, "A Note on Restitution, Equity, and Property," in this chapter for a brief introduction to unjust enrichment in this context, and see chapter 11, "Family Property."

The Ontario Law Reform Commission has recommended the extension of the *Family Law Act*'s property provisions to statutory spouses,[10] and also the novel means of a "registered domestic partnership" whereby same-sex couples may also obtain the benefits of the Act.[11]

1) A Note on Common Law Relationship

Many people, some lawyers and judges included, refer to cohabiting couples as living "common law" or in a "common law" relationship. This is misleading language, principally because most of the rights that cohabiting persons have against each other flow from statute law and not from the common law. And, second, "common law marriage," which is the principal phrase from which these others derive, originally described a marriage valid at the common law.[12] Because the common law has nothing whatever to do with informal relationships, and most of the rights that flow from them are the result of statutory intervention, the term "statutory spouse" will be used throughout this book to describe unmarried persons who are deemed by legislation to be spouses. Their relationships will be called "informal unions," "cohabitation" or, where the means of its formation is irrelevant, simply a "family."

B. STATUTORY SPOUSES

1) Legislation Overview

When legislation seeks to affect the rights and obligations of persons who are cohabiting in an intimate relationship, it will describe the affected persons as "spouses." At present some sixty-five Ontario and forty-five federal statutes make use of the term. However, there is no standard definition of "spouse." Some acts fail to define the word at all,

---

10 *Report on the Rights and Responsibilities of Cohabitants under the Family Law Act* (Toronto: Ontario Law Reform Commission, 1993) at 31 [OLRC *Report on Cohabitation*].

11 *Ibid.* The OLRC refrained from recommending that the Act be reformed so as to include same-sex couples in the extended definition of spouse, and called instead for the gathering of more information from the gay and lesbian communities as to whether such inclusion would suit the needs of these communities.

12 See section B(2)(c), "Common Law Marriage," in chapter 2, "Marriage."

others make use of one of the three or four recurring definitions,[13] and still others construct meanings specific to their purposes. This widespread use of "spouse" reveals the diminishing importance of legal marriage as the source of family-related rights and obligations.

The definition of primary interest here is the one under the *Family Law Act*, which regulates many of the matters of substance between family members. This definition is examined in the section immediately below.

2) The *Family Law Act*

The Act makes a number of rights and obligations depend upon a person's being a "spouse." That relational term is basically defined in section 1(1) to include persons married to each other and those persons who in good faith entered into a marriage that proved to be voidable or void. An extended definition occurs in section 29 and is applicable only to Part III of the Act, dealing with support obligations.

The extended definition, which creates what are called here "statutory spouses," reads as follows:

> 'spouse' means a spouse as defined in subsection 1 (1), and in addition includes either of a man and woman who are not married to each other and have cohabited,
>
> (a) continuously for a period of not less than three years, or
> (b) in a relationship of some permanence, if they are the natural or adoptive parents of a child.

This is a category of limited though important utility. A "spouse" within the meaning of this definition would be obliged to "provide support for himself or herself and for the other spouse, in accordance with need, to the extent that he or she is capable of doing so."[14]

---

13   Two popular definitions used in Ontario legislation, which might be compared to that under the *FLA*, are as follows:

"'[S]pouse' means the person to whom a person of the opposite sex is married or with whom the person is living in a conjugal relationship outside marriage": see, for example, *Loan and Trust Corporations Act*, R.S.O. 1990, c. L.25, s. 1.

"'[S]pouse' means a person of the opposite sex, (a) to whom the person is married, or (b) with whom the person is living outside marriage in a conjugal relationship, if the two persons (i) have cohabited for at least one year, (ii) are together the parents of a child, or (iii) have together entered into a cohabitation agreement under section 53 of the Family Law Act": see, for example, *Municipal Act*, R.S.O. 1990, c. M.45, s. 1(1).

14   *FLA*, above note 1, s. 30. See chapter 12, "Financial Support," for a discussion of support obligations.

But only section 1(1) spouses—those married or whose good faith marriages are void or voidable—have property rights against each other under this Act. Note, too, that whether or not a person is a spouse has no bearing on a parent's obligation to support his or her children, or on issues of custody and access.

a) A Man and a Woman

As was the case with cohabitation agreements, the language of the *FLA* confines the benefits of the legislation to heterosexual couples. As yet, challenges to the heterosexual nature of marriage law have been unsuccessful in Canada, and there have been no recorded attempts to test the Act concerning cohabitation agreements. After a number of challenges in the courts to the exclusively heterosexual nature of family laws, and a strong set of recommendations from the Ontario Law Reform Commission,[15] the Ontario government introduced a bill[16] that, among other things, would have included same-sex couples in the definition of "spouse"; but instead of using its majority to ensure passage of the bill, the government allowed a free vote, and the bill was defeated on Second Reading.[17]

However, a recent 2 to 1 decision of the Ontario Court of Appeal held that section 29 must be extended to cover same-sex couples.[18] It was conceded by all parties and intervenors, the attorney general of Ontario included, that section 29 violated section 15 of the *Charter*,[19]

---

15   OLRC *Report on Cohabitation*, above note 10.

16   Bill 167, *Equality Rights Statute Law Amendment Act*, 3rd Sess., 35th Leg., Ontario, 1994.

17   See B. Cossman, "Same-Sex Couples and the Politics of Family Status" in J. Brodie, ed., *Women and Canadian Public Policy* (Toronto: Harcourt Brace, 1996) at 223–24. In July 1997, British Columbia altered the definition of spouse in its *Family Relations Act* in order to encompass same-sex couples for the purposes of support, custody, and access matters (but not matrimonial property or division of pension benefits): *Family Relations Act*, R.S.B.C. 1996, c. 128, as amended by S.B.C. 1997, c. 20, s. 1(c).

18   *M. v. H.* (1996), 31 O.R. (3d) 417 (C.A.), leave to appeal granted (24 April 1997) S.C.C. Bulletin, 1997, p. 1106.

19   The majority (*per* Charron J.A.) said that this concession was "properly made having regard to both the record before the court and the relevant jurisprudence." They referred particularly to the trio of recent cases decided by the Supreme Court of Canada having to do with discrimination on the basis of sex or sexual preference— *Miron v. Trudel*, above note 8; *Egan v. Canada*, [1995] 2 S.C.R. 513, and *Thibaudeau v. Canada*, [1995] 2 S.C.R. 627—and they adopted the two-step approach to s. 15 of the *Charter* set out by McLachlin J. in *Miron* (at 485–92) in which the applicant must show first that her right to equality has been denied due to discrimination, and, second, that this distinction constitutes discrimination by coming within an enumerated or analogous ground. Using this approach the court decided that the definition of "spouse" in s. 29 violates s. 15 of the *Charter*, above note 8.

and was held by the court that the infringement could not be justified under section 1. Accordingly, when the court-ordered remedy takes effect,[20] the words "a man and woman" are to be severed from the section 29 definition of spouse, and the words "two persons" are to be read in substitution. Thus, if the judgment is not overturned on further appeal,[21] it seems likely that the legislation will be changed to accommodate the needs of same-sex couples.

b) Persons Who Cohabit

To qualify for support under the section 29 extended definition of spouse, the parties to the action must have cohabited within the meaning of the Act. "Cohabit" is defined in section 1(1) as meaning "to live together in a conjugal relationship, whether within or outside marriage." Basically, the courts have determined that the word "conjugal" refers to marriage, and, given that it is not possible to "live together in a [marriage] relationship . . . outside marriage," they have understood the legislature to require that the relationship be "marriage-like."[22]

The difficulty, then, to be confronted in this comparison approach is the nature of marriage or the marriage relationship. Courts have by and large adopted an unexamined view of marriage, asserting without evidence or doubt that the marriage relationship has certain characteristics and that these ought to form the basis for a comparison with the relationship in question. If a significant (but unspecified) number of correspondences are found, the relationship under scrutiny will be held to be a "conjugal relationship."

In *Molodowich* v. *Penttinen*[23] the court identified seven "descriptive components" of marital cohabitation, and, therefore, of marriage-like

---

20   This remedy was suspended for a year, that is, until 18 December 1997, in order to give the legislature time to fashion an effective reform.

21   The judgment is under appeal to the Supreme Court of Canada. The Supreme Court of Canada decided *Egan* v. *Canada*, above note 19, shortly before the Ontario Court of Appeal considered *M.* v. *H.*, above note 18. *Egan* challenged the heterosexual definition of "spouse" in the federal *Old Age Security Act* (now R.S.C. 1985, c. O-9); the majority ruled that the definition violated s. 15 of the *Charter*, above note 8, but was a supportable infringement under s. 1. In *M.* v. *H.*, Charron J.A. decided that Egan was distinguishable in this latter respect because the objectives of Parliament in the *Old Age Security Act* were significantly different from those of the Ontario legislature as expressed in the *Family Law Act*.

22   *Sanderson* v. *Russell* (1979), 24 O.R. (2d) 429 at 432 (C.A.); see also: *Feehan* v. *Attwells* (1979), 24 O.R. (2d) 248 (Co. Ct.); *Harris* v. *Godkewitsch* (1983), 41 O.R. (2d) 779 (Prov. Ct.).

23   (1980), 17 R.F.L. (2d) 376 (Ont. Dist. Ct.).

cohabitation as well: arrangements concerning shelter; sexual and personal behaviour; domestic services; social activities; societal attitudes; arrangements concerning financial affairs; and conduct respecting children. The judge proceeded to formulate a series of some twenty-two questions under these headings, which courts subsequently have found useful in making the determination about cohabitation. A sampling will give the sense of the level of analysis involved:

1. (b) What were the sleeping arrangements? . . .
2. (a) Did the parties have sexual relations? If not, why not? . . .
   (g) Did they buy gifts for each other on special occasions? . . .
3. What was the conduct and habit of the parties in relation to:
   (a) preparation of meals . . .
   (b) washing and mending of clothes . . .
5. What was the attitude and conduct of the community toward each of them and as a couple?
6. What were the financial arrangements between the parties regarding the provision of . . . the necessaries of life . . .[24]

This measuring of proximity to the "real thing" might work as long as everyone had a reasonably similar view of the "normal" marriage, and consequently was able to understand the significance of possible answers to these questions.[25] However, whatever might have been true when the approach was devised, it is unlikely to be the case today that all marriages in Ontario tend towards some norm or common set of features.[26]

---

24 *Ibid.* at 381-82.
25 For example, the *Molodowich* (above note 23) approach was applied in *Zegil v. Opie* (1995), 8 R.F.L. (4th) 91, additional reasons at (1995), 18 R.F.L. (4th) 347 (Ont. Gen. Div.), approved on this point (1997), 28 R.F.L. (4th) 405 (Ont. C.A.). The court found among other things that the woman "did not provide any meals, do any shopping or provide any domestic services. There is no evidence that [she] ever washed or mended clothes." There was no further discussion in the judgment, explaining why in this case it was appropriate to impose the burden of domestic services on the woman. See also *Harris v. Godkewitsch*, above note 22 at 782: "[The respondent] asks me to take judicial notice of what I see as a normal standard for marriage."
26 The OLRC *Report on Cohabitation*, above note 10 at 62, criticizes the use of a notion of "normal" marriage:
    This jurisprudence propagates a stereotypical model of marriage that fails to account for the existing diversity of marital relationships. Reliance on this approach also leads courts to engage in inquiries into the intimate details of relationships, intruding on personal privacy. The tendency to measure common law relationships against a stereotypical view of marriage is regrettable and should be resisted.

Moreover, the approach fails to assist courts in explaining the rational connection between these questions, or answers to them, and the claim being made by the plaintiff for financial support. What is the relevance of sexual relations to financial support? There may arguably be one in a particular case, but the comparison approach evades the issue by moving in two discrete steps, first from sexual practices to (marriage-like) status, and then from status to support.

A somewhat different tack was taken in *Stoikiewicz* v. *Filas*.[27] The court observed that the intent of the *FLA* was "to view the marriage relationship, for its purposes, primarily in the nature of an economic partnership."[28] Particularly, the support provisions were to be responsive to "the intermeshing of the relative productivities of each of the spouses together with their economic needs resulting from the way they have divided up their respective duties and obligations in the marriage."[29] Relevant questions would direct themselves at determining the degree of economic intimacy between the parties, for it is out of such financial interdependence that need attributable to the relationship can arise. In such a focused calculus, matters like sexual behaviour are of no intrinsic importance, but may be relevant insofar as they go to establish economic intimacy. The *Stoikiewicz* approach, however, has not found favour with the courts,[30] and the *Molodowich* approach continues to be found useful.[31]

c) Three-Year Spouses

The requirement under section 29(a) of the *FLA* is that the parties have cohabited "continuously for a period of not less than three years." The point has been made that the requirement of three years serves to create

---

27 (1978), 21 O.R. (2d) 717 at 719 (U.F.C.). "Somewhat different," because the court did, after all, observe at one point: "There is much to support a positive finding in that regard. For example . . . [t]he applicant [woman] cooked and washed for the respondent."

28 *Ibid.* at 720.

29 *Ibid.*

30 See, for example, *Armstrong* v. *Thompson* (1979), 23 O.R. (2d) 421 at 423 (H.C.), where that case was explained as dependent upon its "peculiar facts." The court said that "[t]he economic dependence theory is not applicable to this situation . . . [T]here is nothing in the material to indicate that this was anything but a traditional married couple." There was no indication as to whose tradition was meant. See also *Labbe* v. *McCullough* (1979), 23 O.R. (2d) 536 at 538 (Prov. Ct.), where the court referred to "the peculiar economic arrangements" in *Stoikiewicz*. But see *Batiuk* v. *Pride*, [1989] O.J. No. 1567 (Prov. Ct.).

31 See, for example, *Charbot* v. *Hood*, [1990] O.J. No. 2614 (Prov. Ct.).

"a time period as a proxy for evidence that the couple has a relationship of economic interdependence meriting the imposition of rights and responsibilities under the Act."[32] Thus, if some sufficient degree of domestic intimacy is found and persists for three years, it can be presumed that there will by then be an economic intimacy. It would seem simpler, less intrusive, and more to the point, however, to go directly to the issue of financial interdependence.

The issue of continuousness is, in a sense, resolved by the same means used to discover whether a couple were cohabiting at all; that is, by asking, was the intensity of their relationship—the frequency of their dealings across a sufficiently broad range—such that for three years it fell within limits set by reference to normal or traditional marriages?[33] It is impossible to say with any precision how much off-again/on-again in the union, or how much occasional attenuation in relations would be permissible and still have continuous cohabitation.[34]

Within this broader problem is the special practical difficulty of determining when cohabitation has ended. This will be important, of course, because of the three-year deadline. And it may be a special difficulty because of the nature of many couples' relationships, which will perhaps tend to begin with a bang and end with a whimper. The intensity of a relationship may be highest at the outset, so that there is no difficulty in identifying it as "conjugal," however that term might be construed; but when passions cool or goodwill dissipates, the relationship may begin to deteriorate, first in this and then in that respect, until at last it must be regarded as at an end. But identifying the critical moment is not an easy task for courts.

To assist in this respect, courts resorted to the device of intention, as is done when considering whether married persons are living "separate and apart" for the purposes of the *Divorce Act*.[35] In determining

---

32 OLRC *Report on Cohabitation*, above note 10 at 63.

33 See, for example, *Zegil v. Opie* (1995), 8 R.F.L. (4th) 91 at para. 105, in which the court said: "The varying degrees . . . of the descriptive components detailed in *Molodowich* need to be examined . . . to determine when the parties demonstrated a settled intention in a convincing manner that their marriage-like relationship was at an end."

34 See *Feehan v. Attwells*, above note 22 at 252: "The separation [of three weeks] was no more than a period of reflection—of reassessment . . ." In *Sanderson*, above note 22 at 432, a four-day separation (at a point five months shy of the deadline) did not end cohabitation but was a "brief cooling-off period." See also *Harris v. Godkewitsch*, above note 22, for an example of a court struggling to apply the requirement of continuousness to a relationship of fluctuating intensity.

35 *Divorce Act*, above note 1, s. 8(2)(a).

when cohabitation ended, the Ontario Court of Appeal in *Sanderson* v. *Russell* said:

> Without in any way attempting to be detailed or comprehensive, it could be said that such a relationship [i.e., "cohabitation . . . in a conjugal relationship . . . outside marriage"] has come to an end when either party regards it as being at an end and, by his or her conduct, has demonstrated in a convincing manner that this state of mind is a settled one.[36]

This turning to a (constructed) mental phenomenon permits the court to make a decision as to the critical moment a relationship ended without having to place inordinate stress upon any particular event or lack of action. It allows for the bridging of gaps in the relationship as being "brief cooling-off period[s]"[37] and perhaps gives courts some freedom to protract the continuation of cohabitation past the last physical symptom, where to do so might be just.

It seems likely that the reference to "conduct" in the quotation from *Sanderson* above simply means to acknowledge that not only must there be an intention to end cohabitation by one of the parties but there must also be, of course, no further significant acts of cohabitation. There is no reason to require that the intention to end cohabitation be demonstrated in any particular objective way.

d) Parent Spouses

i) *Relationship of Some Permanence*

Section 29(b) of the *FLA* deems to be spouses those who have cohabited "in a relationship of some permanence" and are the parents of a child. This is a difficult and puzzling requirement, not the least because of the seeming contradiction in terms contained within it: one normally regards permanence as an absolute not capable of qualification by "some."

The predominant sense of "permanence," in ordinary use at least, has to do with duration, persistence across time. But simple duration is dealt with in the previous paragraph of the legislation, which sets three years as the length of time for rights to ripen. Thus, the difficulty of interpretation has entailed, essentially, a search for the proper features beyond duration of this limited form of permanence.

---

36   Above note 22 at 432.
37   *Ibid.*

In the case of *Labbe* v. *McCullough* the court said of the matter before it: "I place great weight on the fact that the parties discussed the possibility of marriage some day. In my view, this gives the relationship a touch of permanence."[38] The discussion of marriage seems to have provided the courts in a number of other cases as well with the hook on which to hang the conclusion of "some permanence."[39] No other important factor or interpretation has emerged from the case law.

The fundamental difficulty is that no clear purpose has been devised for the requirement of "some permanence." The imposition of support obligations on "parent spouses" appears aimed at recognizing that the birth (or adoption)[40] of a child may mean that one parent will be temporarily unable to be self-supporting because of childcare responsibilities. (This will typically be the mother, who, in the case of a birth, may also need a reasonable time to recuperate from the experience.) Because the other parent shares responsibility for the creation of this need, he ought to provide support if he is able to do so.[41]

However, this argument would seem to hold true whether or not the parents of the child ever cohabited; that is, cohabitation is not necessary as a need-causing factor: the creation of a child accomplishes this adequately on its own. Why, then, was it legislated that only those child-rearing parents who were in "a relationship of some permanence" might have their need met?

The answer very likely has to do with a morally disapproving attitude towards women who become pregnant in the absence of even the

---

38 Above note 30 at 538. The parties in that case cohabited for one period of four weeks and another period of two weeks. So much for duration.

39 *Donheim* v. *Irwin* (1978), 6 R.F.L. (2d) 242 (Ont. Prov. Ct.): cohabitation for eleven months; the respondent had promised marriage upon the completion of his divorce. *Rook* v. *Mahoney*, [1983] O.J. No. 713 (Prov. Ct.): cohabitation for nine months; "[t]hey had discussed marriage as a future commitment when the respondent obtained his divorce." But see *Batiuk* v. *Pride*, above note 30: cohabitation for four and a half months; engagement to marry; the court said, "[t]he engagement is an indication to me of an intention to establish a permanent relationship but not, in my view, proof of the establishment of the permanent relationship, particularly when no marriage date was set."

40 Adoption was added in S.O. 1986, c. 4, s. 29.

41 Test this notion with the following thought experiment: A man and woman cohabit briefly, and the woman becomes pregnant; the couple separate; the child is born and the woman assumes responsibility for childcare; the man loses his job and sues the woman, who has some ability to pay, for spousal support on the basis that they are "parent spouses." Most people would feel that the provision was not intended to work in this "reversed" way, and the man would likely not succeed. But the reason would have to be that the rationale behind the provision has to do with meeting need caused in a certain way.

parodic "touch of permanence" that discussion of marriage provides. In the light of the diminishing social disapproval of birth out of wedlock,[42] this provision hardly seems justifiable and ought to be replaced with a straightforward obligation to support the parent who bears the initial burden of childcare.

ii) Parents of a Child

Because this definition of spouses as "parents of a child" is aimed at meeting the need caused by the appearance of a child, it is essential that the parties be "the natural or adoptive parents of a child."[43] And it would seem sensible, in the light of the above argument, to require that the child be a clear, if not the primary, factor that causes the need of the spouse applying for support; otherwise, there would be little point in distinguishing between parent spouses and three-year spouses.[44] This position is supported by observing that the provision is worded so as to exclude adults who are "parents" because they stand in the place of a parent;[45] this makes it clear that the mere presence of a child within the family—even if it entails need in the parent responsible for child-care—will not be enough; there must be a child whose very existence in the family has been caused by the parent.[46] Indeed, if one were to

---

42 See B. Ram, "Current Demographic Analysis, New Trends in the Family," Statistics Canada, Catalogue 91-535E (Ottawa: Ministry of Supply and Services, 1990) at 33. The number of reported births to unmarried women between 1975 and 1986 more than doubled: *ibid.* at 31–32.

43 "Natural" is an unfortunate choice of terms with connotations of moral approval, and a term that some take as implying that adoption is not "natural." "Biological" or "genetic" might be better words.

44 In order to see the effect of treating the parental requirement as a technical matter, consider a case in which a couple have cohabited in a relationship of some permanence and are parents of an adult, self-supporting child. (There is no explicit statement in the Act that the child in question be a minor child, and the definition of "child" in the *FLA*, above note 1, s. 1(1), does not require it.) It would be absurd, surely, to treat them as spouses if they have not cohabited for at least three years.

45 See the definition of "parent" in the *FLA*, above note 1, s. 2(1), and the discussion of parents of intention in section D, "Parents of Intention," of chapter 5, "Parentage."

46 The OLRC *Report on Cohabitation*, above note 10 at 63–64, makes the point that the presence of a child may bring about the parents' financial interdependence; but even if it is true that this cause of *de facto* interdependence is more effective than others and, so, worthy of a separate category, it would seem that by its failure to acknowledge parents of intention in this part of the legislation, the legislature did not intend this interpretation. The OLRC has recommended (at 64) the removal of the words "natural or adoptive" from the definition of parent spouses, in order to bring about the inclusion of parents of intention.

adopt the position just set out that the requirement of "some permanence" has a moral thrust, the phrase "if they are the natural or adoptive parents" ought logically to be interpreted such that the child must be conceived during the cohabitation, the socially approved period for permitting pregnancy.

C. A NOTE ON RESTITUTION, EQUITY, AND PROPERTY

Currently, the FLA only makes provision for the sharing of the value of assets between persons who are section 1(1) spouses, that is, those who have gone through a marriage. However, at just about the same time that the Ontario legislature was beginning to respond to the financial plight of married women, the courts were developing a remedy based in the law of restitution and equity for the same economic injustice.[47] The statutory remedy became the principal means for married couples to resolve their property disputes; but, because the Act made no provision with respect to the property of cohabiting couples, unmarried women turned to the courts.

In Pettkus v. Becker, a case involving an unmarried heterosexual couple, the court held that in dividing property there was no basis for distinguishing between "marital relationships and those more informal relationships which subsist for a lengthy period,"[48] and that unjust enrichment in the case at bar gave rise to a constructive trust in favour of the plaintiff, Rosa Becker, entitling her to a half share in the property in question.[49] In what might be described as the heart of the ruling, Dickson C.J. said:

---

47   In Murdoch v. Murdoch, [1975] 1 S.C.R. 423; (1973), 41 D.L.R. (3d) 367, only one of the judges, Laskin J., was prepared to award the wife a share of the ranch property in question; to do this, Laskin J. made use of a novel view of the constructive trust. Following Murdoch, the Ontario legislature passed the first and partial Family Law Reform Act, 1975, S.O. 1975, c. 41. This was succeeded by a much more comprehensive reform to marital property laws in the Family Law Reform Act, 1978, S.O. 1978, c. 2. By that time Rathwell v. Rathwell, [1978] 2 S.C.R. 436 was decided, a 5 to 4 decision, in which three judges in the majority adopted the new remedial constructive trust as applicable to intimate couples. It was not until Pettkus v. Becker, [1980] 2 S.C.R. 834, that a plurality of judges on the Supreme Court adopted the new remedial approach to property division in family cases.

48   Ibid. at 850.

49   Ibid. at 849.

[W]here one person in a relationship tantamount to spousal preju-
dices herself in the reasonable expectation of receiving an interest in
property and the other person in the relationship freely accepts benefits conferred by the first person in circumstances where he knows or
ought to have known of that reasonable expectation, it would be
unjust to allow the recipient of the benefit to retain it.

In subsequent cases the doctrines of unjust enrichment and constructive trust have continued to develop.[50] Judicial concerns have
arisen as to the degree to which the non-title holder must make a direct
or financial contribution to the acquisition of particular property, and
when it is proper to remedy unjust enrichment with monetary compensation rather than a share of property.[51] The remedies have been applied
in the case of a same-sex couple.[52]

Although the common law is prepared to afford relief to unmarried
spouses, judicial remedies are inferior to statutory provisions for property sharing in a number of respects, the full examination of which will
have to await the discussion of family property in chapter 11. Here it
may simply be pointed out that the statute operates from a presumption
that married couples are entitled to a half share of wealth accumulated
during their time together,[53] whereas at the common law one's deservingness has to be argued for on the facts. As well, the property provisions
in the Act enable married spouses to judge their rights and obligations
with some certainty and ease; but there must always be a fair degree of
uncertainty in unmarried couples about the specific applicability of the
common law doctrines.

---

50   This complex body of law is examined in detail in section E, "The Role of
     Common Law Remedies," in chapter 11, "Family Property."
51   See, for example, *Sorochan v. Sorochan*, [1986] 2 S.C.R. 38, in which the property
     in question had already been acquired by the husband when the wife's labour was
     expended, holding that constructive trust need not be confined to cases of
     acquisition but can be applied as well to cases of maintenance, preservation and
     improvement of property; and *Peter v. Beblow*, [1993], S.C.R. 980, in which the
     argument was defeated that the domestic labour of a cohabiting spouse ought to be
     regarded as issuing out of "love" and therefore inapt as a contribution of financial
     value, and in which the court decided that as a general rule a constructive trust
     will not be imposed if damages or monetary compensation is an adequate remedy
     for unjust enrichment.
52   *Brunet v. Davis*, [1992] O.J. No. 1586 (Gen. Div.).
53   *FLA*, above note 1, s. 5(7).

D. PROPOSED REFORM

The Ontario Law Reform Commission has recently made a number of recommendations for legislative reform concerning the formation of legal relations among family members who are cohabiting.[54] These fall roughly into two main categories: recommendations respecting the meaning and rights of "spouses" under the Act, and recommendations respecting a new "registered domestic partnership."

1) The Definition and Rights of a Spouse

The Ontario Law Reform Commission recommended that the definition of "spouse" contained in section 1(1) of the *FLA* should be amended to ensure that those who are currently section 29 statutory spouses (in a slightly amended definition)[55] should in the future have the same rights and responsibilities as married spouses.[56] Essentially this means to extend to statutory spouses those provisions of the Act that deal with the possession of any matrimonial home and the division of net family property at the end of a relationship.

The Commission recommended against including same-sex couples in the reformed definition of "spouse" on the ground that "we do not have adequate evidence before us about the nature of relationships between same-sex cohabitants and the expectations of members of those relationships to justify imposing these rights and obligations upon them."[57]

This collapsing of distinctions between formal and informal unions is supported on the basis of their functional similarity: couples do not behave differently in the two kinds of relationship. Consequently, the logic that makes it appropriate to designate and protect the matrimonial home and to share the wealth accumulated during cohabitation within marriage, also argues for these rights where cohabitation occurs out-side marriage, particularly when considered within the context of the *Charter* and legislation requiring equality.

---

54 OLRC *Report on Cohabitation*, above note 10.
55 The amendment would include parents of intention in the definition of parent-spouse. See note 46.
56 The OLRC *Report on Cohabitation*, above note 10 at 61.
57 *Ibid.* at 56. The Commission recommended that instead same-sex couples be permitted to make cohabitation agreements (see section B(1), "A Man and a Woman," in chapter 3, "Cohabitation Agreements"), and that registered domestic partnerships be instituted (see the section immediately below).

2) Registered Domestic Partnership

The Ontario Law Reform Commission has recommended the creation of a new institution: the registered domestic partnership.[58] Upon the filing of a signed and witnessed registration form, any two persons—whether of the same sex, or whether otherwise related to each other[59]—would become "domestic partners." The only restrictions on partnership would be that couples not be married to each other or already the registered domestic partner of another,[60] and that each person be at least eighteen years old. The Commission felt that this would provide to gay and lesbian couples especially the appropriate alternative to formal marriage, which lay outside its power to affect in any event.[61]

Registered domestic partners would, with some qualification, have all the rights and obligations under the Act that are now given to section1(1) spouses. This would mean that, in the Commission's scheme of things, there should be three different ways of obtaining the full benefits of the Act: formal marriage, registered domestic partnership, and cohabitation of the kind that makes the parties statutory spouses. Each would be open to a somewhat different class of persons.[62]

---

58   *Ibid.* at 53.

59   *Ibid.* "[T]wo sisters or two friends could choose to have their economic relationship governed by the terms of the *Family Law Act*, both during its course and at its end. If the opportunity to register as domestic partners is open to all forms of relationship, registrants will not have to reveal intimate details about their relationship in order to acquire status." Given that the Report was so broadminded in this respect, it is a bit curious that it restricted partnerships to two persons.

60   *Ibid.* The recommendation is that where this restriction is violated, the registered domestic partnership be void, but, as with marriages that are voidable or void, persons who entered into them in good faith should have all the rights that would have accrued had the partnership been valid.

61   See section A(1), "The Division of Powers," in chapter 2, "Marriage": capacity to marry is within federal legislative jurisdiction. The Commission addressed the possibility that legislation creating registered domestic partnerships might be *ultra vires* the province, and decided that it would not: *ibid.* at 60.

62   Re *marriage*: unmarried persons of different sexes who meet the traditional requirements; re *registered domestic partnership*: unmarried persons of eighteen years not already in a partnership; re *statutory spouses*: persons of different sexes who have cohabited under the circumstances described above. As well, of course, couples might choose to devise particular regimes for themselves through the use of cohabitation agreements.

The recommendations provide that deregistration from a domestic partnership should be available at the instance of either partner, upon giving notice to the other partner.[63]

FURTHER READINGS

COSSMAN, B., & B. RYDER, *Gay, Lesbian and Unmarried Heterosexual Couples and the Family Law Act: Accommodating a Diversity of Family Forms, A research paper prepared for the Ontario Law Reform Commission* (Toronto: Ontario Law Reform Commission, 1993)

HOLLAND, W., & B. STALBECKER-POUNTNEY, eds., *Cohabitation: The Law in Canada* (Toronto: Carswell, 1990) looseleaf service

HOLLAND, W., "Cohabitation and Marriage—A Meeting at the Crossroads?" (1991) 7 C.F.L.Q. 33

MACDONALD, J.C., *et al.*, *Law and Practice under the* Family Law Act *of Ontario*, rev. ed. (Toronto: Carswell, 1994) looseleaf service, Part III

ONTARIO LAW REFORM COMMISSION, *Report on the Rights and Responsibilities of Cohabitants under the* Family Law Act (Toronto: The Commission, 1993)

---

63 Above note 56 at 55. This is the administrative, non-justiciable procedure that some have recommended for divorce: see section A(2), "Sources of Law," in chapter 10, "Custody and Access."

CHAPTER 5

PARENTAGE

A. INTRODUCTION

1) Who Is a Parent?

The law knows at least two kinds of parents: those who have the status of parent for general purposes, and those who are defined as parents by a particular piece of legislation for more narrow reasons. There are, as well, other adults who may be recognized by courts or legislation as exercising some of the functions of parents, but who are not described or defined as such within the relevant law.[1]

As is the case with marriage, parentage is a status freighted with legal and social consequence. This status is accorded to the genetic parents of a child by section 1 of the *Children's Law Reform Act*:[2] "[F]or all

---

1   For example, a person who is not anywhere defined as a parent may be awarded custody of or access to a child; the *Children's Law Reform Act*, below note 2, says in section 20(2) that "[a] person entitled to custody of a child has the rights and responsibilities of a parent." Such custodians, when not biological parents, might be said to be "psychological parents." See chapter 10, "Custody and Access."

2   R.S.O. 1990, c. C.12, as amended by S.O. 1994, c. 27, and S.O. 1996, c. 2, s. 63 [*CLRA* or the Act].

purposes of the law of Ontario a person is the child of his or her natural parents."[3] This dependence on the biological connection[4] permits easy identification of a child's mother[5] but can give rise to problems in identifying the father of a child. The status of parent may also be acquired through legal adoption of a child.[6]

Although most statutes rely upon the general definition of parent, there are a few that make use of a special purpose definition.[7] Two important instances, examined below, are the definitions creating parents of intention for the purposes of financial support under the *Family Law Act*[8] and the *Divorce Act*.[9]

---

3   *CLRA*, above note 2, s. 1(2), makes an adopted person the child of the adopting parents "as if they were the natural parents." The use of the word "natural" in this way is unfortunate, suggesting perhaps that other means of being a parent are "unnatural."

4   Compare *L.(T.D.)* v. *L.(L.R.)* (1994), 114 D.L.R. (4th) 709 (Ont. Gen. Div.), where the court decides that the "relationship of father and child" in s. 5 of the *CLRA* need not be biological, because the phrase "natural," which occurs in s. 1 of the Act, is not used in this section. This ruling does not seem correct in this and a couple of other respects (see section C, "A Note on Reproduction Technology," in this chapter). Section 1 is structured to place the child at the fore: ". . . a person is the child of his or her natural parents . . ." and, because the child-father relationship described in the *CLRA* is exclusive, this must mean that a person cannot be the child of a man who is not his or her natural parent.

5   Events subsequent to birth can, of course, mean that the evidence of the connection originally established between mother and child has been lost or forgotten; and the developments of reproduction technology have recently created uncertainty as to the meaning of biological "mother." See section C, "A Note on Reproduction Technology," in this chapter.

6   See section B, "Statutory Framework," subsection "Effect of the Order," in chapter 6, "Adoption."

7   In addition to those statutes discussed here, see: *Child and Family Services Act*, R.S.O. 1990, c. C.11, ss. 37(1) & 137(1); *Employment Standards Act*, R.S.O. 1990, c. E.14, s. 34; *Provincial Offences Act*, R.S.O. 1990, c. P.33, s. 93. A child may also have a guardian of his or her property appointed by a court: *CLRA*, s. 47 ff.

8   R.S.O. 1990, c. F.3, s. 1(1) [*FLA*].

9   S.C. 1986, c. 4 (as amended by S.C. 1990, c. 18, ss. 1 & 2; S.C. 1992, c. 51, s. 46; S.C. 1993, c. 8, ss. 1–5; S.C. 1993, c. 28, s. 78; S.C. 1997, c. 1, ss. 1–15), s. 2(1) & (2).

2) Duties of a Parent

There is no compendious statement in our law of the duties of a parent or the rights of a child.[10] But it is fair to say that parents are expected to exercise a general tutelary responsibility over their children, involving duties of protection, support, education, guidance and, perhaps, love.[11]

In the family law context, three sets of responsibilities are seen as most important. The first has to do with the parents' general duty to protect a child from harm. Failure to meet this duty may result in the community's intervention in the family through the agency of a children's aid society and perhaps the courts, acting under the *Child and Family Services Act*.[12] In such cases disputes about who is a parent, and thus entitled to resist community intervention, for instance, turn on special definitions in the legislation and will be considered later, when child welfare is examined.[13]

The other two sets of responsibilities relate to financial support and to custody, and are important because they represent in legal terms those aspects of the parent-child relationship that parents are themselves likely to disagree about. Most commonly, disputes about support and custody arise when parents who were once living together have separated, and so these matters will be dealt with contextually in Part III of the book, which addresses family breakdown.

---

10   But see *The United Nations Convention on the Rights of the Child*, adopted by the General Assembly on 20 November 1989, and ratified by Canada on 26 January 1990, and in force on 2 September 1990. Article 18.1 provides in part: "Parents or, as the case may be, legal guardians, have the primary responsibility for the upbringing and development of the child. The best interests of the child will be their basic concern." Article 27.2 provides: "The parent(s) or others responsible for the child have the primary responsibility to secure, within their abilities and financial capacities, the conditions of living necessary for the child's development."

11   *Child and Family Services Act*, above note 7, s. 1, sets out the purposes of that legislation and in so doing makes clear that protection of the child is primary. (See chapter 7, "Child Protection.") The *Family Law Act*, above note 8, s. 31, and the *Divorce Act*, above note 9, s. 15(2), impose financial support obligations on parents. (See chapter 12, "Financial Support.") And although child custody is presented as being the right of the adult, it is awarded by courts according to the "best interests" of the child, which are defined in s. 24(2) of the CLRA. (See chapter 10, "Custody and Access.") See also s. 20(2) of the CLRA, which says that a custodian must "exercise those rights and responsibilities in the best interests of the child." The *Education Act*, R.S.O. 1990, c. E.2, s. 21(5), imposes on parents a duty to educate children. Much other legislation, of course, also touches on rights and responsibilities towards children.

12   Above note 11.

13   Chapter 7, "Child Protection."

Financial support for a child can also become an issue between adults who have never lived together and whose only relationship, proven or alleged, is one of being parents of a child. It is in this type of case that the issue of paternity is commonly raised, and in such cases it is typically the man who takes the position that he is not the father.

B. PATERNITY

1) Legal Contexts

Part II of the *Children's Law Reform Act* is titled the "Establishment of Parentage," but for the most part it has to do with the establishment of paternity. Provision is made for an application to determine that "a female person is the mother of a child";[14] and other sections, particularly those dealing with blood tests, might well be of use in any such application. However, the fact of the matter is that maternity is rarely a dubious or contested issue.[15]

a) Declaratory Orders
The issue of parentage—or paternity—can be raised directly. Under the *Children's Law Reform Act* there are three circumstances under which a person may make an application for a declaration as to parentage,[16] each of which has somewhat different legal constraints:

1. *A person may apply for a declaration that a female person is the mother of a child.*
   - Section 4(1) of the *CLRA* permits "any person having an interest" to apply. There is no necessity, therefore, that the applicant be the child.[17]

---

14 *CLRA*, above note 2, s. 4(1).
15 See, however, section B(1)(a), "Declaratory Orders," para. 1, in this chapter. And see section C, " A Note on Reproduction Technology," in this chapter for a discussion of problems that are posed by reproduction technology.
16 *CLRA*, above note 2, s. 3, restricts jurisdiction to make a declaratory order to the Ontario Court (General Division) and the Unified Family Court. It may be that the Court of Appeal and the Ontario Court (General Division) have jurisdiction to make declarations as to parentage ("binding declarations of right") under s. 97 of the *Courts of Justice Act*, R.S.O. 1990, c. C.43: see *Raft v. Shortt* (1986), 2 R.F.L. (3d) 243 (Ont. H.C.), in which Potts J. finds that he has also inherent jurisdiction to make a declaration as to paternity.
17 Be aware that the *CLRA* uses child in this context in a relational sense alone; an adult may be a "child" for the purposes of this part of the Act.

Neither is there a requirement that the person whose maternity is alleged be a living person.[18]

- The Act does not say what will qualify as "an interest" sufficient to give a person standing. This term might sensibly include an asserted familial relationship between the applicant and the woman, or a pecuniary interest in the relationship in question. The social importance of family relationship is clearly sufficient when the relationship is the central one of mother and child; beyond that, it is a matter of judgment as to where, if anywhere, the line is to be drawn through the extended family. Pecuniary interests may involve, for instance, obligations to support a child, or the descent of title to property.

- In a recent case a woman applied for, among other things, a declaration that she was "a mother" of a child who had been born to her lesbian partner; she wished to be named a mother in addition to, not in substitution for, the birth mother.[19] The court refused the application on the ground that this provision in the Act uses the definite article "the," revealing legislative intention that only one mother was contemplated under the Act.[20]

- The standard of proof required is the normal civil standard of "balance of probabilities."[21]

2. *A person may apply for a declaration that a male person is recognized in law to be the father of a child.*

- "Any person having an interest" may apply under section 4(1) for the declaration that paternity is recognized in law. The meaning of "interest" ought to be the same in this context as in the application for a declaration of maternity.

- Again, the applicant does not have to be the "child" or the "father" in question.

- The *CLRA* permits a declaration to be made only "[w]here the court finds that a presumption of paternity exists under section 8."[22] And unless it is proven on a balance of probabilities that "the pre-

---

18 Unless the present tense in "a female person *is* the mother of a child" (emphasis added) is construed so as to require it. There seems no good reason, however, to read it this way, and good reasons to allow historical relationships to be examined and determined after the death of the mother or child in question.

19 *Buist v. Greaves*, [1997] O.J. No. 2646 (Gen. Div.).

20 *Ibid.* at para. 35. The court also said that the section permitted the court to make the order where it finds "that the relationship of mother and child has been established" (*CLRA*, above note 2, s. 4(3)) and the applicant did not have that close a social or emotional relationship with the child.

21 *CLRA*, above note 2, s. 4(3).

22 *Ibid.*, s. 4(2).

sumed father is not the father . . ., the court shall make a declaratory order confirming that the paternity is recognized in law."[23] The requirement that there be an existing presumption of paternity means to restrict applications by "any person with an interest" to those cases where there is already something like a *prima facie* case. This is probably because proof of paternity has until recently[24] depended upon inferences drawn from other facts, and when the difficulty of proof is coupled with the serious social consequences of a declaration, it was felt appropriate to limit applications by those with merely "an interest" in the issue.[25]

3. *A child or a father may apply for a declaration that the relationship of paternity exists.*

- If there is no operating presumption of paternity under section 8 (and thus no *prima facie* case that the man in question is the father) only someone who claims to be a child or a father may apply for a declaration of paternity.[26] This filters out all but the most directly "personal" interest in paternity when there is no strong (i.e., legislatively recognized) social evidence for the claim.
- The application cannot be brought unless both father and child are living.[27] An order made says that "the relationship of father and child has been established."[28]

It may be as well that a person can apply, either under the Act or otherwise,[29] for a declaratory order that he is *not* the parent of a child.[30]

---

23 *Ibid.*
24 DNA tests are now taken more or less as proof positive of genetic relationship, although there may be cases where such testing is not possible—for instance, if tissue samples are not available or the test is too expensive for the parties. See D. Faigman *et al.*, *Modern Scientific Evidence: The Law of Scientific Expert Testimony* (St. Paul, Minn.: West Publishing Co., 1997) at 754.
25 Note the apparently guarded nature of the declaration, which says only that the man is "recognized in law" to be the father. This contrasts with the declaration of maternity, where the order says the woman "is" the mother, and with the declaration of paternity described next. There appears to be no difference in legal effect between being "recognized in law" as the father and being found to be the father, however.
26 *CLRA*, above note 2, s. 5(1).
27 *Ibid.*, s. 5(2).
28 *Ibid.*, s. 5(3).
29 Above note 16.
30 See *Raft v. Shortt*, above note 16, where a motion to strike such an application was dismissed. See also *L.(T.D.) v. L.(L.R.)*, above note 4, where cross-applications for declarations pro and con paternity were tried.

The Act provides that where "evidence becomes available that was not available at the previous hearing," the court may discharge or vary the declaratory order.[31]

b) Incidental Finding

In many actions it may be necessary to make an incidental finding as to parentage or, more likely, paternity. The simplest example may be that of an application by a child for support from the child's father under the *Family Law Act*.[32] The respondent in such an application may deny that he is the father, and the court[33] will be faced with the necessity of trying the issue of paternity.

With applications for declarations of paternity by a person other than the child (or the father), it is necessary to show that a presumption of paternity exists before being allowed to proceed; however, such restrictions do not affect applications by "third persons" that raise the issue of paternity incidentally.[34]

2) General Matters of Proof

The point has been made briefly already that proof of paternity can be difficult. With maternity, the physical connection between mother and child at the moment of birth typically makes evident the genetic connection, but there are no visible or readily observable indicia of a man's genetic connection to his child. The closest we can come is the fact of sexual intercourse with the mother at the time of conception. But even here we are dealing with an imperfect proxy for the invisible biological connection, and there may be doubt about the time of con-

---

31 *CLRA*, above note 2, s. 6.
32 Above note 11, s. 31(1). Application may also be by the "dependant's parent": s. 33(2).
33 *CLRA*, above note 2; the s. 3 jurisdictional restrictions (above note 16) concerning declarations of parentage do not apply to incidental findings of paternity, and Provincial Division courts faced with such issues may use the helpful provisions of ss. 8–13 of the *CLRA*: *K.S.* v. *G.R.*, [1980] O.J. No. 246 (C.A.); and *Sayer* v. *Rollin* (1980), 16 R.F.L. (2d) 289 (Ont. C.A.).
34 Thus, for example, there would be no necessity that a presumption of paternity exist before a woman could apply for spousal support on the basis that she was a parent spouse because the respondent was the father of her child. (See section B(2)(d), "Parent Spouses," in chapter 4, "Cohabitation.")

ception[35] or whether the woman had sexual intercourse with others at the same time.

Moreover, sexual intercourse is not an act like others: it is performed in privacy, and unlikely to have any witnesses; it is often surrounded with serious moral and social implications, which means that the parties may have reasons for misremembering or distorting the truth. Thus, it is often necessary to turn to a proxy for sexual intercourse as well, and to find from certain kinds of social connection that it is probable that sexual intercourse took place.

There are no requirements in the *Children's Law Reform Act* (or other Ontario statutes) that claims of paternity be corroborated or proved in any special way. And in some contested cases the court will have to depend upon findings of credibility as to whether acts of intercourse took place.[36]

However, two aids to proof are available in many, if not most, cases. These are presumptions of paternity and tissue typing, and they are discussed in turn immediately below.

3) Statutory Presumptions

Almost all fathers are legally constituted as such because of presumptions, the majority of which depend upon men's relationships with the mothers of the children. Section 8(1) of the *CLRA* sets out six circumstances under which "[u]nless the contrary is proven on a balance of probabilities, there is a presumption that a male person is, and he shall be recognized in law to be, the father of a child." These could be said, by and large, to describe social relations that make the genetic connection probable or at least arguable (and, to an extent, social relationships that make sexual intercourse morally acceptable).

---

35 The human gestation period varies considerably, such that calculating backwards from the time of birth may not be done with any real accuracy, even on the assumption that the period was of normal length. See, for example, *S. (E.A.) v. B. (K.M.)* (1989), 24 R.F.L. (3d) 220 at 223 (Ont. Dist. Ct.), where the judge took judicial notice of the fact that the human gestation period is "about 9 months"; and *Re Ruby* (1983), 43 O.R. (2d) 277 (Surr. Ct.), in which Haley Surr. Ct. J. surveyed the case law and found that the period between insemination and labour, the important period in paternity cases, has been taken to range between 265 to 270 days, though courts have taken judicial notice of periods as long as 280 days.

36 See *P.C. v. G.H.*, [1984] O.J. No. 650 (Prov. Ct.) for a typical example of proving paternity in the absence of blood tests or presumptions.

The following is a list of circumstances that give rise to the presumption of paternity:

1. *Where the man is married*[37] *to the mother at the time the child is born*
   This is the modern version of the old, common law "presumption of legitimacy," which presumed that children born in wedlock were the children of the married couple and therefore not bastards. Now that the concept of illegitimacy has been abolished,[38] the presumption from marriage directs itself, more sensibly, at paternity. The notion would seem to be that marriage implies sexual intimacy (and perhaps sexual fidelity), which in turn implies insemination.

2. *Where the man was married to the mother within 300 days of the birth of the child*
   If conception took place during a now-terminated marriage,[39] the man is presumed to be the father. Note the long gestation period, a month longer than "normal."[40]

3. *Where the man marries the mother after the birth and acknowledges paternity*[41]
   The acknowledgment must be that he is the "natural father," and, presumably, not simply that he is prepared to assume the responsibilities of paternity. This latter notion does, however, seem to be the sense behind the presumption, because a man has only limited knowledge about whether in fact he is the father and his acknowledgment may well be inaccurate. The requirement of *ex post facto* marriage seems aimed at protecting the mother and the

---

37   *CLRA*, above note 2, s. 8(2), provides that for the purposes of the presumptions that "where a man and woman go through a form of marriage . . . in good faith, that is void, and cohabit, they shall be deemed to be married during the time they cohabit and the marriage shall be deemed to be terminated when they cease to cohabit." Compare the definition of "spouse" in s. 1(1) of the *Family Law Act*, above note 11, and note that voidable marriages are not referred to here, for the likely reason that they are to be considered valid marriages for this purpose until annulled. (See section C(1), "The Void-Voidable Distinction," in chapter 2, "Marriage.")

38   *CLRA*, above note 2, ss. 1 & 2.

39   *Ibid.*, s. 8(1)2. The marriage is to be terminated "by death or judgment of nullity . . . or by divorce" and the terminating event (or decree *nisi*, in the case of divorce) is to occur "within 300 days before the birth of the child."

40   Above note 35.

41   Although there is no specific form required for the acknowledgment, the *CLRA*, above note 2, provides in s. 12 for the filing in the office of the Registrar General of a statutory declaration as to parentage.

child from undesirable volunteers for paternity[42] and perhaps at providing a moral blessing for the sexual intercourse that must have taken place.

4. *Where the man and the mother were cohabiting in a relationship of some permanence at or within 300 days of the birth*

 Here cohabitation in a relationship of some permanence[43] acts as a substitute for marriage; that is, this sort of relationship makes sexual intercourse likely and that in turn implies insemination.

5. *Where the man, as the child's father, has certified the birth under appropriate legislation*

 In Ontario the appropriate legislation, referred to in the Act,[44] is the *Vital Statistics Act*,[45] which provides for registration of a certified statement of birth by the mother and father,[46] and only permits a father alone to certify birth when the mother is unable to make a statement because of illness or death.[47]

6. *Where, during a man's lifetime, a Canadian court has found him to be the father*

If there are two or more men who would be presumed fathers under these presumptions, then "no presumption shall be made as to paternity and no person is recognized in law to be the father."[48] Such a situation might arise, for instance, if a woman is married but cohabits in a relationship of some permanence with another man.

The question arises whether a plaintiff who is in such a situation might rebut one of the competing presumptions and thus leave the other standing, rather than face the task of persuasion without the considerable benefit of a presumption in her favour. This straightforward

---

42   See *CLRA*, above note 2, s. 9, which provides that a written acknowledgment of parentage "that is admitted in evidence in any civil proceeding against . . . interest . . . " is proof of the fact. Here the context of litigation assures that the person making the acknowledgment will not be an undesirable volunteer because, typically, the mother will be suing for the connection.

43   These terms are the same as those used in the *Family Law Act*, above note 8, ss. 1(1) & 29, to define spouses who have a mutual support obligation. See section B(2), "The *Family Law Act*," in chapter 4, "Cohabitation." It would seem to be even harder in this context to know what "a relationship of some permanence" ought to mean, because cohabitation of some duration alone would be an adequate basis from which to infer sexual relations.

44   *CLRA*, above note 2, s. 8(1)5.

45   R.S.O. 1990, c. V.4.

46   *CLRA*, above note 2, s. 9(2).

47   *Ibid.*, s. 9(1) & (3).

48   *Ibid.*, s. 8(3).

approach seems at first possible because section 8(1) clearly makes presumptions rebuttable. But difficulty is suggested by the language of section 8(3), which says, "[w]here circumstances exist that give rise to" presumptions identifying more than one man, then no presumptions obtain. The "circumstances" giving rise to the presumptions—marriage to a man, in the example above—are not the presumptions themselves, and will continue to exist even if the latter are rebutted—as might be the case if lack of access by the husband were proved, for instance.

4) Tissue Testing

Section 10 of the *CLRA* permits a party to apply for leave to obtain blood tests of relevant persons. No person can be compelled to submit to a blood test; however, where a person named in the order refuses to submit to a test, "the court may draw such inferences as it thinks appropriate."[49]

Two of the issues raised by blood testing will be examined here: When ought leave for testing to be ordered, and what probative effect should be accorded the results?

a) Leave to Order Tests

Section 10 of the *CLRA* provides that, upon application, a court "may give the party leave to obtain blood tests," but it is not entirely clear on what basis the court should exercise its discretion. Three factors have emerged as meriting consideration from time to time: the interests of justice, possible inconvenience or physical harm to resisting parties, and the best interests of any minor children involved.

The interests of justice would argue most of the time for the granting of leave, for the simple reason that blood tests offer very valuable evidence concerning the matter in question. As simply put in the House of Lords judgment in *S. v. S.*: "The interests of justice will normally require that available evidence be not suppressed and that the truth be

---

49   *Ibid.*, s. 10(3). This is fairly clearly an *in terrorem* provision, and so the inference is likely to be that a man who refuses is the father, and, where a woman refuses, that the man is not the father. A strictly rational inference from a refusal might be very weakly probative: a man's refusal, for instance, could at its worst only imply that he believed he was the father, which belief might or might not be well-founded, or, indeed, accurate. The inference from refusal will not necessarily be dispositive, however: see, for example, *Teves v. Gilipe* (1985), 48 R.F.L. (2d) 324 (Ont. Prov. Ct.), in which the court found the inference was not enough to rebut a presumption that another man was the father.

ascertained whenever possible."[50] Where, however, the persons seeking leave have discredited themselves, by inordinate delay[51] or by *mala fides*[52] in bringing the application for paternity, for example, the interests of justice may dictate refusing leave, particularly where factors discussed below argue against leave as well.

Courts are cognizant of the fact that a blood test involves an invasion of the person (albeit minor) and that this physical harm, though small, is nonetheless an inconvenience.[53] There are also (small) risks of serious harm from this invasion of the body, such as infection or lasting injury to tissue.[54] It is this harm and inconvenience, and the interests of children, that stand against the simple automatic granting of leave in every case in order to assist the finding of truth.

The best interests of minor children are of concern to the court.[55] Some earlier decisions in other jurisdictions have held that leave should be refused where the proof of the paternity sought would likely result in emotional or psychological harm to the child.[56] However, recent decisions take the position that although the best interests of the child are a relevant factor, it is normally "in the best interests of the child that the truth be ascertained on the best evidence possible."[57]

---

50 *S.* v. *S.*; *W.* v. *Official Solicitor*, [1972] A.C. 24 at 43, [1970] 3 All E.R. 107, Lord Reid and Lord Morris of Borth-y-Gest.

51 See, for example, *McCartney* v. *Amell* (1982), 35 O.R. (2d) 651 (Prov. Ct.).

52 *H.* v. *H.* (1979), 25 O.R. (2d) 219 (H.C.); *D.H.* v. *D.W.*, [1992] O.J. No. 1737 (Gen. Div.).

53 Section 10 of the *CLRA*, above note 2, does not compel any party to submit to tests; however, the ability of the court to draw adverse inferences from a refusal is a coercive force. Section 10 does not violate the *Charter* (*Canadian Charter of Rights and Freedoms*, Part 1 of the *Constitution Act, 1982*, being Schedule B to the *Canada Act 1982* (U.K.), 1982, c. 11): see *Silber* v. *Fenske* (1995), 11 R.F.L. (4th) 145 (Ont. Gen. Div.).

54 Such possible harm will not be assumed, but must be supported with evidence; see *Silber* v. *Fenske*, ibid.

55 See, for example, *D.* (*J.S.*) v. *V.*(*W.L.*), [1995] 5 W.W.R. 495 (B.C.C.A.), where, after canvassing the English case law on the role that the best interests of the child should play, the court decided that the benefits to be obtained from blood tests in this case were so small as not to outweigh "the possible disadvantages" to the child. But the applicant did not have to satisfy the court that the outcome of the test would benefit the child: *S.* v. *S.*; *W.* v. *Official Solicitor*, above note 50, Lords Reid, MacDermott, and Hodson; this case is quoted extensively in *D.* (*J.S.*) v. *V.*(*W.L.*).

56 See, for example, *M.* v. *W.* (1985), 45 R.F.L. (2d) 337 (B.C.S.C.). In that case the results might show that the husband was not the father and this would place on the child the stigma of illegitimacy (no longer a concern in Ontario: see section B(3), "Statutory Presumptions," in this chapter) and would disrupt the family unit.

57 *D.H.* v. *D.W.*, above note . See also *S.* v. *S.*; *W.* v. *Official Solicitor*, above note 50.

It seems that reluctance to give leave for blood tests, particularly where concern is raised about the best interests of a child, stems in part from doubt about the wisdom of pursuing genetic truth; that is, a child does not know about genetic paternity, and, until taught by society, does not care about such things. Thus, an argument can be made for restricting the ability of adults to put a minor child's paternity into question (and, indeed, for redefining paternity so as to base it upon a man's behaviour rather than his genetic relationship). But that argument goes to the nature of the various causes of action and not to the subsidiary issue of means of proving the elements of an action; currently, there is no requirement to address the best interests of minor children before paternity is put in question.

Most rulings appear to take the position that the pursuit of truth in the interests of justice will dictate that leave should be granted unless those interests are outweighed by other factors.[58] However, some courts have seemed to put the matter on a different footing by requiring that before leave can be granted, the applicant must have a case of some potential merit, which seems to be a way of giving force, if not precedence, to the factor of inconvenience and harm. Thus, in *Rhan* v. *Pinsonneault*[59] the court canvassed the material put forward in the parties' affidavits apparently in search of a *prima facie* case for paternity or more; and, on finding too little, the court decided that its "duty to see that the interests of the child are not neglected . . . and that the personal rights of the respondent are not infringed" meant refusal of leave. And in *G.(F.)* v. *G.(F.)*[60] the court decided that the applicant had the burden of first rebutting the presumption in favour of another man before there would be an issue of paternity that would permit the ordering of blood tests.

The better view is that expressed in *D.H.* v. *D.W.*[61] In that case the court pointed out that the position taken in *G.(F.)* v. *G.(F.)* meant the applicant must essentially prove paternity before tests could be ordered. The court agreed that the strength of the case was one relevant factor to

58   See *G.R.* v. *L.H.*, [1995] O.J. No. 1997 (Prov. Div.); *D.H.* v. *D.W.*, above note 52; *McCartney* v. *Amell*, above note 51; *H.* v. *H.*, above note 52; but see, *contra*, *G.(F.)* v. *G.(F.)* (1991), 32 R.F.L. (3d) 252 (Ont. Gen. Div.); and *Rhan* v. *Pinsonneault* (1979), 27 O.R. (2d) 210 (Co. Ct.).

59   *Rhan* v. *Pinsonneault*, *ibid.*

60   Above note 58.

61   Above note 52.

be considered,[62] but said that the proper test was whether the applicant alleged facts such that there was "a real issue to be tried on the question of paternity."[63]

b) Probative Value

It is not always easy to know how to treat the results of blood tests. The proper use of scientific evidence is a very complex matter that cannot be gone into here,[64] but a few comments on testing in the context of paternity might be helpful.

There are a number of tests that can be performed on blood (and to an extent on other tissue as well) ranging in complexity, effectiveness, and cost from the simple A-B-O blood-typing test to highly sophisticated DNA "fingerprinting" techniques. Each is based more or less on the fact that, because certain measurable attributes of human tissue are inherited from genetic parents, they make useful markers of that genetic linkage.

From this fact it follows that it is possible for tests to exclude a man as a possible father of a child: the child possesses a trait that must have come from a parent, but that is possessed by neither the mother nor the tested man. Exclusion is accepted as proof positive of no paternity.

Any of the standard tests may result in exclusion. However, tests have varying powers of exclusion, which are typically described in percentage terms. Thus, for instance, a test that has the power of exclusion of 95 percent is one that 95 times out of 100 will exclude a wrongly named father.[65] It seems to be the case that DNA testing has a power of exclusion of 99 percent or higher.[66]

---

62   It might be better to see this not as an independent factor but as a means of weighing the interests of justice in pursuing truth against the other two factors of inconvenience/harm and the best interests of children. Thus, for example, in *D.(J.S.) v. V.(W.L.)*, above note 55 at 505–6, the British Columbia Court of Appeal (quoting from *Re F*, [1993] 3 All E.R. 596 (C.A.)) decided that where the probable outcome of the proceedings will be the same whoever is determined to be the father, "there is no point in exposing [the child] to the possible disadvantages of a blood test." Our interest in the truth in this particular context becomes minimal and so is outweighed by our concern for the interests of the child.

63   *D.H. v. D.W.*, above note 52. The application ought to be "not simply based on bare allegations or speculation but on alleged facts which, if proven, could substantiate his claim that he is the father."

64   See generally D. Faigman *et al.*, *Modern Scientific Evidence*, above note 24.

65   These powers of exclusion are determined by the use of experiments with groups whose genetic relationships are known for a fact.

66   DNA testing of blood is permitted under s. 10 of the *CLRA: S.(C.) v. L.(V.)* (1992), 39 R.F.L. (3d) 298 (Ont. Gen. Div.). aff'g *C.S. v. V.L.* (1992), 39 R.F.L. (3d) 294 (Ont. Prov. Div.).

When a test fails to exclude a man, this is not simple proof positive of his paternity. To use the example just given, the failure of a test with the power of exclusion of 95 percent to exclude a man means that he might be the father or he might be innocently among the 5 percent of the population of men who are not the father but whom the test is likely not to exclude.

The difficulty of this is that 5 percent of the male population is a large group of people. Or, to put it another way that takes better account of geographical context, any untested man in the "vicinity" also has a one-in-twenty chance of being the father.

How persuasive this sort of evidence ought to be depends entirely on the context. If it is accepted on other bases that the man in question had sexual intercourse with the mother at the crucial period, for instance, a court might regard failure to exclude by this test as very highly probative.[67] Whereas, if the evidence accepted by the court simply points to a few social contacts between the couple, it might be felt insufficient to cause a finding of paternity.

C. A NOTE ON REPRODUCTION TECHNOLOGY

Reproduction technology has begun to introduce possibilities for the creation of children that the law does not yet comprehend.[68] Merely one source of difficulty for the law lies in our ability to remove gametes from men and women, and to use this genetic material, sometimes many years later, to create children. And a question—only one of many—is then posed whether and to what degree parentage in such cases ought to be based on genetic connection, on features of the context in which the child is created, or on some other basis altogether.

Removal for later use of gametes—sperm—from men is nothing new: simple artificial insemination by donor has been known and practised for years.[69] Even so, our statutes provide no explicit solutions to

---

67   See, for example, *D.(D.P.)* v. *K.(J.A.)* (1992), 43 R.F.L. (3d) 251 (B.C.C.A.), where the court considered a test that was said to prove a 94.76 percent probability of paternity.

68   See Canada, Royal Commission on New Reproductive Technologies, *Overview of the Legal Issues in New Reproductive Technologies* (Vol. 3 of the Research Studies) ([Ottawa]: Royal Commission on New Reproductive Technologies, 1993).

69   See, for example, *Orford* v. *Orford* (1921), 58 D.L.R. 251 (Ont. H.C.), a case in which it was decided that artificial insemination could constitute adultery.

the legal problems that this practice can raise; and, because the laws are framed upon the assumption of insemination by sexual intercourse, they present stumbling blocks, in fact, for courts who wish to fashion responsive judgments.

An illustrative case is *L.(T.D.)* v. *L.(L.R.)*,[70] where a married couple decided on artificial insemination by an anonymous donor (AID) because, as was known to the wife before the couple married, the husband had a low sperm count. As the pregnancy developed, relations soured and shortly after the birth the parties separated. Subsequently, when access to the child was denied him, the husband applied for, among other things, a declaration that he was the father of the child.

The court made a declaration under section 5[71] of the *CLRA* that the husband was the father.[72] Although the result—paternity when AID occurs by agreement within marriage—may be desirable, it is a strained interpretation of the Act that fails to come to grips with the fact that under section 1(1) "a person is the child of his or her natural parents." Thus, Mr. Low is ruled to be the child's father, but the infant is, by definition, not his child. The court ought, perhaps, to have challenged the notion that one may only have a single pair of parents, or the notion that "natural" means biological.[73] The important point,

---

70 Above note 4. See *Zegota* v. *Zegota-Rzegocinski* (1995), 10 R.F.L. (4th) 384 (Ont. Gen. Div.). See also dicta in *Keeping* v. *Pacey*, [1995] O.J. No. 1982 (Prov. Div.), aff'd (1996), 91 O.A.C. 273 (C.A.).

71 See section B(1)(a), "Declaratory Orders," in this chapter. The court apparently does not see the paradox involved in its use of s. 5: this section is applicable where no presumption exists; no presumption exists in this case because the presumption of paternity that arises from his marriage to the mother has been rebutted by the fact of AID; but if a presumption has been rebutted, then, according to the language of s. 8, the "contrary [of his paternity] is proven."

72 This decision was based on the fact that although the adjective "natural" is used to modify "parent" in s. 1(1) of the Act ["a person is the child of his or her natural parents"] and also "father" in s. 8(1)3 [a presumption of paternity exists where "the person marries the mother . . . and acknowledges he is the natural father"] it is not used to modify "father" in ss. 4 and 5, which "suggests the intention of a meaning broader than mere 'biological' father, in those sections." (*L.(T.D.)* v. *L.(L.R.)*, above note 4.) This was reinforced by the fact that s. 5(3) speaks of "the relationship of father and child." The court cited a New Jersey case that reasoned that public policy is best served by deciding "problems presented by the use of AID techniques" in such a way that family units and parent-child relationships are created: *S.* v. *S.*, 440 A.2d 64 at 68 (N.J. Superior Ct. 1981).

73 See also *Buist* v. *Greaves*, above note 19, where the court made the point that the Act contemplates one mother because of the use of the definite article "the" in the section permitting declaration of parentage.

however, is that the legislation did not, and still does not, address the situation directly.[74]

If something that is fairly common creates unresolved issues, how much more difficulty must other technological possibilities pose. Who is "the mother," for instance, where an ovum from woman A is fertilized *in vitro* and implanted in the uterus of woman B, who subsequently gives birth to the child?[75]

D. PARENTS OF INTENTION

1) Under the *Family Law Act*

For limited purposes, the *Family Law Act*[76] recognizes the possibility of more than two parents for a child. A pair of reciprocal definitions in section 1 extends the notions of "parent" and "child" beyond the genetic relationship to include persons who have participated in certain conduct. Thus a parent "includes a person who has demonstrated a settled intention to treat a child as a child of his or her family . . ."[77]

---

74 Legislation was introduced in Parliament in response to the report of the Royal Commission on New Reproductive Technologies (see note 75, below); it was aimed, among other things, at preventing the commercialization of human reproduction, rather than at resolving legal problems resulting from use of technology. The bill died on the order paper, 27 April 1997: Bill C-47, *Human Reproductive and Genetic Technologies Act*, 2nd Sess., 35th Parl., 1996.

75 See Royal Commission on New Reproductive Technologies, *Legal and Ethical Issues in New Reproductive Technologies: Pregnancy and Parenthood* (Research Studies, Vol. 4) "The Challenges of the New Reproductive Technologies to Family Law" by E. Sloss & R. Mykitiuk (Ottawa: Minister of Supply and Services, 1993) at 340. See also Ontario Law Reform Commission, *Report on Human Artificial Reproduction and Related Matters*, Vols. I and II (Toronto: The Commission, 1985), which over a decade ago made clear and comprehensive recommendations for legislative reform that were almost wholly ignored.

76 Above notes 8 and 11. That Act deals essentially with financial matters. Thus, the principal purpose of the extended definition is to impose child support obligations on "every parent": s. 31. See also s. 61 and ff., giving "children" the right to sue for the tortious injury to or death of a "parent" and vice versa. And see references to "parent" in ss. 65–68 of the *FLA*, dealing with amendments to the common law.

77 "except under an arrangement where the child is placed for valuable consideration in a foster home by a person having lawful custody": *FLA, ibid.*, s. 1.

a) Child of the Family

An analysis of when an adult has treated a child "as a child of his or her family" has something in common with the examination of when two persons are "cohabiting" such that they are statutory spouses.[78] As the courts in the latter instance compare the relationship in question with a "normal" marriage relationship, so here the courts tend to compare the adult-child relationship at issue with that between a child and a "normal" or "ideal" father or mother.

Thus, for example, in concluding that a man was a "parent" and indeed satisfied virtually all "societally known indicia of parenting," a court took note that a child called the man in question "Daddy"; the child's surname was changed to his; he attended all parent-teacher events at the child's school; he regularly picked the child up from school; he pooled his income with the child's mother's income; he attended and helped pay for the child's ballet lessons; he regularly put the child to bed and read the child stories at bed time; he expanded his life insurance policy to cover the child; he expressed feelings of love for the child directly to the child and to the child's mother; he exercised discipline over the child; and he presented her in society as his child.[79]

There is, however, no source ever cited in judgments for these "indicia of parenting." And there is scant discussion of how a court is to know which are the important ones and when a sufficient number of these are satisfied. There must be more than "a mere display of common courtesy or hospitality"[80] by the person, or "'making nice' to the child in order to curry favour with the spouse,"[81] but how much more?

It would assist to have a clearer sense of why certain adults are to be required to support children, but the courts are not particularly helpful in this regard.[82] The best answer available seems to be that once an adult has voluntarily assumed a support obligation, it ought to be

---

78   See section B(2)(b), "Persons Who Cohabit," in chapter 4, "Cohabitation."

79   *Cassar-Fleming* v. *Fleming* (1996), 20 R.F.L. (4th) 201 (Ont. Gen. Div.).

80   *Spring* v. *Spring* (1987), 61 O.R. (2d) 743 at 749 (U.F.C.).

81   *Cassar-Fleming* v. *Fleming*, above note 79 at 216.

82   See, for example, *Spring* v. *Spring*, above note 80 at 750: "The legislative purpose of the definition is to enact a relationship between respondent and child that as a matter of public policy is considered appropriate to ground the support obligation."

continued[83]—that the child ought not to be regarded as simply a fortunate beneficiary of a volunteer's generosity. This rationale for imposing a support obligation suggests the importance of financial aspects in the adult-child relationship. But the courts have resisted any such narrowing of focus[84] and continue to examine social, emotional, and psychological factors in the relationship, without being able to say what relevance reading a bed-time story yesterday could have to a duty to support today. The child's emotional or psychological need for a parent who reads bed-time stories will hardly be met by the exaction of money from a person who does not live with the child and resists voluntary payment.[85] Indeed, to freight acts of love or consideration with a duty to

---

83   *Theriault v. Theriault* (1994), 113 D.L.R. (4th) 57 at 61 (Alta. C.A.):
    Our society values parenthood as a vital adjunct to the upbringing of children. Adequate performance of that office is a duty imposed by law whenever our society judges that it is fair to impose it. In the case of the natural parent, the biological contribution towards the new life warrants the imposition of the duty. In the case of a step-parent, it is the voluntary assumption of that role.
    It is unusual to have a duty arise without a requirement of detrimental reliance. Because children are unable to support themselves, they are almost always completely dependent on adults. Reliance on support from a volunteer cannot increase their dependence, unless the supporting adult might be said by his conduct to have precluded other and more faithful supporting adults from assuming a parental role. (See *Cassar-Fleming v. Fleming*, above note 79, where the man excluded the child's uncle.) But this logic would dictate, in part, at least, a focus on relationships between the adults which the courts do not use.

84   See, for example, *Ogden v. Anderson* (28 March 1983), Doc. York D1263/82 (Ont. Prov. Ct.), 20 A.C.W.S. (2d) 206 at para. 17:
    I think the cases make it clear that one should look at the whole relationship between the two parties and not just at one or two factors. One should look at such things as, whether financial support was provided; did the parties marry; how long were they together; what was the day-to-day care of the children; what was the role of this person . . . in vital activities such as education and discipline; how did the child and this person acknowledge one another in their respective roles?
    Indeed, in *Do Carmo v. Etzkorn* (1995), 16 R.F.L. (4th) 341 (Ont. Gen. Div.), the court found that the man had encouraged in the children and their mother "complete financial dependency" on him, and yet ruled that he was not a "parent" because he had not cohabited with the mother.

85   It might be interesting for the courts to examine as a rationale the possibility that "parents" benefit from close relationships with children, and ought to recompense the child for the benefits received.

support may act to discourage, among the knowledgeable and calculating at least, these important benefits to children.[86]

b) Settled Intention

The adult must "demonstrate a settled intention to treat the child" in the ways discussed above in section D(1)(a). The emphasis, then, is on an adult's stance with respect to the future, rather than on the weight of past events.[87] This is consistent with the view that sees the support obligation as based on the assumption of a responsibility, which might only be the work of a brief period.

The adult's intention is to be "demonstrated"; that is, it should be determined from his or her conduct.[88]

Once he or she demonstrates the settled intention, the adult's change of mind is unlikely to remove him or her from the category of "parent" and eliminate the obligation to support.[89] This makes good sense, given that the primary use of the extended definition is to impose

---

86 See *Carignan* v. *Carignan* (1989), 22 R.F.L. (3d) 376 at 392 (Man. C.A.), Huband J.A., speaking there of the obligation arising under the *Divorce Act*. And see the "Annotation" to *Andrews* v. *Andrews* (1992), 38 R.F.L. (3d) 200 at 202 (Sask. C.A.) by J.G. McLeod.

   And, seemingly *contra*, see *Siddall* v. *Siddall* (1994), 11 R.F.L. (4th) 325 at 337 (Ont. Gen. Div.) where the court says: "If requiring men to continue their relationship, financially and emotionally with the children is a discouragement of generosity then, perhaps such generosity should be discouraged. This type of generosity which leaves children feeling rejected and shattered once a relationship between the adults sours is not beneficial to society in general and the children, in particular."

87 "The word 'settled', in my opinion, denotes quality and not duration. What is required is a state of mind consciously formed and firmly established. The brevity of the intention — or the brevity of the relationship in issue — is not, of itself, decisive, although it is one piece of evidence from which the prescribed intention may be deduced": *Spring* v. *Spring*, above note 80 at 749.

88 *Barlow* v. *Barlow* (1978), 8 R.F.L. (2d) 6 (Ont. Prov. Ct.); *Spring* v. *Spring*, above note 80.

89 Although the Ontario Court of Appeal has not ruled on the issue, the majority of recent lower court judgments decided against the ability unilaterally to terminate the duty. See: *Cassar-Fleming* v. *Fleming*, above note 79; *Siddall* v. *Siddall*, above note 86; *Bradbury* v. *Mundell* (1993), 46 R.F.L. (3d) 184 (Ont. Gen. Div.); *Delorme* v. *Delorme*, [1993] 45 R.F.L. (3d) 373 (Ont. Gen. Div.); *Spring* v. *Spring*, above note 80. It may be different where an older child rejects the adult as well, making the termination realistically "mutual": see *Andrews* v. *Andrews*, above note 86, decided under the *Divorce Act* definition of parent of intention.

support obligations on unwilling adults, who would rarely continue or admit to continuing the original intention if it meant liability.[90]

2) Under the *Divorce Act*

Upon divorce, the court may make an order respecting the custody[91] or support[92] of any "children of the marriage." This term is defined in part to include a child for whom one or both of the spouses "stand in the place of a parent."[93]

Because there is an overlap between the federal and Ontario legislation providing for child support,[94] there has been a tendency for decisions under them to converge, such that there may be little if any difference between their definitions of parents of intention.[95] However, there remains some uncertainty whether under the *Divorce Act* provisions, it is possible for an adult unilaterally or wilfully to cease to stand in the place of a parent and, thus, to determine his obligation to support a child. In *Carignan* v. *Carignan*,[96] the Manitoba Court of Appeal, stressing the voluntary and intentional nature of the relation, argued for the ability of a parent to terminate it. Whereas, in *Andrews* v. *Andrews*[97] the Saskatchewan Court of Appeal decided that a parent ought not to be able to bring the relation to an end by will.

The weight of opinion, certainly in Ontario,[98] favours the view expressed in *Andrews* that the obligation of support ought to be beyond the control of the parent of intention to terminate.

---

90   It also makes sense that, once it is determined for whatever reason that an adult is a "parent," the duty be imposed regardless of the adult's conduct after separation of the parents, in order not to discourage the adult from maintaining as full a relationship with the child as may be possible. See *Bradbury* v. *Mundell*, above note 89.

91   *Divorce Act*, above note 9, s. 16(1).

92   *Ibid.*, s. 15.1(1).

93   *Ibid.*, s. 2(2). Under predecessor legislation (*Divorce Act*, R.S.C. 1970, c. D-8, s. 2) the term used was "*in loco parentis.*"

94   See, for example, *Siddall* v. *Siddall*, above note 86, where the court observes that "[n]either counsel made any explicit submissions with regards to which legislation their client was relying on . . ." and goes on to examine both definitions of parent of intention.

95   *Cote* v. *Cote* (1995), 12 R.F.L. (4th) 194 (Ont. Gen. Div.); *Delorme* v. *Delorme*, above note 89.

96   Above note 86. Foll'd *Chartier* v. *Chartier*, [1997] M.J. No. 371 (C.A.); the court said that the Supreme Court would have to arbitrate the different views of the provinces on this point, and according to D. Roberts, "Stepparents in child-support limbo" *The Globe and Mail* (15 July 1997) A1, the case will be appealed.

97   Above note 86.

98   See above note 89.

FURTHER READINGS

ONTARIO LAW REFORM COMMISSION, *Report on Human Artificial Reproduction and Related Matters*, Vols. I and II (Toronto: The Commission, 1985)

PAYNE, J.D., & M.A. PAYNE, *Introduction to Canadian Family Law* (Scarborough, Ont.: Carswell, 1994)

ROYAL COMMISSION ON NEW REPRODUCTIVE TECHNOLOGIES, *Legal and Ethical Issues in New Reproductive Technologies: Pregnancy and Parenthood* (Research Studies, Vol. 4) "The Challenges of the New Reproductive Technologies to Family Law" by E. Sloss & R. Mykitiuk (Ottawa: Minister of Supply and Services, 1993)

CHAPTER 6

ADOPTION

A. INTRODUCTION

Formal adoption of children was unknown to the common law, and was introduced in Ontario by statute as recently as 1921.[1] The current legislation, Part VII of the *Child and Family Services Act*,[2] sets out an administrative procedure whereby the Ontario Court (Provincial Division)[3] may make an order for the adoption of a minor or an adult.[4] The effect of an order is to make the adopted person the child of the adoptive par-

---

1   The *Adoption of Children Act, 1921*, S.O. 1921, c. 55.
2   R.S.O. 1990, c. C.11, as amended by S.O. 1994, c. 27, s. 43(2), S.O. 1996, c. C.2, s. 62 [*CFSA* or the Act].
3   *CFSA, ibid.*, s. 3(1). Because there is no common law of adoption and because the jurisdiction over adoption is given to a provincial tribunal, the court has no "inherent" jurisdiction to fall back on; it must operate "within the four corners" of the legislation or lose jurisdiction.
4   Apparently the only reported case on adult adoption under the current legislation is *Re Q.(A.L.K.)* (2 February 1996), Doc. Kitchener A76/94, [1996] O.J. No. 353 (Prov. Div.) in which Katarynych Prov. J. sets out five criteria: 1. There must be a family "gap" in the person's life; 2. The interaction between the applicant and the proposed adoptee should be "materially and substantially a parent-and-child interaction"; 3. This should replace a non-existent parent; 4. The existing claims of the existing parents should not be defeated thereby; 5. The application must be made in good faith.

ent for all purposes of law and to sever legal relations between the adopted person and the previous parents.[5]

Although the legislation is quite detailed, not to say complicated, there are significant features of the adoption process that it does not document, and that will only be found in the policies of agencies involved in the process. These are either children's aid societies or licensed private adoption agencies.

Over the last few decades, the number of children given up for adoption in Ontario has declined dramatically. As a consequence, relatively few adoption orders are made for Ontario children placed by societies or licensees.[6] The majority of adoptions nowadays are step-parent adoptions[7] that take place within the context of a second family. And there is a growing number of "international" adoptions; that is, adoptions here in Ontario of children brought into the province from other countries.[8]

B. STATUTORY FRAMEWORK

What follows is a précis of Part VII of the Act, designed merely to give a sense of the important elements in the adoption process, as seen from the legal point of view, at least; there is no intention here to present any particular interpretation of the provisions outlined. The focus is on those provisions that are concerned with the adoption of minor children. And the order of presentation roughly parallels the order that an adoption itself would take. Because of the constraints of space, some aspects of adoption will be addressed only in this précis.

---

5   CFSA, above note 2, s. 158(2); see section D, "Finality," in this chapter.

6   For example, in 1982, 1,690 children were placed for adoption by children's aid societies or others; in 1993 the number had fallen to 541, less than a third of the former: Ontario Ministry of Community and Social Services, Adoption Unit, Statistics Division, unpublished fact sheets for internal Ministry use, April 1997 [MCSS fact sheets].

7   In 1993 there were 1, 155 step-parent or family adoptions in Ontario, which constituted 64 percent of all adoptions: ibid.

8   Something like 500 international adoption homestudies are received for approval each year by the Ministry: ibid. See section E(1), "International Adoptions," in this chapter.

Consent—A child must first be "freed up" for adoption, and this will probably require the written consent of certain people related to the child.

- No adoption order may be made unless the consent of every "parent" is given in writing.[9] [s. 137(2)(a)]
  - "parent" means the child's mother and others who have one of various established relationships with the child. [s. 137(1)]
  - Consenters must be informed about the process [s. 137(4)] and offered counselling [s. 137(7)], such that a court making the order is satisfied that they understand the nature and effect of the order[10] [s. 152(2)(a)].
  - But if the child is a Crown ward,[11] only the consent of a director of child welfare is required. [s. 137(2)(b)]
- Parental consent may not be given before the child is seven days old. [s. 137(3)]
- A parent may withdraw consent freely within twenty-one days after it was given, and the child will be returned. [s. 137(8)]
- After twenty-one days, a parent may only withdraw consent where the court finds it would be in the best interests of the child to permit withdrawal. [s. 139(1)]
  - "best interests" of a child is defined in the Act. [s. 136(2)]
  - But if, after the twenty-one days, the child has been placed for adoption, consent may not be withdrawn. [s. 139(2)]
- The court may, on notice to the person [s. 138(b)], dispense with a required parental consent if it is in the best interests of the child to do so. [s. 138(a)]

Placement—It is important that a child be placed for adoption with care, because in fact and in law it is a significant event for a child. Restrictions on who can be involved in arranging adoptions direct themselves at the ability to place a child. A placement period lets the prospective adoptive parents and the adoption agency judge the suitability of the placement.[12] Placement is not adoption: it precedes the making of an adoption order.

---

9   The consent of the child is required, too, if the child is seven years old or older: *CFSA*, above note 2, s. 137(6).

10   Those whose consent is required are not parties to the application for an adoption order; they are not present in court, and so their understanding must be proved by others, typically the adoption agency involved.

11   A child found to be in need of protection may be made a ward of the state: see section C(2), "Crown Wardship and Adoption," in this chapter.

12   The legislation contains no standards for judging the suitability of parents seeking to adopt. Placement criteria are found in the policies of adoption agencies.

- Only a children's aid society[13] or a licensed adoption agency[14] may place a child for adoption. [s. 141(1)(a)]
- A court may make an adoption order only where:
  - a child has been properly placed, by a society or a licensee [s. 146(1)(a)],
  - a child has been placed otherwise (i.e., improperly) but has resided with the applicants for two years [s. 146(1)(b)], or
  - there are no requirements concerning placement, because it is a family adoption; that is, the applicant for the adoption order is the child's "relative"[15] or "parent"[16] or is a "spouse"[17] of the parent [ss. 141(8) & 146(2)].
- Where the placement is by a society or licensee, and twenty-one days after consents are given and not withdrawn, all rights and responsibilities respecting the child are transferred from parents to the society or licensee until placement is ended or the child adopted. [s. 137(5)]
- Placement by a society or licensee terminates all outstanding orders of access to the child.[18] [s. 143(1)]

Director's Role—The director of child welfare is given certain duties under the Act, principally to play a general supervisory role, to monitor certain of the actions of private licensed adoption agencies, and to provide the court with information necessary to the making of an order.

- Licensees must notify the director of a proposed placement of a child for adoption. [s. 141(3)(a)]
- Licensees must provide the director with an adoption homestudy of a person with whom it is proposed to place the child. [s. 142(1)]

---

13 *CFSA*, above note 2, ss. 3(1) & 15(2).

14 *Ibid.*, s. 136(1).

15 *Ibid.*: "grandparent, great-uncle, great-aunt, uncle or aunt, whether by blood, marriage or adoption"

16 The term as used in this context is undefined in the legislation. Compare the meaning of parent used in connection with consent to adoption: section C(1)(a), "Parent," in this chapter; and on the meaning of parent generally see section A(1), "Who Is a Parent?" in chapter 5, "Parentage."

17 *CFSA*, above note 2, s. 136(1), adopts the extended definition in Parts I and II of the *Human Rights Code*, R.S.O. 1990, c. H.19, s. 10(1): "'spouse' means the person to whom a person of the opposite sex is married or with whom the person is living in a conjugal relationship outside marriage." But see note 24, below, concerning the requirement of heterosexuality. And see section B(2), "The *Family Law Act*," in chapter 4, "Cohabitation."

18 Except those made respecting Crown wards under Part III of the *CFSA*, above note 2. See section C(2), "Crown Wardship and Adoption," in this chapter.

- The director, on the basis of the adoption homestudy, must approve or refuse to approve[19] a proposed placement by a licensee. [s. 142(2)]
- The director may review the decision of a society refusing to place a child and the decision of a society or a licensee to remove a child from a placement for adoption. [s. 144(1)]
- Where a placement breaks down, the director shall be notified and shall review the child's status. [s. 145]
- Except for a family adoption, the director shall file a statement[20] with the court that the child has resided with the applicant for the requisite length of time[21] and that it is (or is not) in the child's best interests to be adopted by the applicant. [s. 149(1)]

Court's Role—The order of the court effects the adoption. The court plays an administrative role, and is not the arbiter of a *lis* between parties but responds to the application of a person.[22] The court may on its own motion summon any person to appear before it to testify or produce any document.[23]

- An application to a court for an adoption order may only be made by persons who meet three criteria:
  - resident in Ontario [s. 146(5)],
  - the child's "relative" or "parent" or a "spouse" of the parent [s. 146(2)], and
  - an individual applicant, or, in a joint application, two individuals who are spouses of one another[24] [s. 146(4)].

---

19 Where the director refuses, the person proposed for placement and the licensee are entitled to a hearing: *CFSA*, above note 2, s. 142(3).

20 Based on a report of the society that placed the child or of a person approved by the director: *CFSA*, above note 2, s. 149(5).

21 Six months, where the child was placed by a society or licensee; two years, where the placement was improper: *CFSA*, above note 2, s. 149(1).

22 See *Catholic Children's Aid Society of Metropolitan Toronto* v. *O.(L.M.)* (1996), 139 D.L.R. (4th) 534 at 563 (Ont. Gen. Div.), Chapnik J. quoting James J. in the judgment appealed from: "There is a . . . statutory requirement of a 'hearing' for adoption proceedings . . . The long-standing practice in most areas of the province is that these 'hearings' consist of a judge's examination, invariably in the solitude of chambers, of affidavit evidence, declarations, various certificates and other pertinent documents."

23 *CFSA*, above note 2, s. 152(1).

24 But see *Re K.* (1995), 23 O.R. (3d) 679 (Prov. Div.) [approved in *M.* v. *H.* (1996), 27 O.R. (3d) 593 (C.A.)]. The applicants, four lesbian couples, were faced with the provision that only "spouses" may apply jointly for an adoption order; and "spouse" is defined to mean persons of the opposite sex. The court held that the definition of spouse in s. 136(1) of the Act was not constitutionally valid because it required that spouses be heterosexual. See also *Re C.E.G.*, [1995] O.J. No. 4072 (Gen. Div.) to the same effect. Note that where one of the adult couple is the birth mother of the child, the other member of the couple cannot apply as an individual to adopt the child, because an adoption order would terminate the birth mother's status as parent.

- The court may make an adoption order if placement requirements were met [s. 146(1)] or where it is a family adoption [s. 146(2)].
- The court may make an adoption order if it is in the best interests of the child. [s. 146(1), (2)]
- The court must be satisfied that the persons involved in the adoption process have an adequate understanding. [s. 152(2), (3)]

Effect of the Order—The order changes the child's status completely and accords it a new family. This new status is protected against subsequent legal challenge, and there are confidentiality requirements that intend to protect the new family from interference by the child's former family.

- In law, the adopted child becomes the child of the adopting parents for all purposes[25] and ceases to be the child of the previous parents. [s. 158(2)]
- An adoption order is final and irrevocable and, although it may be appealed,[26] is not subject to review in any court.[27] [s. 157]
- Official information relating to the adoption is to be kept confidential [s. 165(1)] and documents used in the application[28] are to be kept sealed up unless the court orders otherwise [s. 162(2)].
- Information may be disclosed under certain circumstances:
  - non-identifying information may be disclosed to the adoptive parents, the adopted person, or close birth relatives of that person [s. 166]; and
  - identifying information may be disclosed:
    - to protect the health, safety or welfare of any person [s. 168];
    - if both the adopted person and a close birth relative register in the adoption disclosure register [s. 167].

---

25 Except for the purposes of the laws relating to incest and the prohibited degrees of marriage (see section B(1)(f), "Lack of Close Relationship," in chapter 2, "Marriage."): *CFSA*, above note 2, s. 158(6).

26 Only the director or the applicant may appeal an order respecting adoption: *CFSA*, above note 2, s. 156(1).

27 Despite "privative clauses" like that in s. 157, courts have in fact reviewed administrative decisions: see S. Blake, *Administrative Law in Canada*, 2d ed. (Toronto: Butterworths, 1997) at 170. Courts have taken the view that if the adoption order was made without jurisdiction—where a fraud was practised on the court, for example—the order is a nullity and might be so pronounced and set aside; but in no reported Canadian case has an adoption order actually been set aside. See *Children's Aid Society of Metropolitan Toronto* v. *Lyttle*, [1973] S.C.R. 568 and dicta in *K.(I.)* v. *Saskatchewan (Minister of Social Services)* (1996), 23 R.F.L. (4th) 423 at 425 (Sask. C.A.).

28 Note that the application is to be heard and dealt with in private: *CFSA*, above note 2, s. 151(1).

– An adopted person of eighteen may ask the Registrar of Adoption Information to make a discreet search for a parent or birth sibling (and vice versa) and "ascertain whether that person wishes to be named in the register" with the consequence that disclosure will follow. [s. 169]

C. CUTTING TIES WITH THE BIRTH FAMILY

The view that has generally been taken of adoption is that it serves to fill a gap in a child's life by replacing parents (and family) who are missing or unable to perform their roles. It is seen as a drastic legal reordering in response to dire circumstances[29] rather than, for instance, an opportunity to share children or child rearing, to enhance a child's fortunes, or to add additional members to a child's kindred.

This view rests, in part, on the assumptions that parents are the crucial elements in a child's life and that there may only be two of them. As a consequence, it becomes important to ensure that a child is disentangled from legal ties to previous parents before new ties are set in place. This is not merely law's concern with order and neatness at work here, but a reflection of the importance that the status of being a parent has in law: even inadequate or unwilling parents occupy an important legal position that must be respected if the rights and obligations of parents generally are to be protected.

1) Consent to Adoption

The device used to free up a child is that of parental consent. And a good number of cases have been tried on the issues of whether parental consent to adoption, once given, may be withdrawn, and of when the requirement of parental consent may be dispensed with. Broadly speaking, there was for many years a see-saw struggle between the legislature and the courts, with the former promoting an adoption scheme that gives precedence to the best interests of children and the latter acting as champions of the rights of parents.[30] That struggle appears to have come

---

29   See *Re Q.(A.L.K.)*, above note 4, at paras 7, 8: "[A]doption . . . [is] a remedy of last resort, within the intentions of this legislation . . . An adoptive family arises from a gap in the child's life left when the child's parents are permanently lost to him or her. Adoption is an expression of society's responsibility to plan for such children if their parents will not, or are incapable of doing so."

30   See *L. v. L.* (1985), 51 O.R. (2d) 345 (Ont. U.F.C.) for an overview of the history.

to an end, and the predominant (though not exclusive) position accepted by the courts is the "child-centred" position in which one does not speak of parental rights but rather of the interests of the child.[31] Wilson J. in the case of *Racine* v. *Woods*[32] expressed the Supreme Court's position succinctly: "[T]he law no longer treats children as the property of those who gave them birth but focuses on what is in their best interests."

Yet, it is only sensible at some point to understand parents as possessing rights to the custody of their children. The fact of the matter is that children are assigned to the care of their parents at birth, and are removed from their care only with reluctance, legal and otherwise.[33] The difficulty facing the courts is to find language that emphasizes the centrality of children's interests while at the same time acknowledging the social and political reality of parents' power.

a) Parent

Every parent must give written consent to the proposed adoption of a child.[34] "Parent" is defined in section 137(1) of the *CFSA* to include the child's mother but not the child's father in so many words; fathers may find themselves to be "parents" depending on what their relationship with the child or the child's mother has been in fact. The failure to include biological fathers as such has been held not to violate the *Charter*: the biological and social-role differences between mothers and fathers

---

31   See *Manitoba (Director of Child Welfare)* v. *Y.*, [1981] 1 S.C.R. 625. And see, for example, *S.(C.E.)* v. *Children's Aid Society of Metropolitan Toronto* (1988), 64 O.R. (2d) 311 at 314 (Div. Ct.):

> [The legislature] has obviously considered that the best interests of the child are the paramount concern and that all so-called rights of the biological parents are subsidiary to what is best for the child. Debate could go on forever as to whether or not the legislative scheme that is embodied in the law of Ontario is the best one that can be devised by human beings. But the legislature considered all of the competing positions and decided the issue as it saw it in the best interests of the child.

32   [1983] 2 S.C.R. 173 at 174, an adoption case from Manitoba.

33   See section C(1)(a), "Family and State," in chapter 7, "Child Protection." As a thought experiment to test the notion that parents have no rights to custody, imagine going to a nursery and picking a child to take home, on the footing that in every respect the child would be better off in your custody: clearly a custody application on this basis would be resisted by the courts; and even if the reasoning was that as a routine matter children were better off with their birth parents (which might be difficult to argue without the circularity that relied on social values), it would make sense to conclude that, in general, parents have a right to the custody of their children.

34   *CFSA*, above note 2, s. 137(2)(a).

provide a rational basis for the legislative distinction, which is said to be not unfair, in that it excludes none but the "casual fornicator."[35]

The *CFSA* describes five circumstances that will constitute a person a "parent":[36]

1. *The man is described in one of the presumptions of paternity in section 8 (1) of the* Children's Law Reform Act.[37]

   The presumptions are based upon sets of social circumstances from which, in the original context, at least, an inference of insemination can be drawn. In the context of adoption, however, because the fact of paternity is not in and of itself relevant, the inference to be drawn from these social circumstances is presumably one of caring about or commitment to the child on the part of the man. Thus, for example, a man who impregnates a woman while cohabiting with her in a relationship of some permanence[38] is, it seems, to be taken on that basis alone to have displayed a sufficient degree of commitment to fatherhood to warrant a say in the child's fate.[39] The commonest use of the presumptions will be to make "parents" out of men who are married to mothers.[40]

---

35   *Re S.* (1987), 63 O.R. (2d) 114 (Prov. Ct.), reversed *S. (C.E.)* v. *Children's Aid Society of Metropolitan Toronto* (*sub. nom. Ontario (A.G.)* v. *Nevins*), above note 31. The reversing Divisional Court judgment dismissed as the product of a fertile imagination the "scenario where a casual fornicator is not told about the pregnancy and, despite his best efforts to do so, is unable to find out the good news that he is to be a father, has any prospect of being a real father to the child frustrated because of s. 131 [now 137] of the Act." See also: *Re T and Children's Aid Society and Family Services of Colchester County* (1992), 92 D.L.R. (4th) 289 (N.S.C.A.). But, *contra*, see: *M. (N.)* v. *British Columbia (Superintendent of Family and Child Services)* (1986), 34 D.L.R. (4th) 488 (B.C.S.C.); and *Waddell* v. *Hunter* (1993), 84 B.C.L.R. (2d) 104 (S.C.).

36   *CFSA*, above note 2, s. 137(1)(b)–(f). These are discussed in order here. It should be noted that though it will typically be the father who makes use of these sections, it need not be so; and others may qualify as a "parent" under some of these definitions.

37   R.S.O. 1990, c. C.12. See section B(3), "Statutory Presumptions," in chapter 5, "Parentage," for a discussion of the presumptions of paternity.

38   See section B(2)(d)(i), "Relationship of Some Permanance," in chapter 4, "Cohabitation."

39   See *S. (C.E.)* v. *Children's Aid Society of Metropolitan Toronto*, above note 31 at 317: "The statute recognizes as a parent a father who demonstrates the minimum interest in the consequences of his sexual activity. Most fathers are defined as parents. Only those who do not demonstrate some responsibility to the child are not." The court called these men "casual fornicators."

40   *Children's Law Reform Act*, above note 37, s. 8(1), para. 1.

2. *The person has "lawful custody of the child."*

There is an argument that the word "custody" in this context ought to be interpreted to mean *de facto* custody. This is best seen by examining the alternative meaning, which is *de jure* custody—that is, having a declared right to custody. This declared right can derive from the order of a court or a written agreement, or as a consequence of section 20(1) of the *Children's Law Reform Act*, which provides that "the father and mother of a child are equally entitled to custody of the child."[41] The man who has custody by dint of court order or agreement is explicitly made a "parent" under another subsection of the Act,[42] which leaves only the *Children's Law Reform Act* provision as the possible source of *de jure* custody that could have been intended by this provision. Because there is no definition of father in that statute, it must be assumed that there the word means biological father. But the effect of this would be to sweep a great many, if not all,[43] fathers into the category of "parent." This cannot be a correct interpretation, the argument goes, given the care taken in other subsections to identify only some men. Therefore, this definition means to include persons (not just fathers) who *in fact* have such care and control of a child as amounts to charge of the child, provided that this custody is not unlawful (as it would be, for example, if it were in breach of an order or agreement).

3. *The person is a parent of intention or acknowledgment.*

The person is a "parent" who has, within twelve months of the placement of the child, "demonstrated a settled intention to treat the child as a child of his or her family or has acknowledged parentage of the child and provided for the child's support." In the context of the *Family Law Act*, this extended definition of parent[44] is aimed at imposing child support obligations on adults, which might suggest a special interest in financial relations between the adult and the child; but in

---

41   *Ibid.* Section 21(2) provides further that "A person entitled to custody of a child has the rights and responsibilities of a parent."

42   *CFSA*, above note 2, s. 137(1)(e). See note 43 below.

43   Excluded, perhaps, would be fathers living "separate and apart" from the mothers, and who have consented to or acquiesced in the fact that the child lives with the mother; according to the *Children's Law Reform Act*, above note 37, s. 20(4), their rights of custody are "suspended." Apart from the difficulty of knowing when there is acquiescence, there is the argument that the father's custody right would revive once the child was no longer living with the mother.

44   R.S.O. 1990, c. F.3, s. 1(1). For a discussion of parents of intention, see section D, "Parents of Intention," in chapter 5, "Parentage."

the adoption context it would seem that all forms of parenting behaviour should be equally important in assessing the person's intention.

As for acknowledgment of parentage, official acknowledgment is provided for in another portion of the definition, so this reference must mean something relatively informal, but corroborated—as a demonstration of seriousness of purpose—by the fact that the man has in fact provided support prior to any adoption application.

4. *The person has a right of custody of or access to a child under a court order or separation agreement.*

5. *The person has acknowledged parentage in a statutory declaration filed in the office of the Registrar General.*[45]

b) Withdrawing Consent

The Act permits consent to be withdrawn freely within a twenty-one-day period after it was given.[46] Beyond that period consent may only be withdrawn if "the court is satisfied that it is in the child's best interests,"[47] and not at all if the child is placed for adoption.[48] Because placement will typically occur fairly soon after the expiry of the twenty-one-day period, there have been very few occasions in Ontario when the issue has in fact arisen of whether late withdrawal is in the child's best interests.

Although it is difficult to generalize across various statutes and differing fact situations, it seems that courts in other jurisdictions have tended recently to find that it will be in the best interests of children to be adopted and not returned to the parent.[49] This is the result of the courts' view that birth parents (and consenting parents, certainly) have no longer any superior legal position with respect to their children, and

---

45 *CFSA*, above note 2, s. 137(1)(f): official acknowledgment is to be via s. 12, *Children's Law Reform Act*, above note 37.

46 *CFSA*, above note 2, s. 137(8).

47 *Ibid.*, s. 139(1).

48 *Ibid.*, s. 139(2). See *Manitoba (Director of Child Welfare)* v. *Y.*, [1981] 1 S.C.R. 625, in which the court decided that a mother had no absolute right of revocation of consent; under the Manitoba adoption legislation, she had lost her right of revocation upon placement of the child, and it did not matter that she had changed her mind. This case marked a change in the approach of the Supreme Court to parental or, at least, mother's, rights. See: *Martin* v. *Duffel*, [1950] S.C.R. 737: *Hepton* v. *Maat*, [1957] S.C.R. 606; *McNeilly* v. *Agar*, [1958] S.C.R. 52; in which the court sided with the mother against adoption legislation. See also *Re Mugford*, [1970] 1 O.R. 601 (C.A.).

49 See, for example, *King* v. *Low*, [1985] 1 S.C.R. 87 from the Northwest Territories; *Racine* v. *Woods*, [1983] 2 S.C.R. 173, a case from Manitoba; *Re British Columbia Birth Registration #030279* (1990), 24 R.F.L. (3d) 437 (B.C.S.C.).

so, in the adoption context, likely have no advantage at all over typically well-situated prospective adoptive parents.

c) Dispensing with Consent and Step-Parent Adoptions

A required consent may be dispensed with "where the court is satisfied that it is in the child's best interests to do so."[50] Although this is the same language used in connection with the late withdrawal of consent, just discussed, it would seem that it should produce different results. A parent who has given consent ought not to be in the same legal position as a parent who has never consented.

Three ways present themselves of distinguishing between these two kinds of parents. It might be that some implicit parental right to custody will be acknowledged to act as a barrier to easy dispensing with consent, but as has been seen,[51] the courts no longer admit to any such right. Or it might be that the meaning of the best interests of a child will be constructed in such a way that it is generally considered in a child's best interests not to lose a non-consenting birth parent.[52] And, finally, it might be that, although parents have no special rights to custody, and although the best interests test is not used to cloak a parental rights notion, the burden of proof is used to create the distinction between parents who have consented to adoption and those who have not. In this case the person who would dispense with a parent's consent has the onus of proof that it would be in the child's best interests.

The answer will lie partly in the context in which such applications arise. Almost all cases will be proposed family adoptions,[53] and of these the majority will be step-parent adoptions because an adoption agency—society or licensee—rarely plans adoption for a child unless the child's parents are consenting. (And no agency would think of descending on parents with the aim of taking the child away for adoption where there was

---

50 CFSA, above note 2, s. 138(1); and where proper notice has been given to the person whose consent is to be dispensed with, or "a reasonable effort to give the notice has been made": s. 138(2). On this latter point, see J.(A.H.) v. C.(K.) (20 June 1995), Doc. Kitchener A30/95 (Ont. Prov. Div.), where it seems it was decided that it cannot be "reasonable effort" to make no effort, even when one is well motivated.

51 Section C(1), "Consent to Adoption," in this chapter.

52 The "best interests" of a child is defined, non-exhaustively, in s. 136(2) of the CFSA, above note 2. One of the nine named "circumstances" to be considered is "the child's relationships by blood." Thus, the issue is not whether a court could take the importance of a biological link into consideration, but how important it will turn out to be in the court's calculus.

53 Section B, "Statutory Framework," in this chapter.

merely a comparative advantage for the child in adoption.) This means that to some extent there is institutional policy and practice that might reasonably be said to constitute a parental right to custody.

Many, if not most, judgments observe that the applicant does indeed bear the burden of proof.[54] And if in nearly all reported judgments courts in fact dispense with the parent's consent, it will be because the child's relationship with the prospective adoptive parent— typically the new spouse of the custodial parent—has been functioning well for some time; whereas the child's relationship with the non-custodial parent is attenuated, non-existent, or potentially harmful.[55] These non-consenting parents are those who might very likely not even be granted access to the child;[56] and where the child's relationship with the birth parent exists in fact and has some value to the child, the court will probably refuse to dispense with consent.[57] This treatment of children's best interests may not amount to the construction of a parental right, but it does seem to demonstrate a reluctance to dispense with the involvement of birth parents, at least.[58]

More broadly, there are those who believe that it is often wrong to use the adoption process to solidify second families, certainly over the objection of one of the birth parents.[59] The objections are that adoption is a process meant for children who have no parents; and in the context

---

54   See, for example, L. v. L., above note 30; R.(N.J.) v. M.(R.J.) (1994), 5 R.F.L. (4th) 375 (Ont. Prov. Div.).

55   Ibid. And see: J.(S.E.) v. C.(M.) (1994), 6 R.F.L. (4th) 41 (Ont. Prov. Div.); C.(R.) v. M.(G.T.) (5 April 1995), Doc. Lindsay A26/93 (Ont. Prov. Div.).

56   See J.(S.E.) v. C.(M.), ibid.; T.(K.) v. C.(R.W.B.) (1990), 25 R.F.L. (3d) 433 (Ont. Prov. Ct.).

57   See B.(S.M.) v. K.(J.N.) (29 June 1994), Doc. North Bay A3/94 (Ont. Prov. Div.).

58   See, for example, L. v. L., above note 30, and the summing-up language used even by a judge who proclaims (at 357) that "the concept of 'parental rights' [has] echoes of the law of property"; and at 359: "The court should be ever conscious of the awful finality of an adoption order and of the fact that such an order severs the relationship . . . between the child and the child's natural parents . . . The wish of the natural parents to maintain the parent-child relationship is a relevant and substantial consideration that demands the court's attention. But . . ." And see R.(N.J.) v. M.(R.J.) (1994), 5 R.F.L. (4th) 375 (Ont. Prov. Div.): the best interests test is a "rigorous" test in this context.

59   See, for example, P. B. Weiss, "The Misuse of Adoption by the Custodial Parent and Spouse" (1979) 2 Can. J. Fam. L. 141; reprinted in N. Bala, H. Lilles, & G. Thomson, Canadian Children's Law: Cases, Notes and Materials (Toronto: Butterworths, 1982); and see A. Bissett-Johnson, "Step-Parent Adoptions in English and Canadian Law" in I.F.G. Baxter & M.A. Eberts, eds., The Child and the Courts (Toronto: Carswell, 1978) 335.

of second families not only is this not the case, it is largely unnecessary as a legal step, may not do much to enhance the children's emotional or psychological lives, and will usually entail loss of access to the children's birth father.

A step-parent is able to obtain a custody order, for example, so that together with the mother he becomes the joint custodian of the children,[60] which would accord him all "the rights and responsibilities of a parent."[61] There would be nothing to prevent a step-parent from making a will to benefit the step-children. And it is likely that a step-parent willing to apply for an adoption order would be regarded as a parent of intention under the *Family Law Act* and, so, subject to an obligation to support the children.[62] Children's names may be changed without adoption, so that all may appear to be one family.[63]

2) Crown Wardship and Adoption

A child who is in need of protection may be made a Crown ward under Part III of the Act.[64] This drastic "solution" to a very serious problem results in the termination of parental rights,[65] and consequently removes the necessity of parental consent to adoption of the child. Only the consent of the director is required.[66]

It was once fairly routine to make orders of Crown wardship for children who were given up for adoption. Their parents, usually unmarried mothers, would appear before the court and submit the children to

---

60 See, for example, *Children and Family Services Act*, S.N.S. 1990, c. 5, s. 79(1), which explicitly provides for this as an alternative to step-parent adoption: "Where a step-parent and the father or mother with custody of the child make application for the adoption of a child, the court may in lieu thereof, in the best interests of the child, grant an order for joint custody by the step-parent and father or mother rather than an order for adoption."

61 *Children's Law Reform Act*, above note 37, s. 21(2).

62 See the *Family Law Act*, above note 44; and see section D(1), "Under the *Family Law Act*," in chapter 5, "Parentage."

63 *Change of Name Act*, R.S.O. 1990, c. C.7, s. 5. See: *Herniman v. Woltz* (1996), 22 R.F.L. (4th) 232 at 236 (Ont. Gen. Div.): "The onus is on the parent proposing such change to demonstrate that the child will benefit from the change."

64 See section B, "Statutory Framework," subsection "Disposition," in chapter 7, "Child Protection."

65 *CFSA*, above note 2, s. 63(1), with limited rights in the parents to have access granted (s. 59(2)) and to initiate a review of the child's status (s. 64(4)(b)).

66 *Ibid.*, s. 137(2)(b). Once a Crown ward has been placed for adoption, no parent may apply for a status review: s. 64(9).

wardship.[67] Children's aid societies took this route to adoption in order to prevent parents from changing their minds and attempting to withdraw their consent. However, now that the legislation makes successful withdrawal of consent against the wishes of the adoption agency a very small likelihood, there is no longer any need to seek protection for the adoption scheme in what was essentially a perversion of the child welfare process.

Children's aid societies are under a statutory obligation to seek the adoption of all Crown wards.[68]

D. FINALITY

Once an adoption order is made the child becomes the child of the adopting parents (and a member of their family) for all legal purposes.[69] But because the law is based on the premise that a person may have only two parents,[70] gaining new parents means old parents must be lost. And, so, upon adoption "the adopted child ceases to be the child of the person who was his or her parent before the adoption order."[71] Moreover, the Act takes pains to ensure that any non-parental legal ties are also severed, principally those of court-ordered access. And the legislation also goes some way to ensuring that these ties will not be re-established once the adoption order is made.

This legal extinction of the past is protected by a practical cordon around the newly constituted family that, where the adoption takes place through a society or licensee, usually ensures that identifying details of the new family will be kept secret from the old, and vice versa.[72]

---

67   The section defining a child in need of protection (*CFSA, ibid.*, s. 37(2)(l)) that was used in this process still exists, though the practice has largely ceased: "the child's parent is unable to care for the child and the child is brought before the court with the parent's consent." See also s. 55, which requires the court to take special steps before finding a child is in need of protection under this paragraph.

68   *CFSA*, above note 2, s. 140(1)(a).

69   *Ibid.*, s. 158(1) & (2).

70   That is, two persons with the status of parent. It is possible for many persons to be included in the extended definition of parent found in s. 1(1) of the *Family Law Act* (above note 44), for example, but only for the limited purpose of liability for child support: see section D(1), "Under the *Family Law Act*," in chapter 5, "Parentage."

71   *CFSA*, above note 2, s. 158(1).

72   Usually, but not always: see *M.(R.)* v. *M.(S.)* (1994), 20 O.R. (3d) 621 (Ont. C.A.), where, in an adoption placement by a licensee, the birth mother helped select the adoptive parents. This knowledge permitted a custody application by the child's birth grandparents after placement: see section D(1)(a), "Before Adoption," in this chapter.

Over the last decade or so, pressure has been growing for a change in the legislation to permit more ready access by adopted persons to information about their birth parents. Changes have been made that permit disclosure under certain circumstances, but these do not fully satisfy many adopted persons. And, as second (and third) families become increasingly common in the general population, the premise of no more than two parents is being re-examined generally and may be changed in the near future.[73]

1) Custody and Access Rights

a) Before Adoption

i) Custody
For many years parents who had changed their minds about giving up their children for adoption were able to challenge and halt the adoption process by making use of the law of custody, which gave mothers, particularly, strong rights to custody of their children.[74] At that time this tactic was effective, in part, because the legislation setting out the adoption process did not make explicit reference to custody law, and so permitted the courts to use the latter to "trump" the former. Now, however, the CFSA addresses rights respecting custody and access more directly, and subordinates them to rights accorded by the Act.

According to section 137(5) of the Act, where the child is being placed by a society or a licensee and all required consents are given and may no longer be freely withdrawn,[75] "all rights and responsibilities of the child's parents with respect to the child's custody, care and control are transferred to the society or licensee . . ."[76] Because anyone who has "lawful custody"[77] or custody "under a written agreement or a court

---

73 On the "new realities in family life" in this context, see the comments of Nevins Prov. J. in *H.(J.)* v. *G.(B.)* (9 March 1993), Doc. Toronto D1711/86 at 18, 38 A.C.W.S. (3d) 1189 (Ont. Prov. Div.), aff'd (31 May 1993), (Ont. Div. Ct.); and in *P.(M.A.R.)* (*Litigation Guardian of*) v. *Catholic Children's Aid Society of Metropolitan Toronto* (1995), 9 R.F.L. (4th) 385 at 399–400, aff'd (1995), 11 R.F.L. (4th) 95 (Ont. Gen. Div.), aff'd (1995), 126 D.L.R. (4th) 673 (Ont. C.A.), application for leave to appeal dismissed without reasons, (15 February 1996), S.C.C. File No. 24961, S.C.C. Bulletin, 1996, p. 215.

74 See the cases cited above in note 48.

75 See section C(1), "Consent to Adoption," in this chapter.

76 "Until the consent is withdrawn under subsection 139(1) [late withdrawal with leave of court] or an order is made for the child's adoption under section 146": *CFSA*, above note 2, s. 137(5).

77 *CFSA, ibid.*, s. 137(1)(c).

order"[78] is a "parent" for the purposes of section 137,[79] this provision ought effectively to put an end to any existing custody rights that might otherwise compete with rights under the Act.[80]

Family adoptions—where children are adopted by relatives or spouses of their parents[81]—do not depend upon placement by a society or licensee, and so are not affected by this section. Thus, the existing arrangements within the family as to custody and access will not be disturbed until the adoption takes place, when birth parents cease to be parents and, consequently, may lose custody and access rights.[82]

Finally, there is the prospect that a fresh application for custody under the *Children's Law Reform Act*[83] will be attempted during the placement period (which is commonly six months).[84] However, the Ontario Court of Appeal has decided that

> [o]nce the choice of adoption has been made by persons entitled to make that choice, and where the route of adoption has been followed to the point of placement [there is] no room for the operation of s. 21 of the C.L.R.A.[85]

A judge has no jurisdiction under the general legislation; and although a General Division judge may have an inherent *parens patriae* jurisdiction[86] over children, it is not appropriate to exercise it during an adoption placement.[87]

---

78   *Ibid.,* para. (e).

79   See section C(1)(a), "Parent," in this chapter.

80   *M.(R.)* v. *M.(S.),* above note 72. The only possible exception is a biological father who is not constituted a "parent" under this section, but who, nevertheless, is held by a court to have a custody right because of his paternity of the child. But see section C(1)(a), "Parent," in this chapter. Compare *Children's Aid Society of Metropolitan Toronto* v. *Lyttle,* above note 27.

81   See section B, "Statutory Framework," in this chapter.

82   See section D(1)(b), "After Adoption," in this chapter.

83   Above note 37.

84   *CFSA,* above note 2, s. 149(1).

85   *M.(R.)* v. *M.(S.),* above note 72 at 630. The court goes on immediately to say: "In any case, when a child is placed for adoption, the provisions of s. 137(5) of the C.F.S.A. (which transfer the custodial rights and responsibilities of the child's parents to the licensee) do . . . conflict with s. 21 of the C.L.R.A."

86   See section A(2), "Sources of Law," in chapter 10, "Custody and Access."

87   *M.(R.)* v. *M.(S.),* above note 72 at 632: "[A] court having parens patriae jurisdiction would only exercise that jurisdiction in the clearest of cases where grounds of manifest necessity exist."

ii) Access

Rights respecting access, as differentiated from custody, are dealt with in other sections. Section 143(1) of the *CFSA* provides that

> [w]here a child is placed for adoption by a society or a licensee, every order respecting access to the child is terminated, except an order made under Part III (Child Protection).

The exception refers to access orders made in respect of children who have been found in need of protection.[88] No society may place a child for adoption until any such outstanding access order has been terminated.[89] This appears to be a means of ensuring that the more important or urgent matters in a child's life, those touching upon his or her need for protection and safety are dealt with first, and are disposed of under the part of the legislation that explicitly aims to protect children, rather than incidentally under the adoption part. (Note, however, that the provision does not prevent a licensee, as opposed to a society, from placing a child where there is an outstanding access order under Part III.)[90]

Opinion is divided on the question of whether outstanding access orders survive family adoptions.[91] Since placement is not involved, the sections terminating access orders upon placement do not apply.

b) After Adoption

In most cases, where a child is placed for adoption by a society or licensee, the new family is protected by a screen of secrecy that effectively prevents later applications for access to or custody of the adopted child.[92] However, in cases where the identity of the adoptive parents is

---

88 See section C, "Child in Need of Protection," in chapter 7, "Child Protection."

89 *CFSA*, above note 2, s. 140(2)(a).

90 See section D(1)(b), "After Adoption," immediately following, for a case that presents an unusual turn on this exception of Part III access orders where the placement is by a licensee.

91 Compare *B.(S.M.)* v. *K.(J.N.)*, above note 57, where the court says access rights of a father will terminate upon adoption by the step-father, and *M.(R.)* v. *M.(S.)* (1995), 14 R.F.L. (4th) 180 (Ont. Prov. Div.), where the court says that a mother's right under an access order will survive adoption by the sister and her husband. See also: *K.(S.)* v. *D.(M.S.)* (1980), 21 R.F.L. (2d) 271 (Ont. U.F.C.), decided under predecessor legislation, also of the opinion that an access order will survive a family adoption.

92 An application for access cannot be used to overcome the secrecy: *W.(C.G.)* v. *J.(M.)* (1981), 34 O.R. (2d) 44 at 49 (C.A.): "The new adoptive parents on their part are given security from such upset and interference by the secrecy provisions of the Act. Such applications for access, if permitted, would set the secrecy provisions of adoption orders at naught and render them meaningless." See also s. 39(2) of the *Children's Law Reform Act*, above note 37.

known to the child's birth family, applications for custody or access after adoption are practically possible.

Where an adoption order has been made, the Act prohibits a court from making an order for access to the child in favour of a birth parent or a member of a birth parent's family under the part of the Act relating to adoption.[93] However, two other possibilities exist for the making of post-adoption access orders.

First, access may be ordered under Part III of the Act in connection with a child found to be in need of protection.[94] In an unusual case, a Crown ward applied under section 58 (in Part III) of the Act for access to his birth sister, who had been adopted. The adoptive mother opposed the application, arguing that the Act should be read so as to prohibit any and all applications by members of a child's birth family for access after adoption. The Court of Appeal decided, however, that the Act in fact permitted the application for access in the instant case.[95]

Second, and of greater interest, is the possibility of an application for access under section 21 of the *Children's Law Reform Act*.[96] Under the terms of that provision, "[a] parent of a child or any other person" may apply for an order respecting custody and access. Clearly, even after an adoption, a member of a child's birth family would qualify as "any other person." In a case in which a birth mother applied for access to a child three weeks after the adoption order, the Ontario Court of Appeal, dealing with the similar language of the predecessor to section 21,[97] decided that the policy and intent of the then adoption legislation[98] were to cut off contact with the birth family on adoption, at least where adoption through a society was concerned.[99] The court also said that if "the natural parent establishes a relationship with the child after the adoption . . . then such parent is 'any person' and might apply for custody or access to the child under" [appropriate legislation].[100]

---

93   *CFSA*, above note 2, s. 160(1).

94   See section D(1)(a)(ii), "Access," in this chapter.

95   P.(M.A.R.) (*Litigation Guardian of*) v. *Catholic Children's Aid Society of Metropolitan Toronto*, above note 73. Section 160 of the *CFSA*, above note 2, prohibits only the making of access orders under Part VII of the Act; and s. 143(1) saves access orders under Part III from termination upon placement by a licensee, revealing the unusual status of Part III of the Act within the adoption scheme.

96   Above note 37.

97   See "any person": *Family Law Reform Act*, S.O. 1978, c. 2, s. 35(1).

98   *Child Welfare Act*, S.O. 1978, c. 85. The provisions of that legislation were very similar to those in the Act currently, with the exception that s. 160 has been added to bar the making of access orders under Part VIII.

99   *W.(C.G.)* v. *J.(M.)*, above note 92.

100   *Ibid.* at 51.

This view seems to have retained the approval of the Court of Appeal.[101] The current post-adoption position appears to be that, although a court may have jurisdiction to make an access or custody order under general custody legislation, there ought to be an obligation on members of the birth family to establish a strong case based on the best interests of the child before a court should entertain such an application seriously.[102] This will likely not be possible where the allegation is essentially that access by the applicant will be in the child's best interests regardless of what post-adoption situation the child finds himself or herself in. By contrast, it will be relatively easier to do when the claim is based upon a post-adoption relationship with the child.

2) Disclosure

The provisions governing post-adoption disclosure of information describe a scheme that is too complex to be explored in detail here; and, so, only the main features will be examined.[103]

All records concerning an adoption are to be kept confidential, unless the *CFSA* provides otherwise. Thus, court records are to be sealed up and are not to be opened except under a court order or the written direction of the Registrar of Adoption Information.[104] Curiosity about one's origins is not a sufficient reason for the opening of the records[105] and neither are the improvement of one's emotional health or the satisfaction of an obsession of a birth mother to know her child.[106] Records (and the information they contain) held by any other agencies involved in an adoption are to be kept confidential except as the Act otherwise provides.[107]

---

101   *P.(M.A.R.) (Litigation Guardian of)* v. *Catholic Children's Aid Society of Metropolitan Toronto,* above note 73 at 394. The concession by counsel for the CCAS that an application for access by a member of the birth family would be possible if based on a post-adoption relationship was treated by the court as one reason why s. 160(1) is not an absolute bar to access applications.

102   See, for example, *H.(J.)* v. *G.(B.),* above note 73, and *G.(L.E.)* v. *O.(B.D.)* (13 April 1995), Doc. Belleville 25/92 (Ont. Prov. Div.).

103   For more on adoption disclosure, see R. Garber, *Disclosure of Adoption Information* (Toronto: Ministry of Community and Social Services, 1985).

104   *CFSA,* above note 2, s. 162(2).

105   *Ferguson* v. *Director of Child Welfare for Ontario* (1983), 44 O.R. (2d) 78 at 80 (C.A.): "[S]ufficient cause must be shown . . . [T]his sufficient cause must be a cause of such gravity and importance to displace the statutory rights of the other parties as well as the interest of the province in maintaining the integrity of the adoption system."

106   *Tyler* v. *Ontario (District Court)* (1986), 1 R.F.L. (3d) 139 (Ont. Dist. Ct.).

107   *CFSA,* above note 2, s. 165(1) & (2).

The Act establishes a registry of adoption information and a registrar, whose job is to maintain the adoption disclosure register, to monitor the release of information, and to ensure the provision of counselling to those who require it consequent upon their getting information about the adoption. Such information is divided into two categories: non-identifying and identifying.

a) Non-Identifying Information

Non-identifying information is that which will not, if disclosed, materially assist in identifying the person to whom it relates.[108] This sort of information is freely available upon a request to the registrar by the adult adopted person, an adoptive parent, a close member of the birth family, and others with appropriate permissions.[109] The registrar is under an obligation to ensure that counselling is made available to a person receiving non-identifying information.[110]

b) Identifying Information

Identifying information may be disclosed in one of two ways under the Act. The registrar may disclose it (and non-identifying information) to any person if "the health, safety or welfare of that person or any other person requires the disclosure."[111] And the registrar may disclose it where there is a coincidence of registration under the registry by the adult adopted person and his or her birth parent, birth grandparent or birth sibling (or a person the registrar deems desirable to register).[112]

Any of the just-named persons may register, in hopes of there being the necessary corresponding registration, and may ask the registrar to conduct a discreet search for certain members of the other family to inquire whether they would wish to be named in the register.[113] Before the release of identifying information where there is common registration, the registrar must ensure that the persons obtaining the disclosure receive counselling.[114]

---

108   *Ibid.*, s. 166(2).
109   *Ibid.*, s. 166(4). The classes of persons able to request information are defined in s. 166(3).
110   *Ibid.*, s. 166(6), (7), & (8).
111   Ibid., s. 168(1).
112   *Ibid.*, s. 167(5), (8), & (9). Again, these classes of persons are defined in s. 166(3).
113   *Ibid.*, s. 169(1), paras. 1–4, (2), & (3).
114   *Ibid.*, s. 167(8), (11), & (13).

E. A NOTE ON THE ROLE OF SUPRAFAMILIAL GROUPS

The adoption process invites consideration of a child's "belonging" in a broader context, one that questions the role in the legal process of groups in society that are larger than or "beyond" the family. A suprafamilial group in this sense might be a community, a tribe, a race, a nation, a religion or any other group for which membership is largely a matter of heritage or birth. The *CFSA* itself refers to suprafamilial groups, directly and indirectly, but offers only limited guidance on how their views and interests are to be taken into account when assessing the best interests of a child. There is as well the problem of knowing how the views and interests of a suprafamilial group are to be put before the court, whether a group member ought to have standing or whether the information ought to be garnered in some other way.

These questions are part of a much larger issue that explores the fact that our legal system usually operates by according rights to individuals, who are taken to be independent, freely acting agents. Indeed, as the study of family law shows, the legal system has a hard time recognizing the family group as an entity in any useful or important respect, and will commonly address only disputes between family members as individuals, leaving the familial context to be taken into account through the exercise of judicial discretion or, perhaps, through certain special structural arrangements, such as special family courts.

It must be noted that at the very heart of the child welfare process, and to a lesser degree the adoption process, there is a structural division based on religion. In three districts in Ontario there is a Catholic Children's Aid Society in addition to the non-denominational (or "Protestant") society.[115] Therefore, because societies still play an important role in the adoption process, one religion, at least, has its views and interests taken into account and, of course, has no difficulty with standing before the court.

Even more explicitly within the Act, Aboriginal groups are accorded recognition in connection with the adoption process. This special treatment

---

115 Toronto, Hamilton and Windsor. And in Toronto there is a Jewish Family and Child Services. *CFSA*, above note 2, s. 86(2), provides, for example, that "a Protestant child shall not be committed under this part to the care of a Roman Catholic society or institution" (and a "Protestant child" is to be cared for by a "Protestant society," etc.). Section 47(2) requires that "as soon as practicable" at a hearing under the child protection part of the Act, "the court shall determine . . . (b) the religious faith, if any, in which the child is being raised."

is an attempt to remediate the often disastrous effect that earlier child welfare policy had upon native communities, in which many Aboriginal children were removed because of "neglect" and then given up by children's aid societies for adoption into non-Aboriginal families.[116] It is stated in section 1(f) that one purpose of the *CFSA* is

> to recognize that Indian and native people should be entitled to provide, wherever possible, their own child and family services,[117] and that all services to Indian and native children and families should be provided in a manner that recognizes their culture, heritage and traditions and the concept of the extended family.

More specifically, where a society proposes to place a native child for adoption, it must give notice to the child's "band or native community."[118] There is, however, no provision for the band or community to be a party or to have standing before the court, and it would be unable itself, in all likelihood, to adopt a child.[119]

For the rest, there are only general references to the importance of providing services "in a manner that respects cultural, religious and regional differences"[120] and of taking into account "[t]he child's cultural background" and "[t]he religious faith, if any, in which the child is being raised" when determining the child's best interests.[121] No guidance is given as to what counts as culture—whether race, for instance, is to be addressed in this context[122]—or how to bring such matters into the calculations.

---

116   See A. McGillivray, "Transracial Adoption and the Status Indian Child" (1985), 4 Can. J. of Fam. L. 437.

117   There are at present three native children's aid societies.

118   *CFSA*, above note 2, s. 140(3). See also s. 136(3), which provides as a consideration in the calculation of the child's best interests "the importance, in recognition of the uniqueness of Indian heritage and traditions, of preserving the child's cultural identity."

119   See *S.(S.M.) v. A.(J.)* (1992), 89 D.L.R. (4th) 204 at 215 (B.C.C.A.), in which the court says of a tribe (that had intervenor status in California in an earlier aspect of the case): "[T]he tribe is not a person eligible to apply for or be granted child custody under the Family Relations Act . . . In its simplest, organic form a tribe is an agglomeration of individuals like a congregation or a club."

120   *CFSA*, above note 2, s. 1(e).

121   *Ibid.*, s. 136(2), paras. 3 & 4.

122   See, for example, *S.(S.M.) v. A.(J.)*, above note 119, where the mother was born into the Alaskan Akhiok tribe, adopted out to a non-native family before she was two, gave birth to the child in question whose father was non-native, and wished to have him adopted by a non-native family. Would a court say under Ontario legislation that the child had an Akhiok "cultural background"?

Generally the courts have subordinated race to other factors bearing on the best interests of a child. In the leading case in the adoption context, *Racine v. Woods,* the Supreme Court downplayed the role of race, saying, *per* Wilson J., that as the child's bonds with the prospective adoptive parents increase over time, so the "significance of cultural background and heritage . . . abates over time" and the "racial element" becomes less and less important.[123]

It is clear that the courts would not permit the interests of the group to obtrude into the adoption process, if they could not be reflected in the child's best interests.[124] And, too, the child is not usually conceived of as "belonging" primarily to any group such that the calculation of his or her best interests takes place on that premise; rather the child is seen to exist in a decontextualized place where race, class, religion, heritage, and so forth are factors that can be brought into play when the court wishes it, and the measure of best interests is often an acultural notion of healthy growth and development.[125]

Societies and licensees involved in adoption are unfettered by legislation when it comes to placing children, and so practices here could take the interests of suprafamilial groups into account. In Ontario, concerns about Aboriginal peoples apart, there is no policy against the placement of a child of one race with prospective adoptive parents of another—a practice known as transracial adoption.[126] It seems that here, too, race plays a small role, except insofar as the individual biases of the

---

123   Above note 49 at 187.

124   In *S.(S.M.) v. A.(J.),* above note 119, the court observes that the very concept of a group makes its participation inapt where the interests of an individual child are at stake.

125   See, for example, *S.(S.M.) v. A.(J.), ibid.* at 218: "The only competing factor which the Akhiok Tribe can put forward is the uncertain intangible of cultural heritage. At baby R.A.'s present age that is not a factor which outweighs the provision to baby R.A., in the interim, in the words of Mr. Justice McIntyre, of 'healthy growth, development and education of the child so that [she] will be equipped to face the problems of life as a mature adult.'"

126   The Children's Aid Society of Metropolitan Toronto claims to be the first agency in North America to place a black child with white parents, the adoption occurring in 1952: *The Adoption of Negro Children: A Community-Wide Approach* (Toronto: Social Planning Council of Metropolitan Toronto, 1966). In 1959 the Montreal Open Door Society began a campaign for the interracial adoption of black children that had impact throughout Canada and the United States. I should like to acknowledge the assistance I have received in the area of transracial adoption from an unpublished paper of a student: Sogie Omoruyi, "Does Race Matter? A Comparative Analysis of Transracial Adoption in Canada, the United States and Britain," 1997.

prospective adoptive parents are taken into account. And there has been considerable growth recently in the number of international adoptions, most of which involve children of a different racial background from that of the adoptive parents.[127] This practice is briefly examined next.

1) International Adoptions

In recent years fewer children have been given up for adoption. As a consequence, those in Canada who wish to adopt have looked abroad for children. It has been estimated that even by 1992, three children were adopted from other countries for every two adopted from within Canada.[128] Typically, children are sought from poorer countries, where families and state services might lack the resources to meet the needs of all children in the society, and, consequently, might regard adoption out to residents of a rich country as a desirable alternative for children.

There is concern about the practice of international, or intercountry, adoption on at least two levels. It may be seen as a depredation of the "sending" country akin to the earlier colonialism of rich nations, whereby poverty is taken advantage of and, indeed, perhaps perpetuated through the removal of human resources.[129] More commonly, the concern is for the interests of the children directly involved. Not all countries have or have the means to enforce legislation requiring that an international adoption is permitted only when it would be in the child's best interests; and sales of children to the richer prospective adoptive parents have been reported. Moreover, it is difficult to know to what degree, if any, children are harmed when a cultural heritage is "traded" for the (putative) advantages of financial and psychological well-being.

---

127   There were fewer than ten in Canada in 1970, the first year records were kept; and it is estimated that there were more than 2,400 in 1991: Human Resources Development Canada, The National Welfare Grants Division, *Intercountry Adoption in Canada: Executive Summary* by A. Westhues & J. Cohen (Ottawa: 1994).

128   Royal Commission on New Reproductive Technologies, *Adoption as an Alternative for Infertile Couples: Prospects and Trends* (Ottawa: Minister of Supply and Services, 1992) at 5. This movement of children from poorer to richer countries is a worldwide phenomenon; one estimate has it that over half a million children have been involved in this process since the end of the Second World War: C. Bagley, *International and Transracial Adoptions* (London: Athenaeum Press, 1993) at 135.

129   See, generally, M. Eade, "Inter-country Adoption: International, National and Cultural Concerns" (1993) 57 Sask. L. Rev. 381; E. Jaffe, *Intercountry Adoptions: Laws and Perspectives of "Sending Countries"* (Dordrecht: Martinus Nijhoff, 1995).

In Ontario, the *CFSA* makes scant reference to the practice of international adoption. It provides that only a society or a licensee may bring a child into the province to be placed for adoption[130] and that the court may not make an order for an adoption unless the child is resident in Ontario.[131] The Act also provides that an adoption "effected according to the law of another jurisdiction . . . has the same effect in Ontario as an adoption under this Part."[132] This last provision means that persons seeking to adopt a foreign child might do so within the "sending" country and, provided immigration regulations are satisfied,[133] return to the province with a child who is their child for all purposes of law.

Recently Canada ratified the *Hague Convention on Intercountry Adoption.*[134] This provides for the regulation and coordination of international adoptions between signatory countries.[135] Particularly, each country (and within Canada, each province) is to establish a Central Authority that will monitor intercountry adoptions, work to protect the interests of the children involved, and act as a single point of application for prospective adoptive parents. Canadian immigration regulations now provide that the Central Authorities of the "sending" and "receiving" countries must agree to the placement of the child before a permit may be issued. At the time of writing, Ontario had not taken the necessary legislative steps to implement the Convention and establish a Central Authority in the province.[136]

---

130   *CFSA*, above note 2, s. 141(2).

131   *Ibid.*, s. 146(5).

132   *Ibid.*, s. 159.

133   The regulations require that an adoption in Canada or abroad create "a genuine relationship of parent and child": (Immigration Regulations, 1978, s. 2(1). See D.B.N. Bagambiire, *Canadian Immigration and Refugee Law* (Aurora, Ont.: Canada Law Book, 1996) at 21–22.

134   *Hague Convention on Protection of Children and Co-operation in Respect of Intercountry Adoption* of 29 May 1993, Final Act, Part A, in Hague Conference on Private International Law, Proceedings of the Seventeenth Session, Tome II 523–35 (1993), reprinted in 32 I.L.M. 1134. The Convention came into force in Canada on 1 April 1997.

135   At the time of writing twelve countries in addition to Canada had ratified the Convention: Burkina Faso, Cyprus, Costa Rica, Ecuador, Mexico, Peru, the Philippines, Poland, Romania, Sri Lanka, Spain, and Venezuela. Canada Department of Foreign Affairs and International Trade, News Release No. 38, "Canada Ratifies the Hague Convention on International Adoption" (26 February 1997).

136   Canada Department of Foreign Affairs and International Trade, News Release No. 38, above note 135. British Columbia, Manitoba, New Brunswick, Prince Edward Island, and Saskatchewan have passed implementing legislation.

FURTHER READINGS

ONTARIO MINISTRY OF COMMUNITY AND SOCIAL SERVICES, *Adoption Disclosure* (Toronto: 1994)

PHILLIPS, D.W., *et al.*, *Adoption Law in Canada: Practice and Procedure* (Toronto: Carswell, 1995) looseleaf service

PART TWO

ADMINISTRATION OF THE FAMILY

We believe that the law interferes little with the functioning family. The fact is that many laws and state policies affect the way in which families operate, but it is also true that members of an ongoing family are rarely caught up in legal disputes regarding family matters. Law, with its traditional reliance on the adversarial method, is felt to be inapt to the administration of lives in such intimate relation. Love, not law, should regulate families; law is for strangers.

This reluctance to intervene directly is overcome when the risk of harm to a family member becomes too great. This part examines two such instances. Chapter 7 explores the bases on which the state challenges the way that parents raise their children—when it is that children face unacceptable circumstances. Chapter 8 looks at the matter of spousal violence. Male violence towards women is a problem that transcends family law, but which has a particular importance and character in the family context, the primary site for extensive relations between the sexes.

CHAPTER 7

CHILD PROTECTION

A. INTRODUCTION

The care and upbringing of a child are the responsibility of the child's parents or custodians. Yet occasionally children find themselves in situations such that society must intervene in order to prevent their harm. It is a matter of some debate as to what is and ought to be the definition of harm, or risk of harm, that will prompt this direct intervention into the family. The primary formal legal standard is currently found in the concept of "child in need of protection" in the *Child and Family Services Act*,[1] which will be considered in detail below: if a child is found by a court to be "in need of protection," society may take a number of intrusive measures aimed at remedying the situation.

The principal social agent for the protection of children is the "children's aid society." These are quasi-governmental, local organizations that are provided for under the Act.[2] Where the nature of the population warrants it, additional children's aid societies may be formed to serve the needs of particular religious[3] or other[4] communities.

---

1   R.S.O. 1990, c. C.11, as amended by S.O. 1994, c. 27, s. 43(2), S.O. 1996, c. C.2, s. 62 [*CFSA* or the Act].
2   *CFSA, ibid.*, s. 15(2).
3   Of the fifty-five children's aid societies in Ontario, three are Catholic children's aid societies, and one is a Jewish Family and Child Services.
4   The *CFSA*, above note 1, provides for the creation of native children's aid societies (see Part X, Indian and Native Child and Family Services); there are now three operating in the province.

Children's aid societies (hereinafter CASs or societies) are required primarily to

(a) investigate allegations or evidence that children who are under the age of sixteen years or are in the society's care or under its supervision may be in need of protection;

(b) protect, where necessary, children who are under the age of sixteen years or are in the society's care or under its supervision;

(c) provide guidance, counselling and other services to families for protecting children or for the prevention of circumstances requiring the protection of children;

(d) provide care for children assigned or committed to its care under this Act . . .[5]

Societies do the majority of their work without involving lawyers or courts, offering their services to families on a voluntary basis; however, it should be noted that some families will understand that if they do not agree to accept society intervention, they may find themselves embroiled in litigation to authorize society intervention whether or not the parents wish it.

In the past, societies had a reputation for being too interventionist and for too readily removing children from families to placements in foster homes or other institutions. Today, the great majority of children are served in their homes, within their families, and only rarely are children removed.[6] Indeed, the Act makes clear in a number of respects that removing a child from his or her family ought to be a last resort.[7]

This particular change reflects a shift in philosophy that occurred before the passage of this Act in 1984. Under the predecessor legislation[8] the definition of "child in need of protection" was a good deal

---

5   CFSA, ibid., s. 15(3). See also s. 1: "The purposes of this Act are, (a) as a paramount objective, to promote the best interests, protection and well-being of children."

6   Approximately 87,000 families with 150,000 children received support from the CASs in Ontario in 1995, for example. That same year the CASs provided "substitute care" to roughly 20,000 children, of whom something like 9,000 were received into care (with a similar number released from care) that year. See: Ontario Association of Children's Aid Societies, CAS Facts, Fact Sheet #3, December 1996; and Ontario Association of Children's Aid Societies, Info 1995, October 1995.

7   CFSA, above note 1, s. 1: "The purposes of this Act are . . . (c) to recognize that the least restrictive or disruptive course of action that is available and is appropriate in a particular case to help a child or family should be followed." See also s. 57(3) & (4), which impinge on a court's ability to make an order removing the child from the care of a parent or custodian.

8   Child Welfare Act, R.S.O. 1980, c. 66.

broader or vaguer,[9] and there were fewer procedural safeguards to ensure that parents and children could participate fully and adequately in the process. The conception behind this earlier language was that societies ought not to be frustrated in their efforts to help children by narrow or legalistic definitions that did not take into account the complex nature of each child's situation; societies were to have considerable discretion to be flexibly responsive.

A reaction set in that saw societies as having too much power and using it too freely or arbitrarily. Family or parental autonomy and integrity became important notions, as did the right of children to participate in the processes that affected them. Consequently, the legislation was reformed, and the definition of "child in need of protection" was tightened in order to raise the threshold that societies must get over before their intervention can be forced on unwilling families.[10] The pendulum may be swinging back the other way, however, and there are now pressures to amend the legislation to make it clearer that the interests of children (as opposed to parents or "families") are paramount.[11]

Finally, it ought to be noted that part of the problem, at least, is money. Many children live in poverty, which harms them in various ways that children's aid societies are not equipped to prevent or remediate. We as a community demonstrate concern about the welfare of children

---

9 Almost all the particular definitions of "child in need of protection" depended on versions of the word "proper"; thus: "care properly," "improper place," "improper person," "proper medical . . . care." *Child Welfare Act*, s. 19(1).

10 See also *CFSA, ibid.*, above note 1, s. 1: "The purposes of this Act are . . . (b) to recognize that while parents often need help in caring for their children, that help should give support to the autonomy and integrity of the family unit . . ." L'Heureux-Dubé J. in *Catholic Children's Aid Society of Metropolitan Toronto v. M.(C.)*, [1994] 2 S.C.R. 165 at 191 has called the Ontario legislation: "one of the least interventionist regimes," citing R.F. Barnhorst, "Child Protection Legislation: Recent Canadian Reform" in B. Landau, ed., *Children's Rights in the Practice of Family Law* (Toronto: Carswell, 1986) 255.

11 See, for example, "Jury calls for overhaul of Ontario child-welfare system" *The Globe and Mail* (11 July 1997) A6: "Among the [coroner's] jury's other recommendations: . . . Changes to the Child and Family Services Act to make the best interests of the child 'the paramount emphasis'." And see "The Ontario Child Mortality Task Force Final Report," Journal of the Ontario Association of Children's Aid Societies, special edition published with the Office of the Chief Coroner of Ontario, July 1997, which recommends in part that there be amendments to the Act to include neglect and a prior history of parental neglect as grounds for intervention. See, also, *Catholic Children's Aid Society of Metropolitan Toronto v. M.(C.)*, above note 10, where the court emphasized repeatedly the child-centred nature of the legislation and the paramountcy of the best interests of the child.

through the *Child and Family Services Act*, it is true; but at the same time we countenance widespread harm by failing to relieve child poverty.[12]

B. STATUTORY FRAMEWORK

Parts II and III of the *CFSA*, which deal with child protection, are very complex, particularly in procedural matters; and it will only be possible within the confines of this chapter to explore a few of their provisions in any detail, principally those that define the need for protection and, consequently, that license compulsory intervention by societies. However, it is important first to sketch the context within which these provisions operate.

The précis of the Act that follows aims to show broadly how, from a legal perspective, intervention in the family is controlled. Much is omitted, and, so, the propositions must be understood merely as general guides, and not as interpretations of the legislation.

Care Agreements—The primary means of delivering services to families is on a voluntary basis, whereby the family[13] simply agrees to accept the assistance offered by the society. The Act does not refer to or control such informal arrangements. Where there is a need to remove the child from the home, the Act provides for it to be done on the basis of care agreements between the society and the family.

- A custodian who is temporarily unable to care for a child under sixteen may make a care agreement with a society for the society's care of the child. [s. 29(1)]
  - Children twelve or older must be parties to an agreement. [s. 29(2)]
  - A society cannot make an agreement unless it has determined that
    - a beneficial residential placement is available for the child, and
    - the child cannot be cared for at home. [s. 29(4)]

---

12 See, for example, Canadian School Boards Association, *Students in Poverty: Toward Awareness, Action and Wider Knowledge* (Ottawa: Canadian School Boards Association, 1997). In 1995, 1.5 million Canadian children—21 percent of all children—lived in poverty (as measured by the low-income cutoffs established by Statistics Canada).

13 The *CFSA*, above note 1, uses various terms to describe those who have responsibility for a child and whose rights or position societies must acknowledge. Most common is "parent." This term is defined in s. 37(1) in essentially the same way as for the purposes of adoption (see section C(1)(a), "Parent", in chapter 6, "Adoption"), and includes the child's mother and those fathers (and others) who have had a particular relationship with the mother or child. A "parent" is a proper party to a proceeding under this part: s. 39(1), para. 3.

- A temporary care agreement may only last for six months, and may only be extended for a total of twelve months. [s. 29(5)] No temporary agreement may be made that (in combination with a court order) results in a child being in a society's continuous care for more than twenty-four months. [s. 29(6)]
- Agreements may be made between custodians and societies (or the Minister) for the provision of services in respect of children with special needs. [s. 30(1)(a) & (2)(a)]
  - These services may be provided in the home under society supervision or where the society has custody of the child. [s. 30(1)(b) & (2)(b)]
  - Special care agreements must be made for specified periods. [s. 30(3)]
- Any party to an agreement may terminate it at any time by giving written notice of intent to terminate. [s. 33(1)]

Commencing Proceedings—The hearing to determine whether a child is "in need of protection" and, thus, whether society intervention ought to be compulsory, may be commenced in a number of ways. Some involve apprehension of a child from the family prior to the hearing, which is in and of itself an emergency means of protecting a child and not simply a way of prompting an inquiry. Societies are given great powers in these provisions, raising important civil liberties questions.

- Proceedings may be begun upon application by:
  - a society, to determine whether a child is in need of protection [s. 40(1)], or
  - a person, who must first satisfy a court that
    - there are reasonable and probable grounds to believe that a child is in need of protection;
    - a society has not applied or taken steps to apprehend the child despite a report of the matter [s. 40(4)(a)]; and
    - the child cannot be adequately protected otherwise than by being brought before the court [s. 40(4)(a)].
- Where a child is apprehended there must be a hearing within five days to determine whether the child is in need of protection.[14] [s. 46(1)]
  - A child may be apprehended upon a warrant issued by a justice of the peace who is satisfied:

---

14 See also *CFSA*, above note 1, s. 46(2), which provides for a hearing within twenty-four hours of apprehension ("or as soon thereafter as is practicable") to rule on the suitability and terms of detention.

- by a child protection worker that apprehension may be necessary to protect the child [s. 40(1)], or
- by a parent or custodian that apprehension is necessary to protect a child's health or safety [s. 43(1)].[15]
– A child may be apprehended without a warrant[16] by a child protection worker who has good grounds to believe that the child's
  health or safety would be at risk if the time were taken to obtain a
  warrant. [s. 40(7)]

Determination Hearing—The hearing proceeds in two stages, the first
of which is the determination of whether the child in question is in need
of protection.[17] The Ontario Court (Provincial Division) has jurisdiction to make the determination,[18] and, because it has no inherent jurisdiction, may operate only with the sanction of the *CFSA*.

- The court is required to hold a hearing upon application or where the
  child was apprehended in order to determine whether the child is in
  need of protection. [s. 47(1)]
- A child is in need of protection who:
  – because of the action or inaction of the person in charge, has suf-
    fered, or faces a substantial risk of, physical, sexual or severe emo-
    tional harm, or
  – needs medical treatment that is not being provided, or
  – suffers from a condition that could seriously impair development
    and is not being given treatment, or
  – has no available parent or parent-substitute, or
  – is under twelve and has engaged in serious criminal behaviour, or
  – has parents who are unable to care for him or her.[19] [s. 37(2)]
- The hearing is usually held in private. [s. 45(4)]

Disposition—The court has the ability to make a limited number of
orders respecting the child in need of protection, all essentially commit-
ting the child to degrees of society care. There is comparatively little

15   See also *ibid.*, s. 41(1).
16   See also *ibid.*, s. 42(1).
17   Evidence relating only to the second stage of disposition is not to be admitted into
     evidence until the court has determined that the child is in need of protection:
     CFSA, ibid., s. 50(2). For a judicial description of the process to be followed by a
     court, see *Catholic Children's Aid Society of Metropolitan Toronto* v. *M.(C.)*, above
     note 10 at 185.
18   *CFSA*, above note 1, s. 3(1).
19   See also s. 55, *ibid.*

ability in the court to make detailed plans for the child's future, such matters being up to the society or other chosen custodians.[20]

- Where the child before it is found to be in need of protection, the court must determine whether intervention through a court order is necessary to protect the child in the future.[21] [s. 57(1)]
- If so, the court must choose one of four possible orders [s. 57(1), paras. 1–4]:
  - placement with any person, including the parent, under society supervision, for between three and twelve months (a supervision order), or
  - placement in the society's care as a society ward, for no more than twelve months (a society wardship order), or
  - placement in the society's care as a Crown ward until adopted, married, eighteen years old, or the order is terminated upon review (a Crown wardship order), or
  - society wardship, followed by return to the parent under society supervision, for a total of twelve months.
- In making the choice among the possible orders, the court must consider a number of factors:[22]
  - The choice must be in the child's best interests.[23] [s. 57(1)]
  - The court must learn from the parties what efforts have been made to help the child previously. [s. 57(2)]
  - The society must provide the court for its consideration a detailed plan for the child's care. [s. 56]
  - When choosing between leaving the child with the parent (under supervision) or removing the child from the parent's care, the court must be satisfied that less drastic alternatives than removal have been tried and would not protect the child. [s. 57(3)]

---

20 Societies are constrained by the *CFSA*, *ibid.*, in the formation of their plans to some degree: see s. 61.

21 It may be, for example, that a child is "in need of protection" because harm has been suffered—the definition uses the past tense—but that the source or cause of the harm is no longer present. In such a case there may be no need for protection in the future. See also *ibid.*, s. 57(9), requiring the return of the child to the parent in such a case.

22 Evidence relating to these factors may only be introduced after the child has been found to be in need of protection: *CFSA*, above note 1, s. 50(2).

23 There is a guide to determining the best interests of a child under this part of the *CFSA*, *ibid.*, that contains twelve considerations and an invitation to consider "any other relevant circumstance": s. 37(3). Section 57(1) makes clear that it is only upon a finding of need for protection that the court turns to the best interests test.

- Where it is necessary to remove the child from the parent's care, the court shall consider whether placement under society supervision with a relative or member of the child's community is possible.[24] [s. 57(4)]
- Before making a Crown wardship order, the court must be satisfied that the circumstances affecting the child are unlikely to change within the next twenty-four months. [s. 57(7)]

- To assist the court in making these choices, the court may order the child or parent to undergo an assessment by a person qualified to perform various assessments of the situation.[25] [s. 54(1)]
- Where an order has been made removing a child from the parent's care, an order for access by the parent shall be made unless inappropriate [s. 59(1)], except that the presumption is against access where the order is for Crown wardship.[26] [s. 59(1)]
- Orders may be reviewed at the instance of the society, a child of twelve or older, and the parent, except that certain restrictions apply where the child is a Crown ward.[27] [s. 64]

Role of the Child—The current legislation gives older children participatory rights in the proceedings affecting them.

- This part of the *CFSA* aims to protect children under the age of sixteen, unless a child of sixteen or seventeen is already the subject of an order made when he or she was under sixteen. [s. 37(1)]

---

24 Where the child is a native person, the court ought to place the child with a member of the extended family, a member of the child's native community, or a native person, unless there is a substantial reason not to do so: *CFSA*, *ibid.*, s. 137(5).

25 According to the provision, assessments may be "medical, emotional, developmental, psychological, educational or social" in nature.

26 See *Catholic Children's Aid Society of Metropolitan Toronto* v. M.(C.), above note 10 at 207: "Once Crown wardship has been ordered, s. 58(1) of the Act creates a presumption against access." Crown wardship usually entails the effective termination of most parental rights.

27 As to the proper standard to be used upon a review under s. 64, see *Catholic Children's Aid Society of Metropolitan Toronto* v. M.(C.), above note 10 at 200, L'Heureux-Dubé J.:

> The examination that must be undertaken on a status review is a two-fold examination. The first one is concerned with whether the child continues to be in need of protection and, as a consequence, requires a court order for his or her protection. The second is a consideration of the best interests of the child, an important and, in the final analysis, a determining element of the decision as to the need of protection. The need for continued protection may arise from the existence or the absence of the circumstances that triggered the first order for protection or from circumstances which have arisen since that time.

- The age of twelve is a critical age under this part. Children between twelve and sixteen are accorded significant rights under the Act. (Children under 12 may be accorded similar rights if a court determines they can understand and will not be harmed.)
  - Unless the court determines that it would cause the child harm, a twelve-year-old shall receive notice of the proceeding concerning him or her and may be present at the hearing [s. 39(4)], with the right to participate "as if he or she were a party."[28] [s. 39(6)]
  - A child given notice may appeal an order. [s. 69(1)(a)]
  - A twelve-year-old child who is the subject of an order may seek a review of his or her status. [s. 64(4)(a)]
  - Where, after a finding of need for protection, an assessment is performed, a twelve-year-old shall receive a copy of the assessment, unless it would cause him or her harm. [s. 54(5)]
- Where the court is to consider the best interests of the child (which is essentially after a finding of need for protection), the child's views and wishes shall be taken into account, if they can reasonably be ascertained. [s. 37(3), para. 9]
- A child may have legal representation in the proceeding; and a protocol[29] is established for determining when the court should appoint legal representation for an unrepresented child. [s. 38]

C. CHILD IN NEED OF PROTECTION

1) Introduction

a) Family and State
In an important sense, the statutory phrase "child in need of protection" governs the boundary between the family and the state. Society in its official guise has the authority to disrupt the ongoing family in order to provide what is determined to be needed protection for a child, which may entail removing the child temporarily or permanently from the care of the parents.

It would be wrong, however, to imagine that the family is ordinarily free of state intrusion or influence concerning the raising of children, and that intervention under this part of the *CFSA* represents a sudden and unique display of state interest. The family and political life are not

---

28   The child is otherwise not defined as a party: *CFSA*, above note 1, s. 39(1).

29   See section E(2), "Appointment by the Court under Section 38 of the *Child and Family Services Act*" in this chapter.

discrete spheres of activity, but interact at all levels to support and shape each other. The clearest examples of continuing state involvement in the raising of children are the requirement that children be educated[30] and the provision of a public school system to carry out that objective. Other obvious examples would be the requirement that children be vaccinated against certain diseases,[31] the requirement that day-care facilities operate according to standards,[32] and, indeed, the provision of tax benefits to parents.[33] The appropriate degree of evident or direct state involvement is a perennial issue.[34]

Recently this discussion has been carried in terms that oppose parental rights to the best interests of the child, and has more often than not concluded that parents have no rights as such.[35] Any advantages that parents may have over other potential custodians of the child are, in this view, attributable to the interest the child has in some aspect of the familial situation.[36]

A good illustration of this, in the context of child protection, is the case of *Catholic Children's Aid Society of Metropolitan Toronto* v. M.(C.),[37] in which the Supreme Court dealt with the issue of the proper judicial approach to the subsequent review of orders made upon finding a child in need of protection. According to the Act, a review decision is to be

---

30　*Education Act*, R.S.O. 1990, c. E.2, s. 21(1).

31　*Immunization of School Pupils Act*, R.S.O. 1990, c. I.1, s. 3.

32　*Day Nurseries Act*, R.S.O. 1990, c. D.2, s. 11(1).

33　*Income Tax Act*, S.C. 1992, c. 48, s. 122.6.

34　See, for example, J. Singer, "The Privatization of Family Law" [1992] Wisc. L. Rev. 1443; and J. MacKinnon, "Best Interests of the Child in Protection Hearings: A Move Away from Parental Rights?" (1980) 14 R.F.L. (2d) 119; and P. Coleman, "A Proposal for Terminating Parental Rights: Spare the Parent, Spoil the Child" (1993) 7 Am. J. Fam. L. 123.

35　See, also, section C(1)(c), "Dispensing with Consent and Step-Parent Adoptions," in chapter 6, "Adoption."

36　There has not developed a serious case law position that would accord the family *per se* the right to protection from interference. The law tends to think almost exclusively in terms of an individual's interests (see, also, section E, "A Note on the Role of Suprafamilial Groups," in chapter 6, "Adoption."), and so in this context it must be the child's interests opposed to the interests of the individual parents. See *B.(R.)* v. *Children's Aid Society of Metropolitan Toronto*, [1995] 1 S.C.R. 315 at 363 "[Section] 7 of the Charter does not afford protection to the integrity of the family unit as such. The Canadian Charter, and s. 7 in particular, protects individuals." LaForest J. *Canadian Charter of Rights and Freedoms*, Part 1 of the *Constitution Act, 1982*, being Schedule B to the *Canada Act 1982* (U.K.), 1982, c. 11 [*Charter*].

37　Above note 10. But see *B.(R.)* v. *Children's Aid Society of Metropolitan Toronto*, *ibid.* (discussed in section C(3), "Required Medical Treatment," in this chapter, for a statement of parental rights protected by the *Charter*.

based on differently expressed criteria from an original finding that a child is in need of protection,[38] so strictly speaking, the judgment is limited in application. However, Justice L'Heureux-Dubé used general language a good deal and took the opportunity to address some of the potentially conflicting aims of the legislation.

She observes that section 1 of the *CFSA* establishes that "the first and 'paramount' objective of the Act is to promote 'the best interests, protection and well-being of children,'" and that "the Act carefully seeks to balance the rights of parents . . . with the rights of children to protection and well-being." This results in a relatively "non-interventionist" approach, in her opinion, but one that

> is premised not with a view to strengthen parental rights but, rather, in the recognition of the importance of keeping a family together as a means of fostering the best interests of children. Thus, the value of maintaining a family unit intact is evaluated in contemplation of what is best for the child, rather than for the parent. In order to respect the wording as well as the spirit of the Act, it is crucial that this child-centred focus not be lost . . .[39]

And a little later: "The paramountcy of the best interests of the child is clearly apparent . . . throughout the Act."[40] And later still she continues to speak of balancing interests and then quotes an American scholar who says:[41]

> Focus on parental fitness is inappropriate in many termination cases. Rather, when the child is young, emphasis should be on needs and interests of the child. . . . [P]arental rights should be terminated if . . . it is determined it would be in the best interests of the child to terminate.

Her approach would seem to convert "the rights of parents" into a judicially legislated value that says the best interests of a child are (ordinarily?) met within an intact "family unit." (Other statutory values concerning the best interests of a child are expressed merely as considerations for a judge, and not as universal assertions.)[42]

---

38   See section B, "Statutory Framework," subsection "Determination Hearing," in this chapter.
39   *Catholic Children's Aid Society of Metropolitan Toronto* v. *M.(C.)*, above note 10 at 191.
40   *Ibid.* at 195.
41   *Ibid.* at 201, quoting P. Coleman, above note 34 at 148.
42   See *CFSA*, above note 1, s. 37(3), for the definition of the best interests of a child.

Whatever the correctness of this view when considering review of an order, it would be wrong if applied so as to justify original intervention in the family when it was "simply" in the best interests of the child, however understood: the Act clearly postpones consideration of the child's best interests until a need for protection as defined is found to exist.[43] Thus, a child must be left with the parent even though he or she might be "better off" in care; the aim is not improvement, but protection from harm.

b) The Role of Experts

From the examination below of the various kinds of children deemed to be "in need of protection," it will become evident that the legislation—any legislation, indeed—is unable to provide more than general guidance. A great deal is left to the discretion of the judge. Were our population homogeneous and stable, it might be possible for all to share a common understanding of what is and what is not so harmful to a child that the state must step in. In fact, however, it is clear that there are different views of where to draw the line.

It is important in this context to draw attention to the role played in this process by social work, medical, and mental health professionals. Certain of the definitions of a "child in need of protection" use language that reveals the hand of such experts in their formulation, and which may, indeed, require expert assistance to understand and apply. Moreover, no court can have the kind of experience in dealing with children and families that professionals in the field possess; and when making difficult, discretionary judgments this experience can be very welcome. As has been seen,[44] the court may order assessments of the child and family by such experts and will probably rely, to a greater or lesser degree, on their findings.[45]

---

43 *Ibid.*, s. 57(1); and see above note 23. Also, s. 1 identifies the promotion of the best interests of a child as the "paramount" aim of the Act, with the consequence that there are other, albeit subsidiary, aims—"family autonomy and integrity," for example—that do not principally have to do with the best interests of the child, or, at least, are not to be subsumed within that calculus.

44 See section B, "Statutory Framework," subsection "Disposition," in this chapter.

45 See, for example, *Children's Aid Society of Hamilton-Wentworth (Regional Municipality)* v. *D.(S.)* (1991), 35 R.F.L. (3d) 136 at 140–41 (Ont. U.F.C.): "Family courts are encountering child abuse cases under the Child and Family Services Act, 1984 with increasing frequency. These are very complex matters, since they usually involve children not yet old enough to adequately express themselves, to understand what has happened to them, or to take an adversarial position against their custodians. Expert evidence is obviously critical in such situations."

The involvement of experts in the child welfare process may appeal to many because it offers the prospect of a "scientific," "objective" standard that ought therefore to be universally acceptable. This standard might best be described by the phrase "normal healthy development."[46] That which seriously endangers "normal healthy development" of a child requires social intervention. Yet it is important to remember that, while the scientific method can indeed provide universally useful knowledge, much of the expertise that is brought to bear in child protection matters is based rather on personal experience than on studies and experimentation, and all science, especially that dealing with people, has subjective and cultural underpinnings.[47]

c) Attention to the Limits

The discussion that follows will often focus on the limits or contested boundaries of the various definitions of child in need of protection. This ought not to mislead anyone into believing that all, or even most, cases brought before the court under this part are legally difficult: unfortunately, a great many of these are cases where repeated efforts by societies[48] have failed to alleviate conditions that most, if not all, would agree are beyond that which any child should have to bear. Societies and courts do not have budgets sufficient to let them deal with the borderline cases in addition to all the clear cases.

2) Harm

There is a sense in which every one of the definitional subclauses in section 37(2) of the *CFSA* aims at protecting a child from harm. Four of the twelve, however, use that very word; other subclauses use different language for the evil to be avoided; and still others describe situations from which a form of harm is to be inferred.

---

46 See, for example, J. Goldstein *et al.*, *The Best Interests of the Child: The Least Detrimental Alternative* (New York; Toronto: The Free Press, 1996) at xx, using the phrase "healthy growth and development."

47 See S.J. Gould, *The Mismeasure of Man*, rev. ed. (New York: Norton, 1996).

48 See, for example, *Child and Family Services Agency of Winnipeg South* v. *S.(D.D.)* (1990), 24 R.F.L. (3d) 290 (Man. Q.B.), in which some thirteen helping professionals testified about their involvement with the family over a period of under two years. These included seven social workers, a homemaker, two psychiatrists, a public health nurse, and a psychologist.

a) Physical Harm

A child is in need of protection where,

(a) the child has suffered physical harm, inflicted by the person having charge of the child or caused by that person's failure to care and provide for or supervise and protect the child adequately;

(b) there is a substantial risk that the child will suffer physical harm inflicted or caused as described above;[49]

Note that the harm may be caused directly by the custodian or as a consequence of the custodian's neglect. Note also that intervention does not need to await actual harm, but may occur where there is "a substantial risk" of harm. Obviously, this calls for speculation about the future, something that courts find more difficult, perhaps, than their usual task of determining what happened in the past.

There is a continuum of physical harm that proceeds from the trivial to the most grievous—from a bump or a scrape to broken bones and gross bodily injury, for example. Although the definition does not qualify the sort of harm that will constitute the need for protection, societies and courts must judge which harms are too trivial or transient to be considered and which merit concern.

However, the seriousness of the harm alone is not sufficient to enable societies and courts to perform the judgment about need for protection. It will also be necessary to take into account the manner in which the harm came about. A child who falls while playing and scrapes a knee would almost certainly not be in need of protection: the child has suffered harm, but it is likely that this harm would not be judged to be caused by parental failure to supervise adequately. Some harms for children are to be expected and form a normal part of growing up. However, if the scrape were inflicted by a parent, the child might be found to be in need of protection, for we most likely do not recognize that sort of parental behaviour as acceptable.

It will be clear from that last statement that a judgment must ultimately be made here about the acceptability of the harm/cause combination. Some courts make this judgment by explicit reference to a "community standard"; however, this poses the question of what is the appropriate community. Those who are less interventionist might approve of the wide conception of community put forward in *Re Brown*:

---

49   *CFSA*, above note 1, s. 37(2)(a) & (b).

Society's interference in the natural family is only justified when the level of care of the children falls below that which no child in this country should be subjected to.[50]

Others might wish the comparison community to be more locally or particularly defined,[51] and still others would prefer the standard to be closer to that of the scientific or child-expert community than to that of the broader population.[52]

b) Emotional Harm

When the predecessor child protection legislation was passed, Ontario was lauded by childcare professionals for its explicit recognition of emotional harm as a form of injury to children.[53] Subsequently, however, this original provision was criticized by many as permitting too easy intervention into the family, too easy removal of children, in part for the obvious reason that an emotion or the emotion-producing facility is not directly observable; the danger is that we will inaccurately project our understanding of a situation onto the child in question. The current Act retains emotional harm that has not been prevented by the parent as a basis for a finding of need for protection but requires that this harm be

demonstrated by severe,

(i)   anxiety,

(ii)   depression,

---

50   (1975), 9 O.R. (2d) 185 (Co. Ct.).

51   See, for example, *Re Warren* (1973), 13 R.F.L. 51 at 53 (Ont. Co. Ct.): "[T]his Court must not be persuaded to impose unrealistic or unfair middle class standards of child care upon a poor family of extremely limited potential." See also *Re E.*, [1980] 4 W.W.R. 296 at 297 (Sask. Prov. Ct.):

> [W]hile there is a minimum parental standard for all society, a secondary standard must be established for parents of the age of the parent in question and for the type of community in which the parent resides. A teen-aged parent cannot live up to the standard expected for a middle-aged parent. Similarly, different standards of parenting apply to parents of Cree ancestry who reside in a small rural community in northern Saskatchewan than would apply to white middle-class parents living, for example, in Regina. What is an acceptable standard for the former might be unacceptable to the latter.

52   B. Dickens, "Parental Discipline: Re O." (1978) 1 Can. J. Fam. L. 601 at 607: "The need for protection . . . may be objectively assessed by concepts of causation rooted in appropriate professional disciplines rather than by reference to the level of harm a given community has been accustomed to tolerate." Quoted with approval in *Children's Aid Society of Ottawa-Carleton v. W.(S.)*, [1987] O.J. No. 1896 (Prov. Ct.).

53   *Child Welfare Act*, above note 8, s. 19(1)(b)(x).

(iii)   withdrawal, or

(iv)   self-destructive or aggressive behaviour . . .[54]

These terms, particularly as modified by the requirement that the symptoms be "severe," would seem to have their origins in the mental health sciences; and although they may have in some respects passed into ordinary language, it will be natural to rely on mental health professionals for their meaning and applicability in a given case.[55] There is, of course, a risk that reliance on experts will mean families are dealt with according to standards not fully comprehensible by the ordinary citizen, and, therefore, standards difficult to evaluate or criticize.

Perhaps more troublesome is the companion definition that says "a substantial risk of emotional harm"[56] as just described constitutes a need for protection. As with physical harm, this requires prognosis from the court, but rather more difficult in this case, one would think; for what is required is that the court determine that there is not simply a risk but a substantial risk that the child will suffer not merely withdrawal, for instance, but severe withdrawal, as a consequence of emotional harm.[57]

---

54   *CFSA*, above note 1, s. 37(2)(f). See as well cl. 37(2)(h), which renders a child in need of protection who "suffers from a mental, emotional or developmental condition that, if not remedied, could seriously impair the child's development" and whose parent does not provide treatment. This clause is not examined in this book.

55   See, for example, *Kawartha-Haliburton Children's Aid Society* v. *D.C.*, [1995] O.J. No. 2936 (Prov. Div.) at para. 194:

J.B.C. and H.A.C. showed very aggressive behaviour towards each other and, in Dr. Virginia Winters' opinion, P.H.C. was depressed when he came into care. The aggression could appropriately be called severe and depression in a child as young as P.H.C. at the time should be labelled as a severe condition. After all, these children were still too young to show the usual anxiety, depression or withdrawal contemplated by this clause that older persons exhibit to indicate their emotional suffering.

Note that the court moves the severity requirement from the "depression" to apply it instead to the broader "condition." The problem of unmanifested emotional harm is made clear here.

56   *CFSA*, above note 1, s. 37(2)(g).

57   In practice the calculation might be considerably less exacting: see, for example, *Kawartha-Haliburton Children's Aid Society* v. *D.C.*, above note 55 at para. 195:

D.C.'s insensitive and demeaning treatment of the children at the shelter was very unloving. It would undermine any sense of self-worth that these little people might enjoy. If the children were left in D.C.'s care, psychiatric intervention and perhaps the criminal justice system would be involved in the children's future lives.

But see *Children's Aid Society of Metropolitan Toronto* v. *P.(J.)*, [1989] O.J. No. 2564 (Prov. Ct.) in which the court makes clear that the emotional harm must be demonstrated by severe anxiety, etc., and that there must be a causal connection between the emotional harm and the anxiety.

c) Sexual Harm

The *CFSA* does not use the term "harm" in this context, but speaks of sexual molestation or exploitation.[58] A child is in need of protection when either of these harms is brought about by the parent or person in charge, or by someone else where the parent or person in charge should have known "of the possibility" and failed to protect the child. As with the other forms of harm, substantial risk of this sexual harm will also constitute a child as being in need of protection.

Sexual abuse, particularly of girls, is a common and under-reported phenomenon. A recent study[59] in Ontario questioned nearly 10,000 individuals to determine, among other things, how many had a history of child sexual abuse[60] by an adult. The study indicated that 12.8 percent of female respondents reported sexual abuse (11.1 percent "severe" sexual abuse); and 4.3 percent of males reported sexual abuse (3.9 percent "severe" sexual abuse). The abuse was most commonly reported to be by an adult other than the "natural" mother or father. Earlier studies, differently constituted, have suggested even more widespread sexual abuse.[61]

This is an area where a number of factors converge to make for serious difficulty. First, the power imbalance between adults and children makes it possible for adults to gratify their needs at the expense of children, and makes it difficult for complaints to be voiced, heard, and taken seriously.[62] Then, as the statistics above clearly show, the relatively

---

58 *CFSA*, above note 1, s. 37(2)(c), (d).

59 H.L. MacMillan *et al.*, "Prevalence of Child Physical and Sexual Abuse in the Community" (1997) 278 J.A.M.A. 131.

60 *Ibid.* Sexual abuse was defined as the following adult behaviour "while the [respondent] was growing up": (i) exposure of genitals to the child more than once, (ii) threat to have sex with the child, (iii) touching the child's "sexual parts," (iv) trying to have sex with the child or sexually attacking the child. Behaviours (ii), (iii) and (iv) were characterized as "severe sexual abuse."

61 C. Badgley, *Child Sexual Abuse in Canada: Further Analysis of the 1988 National Survey* (Ottawa: Family Violence Prevention Division, Ministry of Health and Welfare, 1988), reported that 17.6 percent of females and 8.2 percent of males experienced unwanted sexual acts (not necessarily by adults) before their seventeenth birthday. See also D. Finkelhor, "The International Epidemiology of Child Sexual Abuse" (1994) 18 Child Abuse and Neglect 409.

62 But it is no longer mandatory for a court to give the jury a warning about convicting an accused on the evidence of a child: *Criminal Code*, R.S.C. 1985, c. C-46 (as amended by S.C. 1993, c. 45, s. 9), s. 659. And a child's unsworn testimony need no longer be corroborated: *Canada Evidence Act*, R.S.C. 1985, c. C-5 (as amended by S.C. 1994, c. 44, s. 89), s. 16. See also *R. v. Marquard*, [1993] 4 S.C.R. 223, concerning the testimonial competence of children.

inferior social position accorded to women and girls makes it especially likely that they will be the targets of abuse and that the abusers will be men. Our society's stereotype of children as basically innocent and pure further complicates matters because it may mean that we do not wish to contemplate or discuss the violation of this "perfection," and so refuse to credit the fact of sexual abuse or to plan for its elimination. And, finally, our marked ambivalence about sexuality generally prevents us from discussing the problem of child sexual abuse as freely as is necessary if any solution is to be found.

3) Required Medical Treatment

A child is in need of protection where he or she "requires medical treatment to cure, prevent or alleviate physical harm or suffering" and the custodian does not or cannot consent to the treatment.[63] Note that there is no "substantial risk" clause associated with this definition.

Every aspect of this definition can be made problematic: for example, assuming we know what "harm" is, what then is "suffering"? How much relief must there be for the treatment to be said to "alleviate" the harm or suffering? What cure rate has to be shown in order to say that the treatment is "required . . . to cure" the condition? What constitutes "medical" treatment? Clearly, the practical answers to such questions will result from an exercise of judgment by the society and the court based upon evidence provided by the medical profession. It might be the case that where emotional harm is concerned, for example, courts will often have to obtain assistance from mental health professionals; but here reliance on professional assistance is almost mandatory. This raises questions about how, if at all, it is possible for a court to have a standpoint for judgment that is not a "captive" of professional assumptions and beliefs.

Perhaps more so than other protection issues, disputes about medical treatment will oppose societies to parents who are making conscious, deliberate choices concerning their children. These choices, because they are conscious and deliberate, are often based on belief systems that are at odds with the majoritarian world view. Thus, these disputes can have a clearer political element, and argument will often range into basic liberties and fundamental rights. As well, this is the locus for debate about certain ultimate issues in our society, such as when, if

---

63   *CFSA*, above note 1, s. 37(2)(e). See as well cl. 37(2)(h).

ever, death is preferable to continued life,[64] and who ought to be able to make such decisions for children.[65]

The case of *B. (R.)* v. *Children's Aid Society of Metropolitan Toronto*,[66] decided by the Supreme Court, is illustrative. Medical doctors determined that an infant required surgery and for that and other reasons would require blood transfusions. The child's parents, Jehovah's Witnesses, objected to blood transfusions on religious grounds. A hearing was held before the court on short notice to the parents; and a society wardship order was made under the prior child protection legislation,[67] and later extended for some three weeks, during which time surgery was performed and a blood transfusion administered to the child. The wardship order was terminated and the child was then returned to the care of the parents.

The parents argued that the provisions of the then legislation respecting medical treatment[68] and the powers given to the court in that connection violated their right to choose medical treatment for the child under section 7 of the *Charter* and infringed on the parents' freedom of religion under section 2(a).[69] In a series of judgments difficult to reconcile into a coherent policy, the court upheld the validity of the original decision and the legislation under which it was made. In so doing the judges (all but one) made it clear that the *Charter* is relevant in child protection cases and creates a right in parents of some description to make decisions respecting their children.

The decision of LaForest J. gathered the most support (four judges in all). Speaking of section 7 he observed that:

---

64   See, for example, *British Columbia (Superintendent of Family and Child Services)* v. *D.R.*, [1983] 3 W.W.R. 618 (B.C.S.C.): parents of a severely mentally and physically handicapped child resist the replacement of a device that may prolong life.

65   See, for example, *Re K. (L.D.)* (1985), 48 R.F.L. (2d) 164 (Ont. Prov. Ct.): an eleven-year-old girl with fatal leukemia wishes to refuse medical treatment.

66   Above note 36.

67   *Child Welfare Act*, above note 8. The child was ordered into temporary care in 1983; the appeal to the Supreme Court was decided more than eleven years later.

68   *Ibid.*, s. 19(1)(b)(ix): ". . . a child where the person in whose charge the child is neglects or refuses to provide or obtain proper medical, surgical or other recognized remedial care or treatment necessary for the child's health or well-being . . ."

69   *Charter*, above note 36. The parents conceded that the state may intervene to protect children and that in a true emergency situation a doctor may act without sanction of a court order and against the parents' wishes; they protested, however, the ease and speed with which parental wishes may be overturned in non-emergency situations.

> [T]he right to nurture a child, to care for its development, and to make decisions for it in fundamental matters, such as medical care, are part of the liberty interest of a parent . . . While acknowledging that parents bear responsibilities towards their children, it seems to me that they must enjoy correlative rights to exercise them . . . This . . . translates into a protected sphere of parental decision making.[70]

Intervention must be justified and parental decision making will receive the protection of the *Charter*. In this case the intervention provided for by the legislation complied with the principles of fundamental justice.

With respect to section 2(a) of the *Charter*, LaForest J. said that "the right of parents to rear their children according to their religious beliefs, including that of choosing medical and other treatments, is [a] . . . fundamental aspect of freedom of religion."[71] The legislation in its effect infringed on this freedom, but the consequent section 1 analysis justified the infringement. The security of the child was paramount in this case, and the procedures in the legislation were sufficient to satisfy sections 1 and 7.

4) Foetal Apprehension

> Here is a classic dilemma. An expectant mother sniffs solvent to the probable detriment of her unborn child. If nothing is done, the child when born will surely suffer. Yet, anything which can be done necessarily involves restricting the mother's freedom of choice and, if she persists in the habit, her liberty.[72]

In *Winnipeg Child and Family Services (Northwest Area)* v. *G.(D.F.)* the Manitoba Court of Appeal decided that the use of mental health legislation to declare the glue-sniffing mother incompetent was improper in the instant case and was an indirect attempt to protect the unborn child. It then considered "the much more controversial question of whether the [court] has authority to order the mother to undergo treatment . . . for the protection of the child."[73]

The court decided that it could not use its inherent *parens patriae* jurisdiction to make an unborn child a ward of the court, and that it ought not to restrain the mother's allegedly tortious conduct on behalf of the unborn child. In both instances the court discussed the grave difficulties, particularly the loss of liberty in the mother, that would result

---

70   *B.(R.)* v. *Children's Aid Society of Metropolitan Toronto*, above note 36 at 372.
71   *Ibid.* at 382.
72   [1996] 10 W.W.R. 111 at 113 (Man. C.A.), aff'd [1997] 3 S.C.R. 925.
73   *Ibid.* at 115.

if the interests of the unborn child were permitted to be opposed to those of the mother. The court observed that in the preamble to the United Nations Declaration of the Rights of the Child, to which Canada is a signatory, the child is said to require "legal protection before as well as after birth."[74] This protection, however, would have to be derived from legislation because of the difficult moral and policy issues involved.

On appeal the Supreme Court in a 9 to 2 judgment affirmed its opposition to granting rights to unborn children.[75] McLachlin J. dismissed the appeal on the basis that an unborn child is not a person under current law and has no tort rights; similarly, the court's *parens patriae* jurisdiction does not extend to unborn children. The court ought not, she held, extend the law to cover unborn children; any extension would be properly left to the legislature, if only because of the extreme complexity of the issue.

Some lower courts, however, had earlier made orders for foetal apprehension under local child protection legislation; but the general opinion was against the propriety of such orders.[76]

D. CHILD ABUSE

1) Introduction

Child abuse is defined in the *CFSA* for two purposes. One definition relates to a special duty to report, which is discussed immediately below. That definition identifies children as suffering from abuse who are in need of protection because of having been harmed (rather than because of any risk of harm).[77] The second definition relates to the

---

74   *Ibid.* at 120, quoting U.N. Document A/4354 (1959), with a reference as well to U.N. Document A/RES/44/25 (1989).

75   *Winnipeg Child and Family Services (Northwest Area)* v. *G. (D.F.)*, above note 72. See also: *Tremblay* v. *Daigle*, [1989] 2 S.C.R. 530 (right to life under the Quebec *Charter of Human Rights and Freedoms*); *R.* v. *Sullivan*, [1991] 1 S.C.R. 489 (criminal negligence causing death).

76   See *Re Baby R* (1987), 9 R.F.L. (3d) 415 (B.C. Prov. Ct.), rev'd (1988), 15 R.F.L. (3d) 238 (B.C.S.C.); *Re A* (1990), 75 O.R. (2d) 82 (U.F.C.). But see *Children's Aid Society of City of Belleville* v. *T.(L.)* (1987), 59 O.R. (2d) 204 (Prov. Ct.).

77   *CFSA*, above note 1, s. 72(1): "to 'suffer abuse' . . . means to be in need of protection within the meaning of clause 37 (2) (a), (c), (e), (f) or (h)." Note that this includes as well a child in need of medical treatment and a child suffering from a mental, etc., condition in need of remediation. See also s. 81, which permits the Children's Lawyer to sue for damages or compensation on behalf of an abused child, defined in the same way.

quasi-criminal provision under the Act that prohibits abuse.[78] Anyone who has charge of a child and who inflicts or permits the infliction of abuse on a child may be fined or imprisoned.[79]

In a recent study in Ontario,[80] 31 percent of males and 21 percent of females reported a history of physical abuse[81] during childhood; and 4 percent of males and 13 percent of females reported a history of sexual abuse while they were growing up.[82]

The legal system has not done a very good job of stopping abuse. Until relatively recently, much abuse, physical and sexual, was regarded as "normal" or, at least, tolerable behaviour within a family—a private matter that should not provoke state intervention. Even when it became clear that the rate of child abuse was much higher than had been supposed (because of drastic under-reporting), the view was often held that state intervention ought to be of a limited kind aimed at preserving the family and the place of the child within it.[83]

Currently there appears to be a willingness to use all the tools available in the legal system, including the criminal law and its power to condemn and punish the abusive behaviour.[84] Even so, mistreatment of children will not be stopped without widespread social efforts to alter general attitudes that are permissive with respect to abuse of parental power.

---

78   *Ibid.*, s. 79(1): "'abuse' means a state or condition of being physically harmed, sexually molested or sexually exploited."

79   *Ibid.*, s. 79(2), establishes the prohibition and s. 85(2) creates the offence and punishment.

80   H.L. MacMillan *et al.*, above note 59.

81   *Ibid.* Physical abuse included often or sometimes: being pushed, grabbed, or shoved; and having something thrown at one; [what follows was defined as severe physical abuse] and kicked, bit, or punched; and being hit with something; and being choked, burned, or scalded; and being physically attacked in some other way. Severe physical abuse was reported by 10.7 percent of males and 9.2 percent of females.

82   See section C(2)(c), "Sexual Harm," in this chapter.

83   But see *"Reaching for Solutions": The Report of the Special Advisor to the Minister of National Health and Welfare on Child Sexual Abuse in Canada* (Ottawa: National Clearinghouse on Family Violence, Health and Welfare Canada, 1990) at 57–58: Recommendation #23: "That in each jurisdiction there should be a clear government policy to charge and prosecute child abusers in every case where the Crown Attorney is satisfied that there is sufficient evidence to merit prosecution and that the child will not be unduly traumatized by the process."

84   It is still the case, however, that the criminal law provides that "[e]very schoolteacher, parent or person standing in the place of a parent is justified in using force by way of correction toward a pupil or child, as the case may be, who is under his care, if the force does not exceed what is reasonable under the circumstances": *Criminal Code*, R.S.C. 1985, C-46, s. 43.

2) Obligation to Report

Child abuse must be reported before it can be stopped. Although reporting rates have risen over the past years,[85] there is still a general reluctance to report suspected abuse, and the reluctance is increased where the person noting the abuse has a professional relationship with members of the family that normally includes a duty of confidentiality.

The *CFSA* contains two duties to report, the first, falling on all persons, to report to a society a belief on reasonable grounds that a child is simply in need of protection;[86] and the second, falling on a limited set of persons, to report to a society a *suspicion* on reasonable grounds that "a child is or may be suffering or may have suffered abuse."[87] Breach of the general duty is not punishable under the Act, but there is provision for a fine for breach of the more specific duty.[88]

The limited duty applies to "every person who performs professional or official duties with respect to a child,"[89] including, among others, health care professionals, teachers, social workers, members of the clergy, peace officers, and solicitors. These persons must report when the suspicion of abuse arises "in the course of . . . professional or official duties"; and the obligation exists "despite the provisions of any other Act"[90] or duties of confidentiality.[91]

It might be useful to examine briefly the duty to report imposed on "a solicitor" by these provisions. The Act creates a problem peculiar to lawyers, when it states that "[n]othing in this section abrogates any privilege that may exist between a solicitor and his or her client."[92] Thus, a solicitor (one of the specifically identified classes of professional person), who develops reasonable grounds to suspect abuse while performing a duty, is obliged to report the suspicion and information on which it is based, notwithstanding that "the information reported may

---

85 The approximately 19,000 allegations of abuse investigated by CASs in Ontario represent a 200 percent increase over the previous decade: Ontario Association of Children's Aid Societies, *Info 1995*, October 1995.

86 *CFSA*, above note 1, s. 72(2).

87 *Ibid.*, s. 72(3).

88 *Ibid.*, s. 85(1)(b).

89 *Ibid.*, s. 72(4).

90 *Ibid.*, s. 72(3). The phrase "with respect to a child" is not used in this subsection to modify "duties," as it is in subsection 4, which identifies those persons to whom this duty-creating subsection applies. It is not entirely clear whether, if the information arises while performing a duty with respect to an adult, it ought even so to be reported.

91 *Ibid.*, s. 72(7).

92 *Ibid.*, s. 72(8).

be confidential or privileged." But yet the "privilege" that exists between solicitor and client is not abrogated by the Act.

One means of resolving the apparent conflict is to interpret the unabrogated solicitor-client "privilege" as being a reference to the evidentiary privilege, whereby a lawyer may not be compelled to testify to what a client told him or her while retained as counsel.[93] In this view, the obligation in the Act overrides any professional duty of confidentiality, but stops short of permitting the lawyer to be compelled to testify against the wishes of the client. This interpretation receives some support from the fact that subsection 72(7) distinguishes between information that is "confidential" and that which is "privileged."

It is likely, however, that most lawyers would be loath to breach their obligation of confidentiality. To justify this reluctance, however, the provisions under discussion would have to be interpreted to mean that solicitors must report, despite confidentiality or privilege, but are relieved from the obligation to report where the information is confidential—which will be almost always the case, for information received while performing a professional duty. This analysis does not seem sound.

The rules of professional conduct do not address the specific situation at all,[94] which illustrates one aspect of the problem with professional duties to report abuse. The statutory obligation was imposed on professional persons without their cooperation and agreement, such that the ethic of reporting is not established within the professions. It is possible that professional ethical obligations will be felt to be more compelling than legal obligations.

3) Child Abuse Register

Child abusers may move from place to place to escape detection. In order to respond to this possibility, the *CFSA* establishes a child abuse register with the aim of gathering in one place information that would otherwise be held locally in municipalities and regions throughout the province.[95]

---

93   See S. Shiff, *Evidence in the Litigation Process*, 4th ed. (Toronto: Carswell, 1993) at 1099–1125.

94   Rule 4 of the *Rules of Professional Conduct* (Toronto: Law Society of Upper Canada, 1996) permits a lawyer to disclose confidential information when "required by law to do so." This, of course, is the question under discussion, and the rule is unhelpful.

95   *CFSA*, above note 1, s. 75. There have been calls for the establishment of a national register.

A society that receives a report of suspected abuse must verify the information on which the suspicion is based, and when that information is verified the society must report it to the director of the register.[96] The person identified in the report and in the register is given notice and an opportunity to persuade the director at a hearing that the information is in error and ought to be removed from the register.[97]

Societies and others permitted by the director may inspect the register and remove information from it.[98] However, the register may not be admitted into evidence in proceedings except under very limited circumstances.[99] Thus, the information is to assist societies in forming conclusions about the need for protection of a child, but cannot, in the form of registered information, assist in making a case before a court. For that purpose, presumably, a society must obtain direct evidence from the occasion that gave rise to the report.

E. REPRESENTING THE CHILD

1) Introduction

Section 38(1) of the *CFSA* provides that a child may have legal representation in a proceeding under this part.[100] Legal representation may come about in a number of ways. A child may retain a lawyer on his or her own initiative, provided that the child has sufficient ability to understand the nature of such a contract,[101] or a parent could retain a

---

96   *Ibid.*, s. 75(3).
97   *Ibid.*, s. 76.
98   *Ibid.*, s. 75(8).
99   *Ibid.*, s. 75(14).
100   Note representation is possible even though the child may not be a party to the proceeding. See section B, "Statutory Framework," subsection "Role of the Child," in this chapter. A child may have a right under s. 7 of the *Charter* to have counsel; this may depend upon a number of factors including the potential for the child's liberty to be affected: *Re M.(R.A.)*, [1984] 2 W.W.R. 742 (Man. C.A., Judge in Chambers); however, "a lawyer can only represent an infant through either a next friend, a guardian, or the public trustee; there is no provision for an infant to instruct counsel directly: *Re M.(R.A.)*, [1984] 4 W.W.R. 478 (Man. C.A.), reversing the decision of the Judge in Chambers. See also *H.(T.) v. Children's Aid Society of Metropolitan Toronto* (1996), 138 D.L.R. (4th) 144 (Ont. Gen. Div.): where a thirteen-year-old girl was made a ward in order to transfuse her, there was no breach of fundamental justice (and no question of breach of s. 7), because she had notice, was not heard because of the emergency nature of the situation, and had her position adequately represented by others.
101   J. Wilson, *Wilson on Children and the Law* (Toronto, Ont.: Butterworths, 1994) at 5.34.14.

lawyer for the child. In the latter case, it would have to be made clear in the retainer that the lawyer was to represent the child and not the parent who initiated the arrangement or may pay the bill; and it would have to be the case that both parents agreed to the arrangement, or, at least, were not opposed in interest to each other.[102]

As well, courts may arrange for the appointment of legal representation for the child. In ordinary civil matters this is done under section 89(3) and (3.1) of the *Courts of Justice Act*,[103] and brings about the involvement of the Children's Lawyer, who would typically appoint counsel for the child. But in a proceeding under Part VII of the Act, section 38 gives the court a responsibility and a power to appoint representation if required.

2) Appointment by the Court under Section 38 of the *Child and Family Services Act*

The legislative provision for the appointment of representation is confusingly worded. It is clear that the court has a duty to determine on its own motion whether "legal representation is desirable to protect the child's interests"; and when it is, the court must direct its appointment.[104] The difficulty begins in subsection 38(4), which guides the court's analysis of whether representation is desirable.

The structure of the subsection is as follows: When any of three circumstances exists "legal representation shall be deemed to be desirable" unless the court is satisfied "that the child's interests are otherwise adequately protected"; in other words, that it is not desirable. This would appear to establish rebuttable presumptions in favour of the desirability of representation.

---

102   See *Fiorellino* v. *Fiorellino* (1995), 18 R.F.L. (4th) 301 (Ont. Gen. Div.). In a dispute between parents, the court held that children should never be represented by counsel retained by one parent. In a child protection proceeding, it might be the case that the parents are not in a conflict of interest with each other.

103   R.S.O. 1990, c. C.43, amended in this respect by S.O. 1994, c. 12, s. 37 and c. 27, s. 43(2). See also s. 112. It may be that the Ontario Court (General Division) and the Unified Family Court have the power to appoint counsel for a child under their *parens patriae* jurisdiction, but this is unnecessary because of the availability of the provisions of the *Courts of Justice Act: Strobridge* v. *Strobridge* (1994), 18 O.R. (3d) 753 (C.A.).

104   *CFSA*, above note 1, s. 38(2) &(3). The mechanism for appointment will typically be the Office of the Children's Lawyer, which will arrange for counsel.

The three circumstances are:

(a) when, in the court's opinion, the child's views are different from those of the parents or the society, *and* the society proposes the child be removed from a person's care or made a ward;
(b) when the child is in the society's care, *and* no parent appears, or it is alleged that the child is in need of protection because of one of the serious harm clauses; or
(c) when the child is not permitted to be present at the hearing.

The first circumstance seems to say that when the possible consequences are very serious, the child ought to be a participant if only through an attempt to ascertain his or her views. Then, if these views are not going to be put forward by others who might speak for the child, a lawyer ought to be provided. The second circumstance directs itself at the lack of suitable advocates for a child where the society who has responsibility for the child has allegedly permitted harm to the child. The third is apparently concerned to ensure some minimal participation by the child of the sort that his or her presence would have accorded. This last, it should be noted, makes it more likely that representation will be awarded for young children, who are not presumptively entitled to be present,[105] and who are, one would think, less able to instruct counsel.

If representation is deemed desirable to protect the child's interests because of seriousness of outcome, conflict of interest with other protectors, or exclusion, the court may nonetheless (taking into account the child's "views and wishes[106] if they can reasonably be ascertained") decide that the child's interests are otherwise adequately protected. It may be easiest to see this provision operating against appointment of representation for very young children: they could not have participated in any meaningful sense even were they present, and there are no (presumptive) reasons to suppose that between them the parents and the society cannot protect their interests.

All in all, this section sets up too complex a procedure, which failure represents, perhaps, the basic uncertainty we still feel about whether and when children ought to be treated as possessing the full panoply of civil rights, and, consequently, the right to counsel in order to protect them. But looked at from the view that considers children incompetent to exercise rights, there are clearly difficulties with our system. Parents have the first responsibility for protecting children, but

---

105 See section B, "Statutory Framework," subsection "Role of the Child," in this chapter.
106 Note that the legislation draws a distinction between views and wishes.

they sometimes fail or falter; and when they do, the children's aid society is the child's second line of defence. Acknowledging that societies may also fail children, the law provides for a third line of defence, the lawyer.

3) Role of a Child's Lawyer

The proper role of a child's lawyer is a much vexed question. The difficulty is part and parcel of the uncertainty, mentioned above, of when children ought to be treated as full political actors. Their perceived "difference" from the rest of us—incompetence, specially vulnerability, the lack of power—is reflected in the role that they are accorded in litigation concerning them, which is typically that of interested bystanders rather than of participating parties: "Let the adults handle this for you" is the sentiment from this standpoint, with perhaps the concession that "You can watch, but don't get in the way." Children may see, but not be heard.

At the same time, however, legal matters concerning children, and particularly their custody, are increasingly to be dealt with from a "child-centred" point of view. The suspicion is ripening into knowledge that too often the power imbalance between adults and children has been used to satisfy adult needs to the detriment of children; and, so, it is their needs alone that ideally ought to be met. The difficulty is that needs must be identified and communicated to decision makers; they must be "constructed" by a system. Adults are thought to be able to identify their own needs and, within the legal context, to pursue their satisfaction with the assistance of lawyers working in an adversarial system. But that same system, with its *lis* between parties, active independent litigants, and instruction-taking advocates, does not lend itself easily, if at all, to the construction and pursuit of the needs of children who are, or are believed to be, "different."[107]

---

107   See *Fiorellino* v. *Fiorellino*, above note 102 at 306: "It can never be in the best interests of children to be placed in a position where they become part of the adversarial dispute between parents." And see *Carter* v. *Brooks* (1990), 2 O.R. (3d) 321 at 328 (C.A.), where Morden A.C.J.O. is concerned to avoid an approach that "over-emphasizes the adversary nature of the proceeding and depreciates the Court's *parens patriae* responsibility."

Thus, we find a variety of views regarding the appropriate roles of children in the legal process and, consequently, the roles of their lawyers. One view has it that lawyers for children ought to play no different role than lawyers for adults: they take instructions, they counsel, and they advocate.[108] This view might be held, however, for different reasons. A traditionalist would say that this is the only appropriate role for a lawyer; and if it means that some, or most, children will be unable to participate in decisions affecting them because they cannot properly instruct counsel, then that is as it should be, for these are decisions for adults to make in any event. But a supporter of children's rights and the empowerment of children might also take this view, believing that children can and ought to be allowed to instruct counsel in much the same way as adults and that any other participation will be a lesser form of involvement in the construction and satisfaction of their needs.

Another view would see children's lawyers as *amici curiae*. In this view the lawyer does not represent the child as such but possesses a broad function to assist the court in ensuring that all relevant evidence is before it and is properly addressed.[109] This view might be held by those who believe that children ought to remain incompetent to participate directly, and that the unmodified adversarial system is inapt to discern and address children's needs.

At a more fine-grained level, there are disputes about whether a child's lawyer ought to be able to inform the court directly of the child's views and wishes, or whether these ought to be introduced in some other way;[110] whether a child's lawyer may express to the court his or her

---

108　See Law Society of Upper Canada, *Report of Sub-Committee on the Legal Representation of Children* (Toronto: The Committee, 1981); and see J. Wilson, *Wilson on Children and the Law* (Toronto, Ont.: Butterworths, 1994), looseleaf service, at 6.18. It ought to be noted that children would not be the only inarticulate, vulnerable, powerless clients a lawyer might have; and it can be argued that they present problems that are no different in kind from problems that lawyers address (or ought to address) in other areas of practice.

109　See J. Boyes & M.E. Walden, "The Life and Death of the Amicus Curiae in Custody Litigation in Alberta" (1991) 8 C.F.L.Q. 81.

110　See *C. v. Children's Aid Society of Metropolitan Toronto* (1980), 20 R.F.L. (2d) 259 at 264 (Ont. Co. Ct.): "I can see no reason that the views of the [child] parties, through the mouth of their counsel, should not be presented to the court." But see *Strobridge v. Strobridge*, above note 103 at 759: "Counsel cannot be both an advocate and a witness on an important issue."

view of the child's best interests;[111] and whether it is possible for counsel to represent children too young to instruct.[112] This last point invites consideration of whether, where non-instructing children are concerned, it is necessary to appoint the Office of the Children's Lawyer as a litigation guardian, who in turn might then instruct counsel. In the case of legal representation provided under section 38 of the *CFSA*, it has been decided that the statute mandates the direct appointment of a lawyer and not a litigation guardian, on the basis that section 39(6) provides that when a child has legal representation in a proceeding under Part VII, the child (and not another person on his or her behalf) is to participate "as if he or she were a party."[113]

---

111   See *Catholic Children's Aid Society of Metropolitan Toronto* v. M.(C.) (1991), 35 R.F.L. (3d) 1 (Ont. Prov. Ct.): "[C]ounsel for the non-instructing child may [not] put his own personal opinion as to the best interests of the child . . . before the Court." The judgment was reversed on a broader basis, without addressing this point, at (1991), 35 R.F.L. (3d) 297 (Ont. Gen. Div.). But see *Dumas* v. *Dumas*, [1989] O.J. No. 360 (Dist. Ct.), aff'd as to result (1990), 30 R.F.L. (3d) 127 (Ont. C.A.) to spare the child from testifying. It is consistent with that policy to allow court-appointed counsel for the child to relate the child's views, and to give counsel's observations and recommendations in the context of submissions.

112   See *Wicks* v. *Wicks*, [1990] O.J. No. 2414 (Prov. Div): "When counsel undertakes to represent children, they cannot take a narrow and technical approach and simply follow the perceived instructions of these very young and vulnerable children. If counsel attempted to do that and if they were to remain professionally honest and consistent, I suspect that they would have to refuse to represent infants who are obviously incapable of giving instructions . . ." But see *Catholic Children's Aid Society of Metropolitan Toronto* v. M.(C.), (trial judgment), above note 111: "[I]t is trite law that a counsel acting for a party in a proceeding who is unable to obtain instructions from that party cannot continue to act."

113   *Catholic Children's Aid Society of Metropolitan Toronto* v. M.(C.), (appeal judgment), above note 111. The appeal judgment does not address the concerns raised at trial about how counsel with a non-instructing client ought to act.

FURTHER READINGS

BALA, N., J. HORNICK, & R. VOGL, eds., *Canadian Child Welfare Law: Children, Families, and the State* (Toronto: Thompson Educational Publishing, 1991)

BERNSTEIN, M., *et al.*, *Child Protection Law in Canada* (Toronto: Carswell, 1990) looseleaf service

BERNSTEIN, M.M., & L.M. KIRWIN, *Child Protection: Practice and Procedure* (Scarborough, Ont: Carswell, 1996)

HUDSON, J., & B. GALAWAY, eds., *Child Welfare in Canada: Research and Policy Implications* (Toronto: Thompson Educational Publishing, 1995)

MANG, I., & J. KING, *Annotated Child and Family Services Act 1996* (Toronto: Carswell, 1996)

WILSON, J., *Wilson on Children and the Law* (Toronto: Butterworths, 1994) looseleaf service, c. 3

CHAPTER 8

SPOUSAL VIOLENCE

A. INTRODUCTION

Violence in our society ranges in severity and kind across broad spectra that include such diverse acts as corporal punishment of children, murder, sports, slapping, robbery, shoving, confinement of convicted criminals, rape, and displays of anger. We tolerate and even encourage some forms of violence, and when it comes to violence in the family, we too often turn away, not wishing to know or, when knowledge is forced on us, seemingly unable to devise clear means of dealing with it.[1] Violence within the family has some special features that set it apart as a social phenomenon deserving of particular attention and response.

Families are places of intimacy. For the most part, perhaps—and certainly in our hopes—this intimacy finds expression in love and caring, in gentleness and toleration. But intimacy may also license or give rise to anger, fear, and frustration, which are often expressed violently. And because family intimacy implies physical as well as emotional closeness, violence can easily be directed at those nearest.

Families persist—and are intended to persist. Violence against a stranger is unlikely to be repeated, if only because the opportunity will not present itself. Its consequences, serious enough, can be dealt with privately; whereas violence within the family may occur more than

---

1   See chapter 7, "Child Protection," section C(2)(c), "Sexual Harm," and section D, "Child Abuse."

once, and may indeed become a part of the pattern of behaviour in the relationship. And the consequences of violence for the victim and the perpetrator will often be worked through in each other's presence.

Families are private, we believe. We are reluctant to poke our noses into others' family affairs. This means that there is little chance that a pattern of violence within the family will be discovered and stopped, unless the victim is able to tell us about it. But victims, too, feel the injunction of privacy and are reluctant to take "family matters" public for fear of shame. It may be that we even regard things that happen within the family—"family matters"—as somehow immune from the criminal law and other codes of behaviour that clearly govern public life, meaning that when we discover family violence, we may do little or nothing about it.

Families involve power imbalances. All human institutions deal in part with power, and families are no exceptions. This imbalance is clear to us where children are concerned: children are relatively powerless in the family (and within society) and adults are relatively powerful. The powerful are meant to protect and nurture the weak, but, as was seen in chapter 7, "Child Protection," that does not always happen.

While men and women are meant in theory to be equally powerful in our society, the fact is that as a group, men still have greater access to economic resources and political influence. Gendered social roles, the legacy of history, and, important in the context of violence, disparity in physical size, all contribute to the power imbalance between men and women. Greater power may in and of itself lead some to abuse, but lesser power means that individual victims of violence may be insufficiently able to stop the abuse, either by leaving the abusive situation or by obtaining the necessary assistance from outside the family.

Because of the role played by power imbalances, this chapter will treat spousal violence as being essentially violence against women. It is clear that some women are violently abusive to their spouses.[2] Some research has sought to show that the sexes are equally violent towards each other;[3] however, this claim does not comport with the results of the

2   Men were victims in 10 percent of the spousal assaults reported to the police in Canada: H. Johnson, *Dangerous Domains, Violence against Women in Canada* (Scarborough, Ont.: Nelson Canada, 1996) [*Dangerous Domains*] at xix, citing Canadian Centre for Justice Statistics, Revised Uniform Crime Reporting Survey, unpublished data, 1993.

3   See, for example, M. Straus, R. Gelles, & S. Steinmetz, *Behind Closed Doors: Violence in the American Family* (New York: Anchor Press/Doubleday, 1980); G. Kantor & M. Straus, "The 'Drunken Bum' Theory of Wife Beating," in M. Straus & R. Gelles, eds., *Physical Violence in American Families: Risk Factors and Adaptations to Violence in 8,145 Families* (New Brunswick, N.J.: Transaction Publishers, 1990).

majority of investigations, with reports to police and other social agencies, or, indeed, with our knowledge of the behaviour of men and women in other contexts.[4]

B. PREVALENCE OF VIOLENCE

Recent survey data show how prevalent is violence against women by their spouses. The Violence Against Women (VAW) Survey was commissioned by the federal Department of Health and carried out by Statistics Canada in 1993. A random sample of 12,300 women was surveyed about adult experiences of violence by men. Responses indicate that some 29 percent of all women who have been married or cohabited with a man have been assaulted by a spouse.[5]

When the survey data is disaggregated, it appears that the most common forms of violence by women's spouses are pushing, grabbing, and shoving (25 percent of women surveyed).[6] The next most common are, in descending order: threats of hitting (19 percent); slapping (15 percent); throwing something at her (11 percent); kicking, biting, or hitting with a fist (11 percent). In each of the yet more serious catego-

---

4   H. Johnson, *Dangerous Domains*, above note 2 at xix. See also R.P. Dobash, R.E. Dobash *et al*. "The Myth of Sexual Symmetry in Marital Violence" (1992) 39 Social Problems 71.

5   *Dangerous Domains*, *ibid*. at 49. Spousal violence was defined to mean any of the following acts by a husband or male partner: threatening to hit with a fist or anything else that could hurt; throwing something at the woman that could hurt her; pushing, shoving, or grabbing; slapping; kicking, biting, or hitting, with a fist; hitting the woman with something that could hurt her; beating up the woman; choking; threatening to use a gun or a knife; forcing the woman into unwanted sexual activity by any of these means. The survey also showed that 51 percent of women have experienced at least one physical or sexual assault by a man, whether or not a partner, since the age of sixteen. Compare the result of this survey with the conclusion of the Women's Safety Project that "27 percent of women have experienced a physical assault in an intimate relationship": Canadian Panel on Violence Against Women, *Changing the Landscape: Ending Violence — Achieving Equality*, Executive Summary (Ottawa: Canadian Panel on Violence Against Women, 1993) [*Changing the Landscape*] at 11.

6   The figures in this paragraph are taken from H. Johnson, "Seriousness, Type and Frequency of Violence against Wives" in M. Valverde, L. MacLeod, & K. Johnson, eds., *Wife Assault and the Canadian Criminal Justice System: Issues and Policies* (Toronto: Centre of Criminology, University of Toronto, 1995) at 125 [M. Valverde, *Wife Assault*]. The figures do not add up to the overall finding of 29 percent because of multiple reports.

ries of violence, between 5 and 9 percent of the women surveyed indicated that they had been victims of such violent acts.

The data produced by the VAW Survey surprised some people, who doubted or had not understood that violence against women was so common.[7] Much of our information as to the frequency of violence in society comes from the Unified Crime Reporting (UCR) Survey, which tabulates police statistics. It might not be sensible to rely on police statistics for an understanding of the prevalence of spousal violence against women for a number of reasons.[8] Not all acts of violence will be reported to the police because women fear reprisals from their spouses or because women are ashamed to tell strangers of their abuse, to mention only two reasons. As well, police are required to exercise discretion in deciding what information will become a report, and then which reports will be regarded as substantiated and which dismissed as unfounded and never recorded in the UCR Survey.[9]

C. THE RESPONSE OF LAW

1) Lack of Coordinated Response

Clearly the problem of violence against spouses cannot be eradicated by law alone, no matter how broadly law is understood. It is a problem that has its sources in every aspect of our culture, and only change in many of society's parts can achieve this desirable goal. Equally clearly, however, the law has important roles to play in any attempt to tackle the problem. But at present the legal response is fractioned, partial, and uncoordinated. Part of this disarray may be attributable to the division of legislative jurisdiction in this country between the federal Parliament and the provincial legislatures. But, more deeply, the scattered legal response suggests that we have not been prepared in fact to see

---

7   See A. Doob, "Understanding the Attacks on Statistics Canada's Violence Against Women Survey," *ibid.* at 157.

8   See H. Johnson, *Dangerous Domains*, above note 2 at 26ff.

9   Current policy of the Toronto police requires officers to document fully "their response to every domestic call on an occurrence report regardless of whether or not a criminal offence has been committed": Metropolitan Toronto Police, "Domestic Violence Policy," June 1993, unpublished, at 9. (This document is available in the York University Library.) See also Police Standards Manual 0217.00, Police Response to Wife Assault [Ontario Provincial Police], 13 January 1994, in M. Valverde, *Wife Assault*, above note 6 at 368.

spousal violence as a social problem, or as one deserving of concentrated attention.[10]

The situation may be changing, however. Saskatchewan recently enacted *The Victims of Domestic Violence Act*[11] that seeks in a coordinated fashion to educate the public in the seriousness of spousal violence and to assist victims of violence in various ways. Principally the statute provides for emergency intervention orders, which are available twenty-four hours a day from specially designated justices of the peace, and which use a number of legal devices to promote the victim's safety; victim assistance orders, which create a number of remedies for the victim, such as monetary damages, temporary possession of personal property, and particular restraining orders; and warrants of entry, necessary to enable authorities to examine certain domestic situations without permission of the householder.[12]

Prince Edward Island followed suit with legislation in 1996.[13] And the Alberta Law Reform Institute has since then recommended that a similar law be enacted in that province,[14] partially in response to a private member's bill much like Saskatchewan's law that surprisingly obtained unanimous approval upon second reading.[15]

2) Response of Criminal Law

The main legal response to violence in our society is through the criminal law process, which attempts to make clear our condemnation of violence (in certain of its forms, at least) and to prevent it through deterrence, both individual and general. As with all aspects of law, this legal attempt is not simply a matter of passing clear rules and awaiting complete compliance, but rather an enterprise that may be more or less successful, depending on a large number of factors. It is fair to say that the criminal law process has not been successful either in condemning or in preventing spousal violence against women.

---

10   See above note 7, and accompanying text. See also *Changing the Landscape*, above note 5 at 3, to the effect that "most Canadians have chosen to deny" the reality of violence against women.

11   S.S. 1994, c. V-6.02; the legislation came into force February 1995.

12   See J. Turner, "Saskatchewan Responds to Family Violence: *The Victims of Domestic Violence Act, 1995*" in M. Valverde, *Wife Assault*, above note 6 at 183, for a brief narrative description of the legislation and something of its origins.

13   *Victims of Family Violence Act*, P.E.I.A. 1996, c. 47.

14   Alberta Law Reform Institute, *Protection against Domestic Abuse*, Report No. 74 (Edmonton: Alberta Law Reform Institute, February 1997).

15   Bill 214, *The Victims of Domestic Violence Act*, 4th Sess., 23rd Leg., Alberta, 1996.

A large number of offences under the *Criminal Code*[16] can apply to spousal violence against women. Included are those that pertain to assault,[17] those that criminalize sexual assault,[18] those that are directed at causing fear of harm.[19] Moreover, it is not necessary that an offence has to have been committed before the criminal law process can be invoked: a person who fears on reasonable grounds that another will injure her, her family, or her property can have a justice of the peace require the other to enter into a recognizance, with or without sureties, to keep the peace and to meet certain further terms of an order.[20] Clearly, the problem is not that there are too few fitting rules (though it may be that there are too many aimed at diverse circumstances, in the sense that none explicitly condemns abuse of women by spouses).

Rules do not apply themselves, of course. Thus, police attitudes and behaviour become important, as do those of all the actors in the criminal justice system, the Crown counsel who prosecute, the judges who decide, the parole boards and parole officers who deal with offenders, and others as well.

Police have been reluctant to intervene in occasions of spousal violence for a number of reasons, including the risk of harm to the intervening officers,[21] perception by the officers that the victims exaggerate claims of harm, and a general attitude that much violence within the family ought not to be dealt with by the criminal law. When police did intervene, it was common practice for them to advise the woman that the laying of charges was up to her. Attempts are under way in many parts of the province to provide police with the training necessary for them to deal effectively with spousal violence. Recently the Ontario Solicitor General has issued directives that aim to ensure that charges are laid by the police whenever there are reasonable grounds to support a charge.[22]

---

16 R.S.C. 1985, c. C-46, as amended.
17 *Ibid.*, ss. 266 (assault), 267 (assault with a weapon or causing bodily harm), 268 (aggravated assault), 269 (unlawfully causing bodily harm), and 279 (forcible confinement).
18 *Ibid.*, ss. 268 (aggravated assault), 271 (sexual assault), 272 (sexual assault with a weapon), and 273 (aggravated sexual assault).
19 *Ibid.*, ss. 264 (criminal harassment), 264.1 (uttering threats), 372(3) (harassing telephone calls), and 423 (intimidation, including watching and besetting).
20 *Ibid.*, s. 810. See also s. 811 respecting breach of recognizance.
21 See Metropolitan Toronto Police, "Domestic Violence Policy" June 1993, unpublished, at 5. (This document is available in the York University Library.)
22 *Ibid.* at 9, where it is also stated that "arrest is the preferred response to domestic violence because arrest offers the greatest potential for ending the violence." See also Kelly Hanna-Moffat, "To Charge or Not to Charge: Front Line Officers' Perceptions of Mandatory Charge Policy" in M. Valverde, *Wife Assault*, above note 6 at 35.

Successful prosecution of charged spouses is by no means guaranteed. Crown counsel may not devote (or be able to devote) adequate time to preparation.[23] Physical evidence may not be available. The victim may be unwilling to testify to the violent events, for a number of reasons that include fear of reprisals from the abuser or a need or wish that the relationship continue.

A "get-tough" or "zero-tolerance" policy, coupled with appropriate resources and education, can cause those with discretion to exercise it more frequently in favour of forceful prosecution. However, this is not always in the interests of the women involved. A rigid criminal justice system can, paradoxically perhaps, result in harm to the victim, such as where a reluctant woman is compelled to testify under threat of punishment, or a mother loses support for her children because of the imprisonment of their father. And it needs to be said, even if obvious, that arrest, conviction, and punishment of the offender may not succeed in stopping violence by that man, or by other men in the society; the deterrence value of the criminal law is not certain.

This ambivalent attitude towards the utility of the criminal law process is reflected in two pilot projects currently under way in Ontario. The first, focused on a specialized court in Toronto, is aimed at securing as many convictions as possible and appropriate sentences for convicted men.[24] The team of special prosecutors assigned to the project works closely with the police to obtain and introduce into court as much evidence as possible, such as video-taped interviews with the woman, so as not to have to rely on the victim's testimony alone. As well, the woman is approached by a Victim Witness Assistance Program, in order to help her understand the legal process and to refer her to supporting social agencies where necessary.

---

23   See L. MacLeod, "Expanding the Dialogue: Report of a Workshop to Explore the Criminal Justice System Response to Violence against Women" in M. Valverde, *Wife Assault*, above note 6 at 26: Crown counsel attitudes are formed from the experience that spousal assault cases "are difficult to process and they are unlikely to lead to convictions." Counsel may experience themselves as failing and may blame the victim for that failure.

24   See: "Women's Court Watch Project, Final Report," Tamara Sheats, coordinator (unpublished paper, "funded by the City of Toronto in collaboration with the Metro Woman Abuse Council") June 1996 ["Women's Court Watch"]. (This document is available in the York University Library.)

The second pilot project, originally based at a specialized "plea court" in North York but now expanded to other locations in the province,[25] deals with cases where the victim suffered no serious physical injury at the hands of a first-time offender who pleaded guilty.[26] If the victim agrees, the offender may consent to participate in a program specifically aimed at the re-education of abusers. This project aims to stop the cycle of abuse.

3) Response of Family Law

Although one may be able to speak of the criminal justice system and refer to a more or less coherent process, there is no comparable, coherent family law system of justice. Family law is composed of a wide variety of statutes, both federal and provincial, and common law principles, all of which have as a central objective something other than dealing with spousal violence. Yet, in a number of areas of family law the fact of spousal violence plays a role and so its existence is acknowledged by some laws; these various acknowledgments constitute the response of family law to the problem.

Cruelty is a ground for divorce, for example.[27] But divorce is available to anyone after a year's separation; and so it may be that this legislative acknowledgment of spousal violence is of no particular utility. Some, however, might argue that this fault ground for divorce ought to be retained to enable victims of violence to register and obtain condemnation of the behaviour by the legal process.

More generally, matrimonial fault has almost disappeared as a factor in family law decisions. This is probably a laudable development—a sophistication, perhaps, in our understanding of adult relationships—but it may mean that in removing opportunities for petty blaming and mudslinging, we have lost at the same time rather more important occasions for judging and condemning truly wrong conduct, particularly violence directed at women.

---

25   Ontario Ministry of the Attorney General, Press Release, "Attorney General Announces Six Additional Specialized Courts to Combat Domestic Violence" (2 July 1997).

26   See "Women's Court Watch," above note 24.

27   See section B(2), "By Reason of Cruelty," in chapter 9, "Divorce." A married person who has "treated the other spouse with physical or mental cruelty of such a kind as to render intolerable the continued cohabitation of the spouses" has thereby provided the other with a ground for divorce.

Spousal support, for example, is now determined according to need and other notions of deservingness, and the only reference to marital misconduct in the relevant statutes is found in now neglected section 33(10) of the *Family Law Act*,[28] which provides that "a course of conduct that is so unconscionable as to constitute an obvious and gross repudiation of the relationship" may affect the amount of support awarded but not the entitlement. Attempts to use this provision on behalf of women victims of violence were never really successful.[29]

Child custody and access decisions are meant to be wholly child-centred now, and the use by the court of "past conduct of a person" is proscribed except insofar as it is "relevant to the ability of the person to act as a parent of the child."[30] However, not all courts are prepared to accept that spousal violence is at the same time a form of child abuse, and therefore must be an important consideration in any custody or access case.[31]

Property decisions are made almost wholly without reference to the behaviour of parties during the marriage, and such conduct as is relevant relates more to financial arrangements than to anything else.[32] In one important respect, however, matrimonial property law may be helpful to a victim of spousal violence. Married spouses likely have a "matrimonial home," as defined by statute; if so, they are equally entitled to its possession, regardless of how it is owned or how the lease is held.[33] Either spouse may apply to the court for an order of exclusive possession, and the court must consider, among other things, "any violence committed by a spouse against the other spouse or the children."[34] Various practical difficulties, such as procedural delay and the cost of an application and legal advice, may make this legal ability to exclude a

---

28 R.S.O. 1990, c. F.3.

29 See, for example, *Melanson* v. *Melanson* (1991), 34 R.F.L. (3d) 323 at 327 (Ont. Gen. Div.), where although the husband beat the wife, the court said, "The steamy relationship between the parties and the physical assaults by the defendant standing alone do not, in my view, constitute an obvious and gross repudiation of the relationship." See section C, "Spousal Support," in chapter 12, "Financial Support."

30 *Children's Law Reform Act*, R.S.O. 1990, c. C.12, s. 24(3). See also *Divorce Act*, S.C. 1986, c. 4, s. 16(9). See chapter 10 for a discussion of custody and access.

31 See *Changing the Landscape*, above note 5 at 39.

32 See chapter 11 for a discussion of property issues.

33 *Family Law Act*, above note 28, ss.18 & 19.

34 *Ibid.*, s. 24(3)(f). Penalties are provided for contravention of an order for exclusive possession in s. 24(5); subsection 6 permits a police officer to arrest a person who violates the order.

violent spouse less than fully useful, of course. And, because the property provisions in the *Family Law Act* pertain only to married persons, unmarried women are unable to avail themselves of the remedy.

A man's violent behaviour may affect his spouse's ability freely to negotiate a separation agreement, a contract that can record the parties' resolution of the many substantive issues that arise when a relationship ends. The potential for such an imbalance in power is recognized in contract law, particularly in the family law context, and if it is used to drive an unfair bargain, the resulting contract may be void.[35]

Finally, there is a general provision in the *Family Law Act* that permits a court to make an order

> restraining the applicant's spouse or former spouse from molesting, annoying or harassing the applicant or children in the applicant's lawful custody, or from communicating with the applicant or children . . . and may require the applicant's spouse or former spouse to enter into the recognizance that the court considers appropriate.[36]

It is important to note that this provision applies not only to married persons but also to persons who are spouses by reason of cohabitation.[37]

FURTHER READINGS

ALBERTA LAW REFORM INSTITUTE, *Protection against Domestic Abuse*, Report No. 74 (Edmonton: Alberta Law Reform Institute, February 1997)

CANADIAN PANEL ON VIOLENCE AGAINST WOMEN, *Changing the Landscape: Ending Violence — Achieving Equality*, Final Report (Ottawa: Canadian Panel on Violence Against Women, 1993)

JOHNSON, H., *Dangerous Domains, Violence against Women in Canada* (Scarborough, Ont.: Nelson Canada, 1996)

VALVERDE, M., L. MACLEOD, & K. JOHNSON, eds., *Wife Assault and the Canadian Criminal Justice System: Issues and Policies* (Toronto: Centre of Criminology, University of Toronto, 1995)

---

35   See section B(1)(b), "Unfair Advantage," in chapter 13, "Separation Agreements."

36   *Family Law Act*, above note 28, s. 46(1). A police officer is given power to arrest a person who contravenes a restraining order (s. 46(3)) and penalties are provided for its contravention (s. 46(2)).

37   See section B(2), "The *Family Law Act*," in chapter 4, "Cohabitation."

PART THREE

REORGANIZATION OF RELATIONS

When the family breaks down, it is common for the spouses to turn to the law to assist in the resolution of the issues between them. This is, perhaps, the traditional part of family law, the law of husband and wife, as it used to be called. Typically, a couple will reach an understanding, with or without the assistance of lawyers or mediators, which will be recorded in what is known as a separation agreement.

If there are no children in the family and no arrangement to pay spousal support, the parties might indeed be truly separated, and the agreement, once executed, may mark the end of relations. However, for many couples, a separation agreement may bring about not an end to the relationship but its reorganization: the spouses may remain parents of children and need to confer and to accommodate each other to carry out the obligations of a parent; and it may be that the financial consequences of cohabitation will take some time to work through, perhaps in the form of periodic support payments or in the form of instalment payments designed to transfer property values.

Spouses negotiating a settlement do so in the light (some would say "shadow") of pertinent statute law. Thus, it is convenient to proceed through a discussion of the issues facing most couples as if they were litigating, in order to see what rights and obligations they might have if the courts were to adjudicate their dispute. For this reason Part III begins with divorce, the subject of chapter 9. Although a legal divorce is usually the last thing of concern to separated spouses, it is important to know what the *Divorce Act* says concerning matters of real substance, custody and support. And because orders for custody and support—corollary relief, as it is called—can only be made under that Act where one of the spouses has applied for a judgment of divorce, it makes sense to tackle first when it is that a divorce may be sought and granted.

Chapter 10 begins the examination of issues of real substance with the matter of child custody. Custody is addressed first not only because the interests of children should be given primacy, but also because decisions made concerning custody can have an impact on the other matters of substance, property, and support.

Chapter 11 addresses property rights and obligations between separating spouses. Property issues are dealt with by statutory provisions that aim to provide relatively clear and automatic answers, but succeed even so in raising basic questions about economic justice between spouses. Decisions made here will influence issues of support.

Chapter 12 treats support obligations, both to children and spouses. What has not been satisfactorily resolved by a sharing of property values may need to be the subject of an order for financial support.

Finally, in chapter 13, when the issues of substance have been explored, it is appropriate to examine how their resolution is properly recorded in a contract, the separation agreement.

CHAPTER 9

DIVORCE

A. INTRODUCTION

1) A Brief History

The point ought to be made at the outset that, essentially, anyone who wants a divorce may obtain it. Although this is not quite "divorce on demand," it is very close to it, with the consequence that the apparently elaborate structure found in the *Divorce Act*[1] has less importance than might first be supposed. This structure has a historical explanation.

The federal Parliament has the constitutional jurisdiction over divorce;[2] however, until 1968 there was no nationwide divorce law, but rather different regimes for different provinces. Indeed, judicial divorce was not possible in Newfoundland and Quebec until 1968. The new national law[3] broke with tradition by introducing the possibility of divorce grounded on separation of the parties for a period of three years; whereas, until then only proof of a matrimonial "offence" or fault by one party would have justified a divorce. The traditional fault grounds of

---

1 S.C. 1986, c. 4, as amended by S.C. 1990, c. 18, ss. 1 & 2; S.C. 1992, c. 51, s. 46; S.C. 1993, c. 8, ss. 1–5; S.C. 1993, c. 28, s. 78; S.C. 1997, c. 1, ss. 1–15 [*DA* or the Act].

2 *Constitution Act, 1867* (U.K.), 30 & 31 Vict., c. 3, s. 91(26), gives Parliament power to make laws respecting "marriage and divorce."

3 *Divorce Act*, S.C. 1967–68, c. 24. The grounds for divorce were set out in ss. 3 & 4.

adultery and cruelty were retained, however, and expanded;[4] and various less fault-based "marriage breakdown" grounds were introduced, in addition to three years of separation.[5]

There was considerable worry at the time of the drafting of the 1968 statute and for many years afterwards about the effect on society of "lax" divorce laws. The fear was that this new law, by permitting easier divorce, would bring about the breakdown of families that would otherwise have remained intact and beneficial. In this view, law leads and does not lag behind social trends. The opposing view was that society had changed and no longer held the view, if it ever had, that marriage was forever and that social good was maximized by staying in bad marriages. It was pointed out that marriages came to a functional end in fact, whether or not this was acknowledged by divorce, and refusal to permit remarriage in such cases simply produced misery. The law was lagging behind, in this view.

Courts devoted much anxious consideration to the proper meanings of terms like "cruelty" and "separate and apart"; and a considerable body of jurisprudence grew up on when a divorce was permissible. This legal activity reflected the social uncertainty about the proper role of divorce and also arose from the terms of the statute itself, for an interpretation one way or another could make a big difference in a party's life. A petitioner who had deserted the respondent might find that the resumption of a close relationship with the respondent in the fourth year of separation, for example, restarted the clock and meant another five-year wait for a divorce.

Social attitudes continued to change, to become more tolerant of divorce, and criticism grew of the judgmental, finicky, and at times unclear grounds in the statute. The current Act swept away most of the old grounds and retained only three. Technically there is only one ground for divorce, and that is "breakdown of the marriage," which "is established only if":

(a) the spouses have lived separate and apart for at least one year immediately preceding the determination of the divorce proceeding and were living separate and apart at the commencement of the proceeding; or

---

4   *Ibid.*, s. 3. Fault grounds included as well rape, sodomy, bestiality, a homosexual act, and bigamy. Cruelty was expanded to included mental as well as physical cruelty.

5   *Ibid.*, s. 4. Marriage breakdown was a ground when it was caused by the respondent's alcohol or narcotics addiction, non-consummation, imprisonment or disappearance, or by the petitioner's desertion, and had been evidenced by separation for various lengths of time.

(b) the spouse against whom the divorce proceeding is brought has, since celebration of the marriage,

(i) committed adultery, or

(ii) treated the other spouse with physical or mental cruelty of such a kind as to render intolerable the continued cohabitation of the spouses.[6]

Note that the separation period has been reduced from three years to one, and the time that it takes to prosecute the legal action may be included in the calculation of this year waiting period. Moreover, it no longer matters whether the separation is consensual or not.[7] And now parties who wish to evidence the amicable nature of the process may apply jointly and may both be granted the divorce.[8]

As can be seen from the provision quoted above, cruelty and adultery continue to provide grounds for divorce.

These changes introduce the possibility of true no-fault divorce, and, together with the reduction of the waiting time, make something very like divorce on demand a reality. Moreover, where an application is uncontested, it is possible for parties to obtain a divorce simply by filing the necessary documents and affidavits; and, although it is still necessary for a court to judge that the grounds in fact exist, this can be done in chambers, and a personal appearance by the parties in an uncontested divorce is not required.[9] Thus, we have moved very near to making divorce the non-justiciable, administrative matter that some believe it should be.

Note, however, that a divorce proceeding is still not litigation of which the parties have the sole carriage: divorce may not result directly from agreement or the settlement of a dispute between spouses. Even when the parties are in agreement as to what they want, a court must decide that the grounds for it exist. And the parties must provide the court with the evidence necessary for the making of that judgment. This procedural recognition of the state interest in marriage and divorce is examined below in the context of bars to divorce.[10]

---

6   *DA*, above note 1, s. 8(2).

7   Under prior legislation, if the separation was consensual, either party could obtain a divorce after three years; whereas, if only one party consented to the separation, the party who caused the separation might well be "in desertion" and would have to wait five years. See also section B(3), "By Reason of Living Separate and Apart," in this chapter.

8   *DA*, above note 1, s. 8(1).

9   See section E, "Procedural Matters," in this chapter. These routine procedures have become known as "desk top divorces."

10 See section D, "Bars," in this chapter.

2) Divorce in the Current Context

Ought divorce be a simple administrative matter akin to a deregistration? What, if any, conditions should be imposed on obtaining a divorce? For instance, ought the current one-year waiting period be retained? And what good reasons can be found for retaining fault grounds?

To be able to understand and perhaps answer these questions, one needs first to consider what the purpose of divorce is. There are various ways of approaching this matter. From a narrow legal point of view, divorce is nothing more than the grant of a licence to remarry.[11] All else is ancillary—or "corollary," to use the language of the Act: issues respecting children and financial matters can be dealt with by agreement or under provincial legislation whether or not the parties seek the right to be free to remarry. Divorce and the Act provide an occasion to resolve these issues, it is true, but not the only or an essential occasion.

However, most do not take such a narrow view of divorce—or marriage, upon which it is dependent. Clearly, marriage and divorce are social institutions, with important symbolic and emotional meanings for many citizens. And it is one of the law's functions to support and give shape to social institutions, to facilitate practices whose meanings lie outside the legal. If support and facilitation of the social institutions of marriage and divorce were all that there was at stake, there might be no good reason to resist easy, efficient divorces, provided they offered an adequate degree of ceremonial formality, for such divorces would best facilitate the private wishes of citizens. But we have long attributed to divorce (and marriage) law the function of assisting not just the attainment of individuals' wishes but the achievement of a desirable social order.

The social aim might be expressed as the stability, or at least duration, of relationships. Stable or long-lasting relationships may be presumed to maximize the economic and other social contributions of their members, and to avoid the social costs attendant upon the breakup of relationships and the formation of new ones. Particularly, it is believed that family stability is important for the proper development

---

11   There is a tendency, particularly American, to use the word "divorce" to describe the whole process of family breakdown, separation, and reorganization. The fact is that many married people who separate do not get divorces because of religious or other reasons. It is best, from any legal standpoint, narrow or broad, to reserve "divorce" to refer to a proceeding under the *Divorce Act* or the judgment obtained under it.

of children.[12] Even if one accepts all this as true and desirable, there remain difficult questions about how, if at all, the law alone can contribute to the stability of relationships.

With the advent of the national divorce law, the rates of divorce shot up, and they continued to climb for a number of years.[13] In 1968, the year the first modern, national divorce statute was passed, the divorce rate was 54.8 per 100,000 population; three years later, in 1971, the rate had more than doubled to 135; by 1982, it had risen to 280; and in 1987, the rate had reached a high point of 355. Since that time, the divorce rate has fallen off somewhat and has stayed around 270 during the 1990s. But these data say nothing about whether it is the law or social desire that is driving the increase.

It might once have been the case that people did not (or did not readily) form families without the sanction of marriage; and, consequently, to refuse a divorce and frustrate remarriage would be to inhibit the break-up of existing marriages. The stakes would be high—the loss of this family might mean the loss of family forever—and so there would be reluctance. Easy marriage and hard divorce would arguably promote the social good (even at the expense of individual happiness). But it seems impossible to argue today that there is any strong relationship between legal marriage and family formation. People live together and women have children outside marriage with increasing frequency.[14] Consequently, marriage and divorce may no longer have enough social importance to justify resistance to treating divorce as a simple administrative procedure based entirely on the wish of one party, at least when that resistance is based upon the fostering of stable relationships. And the state interest in stability may no longer outweigh the interests of the individuals immediately involved in being able to obtain a speedy, efficient, and inexpensive divorce.

---

12 See, for example, references to this and allied values in the definitions of a child's "best interests": *Child and Family Services Act*, R.S.O. 1990, c. C.11, s. 37(3), para. 7; *Children's Law Reform Act*, R.S.O. 1990, c. C.12, s. 24(2)(c).

13 Data following in the text are from: P. La Novara, *A Portrait of Families in Canada*, Statistics Canada, Catalogue 89-523E (Ottawa: Statistics Canada, 1993) at 17; and J. Gentleman & E. Park, "Divorce in the 1990s" in *Health Reports*, vol. 9, no. 2 (Autumn 1997), Statistics Canada, Catalogue 82-003-XPB (Ottawa: Minister of Industry, 1997) at 54–55.

14 The number of people living in informal unions in Canada tripled to over one million between 1981 and 1995: J. Gentleman & E. Park, "Divorce in the 1990s," *ibid.* at 53. The number of reported births to unmarried women more than doubled between 1975 and 1986: B. Ram, "Current Demographic Analysis, New Trends in the Family," Statistics Canada, Catalogue 91-535E (Ottawa: Ministry of Supply and Services, 1990) at 33.

3) The National Aspect

As stated above, divorce is within the exclusive jurisdiction of the federal Parliament. The courts have decided that Parliament can also legislate with respect to custody and support under the same authority, as these are matters that are ancillary to divorce.[15] The provinces, too, have the jurisdiction to make laws respecting custody and support, with the consequence that there is an overlap and a possibility of conflict. This issue will be addressed directly when custody and support are dealt with, later in the book. But the federal jurisdiction also brings an advantage in that orders made under the *Divorce Act* are of nationwide force and do not depend on the provisions of local law that provide for the enforceability of foreign—that is, extra-provincial—orders. Thus, although substantive matters such as custody and support are logically distinct from an application for a licence to remarry, it may be advantageous to raise them in that context to obtain the broad enforceability of orders under the Act.

It should be noted that under the Act only superior courts in the provinces are given jurisdiction to order divorces.[16]

B. GROUNDS: MARRIAGE BREAKDOWN

1) By Reason of Adultery

Marriage breakdown, and therefore grounds for divorce, may be established if the spouse against whom the divorce proceeding is brought has committed adultery. This is a fault ground, and so a petitioner cannot rely on his or her own adultery as proof of marriage breakdown, but must complain of the respondent's adultery.

Adultery consists in voluntary sexual intercourse by the married spouse with a person to whom he or she is not married. Other acts of a sexual nature will not constitute adultery. This legal fact may illustrate the nature of the wrong in the act of adultery, which does not seem to be simply the breach of a code of sexual morality, but may, in the words of one judge, be found in "the voluntary surrender to another person of the reproductive powers or faculties of the guilty person."[17] This would

---

15   *Papp* v. *Papp*, [1970] 1 O.R. 331 (C.A.); *Zacks* v. *Zacks*, [1973] S.C.R. 891.

16   *DA*, above note 1, s. 2(1): "'court' in respect of a province means (a) for the Province of Ontario, the Ontario Court (General Division) . . ." etc.

17   *Orford* v. *Orford* (1921), 49 O.L.R. 15 at 22–23 (H.C.), Orde J. The court decided that artificial insemination by the wife amounted to adultery. But see *Maclennan* v. *Maclennan*, [1958] S.C. 105 (Scot. Ct. of Sess.).

certainly comport with the historical anxiety in Western culture concerning paternity and the "family line."

Proof of adultery may be a problem, for the obvious reason that sexual intercourse is a private act, and for the less obvious one that under section 10 of Ontario's *Evidence Act* no one may be asked a question tending to show that he or she is guilty of adultery.[18] Adultery may be admitted, however. But when the divorce is contested, adultery may have to be proved indirectly.

It is not possible to say what social circumstances will lead inexorably to a conclusion of adultery. Proof of opportunity will not be enough; it must as well be proper to infer that the opportunity was used.[19] It should be noted that social practices have changed in recent years, such that we expect women will be in the company of men for reasons of business or friendship in social circumstances now regarded as "harmless" but that in earlier times might have given rise to inferences of a sexual relationship.

Although it is clear that the applicable burden of proof is the ordinary civil onus, the cases are full of judicial expressions of reluctance to find adultery unless an unusual amount or character of evidence is present.[20]

2) By Reason of Cruelty

The ground for divorce is not simply "cruelty" but that the respondent has "treated the other spouse with physical or mental cruelty of such a kind as to render intolerable the continued cohabitation of the spouse."[21]

Under the 1968 statute, the courts developed a dual test for cruelty that recognized both a subjective and an objective aspect. The effects of the particular acts on the plaintiff, given his or her actual qualities, must be taken into account: treatment that would cause one person to suffer might not have a serious effect on another person.[22] Thus, every case is to be decided on its own merits and will not have much, if any, precedential

---

18 No witness or party may be asked or is "bound to answer" such a question "unless such witness has already given evidence in the same proceeding in disproof of his or her alleged adultery." R.S.O. 1990, c. E.23, s. 10. (Similar provisions exist in the other provinces.) Provincial laws of evidence apply to proceedings under the Act: *DA*, above note 1, s. 23(1).

19 See, for example, *Farrell* v. *Farrell* (1972), 4 R.F.L. 261 (Sask. Q.B.).

20 See, for example, *George* v. *George*, [1950] O.R. 787 (C.A.).

21 *DA*, above note 1, s. 8(2)(b)(ii). The same language was used in the prior *Divorce Act*, so the cases under that legislation are pertinent today.

22 *Zalesky* v. *Zalesky* (1968), 1 D.L.R. (3d) 471 (Man. Q.B.). See also: *Knoll* v. *Knoll*, [1970] 2 O.R. 169 (C.A.); *Austin* v. *Austin* (1970), 13 D.L.R. (3d) 498 (Sask. C.A.).

value. Yet at the same time, the conduct causing a person to suffer is, objectively, to be "not a trivial act, but one of a 'grave and weighty' nature."[23]

Personal suffering, particularly in cases of mental cruelty, is typically evidenced by doctors' reports of emotional upset such as anxiety, sleeplessness, loss of appetite, or depression. And though corroboration is not required,[24] evidence of complaints about the cruel treatment is often expected.[25]

Conduct complained of does not have to be "aimed at" or intended to hurt the plaintiff.[26] But there does have to be a course of conduct, or, to put it another way, one spouse has to "treat" the other with cruelty; and some innate quality or aspect of a spouse's being would not alone be capable of producing the requisite cruelty.[27]

According to the *DA*, the cruelty must render continued cohabitation "intolerable." It will commonly be the case that in fact the spouses cease to cohabit before the divorce proceeding, but in some instances the "intolerability" may not lead to separation but be tolerated for reasons most likely having to do with children or poverty.[28]

3) By Reason of Living Separate and Apart

Marriage breakdown exists where the spouses have lived separate and apart for the year "immediately preceding the determination of the divorce proceeding" and were so living at the start of the proceeding.[29] The time the proceeding takes can, therefore, be included in the one-year waiting period.

Under the prior statute it was determined that the requirement of living "separate and apart" had both a physical and a mental component. The parties must be living physically separate lives, and at least one of them must have the intention to bring an end to the matrimonial consortium.[30] Because there is no longer any distinction in divorce law between separations by mutual consent and separations at the instance of one spouse alone, an applicant for divorce may plead a year's living

---

23 *Knoll* v. *Knoll*, above note 22.

24 *Thordarson* v. *Thordarson* (1978), 5 R.F.L. (2d) 92 (Ont. C.A.).

25 *Zalesky* v. *Zalesky*, above note 22; *Lacey* v. *Lacey*, [1970] 1 O.R. 279 (H.C.).

26 *Knoll* v. *Knoll*, and *Austin* v. *Austin*, above note 22.

27 *Baker* v. *Baker* (1969), 8 D.L.R. (3d) 260 (B.C.S.C.); *Peppard* v. *Peppard* (1970), 2 R.F.L. 162 (N.S.T.D.); *Lacey* v. *Lacey*, above note 25.

28 See, for example, *Krause* v. *Krause*, [1975] 4 W.W.R. 738 (Alta. T.D.), varied on other grounds (1976), 64 D.L.R. (3d) 352 (Alta. C.A.).

29 *DA*, above note 1, s. 8(2)(a).

30 *Dupere* v. *Dupere* (1974), 19 R.F.L. 270 (Q.B.), aff'd (1975), 10 N.B.R. (2d) 148 (C.A.). See also *DA*, above note 1, s. 8(3)(a).

separate and apart where the separation was against the wishes of the other spouse.[31]

The degree of physical separation required is not a matter of simple formula. Where there is doubt, the relationship will typically be compared to a "normal" marriage (much as is done when considering "statutory spouses"),[32] in order to ensure that a sufficient number of aspects to the relation are missing. The commonest cases of difficulty are those where the parties continue to live "under one roof."[33] And courts have disagreed about whether certain circumstances could excuse or justify proximate living.[34]

It would perhaps be easier to make borderline decisions if the courts had explored the rationale behind the requirement of living separate and apart. It may be supposed that the object is to bring home to the parties the emotional and psychological consequences of divorce while there is still time for them to change their minds. Thus, where there is a sufficient separation to cause this understanding, the requirements of the Act should be met.

This paternalistic requirement of a foretaste of divorce can be seen to run counter to other things we value, such as supportive and caring behaviour generally and, more narrowly, the amicable resolution of disputes. But the Act attempts to eat its cake and have it too, in this respect: it provides that the one-year period will not be considered to have been interrupted or terminated when the spouses resume cohabitation in order to attempt reconciliation, so long as the period (or periods) of cohabitation is less than ninety days in total.[35]

---

31 All that the Act requires is that either party have had the intention to live separate and apart during the one-year period: *DA*, above note 1, s. 8(3)(a).

32 See section B(2), "The *Family Law Act*," in chapter 4, "Cohabitation."

33 See, for example, *Cooper* v. *Cooper* (1972), 10 R.F.L. 184 at 187 (Ont. H.C.): "Certainly spouses living under the same roof may well in fact be living separate and apart from each other. [This is, generally speaking, where] (i) Spouses occupying separate bedrooms. (ii) Absence of sexual relations. (iii) Little, if any, communication between spouses. (iv) Wife performing no domestic services for husband. (v) Eating meals separately. (vi) No social activities together."

34 See, for example, *Rushton* v. *Rushton* (1968), 1 R.F.L. 215 (B.C.S.C.), where "economic circumstances" were understood to explain living under one roof; and *Dupere* v. *Dupere*, above note 30, where "remaining together 'for the sake of the children'" was rejected as a reason for living too closely.

35 *DA*, above note 1, s. 8(3)(b)(ii). The requirement of a year's separation is arguably unnecessary, given the requirement, explored in the next section, that a court not proceed when there is any prospect of reconciliation between the parties; if only those couples who could not reconcile will obtain divorces, it hardly seems necessary to "promote" reconciliation through a "trial" separation.

C. DUTIES

1) Reconciliation

Ever since 1968 the *Divorce Act* has required lawyers and courts to take steps to ensure that every possibility of reconciliation is explored by the parties. Unless circumstances make it clearly inappropriate, lawyers must draw clients' attention to those provisions of the *DA* that promote reconciliation, discuss with clients the possibility of reconciliation, and inform clients of resources that might assist reconciliation.[36]

In every divorce case, before considering the evidence, a court must satisfy itself that there is no possibility of reconciliation, unless, again, the circumstances make this inquiry clearly inappropriate.[37] If at any stage of the proceedings it appears that there is a possibility of reconciliation, the court must adjourn the proceedings and take steps to obtain assistance for the parties to achieve reconciliation.[38]

It is fair to say that these obligations have never produced any serious results, and they are largely carried out in a perfunctory fashion today, particularly when the proceedings are likely to be nothing more elaborate than the consideration of documents by a judge in chambers.

2) Negotiation

New in the current *DA* is the requirement that lawyers discuss with clients the advisability of negotiating the resolution of custody and support issues, and must inform clients of the availability of mediation facilities known to the lawyer that might assist the negotiations.[39] It would be the rare case indeed in which lawyers did not advise—indeed expect—parties to negotiate concerning contested issues, without the need of legislative prompting. The explicit legislative encouragement of mediation, and what have become known as "alternative means of dispute resolution," is relatively new, however.

---

36   *Ibid.*, s. 9(1).
37   *Ibid.*, s. 10(1).
38   *Ibid.*, s. 10(2).
39   *Ibid.*, s. 9(2).

D. BARS

1) Collusion

A divorce action is not like other lawsuits between private parties, in that relief may not simply be agreed to between the litigants but must be given by a court and only then according to set criteria.[40] The state interest in divorce was, indeed, once personified in the form of a Queen's Proctor, whose job was to ensure that the law's requirements were in fact met by the parties.[41] As might be supposed, when it was more difficult to obtain a divorce, there was a temptation for parties to make arrangements to falsify either evidence or the fact that the plaintiff was aggrieved by the ground put forward, which was typically adultery. Such collusive agreements were illegal and would bar the granting of a decree. Nowadays, the Act still makes collusion a bar to divorce, but defines it in a way that makes it unlikely, given the ease with which a divorce can be obtained, that anyone will fall afoul of the provision.[42]

Under the present Act:

> "collusion" means an agreement or conspiracy to which an applicant for a divorce is either directly or indirectly a party for the purpose of subverting the administration of justice, and includes any agreement, understanding or arrangement to fabricate or suppress evidence or to deceive the court, but does not include an agreement to the extent that it provides for separation between the parties, financial support, division of property or the custody of any child of the marriage.[43]

It is the duty of the court to satisfy itself in all divorce cases that there was no collusion, and to dismiss the application if it finds that collusion existed.[44]

Note that the definition excludes agreements in which the parties make arrangements for the settlement of their affairs consequent upon separation or divorce. This exclusion makes clear that we are no longer anxious that spouses may be tempted by material inducements to bring their marriages to an end.

---

40   The prior *Divorce Act*, above note 3, s. 9(1)(a), specifically provided that "it is the duty of the court to refuse a decree based solely upon . . . consent . . . and not to grant a decree except after a trial."

41   See, for example, *MacPherson v. MacPherson* (1976), 13 O.R. (2d) 233 (C.A.) for an instance of the involvement of the Queen's Proctor.

42   Indeed, it would seem that since the definition was first enacted in 1968, there has been no reported case in which collusion was found.

43   *DA*, above note 1, s. 11(4).

44   *Ibid.*, s. 11(1)(a).

2) Maintenance Arrangements for Children

The court must satisfy itself that "reasonable arrangements have been made for the support of any children of the marriage," and if they have not, it must stay the divorce until proper arrangements have been made.[45] This provision aims at ensuring in a rough fashion that the adults' interests are not met at the expense of those of the children; and, although in most cases one would expect that parents would be sure to provide for the needs of their children as zealously as any court, it will not always be true.[46]

In the past this bar presented some difficulties in uncontested cases that were sought to be decided only on the basis of affidavit and other documentary evidence—"desk top divorces" as they are known—because it was not always clear what evidence was required for the court to make a proper decision, and what would be regarded as "reasonable arrangements" in a particular case. The view was expressed that

> where matters of corollary relief have been agreed upon by parties who have benefitted from independent legal advice, and where the divorce proceeds on an unopposed basis, it will not require extensive evidence to satisfy the court that reasonable arrangements have been made.[47]

An Ontario court remarked that while this approach might be "applicable most of the time," the court ought to take care not to perform its obligation in a perfunctory fashion, and it is always essential that the petitioner make a full disclosure to the court of all the material facts, which might include the availability of financial assistance from any source, the involvement of social assistance, whether there is an agreement between the parents, the effect of income tax, whether there is provision for increasing support in line with inflationary increases,

---

45   *Ibid.*, s. 11(1)(b).

46   See *Harper* v. *Harper* (1991), 78 D.L.R. (4th) 548 at 553 (Ont. Gen. Div.), Kurisko J.: "[T]he . . . sanguine view of consensual child support arrangements does not entirely accord with my experience over many years involving hundreds of unopposed child support agreements. There has been a surprising frequency of inadequate arrangements. At times the degree of inadequacy is appalling." Note that there is no requirement that children have independent legal advice or representation at any stage of divorce proceedings, or during negotiations between their parents.

47   *Money* v. *Money* (1987), 5 R.F.L. (3d) 375 at 379 (Man. C.A.): "The evidence . . . should be primary evidence establishing the factual circumstances, and not just testimony reflecting subjective opinions."

and whether extended medical, dental, or other health care insurance coverage has been arranged.[48]

Now the new rules governing child support under the Act, depending, as they do, upon more or less rigid guidelines, will probably make it easier to provide the court with the necessary basis for making a decision.[49] And the wording of the bar has been changed by the recent amendments so as to require the court to have "regard to the applicable guidelines" when satisfying itself concerning the reasonableness of any arrangements.

It is not clear whether the court will regard this requirement as satisfied when the parties have been unable to agree and the issue of child support is before the court as a matter of corollary relief—that is, whether, in the words of one commentator, "leaving child support to a judicial determination is making reasonable arrangements for child support."[50] The use of guidelines now, however, ought to mean that spouses will agree as to amount in many more cases.

3) Connivance and Condonation

The bars of connivance and condonation originate from a time when matrimonial fault was the sole basis on which a divorce could be obtained, and their meaning and use are bound up with that outdated legal world of marital blame and punishment. Under the present *DA* they apply only with respect to divorce applications based upon adultery or cruelty. In such cases the court must satisfy itself that neither connivance nor condonation exists, and if either does, the application must be dismissed, unless, "in the opinion of the court, the public interest would be better served by granting the divorce."[51] Thus, these bars are not absolute.

---

48 *Harper* v. *Harper*, above note 46.
49 See *DA*, above note 1, s. 15.1(3), requiring the use of guidelines, and subs. (7) & (8) permitting consent orders after the agreed amount of support is examined in the light of the guidelines. See section B(2), "The Federal Child Support Guidelines," in chapter 12, "Financial Support."
50 J. McLeod, Annotation, (1989), 20 R.F.L. (3d) 404. *Marinovic* v. *Marinovic* (1989), 20 R.F.L. (3d) 404 (Ont. H.C.) says that it does; *MacLellan* v. *MacLellan*, [1996] O.J. No. 3606 (Gen. Div.) says that it does not.
51 *DA*, above note 1, s. 11(1)(c). The Act also provides that conduct, once condoned, is not capable of being "revived" so as to constitute a ground for divorce: s. 11(2). Under old law, condoned conduct could be revived into a ground if the forgiven spouse was guilty of behaviour less than a matrimonial offence; thus, condonation used to be a conditional forgiveness.

Both bars direct themselves at the basic requirement that an applicant for divorce founded on adultery or cruelty ought genuinely to be aggrieved by the offence. It is not appropriate for fault grounds to be used simply because it is expedient or to achieve some other ulterior purpose. Connivance is the act of consenting to or even working to bring about the thing complained of, and so when applicants connive at their spouses' adultery, for example, they are authors of the wrong and ought not, therefore, be allowed to complain about it now.[52] Condonation is essentially forgiveness; and a forgiven act of adultery, for instance, is no longer a source of grievance.

The classic legal definition of condonation requires that the aggrieved spouse have knowledge of the offence, intend to forgive the offending spouse, and "reinstate" the offending spouse to his or her former marital position.[53] This last requirement means essentially that the forgiveness must be genuine and evidenced not merely in words but in behaviour. Typically, condonation was evidenced by the resumption or continuation of sexual relations; but it may be that today sexual intercourse would not function so automatically as a proxy for genuine forgiveness.

The Act provides for a trial reconciliation period (or periods) of not more than ninety days, during which the spouses may resume or continue cohabitation without having the conduct regarded as condonation.[54]

Under the Act (and under the prior statute) the court could determine that it is in the public interest to grant the divorce despite connivance or condonation. The courts have never been clear on when it would *not* be in the public interest to grant a divorce in the situation where a marriage has broken down, as evidenced by the application itself, and there is no prospect of reconciliation, a finding that must be made in all cases before evidence can be heard.[55] And it is the rare case, indeed, in which the court has not found that there was little to be gained by keeping the parties together in the legal bond of marriage.[56]

---

52   See *Maddock* v. *Maddock*, [1958] O.R. 810 (C.A.) for a more extensive definition. Note that "passive acquiescence" in a spouse's adultery was there regarded as constituting connivance. Connivance is not an important factor in modern divorce law.

53   *Leaderhouse* v. *Leaderhouse*, [1971] 17 D.L.R. (3d) 315 (Sask. Q.B.).

54   *DA*, above note 1, s. 11(3).

55   See section C(1), "Reconciliation," in this chapter.

56   But see, for example, *Blue* v. *Blue*, [1971] 17 D.L.R. (3d) 226 (Sask. Q.B.), where the court put the matter on a different footing by attempting, and failing, to find a benefit from granting the divorce notwithstanding condonation.

4) Religious Barriers to Remarriage

According to the precepts of some religions, and specifically the Jewish religion, a spouse has the power to block a religious divorce by refusing to grant consent. This, of course, does not affect any power of the civil courts to grant a divorce. However, the social and religious consequences for observant Jews of failing to obtain a parallel religious divorce can be serious and may effectively prevent remarriage. The *DA* empowers a court, among other things, to dismiss the application for divorce or strike out the pleadings of any person who has refused (without genuine religious grounds) to remove barriers to the spouse's remarriage that lie within the refusing spouse's control.[57]

E. PROCEDURAL MATTERS

1) Jurisdiction

Because families and individuals are mobile, and because the *DA* is federal legislation and applicable throughout Canada, there are provisions for determining which province's courts will take jurisdiction of an application for divorce. Section 3(1) provides that the courts of a province have jurisdiction where either spouse has been "ordinarily resident[58] in the province for at least one year immediately preceding the commencement of the proceeding." In Ontario, the appropriate court is the General Division of the Ontario Court.[59]

When spouses in different provinces begin separate proceedings, the place where the action was commenced first has exclusive jurisdiction to

---

57   *DA*, above note 1, s. 21.1. There is a similar provision affecting relief under
      Ontario's *Family Law Act*, R.S.O. 1990, c. F.3, s. 2(4). See: J.T. Syrtash, *Removing
      the Barriers to Religious Remarriage under Canada's Divorce Act and Ontario's Family
      Law Act: Rights and Remedies* (Downsview, Ont.: B'nai Brith Canada, National GET
      Committee, 1990); *Religion and Culture in Canadian Family Law* (Toronto:
      Butterworths, 1992); and S. Van Praagh, Book Review of *Religion and Culture in
      Canadian Family Law* by J.T. Syrtash (1993) 38 McGill L.J. 233.

58   As to the meaning of "ordinary residence," see: *Thomson* v. *M.N.R.*, [1946] S.C.R.
      209 at 231–32, Estey J.: ". . . the place where in the settled routine of his life he
      regularly, normally or customarily lives"; and in the context of the Act:
      MacPherson v. *MacPherson* (1976), 28 R.F.L. 106 at 112–13 (C.A.), Evans J.A.:
      ". . . the arrival of a person in a new locality with the intention of making a home
      in that locality for an indefinite period makes that person ordinarily resident in
      that community."

59   *DA*, above note 1, s. 2(1) definition of "court."

hear the application.[60] Should two actions be launched on the same day, jurisdiction is given to the Trial Division of the Federal Court.[61]

If there is a contested application for a custody order as corollary relief, and the parties are in different provinces, a party may apply to have the divorce proceeding transferred to that province with which the child "is most substantially connected."[62]

2) Presentation of Evidence

The *DA* delegates to a "competent authority" in each province the power to make rules respecting "the practice and procedure in the court" and "the conduct and disposition of any proceedings under this Act without an oral hearing."[63] In Ontario, the Family Court Rules (applicable to the Family Court branch of the General Division of the Ontario Court)[64] provide that

> [i]n an undefended application, any evidence or information required to enable the Court to perform its duties under subsections 10 (1) and 11 (1) of the Divorce Act (Canada) (reconciliation and bars to divorce) and the evidence at the hearing may be presented by affidavit, unless the Court orders otherwise.[65]

3) Judgment

Under the prior statute, a divorce was awarded as a decree and in two stages.[66] The decree nisi was granted upon proof of grounds for divorce. Three months later either spouse could apply for a decree absolute, the issuing of which effectively terminated the marriage. The three-month period, which could be shortened by the court, was designed to be a time during which parties could change their minds or when irregularities might come to light.

The current Act provides for a judgment and a certificate. The judgment of divorce is granted by the court upon proof of grounds, but "a divorce" does not take effect until the thirty-first day after the day on

---

60   *Ibid.*, s. 3(2).
61   *Ibid.*, s. 3(3).
62   *Ibid.*, s. 6(1).
63   *Ibid.*, s. 25(2).
64   See *Courts of Justice Act*, R.S.O. 1990, c. C.43, s. 21.1 & 21.2.
65   *Family Court Rules*, R.R.O. 1990, Reg. 202 as amended by O. Reg. 72/92, O. Reg. 468/93, O. Reg. 282/95, Rule 82 (1).
66   *Divorce Act*, above note 3, c. 24, ss. 13 & 16.

which the judgment was rendered (unless the parties agree, or the court finds that because of special circumstances, it should take effect earlier).[67] When the divorce has taken effect, any person may obtain from the court a certificate that the marriage in question was dissolved as of a certain date, and this certificate is "conclusive proof" of these facts.[68]

4) Effect

Once it takes effect, a divorce dissolves the marriage of the spouses.[69] A divorce alters the status of the parties—is a judgment *in rem*. It may not be appealed once it has taken effect;[70] and, though the judgment can be set aside for fraud[71] and other reasons,[72] care must be taken not to adversely affect those who have in good faith relied on it.[73]

F. A NOTE ABOUT COROLLARY RELIEF

The federal Parliament, having legislative power to make laws respecting divorce, also has, as an ancillary power, the constitutional authority to make laws for the support of spouses or children and for the custody of children.[74] Orders made under the Act for custody[75] or support[76] are known as orders for corollary relief. Because these matters of substance are also within the legislative competence of the province and, so, may be resolved according to provincial laws or according to private agreement, it is appropriate to treat them separately from divorce proper. Each will be discussed in a separate chapter of this book.

It might be useful here, however, to point out that orders for support or custody made under the *DA* have the advantage of having legal effect throughout Canada[77] and may be enforced in any province simply by registration in the relevant court.[78]

---

67 *DA*, above note 1, s. 12(1) & (2).
68 *Ibid.*, s. 12(7) & (8).
69 *Ibid.*, s. 14.
70 *Ibid.*, s. 21(2).
71 *Fromovitz v. Fromovitz*, [1962] O.R. 120 (H.C.).
72 *Rivas v. Rivas*, [1977] 72 D.L.R. (3d) 702 (Alta. S.C.).
73 *Chadderton v. Chadderton*, [1973] 1 O.R. 560 (C.A.).
74 *Zacks v. Zacks*, above note 15.
75 *DA*, above note 1, s. 16.
76 *Ibid.*, s. 15.
77 *Ibid.*, s. 20(2).
78 *Ibid.*, s. 20(3).

Corollary relief may only be granted under the Act where an application for divorce has not yet been determined, in which case the order would be for interim relief, or where a judgment for divorce has been granted. It has been made clear in the current Act that an application for corollary relief may be made at any time after the divorce judgment.[79] Thus, there may in a sense now be "federal families" and "provincial families," the former being divorced persons and the children of their marriage, for whom matters of support and custody may (or perhaps must) be determined under the Act, and the latter being undivorced (perhaps unmarried) spouses and their children, for whom provincial laws are determinative of support and custody.

Provisions governing custody and support under the Act differ to some extent from those under provincial legislation, and it will sometimes be necessary to determine how to resolve the problem of overlapping jurisdictions. This, too, will be addressed when the substance of custody and support are discussed, below.[80]

FURTHER READINGS

PAYNE, J.D., *Payne on Divorce*, 4th ed. (Toronto: Carswell, 1996)

MACDONALD, J., & A. WILTON, *The 1999 Annotated Divorce Act* (Toronto: Carswell, 1998)

MACDONALD, J., & L. FERRIER, *Canadian Divorce Law and Practice*, 2d ed. (Toronto: Carswell, 1988) looseleaf service

---

79   See *DA, ibid.*, s. 4(1): "A court . . . has jurisdiction to hear and determine a corollary relief proceeding if (a) either *former spouse* is ordinarily resident in the province . . ." (emphasis added).

80   See section G, "Overlapping Jurisdictions," in chapter 10, "Custody and Access"; and section F, "The Problem of Overlapping Jurisdiction (Revisited)," in chapter 12, "Financial Support."

CUSTODY AND ACCESS

A. INTRODUCTION

1) Simplicity and Difficulty

No aspect of family law is easier to summarize and harder to apply than that governing custody of children. The applicable rule is, quite simply, that courts are to do what is in the best interests of the child. There are no other rules as such; and, because every case must be decided on its own merits and has no precedential value, none can be constructed. Best interests of the child: beginning and end.

Yet, for a variety of reasons, custody law is very difficult indeed.[1] It is difficult because this simple test is too vague to provide the kind of guidance some disputing parties require in order to come to agreement. It is difficult in that the law does not adequately take into account legitimate adult interests or provide a way of harmonizing them with those of the child. And, too, it is difficult because its subject is children, about whom we have strong feelings and a good deal of ambivalence. In a sense, then, everything that follows is an explication of difficulties that are created by the simple best interests test.

The discussion may make it appear that courts are commonly involved in the resolution of custody disputes, or that disputes as to custody arise whenever parents separate. In fact, most separating couples

---

1   See section B(3), "An Analysis of Difficulty," in this chapter.

are able to agree, often without any trouble, on how the custody of or access to their children ought to be arranged, and courts are relatively infrequently required to make choices for them. It is simply more convenient to cast the discussion in terms that give the court a role. It is convenient, too, to speak of matters as though custody disputes always involved two separating parents, even though other kinds of adults may be caught up in custody issues from time to time.

2) Sources of Law

Two statutes principally[2] govern child custody and access matters: Ontario's *Children's Law Reform Act*[3] (Part III) and the federal *Divorce Act*.[4] The former is more elaborate in its relevant provisions, and so it will be useful to refer to it most frequently and usually to allow its terms to guide the discussion. The differences between them are important in some respects and will be addressed below. But both, however, make "the best interests of the child" the sole test for determining custody and access.[5]

In some cases it can be hard to determine whether provincial or federal law is to govern a situation.[6] But in many if not most cases, it will not matter greatly, because the best interests test is central to both and understood (by the same judges) in the same way in both laws. In the great majority of cases the question will be settled by agreement between the adults involved rather than by a court, so jurisdiction will not arise as an issue. Generally speaking, however, the *Divorce Act* will govern custody matters respecting children of spouses who have applied for a divorce, and the *Children's Law Reform Act* will apply to all other situations.

---

2   The *Child and Family Services Act*, R.S.O. 1990, c. C.11, also deals with custody and access; see: ss. 135(5), 143(1), and 154, in connection with the adoption process (and see section D(1), "Custody and Access Rights," in chapter 6, "Adoption"), and ss. 51(2) & 58, in connection with the child protection process (and see chapter 7, "Child Protection").

3   R.S.O. 1990, c. C.12, as amended by S.O. 1992, c. 32, s. 4; S.O. 1993, c. 27, Sched.; S.O. 1996, c. 2, s. 63; S.O. 1996, c. 25, s. 3 [*CLRA* or the Act].

4   S.C. 1986, c. 4, as amended by S.C. 1990, c. 18, ss. 1 & 2; S.C. 1992, c. 51, s. 46; S.C. 1993, c. 8, ss.1–5; S.C. 1993, c. 28, s. 78; S.C. 1997, c. 1, ss. 1–15; [*DA* or the *Divorce Act*].

5   *CLRA*, above note 3, s. 24(1): "The merits of an application . . . in respect of custody or of access to a child shall be determined on the basis of the best interests of the child." *DA, ibid.*, s. 16(8): "In making an order . . . the court shall take into consideration only the best interests of the child."

6   See section G, "Overlapping Jurisdictions," in this chapter.

Apart from statute, superior courts have an innate *parens patriae* juris-diction respecting children that descends from English Chancery courts' *parens patriae* and wardship jurisdictions.[7] It will be unnecessary for the most part to make use of this jurisdiction because that conferred by legis-lation is broad enough to achieve most aims; and where statutory jurisdic-tion exists, it ought to be used.[8] However, the courts will turn to it "to deal with uncontemplated situations" that call for the protection of children.[9]

3) Custody and Guardianship

There is some uncertainty as to the exact meaning of the terms "cus-tody" and "guardianship." Historically, guardianship was the larger concept, focused at the beginning on protection of the child's estate and embracing the right to custody of the person of the child as simply one element within its broad compass. But things have shifted over time such that now, in Ontario at least, custody is the term that describes the full panoply of rights and obligations an adult may have with respect to a child; and guardianship has come to refer to an extraordinary appoint-ment to manage a child's property.[10]

The *CLRA* defines custody only by reference to the "rights and responsibilities of a parent."[11] Although there is no clear statutory enu-meration of these, social practice shows that parents have authority to make decisions respecting a child's residence, education, property, reli-gious affiliation, medical treatment, and a great many other important, and more mundane, circumstances.[12] These rights and responsibilities must be exercised in the best interests of the child;[13] and where they are not, the state may intervene.[14]

---

7   *CLRA*, above note 3, s. 69: "This Part does not deprive the Ontario Court (General Division) of its *parens patriae* jurisdiction." See *E. v. Eve*, [1986] 2 S.C.R. 388 at 407 for a helpful discussion of the origins of this jurisdiction, particularly as it relates to mental incompetence. See also S.I. Bushnell, "The Welfare of Children and the Jurisdiction of the Court under *Parens Patriae*" in K. Connell-Thouez and B. Knoppers, eds., *Contemporary Trends in Family Law: A National Perspective* (Toronto: Carswell, 1984) 223.

8   See *M.(R.) v. M.(S.)* (1994), 20 O.R. (3d) 621 at 632 (Ont. C.A.).

9   *E. v. Eve*, above note 7 at 411, referring to *Beson v. Newfoundland (Director of Child Welfare)*, [1982] 2 S.C.R. 716.

10   See *CLRA*, above note 3, s. 47. See also a discussion of the scope of custody in *Young v. Young*, [1993] 4 S.C.R. 3 at 39.

11   *CLRA*, above note 3, s. 20(2).

12   See section A(2), "Duties of a Parent," in chapter 5, "Parentage."

13   *CLRA*, above note 3, s. 20(2).

14   See section C(1)(a), "Family and State," in chapter 7, "Child Protection."

4) Relevant Adults

a) Who May Apply

Typically, custody disputes occur between parents. However, anyone may apply for an order respecting the custody of, or access to, a child.[15] In reality, of course, total strangers do not intrude themselves into children's lives by seeking their custody,[16] and "any person" will describe someone who has a family or a social relationship with the child—a grandparent, aunt or uncle, or sibling, perhaps. Although a "stranger" or "officious intermedler" would be able to bring an application, the court would probably require that some connection with the child be demonstrated before permitting the application to proceed.[17]

Because of this provision, it is not necessary for a person who has performed the functions of a parent to have a genetic relationship with the child before being able to apply for a custody order. Thus, step-parents, for instance, or "psychological parents" may obtain custody based on the needs of the child, rather than on any adult view of the importance of genetic ties.

b) Parents and Custody

The Act provides that "the father and the mother of a child are equally entitled to custody of the child."[18] This is the only statutory acknowledgment of the right accorded to parents to raise their own children.

---

15   *CLRA*, above note 3, s. 21: "A parent of a child or any other person may apply . . . for an order respecting custody of or access to the child." *DA*, above note 4, s. 16(1): "A court ... may, on application by either or both spouses or by any other person, make an order respecting the custody of or the access to . . . children of the marriage." A person other than a spouse must get leave of the court to apply for custody, however: *DA*, s. 16(3).

16   See *Smith* v. *Hunter* (1979), 27 O.R. (2d) 683 at 685 (H.C.): "[I]t is suggested [that granting the applicants standing would] open the door to applications by a horde of unqualified non-parents. The answer to that, it seems to me, is that to apply is not necessarily to succeed and the patently unqualified are unlikely to apply. I would not be worried, therefore, about the prospect of a flood of unmeritorious applications."

17   Under the *Divorce Act*, above note 4, a person wishing custody who is not a spouse must obtain leave of the court to apply: s. 16(3). See also *W.(C.G.)* v. *J.(M.)* (1981), 34 O.R. (2d) 44 at 49 (C.A.); and see section D(1)(b), "After Adoption," in chapter 6, "Adoption."

18   *CLRA*, above note 3, s. 20(1).

Most clearly the provision equates the rights of mother and father,[19] but it seems as well to establish that parents, as opposed to any others, have the *initial* right to custody. This broader effect may be inferred from the equation of a custodian's rights to those of a "parent" in section 20(2), and from the reference in section 20(4) to the "entitlement" of a separated parent to custody.

Where a child has two parents, the rights and responsibilities that make up custody are shared. But there is no requirement that parents, or other joint custodians, agree before a decision can be made respecting a child. The Act makes it clear that although more than one person may be entitled to custody each custodian has, and may exercise, the full set of rights and responsibilities.

Where parents cannot agree as to what is best for the child, the courts initially offer only the prospect of removing custody rights from one of them, leaving the other free to implement his or her view of what is best.[20] It will almost always be the case that parents who seek assistance from lawyers (and, potentially, courts) are separated. The Act anticipates that the break-up of a family, and consequent separation of the parents, is a fertile occasion for serious disagreements about the care or custody of a child; and it provides that

> [w]here the parents of a child live separate and apart and the child lives with one of them with the consent, implied consent or acquiescence of the other of them, the right of the other to exercise the entitlement of custody and the incidents of custody, but not the entitlement to access, is suspended until a separation agreement or order otherwise provides.[21]

---

19   Historically, fathers had the right to guardianship of their (legitimate) children. In England, mothers gained rights in Chancery during the nineteenth century; and for much of this century, there was a more or less automatic assumption by the courts that mothers ought to get custody. For a good capsule history, see *Young* v. *Young*, above note 10 at 34ff, McLachlin J.

20   "Law" can provide for negotiation, mediation, or arbitration of disputes, of course; and agreements arrived at with the assistance of lawyers may establish a framework that will assist the parties over difficulties. The point being made here, however, is that, initially at least, courts prefer not to decide particular issues for parents who cannot agree, and tend to resolve disputes by identifying appropriate decision makers.

21   *CLRA*, above note 3, s. 20(4). This provision applies as well, of course, to parents who have never cohabited.

Even where parties agree as to the appropriate custody arrangement upon separation, the potential for difficulty remains, for the obvious reason that custody and access responsibilities entail a continuing and changing relationship between the parents. Much of the reported litigation in this area has to do with disagreements arising after an initial settlement or decision and, in particular, with questions about the respective authority of custodial and access parents. Here, in the context of "relitigation," so to speak, the courts are being increasingly driven to ruling on specific issues of child-rearing practice.[22]

5) Variation

A custody or access order made at the conclusion of litigation is known as a "final" order,[23] but in fact custody arrangements are almost always open to variation. Under the Act, variation of an order respecting custody or access is only possible where there has been "a material change in circumstances that affects or is likely to affect the best interests of the child."[24] The language in the *Divorce Act* is somewhat different, requiring that there must be a "change in the condition, means, needs or circumstances of the child . . . since the making of the custody order" and in making the variation, "the court shall take into consideration only the best interests of the child as determined by reference to that change."[25]

In either case, the court will start from the assumption that the original order was correct, and will not permit the application for variation to become a relitigation or appeal of the original decision.[26] This aim seems to be the reason behind the language of the *Divorce Act*, restrict-

---

22   See, for example, *Chauvin v. Chauvin* (1987), 6 R.F.L. (3d) 403 (Ont. Dist. Ct.), where the court became involved in a dispute about whether the children ought to attend French school. Note that *CLRA*, above note 3, s. 21 provides for an application to a court for, among other things, "an order . . . determining any aspect of the incidents of custody of the child." See also *DA*, above note 4, s. 16(6), to the same effect.

23   In order to distinguish it from an interim order, which is granted pending a final order. Interim orders are granted generally to preserve the status quo unless that would place the child at risk. An interim order will typically be made on the basis of affidavit evidence and, of course, a less than thorough airing of all the circumstances. There is a danger that delay after an interim order will make it increasingly less likely that a court will be prepared to move the child by the time the final hearing is reached.

24   *CLRA*, above note 3, s. 29. Presumably, a change that did not affect the best interests of a child would not be, for that reason, "material."

25   *DA*, above note 4, s. 17(1)(a) & (5).

26   *Gordon v. Goertz*, [1996] S.C.R. 27 at 43 [*Goertz*].

ing a court to a particular view or focus on the best interests of the child. But it hardly seems possible that a court could understand the impact of a change on a child without understanding something, at least, of the history of the situation. In *Gordon v. Goertz,* the Supreme Court has said that, although the *Divorce Act* speaks of restricting attention to the change, "the inquiry cannot be confined to that change alone" and "the material change places the original order in question; all factors relevant to that order fall to be considered in light of the new circumstances"; moreover,

> [I]t is error for the judge on a variation application simply to defer to the views of the judge who made the earlier order. The judge on the variation application must consider the matter anew, in the circumstances that presently exist.[27]

This appears to accord no deference whatever to the original decision, which is taking matters too far. A material change does, in theory, alter the constellation of all circumstances in a child's life, since it is true that matters are all related in complex ways. However, in practice there are constants, and a principle of parsimony suggests a better approach would be to work away from a deference to the original decision as far as is made necessary by the changes.[28]

Because no order for custody is truly final, and because the vicissitudes of life are many and complex, the ability of the non-custodial spouse to apply for variation can easily be converted into an ability to harass a custodian. It might be better if, once a final order were made, the court lost jurisdiction to intervene further in the family's life, absent a child's need for protection; there is little good reason, it could be argued, to subject the lives of separated parents and their children to continued, fine-grained scrutiny, when the rest of us are left alone.

However, the peace of the rest of us is a function of actual harmony—or at least of our disinclination to sue each other for sole custody—rather than of any lack of jurisdiction of the court. Even so, it is important for courts and lawyers to take the position that applications to vary are not merely "tune-ups" or fine adjustments, but are serious intrusions into peoples' lives, as was the original suit.

---

27   McLachlin J., *ibid.* at 46.
28   Yet McLachlin J., *ibid.*, says, somewhat confusingly perhaps, "[the] new inquiry is based on the findings of the judge who made the previous order and evidence of the new circumstances." It will depend, it appears, on what "facts" the original judge finds.

B. THE BEST INTERESTS TEST

1) The Factors Approach

There is no formula or guiding method for determining which outcome of a dispute would be in the best interests of a child.[29] From the point of view of a judge faced with the need to decide, the determination requires an exercise of discretion after the consideration of relevant factors. But this says next to nothing. Taken broadly, the task of knowing what is in the best interests of a child can be dauntingly large.

We lack a generally accepted theory of the "good" that would enable a court to know what to value and how to rank various putative goods. Is stability better than excitement? Is a life of ease preferable to one of struggle? From this wide perspective, all choices of values are evidently political choices; and none is so clearly superior to any other that the decision is easy. But judges, and most disputants, are not trained philosophers, and rarely push matters back to first, or even second, principles in this fashion.[30]

How then are the child's best interests determined? It is important to see at the outset that the decision to be made is rarely, if ever, what in all the world would be best for this child. In actual fact the question is: Which of the real and limited alternatives proposed by these very adults would be in the child's interests? Ballet lessons, for example—or music, or, indeed, any artistic stimulation—may simply not be a realistic possibility. This is not to say that choices at this less abstract level are somehow free of political meaning. It is merely to observe that much potential difficulty is removed by the constraints of the actual situation.

Another focusing device may be found in section 24(1) of the *CLRA*, which sets out a list of some seven factors that must be considered when

---

29   There were once informal but generally adopted guidelines, the most important of which were that children under seven belong with their mother—the so-called "tender years" doctrine (see *Bell* v. *Bell*, [1955] O.W.N. 341 (C.A.)); and siblings ought not to be separated (see *White* v. *White* (1994), 7 R.F.L. (4th) 414 (N.B.Q.B.)). See also *Wereley* v. *Wereley* (1979), 14 R.F.L. (2d) 193 (Ont. H.C.).

30   Compare the relative lack of expressed values in this context with those "virtues" set out in the duties of a teacher under the *Education Act*, R.S.O. 1990, c. E.2, s. 264(1)(c): "to inculcate by precept and example respect for religion and the principles of Judaeo-Christian morality and the highest regard for truth, justice, loyalty, love of country, humanity, benevolence, sobriety, industry, frugality, purity, temperance and all other virtues."

determining the best interests of the child.[31] These include: (a) "the love, affection and emotional ties between the child" and various others; (b) "the views and preferences of the child . . ."; (c) "the length of time the child has lived in a stable home environment"; (d) the respective merits of the applicants as providers of "guidance and education, the necessaries of life and any special needs of the child"; (e) "any plans proposed for the care and upbringing of the child"; (f) "the permanence and stability of the family unit with which it is proposed that the child will live"; and (g) "the relationship by blood" between the child and an applicant.

A couple of points need to be made about this list. First, it is not exhaustive: the requirement of the section is to consider "all the needs and the circumstances of the child" including the listed ones.[32] Note that the potentially overwhelming nature of the task makes its return in this way: if the *general* debate about the good is not to occur, it is still the case that every aspect of this *specific* child's life and person is supposed to be be examined—equally clearly a gargantuan job. But because these factors have been expressly identified, they are typically seized upon as being important ones to explore. There is no guidance given, however, as to whether any are to be weighted more heavily than others.[33]

Second, the factors describe different sorts of "circumstances." Some, such as the views of the child and the proposed custodian's plans, have a procedural aspect; they direct themselves at the provision of important information to the court. Others express values more or less directly; thus, love,[34] stability and education, for instance, emerge as things that are deemed good. The reference to blood ties between the

---

31 There is no comparable listing or definition in the *Divorce Act*, above note 4; there is only the direction in s. 16(8) to determine the best interests of the child "by reference to the condition, means, needs and other circumstances of the child." This absence suggests that no special importance ought to be attached to factors listed elsewhere: Parliament clearly felt that judges were capable of managing without detailed assistance.

32 Compare this list with those found in ss. 37(3) & 136(2) of the *Child and Family Services Act*, above note 2. The former section identifies a dozen factors, some relevant only to a child protection hearing, but others, such as "the child's cultural background" and "the religious faith . . . in which the child is being raised," of possible utility in a custody hearing. Presumably, their explicit presence in legislation elevates them to a sufficient level of importance to compete with the factors identified in the *CLRA*, above note 3.

33 It might be suggested that those that come first are superior to those that come after, but this would seem to be a capricious assumption.

34 The word "love" appears in only two Ontario statutes: in the *CLRA*, above note 3, and in the *Education Act*, above note 30, s. 264(1)(c), where the reference is to "love of country."

child and applicants for custody is presumably also the declaration of a value (that affects the child and not just adults?), rather than the simple direction to pay attention to a neutral fact.[35]

The difficulty is in knowing how to combine these different sorts of factors—the problem of apples and oranges. There is no matrix provided in the statute for the weighing and comparing of such values as stability and genetic relationship.

It should be noted here that two potential factors are singled out in legislation for special attention. A court may not have reference to "the past conduct of a person" unless the "conduct of a person is relevant to the ability of the person to act as a parent of a child."[36] This ought not to be a necessary statement, given that everything considered must be relevant to the best interests of the child; however, judgments under earlier, differently worded legislation did decide that "marital misconduct" might, "as a matter of justice," bear directly on a woman's entitlement to custody.[37] The courts have taken cognizance of the fact that physical abuse of one spouse by the other can have relevance in child custody cases.[38]

Under the *Divorce Act*:

> In making an order under this section, the court shall give effect to the principle that a child of the marriage should have as much contact with each spouse as is consistent with the best interests of the child and, for that purpose, shall take into consideration the willingness of the person for whom custody is sought to facilitate such contact.[39]

Note that this is the only legislated instance of an official value that is required to affect custody. It is debatable whether it was intended to be a fixity within the best interests calculus, or whether it was meant as an extrinsic limitation on the best interests test; the wording suggests, perhaps, that the latter is the more accurate view. There is no provincial counterpart to this "friendly parent" rule.

---

35   This is in part captured by the use of the emotive and inaccurate word "blood" instead of the more neutral "genes," in a section where generally modern terms such as "stable home environment" are used.

36   *CLRA*, above note 3, s. 24(3). The provision in *DA*, above note 4, s. 16(9), is almost identical.

37   See *Talsky* v. *Talsky*, [1976] 2 S.C.R. 292, rev'g [1973] 3 O.R. 827 (C.A.) where this view was given effect.

38   See, for example, *Renaud* v. *Renaud* (1989), 22 R.F.L. (3d) 366 (Ont. Dist. Ct.).

39   Above note 4, s. 16(10). This will be considered again in section D(2), "The Proper Standard," in this chapter.

2) The Use of Experts

The absence of a clear legislated scheme of values has led many courts, understandably, to turn to other areas in search of guidance and a means of delimiting the task of knowing what is best for the child. The various disciplines that concern themselves with child development offer attractive possibilities, in that they can be seen to describe something that might be called "healthy, normal development."

When healthy, normal development (or some version of it) is adopted by courts and lawyers as the supreme "good" for children, a number of benefits follow. It brings with it a system of analysis that permits reliance on experts and so shares the burden of decision with others. Further, it offers the advantage of seeming objectivity and universality: child development is an observable, scientific fact; it normally occurs in a particular fashion, aided by certain environmental factors, and retarded by various others; normal development is healthy development, in this quasi-medical model of aging; and health is a universal value that can hardly be gainsaid.

Moreover, once this aim is accepted as the *summum bonum*, the circumstances in a child's life may be regarded instrumentally, rather than as entailing political values about which hard choices must be made. The problem is now one of means, rather than ends; and the question becomes: Is this circumstance helpful or hurtful in achieving normal, healthy development?

It is impossible, of course, to summarize any prescription for normal, healthy development. That is not the point, particularly: the goal gets adopted and any arguments about the best ways to get there are far less troubling than explorations of "the good life." Besides, disagreements in science are only to be expected. Law is comfortable with them, and is thereby allowed to retain ultimate decision-making authority.

The influence of child development experts can be seen reflected in the Act's identification of important factors in a child's best interests, particularly in an emphasis on "stability."[40] If one lesson has been learned from the various studies it is that continuity of care is highly important to normal, healthy child development, and that changing

---

40 *CLRA*, above note 3, s. 24(2)(c) & (f). Scientific, or pseudo-scientific, phrases in the section, like "stable home environment" and "family unit," may also bespeak the influence of child development experts. See also, for example, the approving reference by L'Heureux-Dubé J. to Goldstein, Freud, and Solnit's *Beyond the Best Interests of the Child*, (New York: Free Press, 1979), a book that was once surely on every judge's desk, in her dissent in *Young* v. *Young*, above note 10 at 41.

custodians brings with it risk of trauma for the child. This simple guide has been used by many courts to assist in making decisions since it was adopted by the Ontario Court of Appeal in *Moores* v. *Feldstein*[41] to overturn a predisposition to award custody to birth mothers in preference to adults unrelated to the child.

Expert involvement in specific disputes will most likely be through "assessment." The Act provides that the court

> may appoint a person who has technical or professional skill to assess and report to the court on the needs of the child and the ability and willingness of the parties or any of them to satisfy the needs of the child.[42]

It is also possible that parties to a dispute will themselves resort to assistance from experts for advice or for support in anticipated litigation, and the Act makes clear that appointment of an assessor does not prevent parties from submitting "other expert evidence as to the needs of the child."[43]

3) An Analysis of Difficulty

There is a mismatch between the task of resolving custody disputes and the resources of the legal system, certainly in its traditional guise as a court-based adversarial procedure, and this produces difficulty. Three aspects of the situation are briefly examined here.

First, as has already been seen, the task as currently structured by the best interests test is open-ended. The court and those bargaining in the light of the law are to consider all circumstances that are rele-

---

41   [1973] 3 O.R. 921 (C.A.).

42   *CLRA*, above note 3, s. 30(1). See, for example, *Green* v. *Green* (15 March 1996), Doc. Vancouver D096884 at para. 8, 1996 CanRepBC 529 (B.C.S.C.), in which the court ordered an assessment by a psychologist, an excerpt from which follows and demonstrates the general point just made about the aim of normal, healthy development:

> The psychological research done in this area (c.F. Hodges, 1991) usually urges prior to the age of 3, frequent access several times a week with the non-custodial parent, and overnight access after the age of 3. This is based on the principle that the emotional and intellectual development of the child is better served by frequent contact with the non-custodial parent, which develops a sense of confidence and security in the relationship to permit overnight access after the age of 3. Frequent access is usually considered to occur two or three times a week for periods of two to three hours each.

43   *CLRA*, above note 3, s. 30(15).

vant to the child's interests. Normally, relevance is a usefully limiting notion within law, confining attention to those features of a situation that are highlit, so to speak, by the illumination of the particular rule. Here, however, there is no limit to what is potentially relevant to a child's interests. The rule, perhaps correctly, invites us to consider the whole person of the child, but in so doing opens up the full complexity of human life for consideration. No adequate "proximity" rule has been developed to delimit the reach of the inquiry, other than the usual transactional costs associated with the use of the legal system. Although these costs are effective in cutting off considerations at some point, there is no sense that this point is particularly appropriate, for it will always be arbitrary.

Second, custody decisions call for predictions about the future. For this reason a "final" decision is always capable of being varied if the circumstances warrant it. But law is far more comfortable with analysis of the past than the future. It has considerable experience in reconstructing historical events and then debating their meaning or import in a more or less leisurely fashion, and from a standpoint that we feel to be detached because the events under discussion are over or finished.

However, with custody the relevance of the past—indeed, the present—is uncertain because it is dependent upon far too many contingencies to be fixed with any degree of confidence. Planning for an unpredictable future is not alien to human beings, of course, but the point is that the law and its officers have no special expertise in this process. There are never any studies done by courts to see whether their predictions have panned out; and, indeed, there could hardly be, given the plethora of "variables."

Moreover, the legal system is itself a participant in the substantive matter, rather than the independent or detached commentator we often suppose it to be. Not only does the court's decision have an obvious impact in the life of the child, but the process as well is important. Delay, for example, may alter the conditions upon which a prediction is to be based, as might the way in which the disputants relate to each other. The child in question is the present and future child, not the child of a dead past now immune from our process.

Third, the way in which our society constructs childhood invites the bafflement of the legal system. We identify certain characteristics of infancy as particularly determinative of what it means to be a child, and then we see young people as having these characteristics until or even past adolescence. It turns out, unsurprisingly, that the "nature" of children, thus constructed, is quite opposed to the "nature" of adult citizens, particularly in their role as actors in a legal system. The system cannot deal with persons who have the characteristics we ascribe to children, at least not as it is currently structured.

For example, we see children as relational beings—this is a primary sense of the word "child" after all. To be a child is to be in relation with another, typically a mother or father. Because children are relational, they are understood to be dependent beings: they cannot provide for themselves. Children are perceived to be changeable; they grow and develop, and are different people from day to day. This, together with their dependent nature, makes them vulnerable to environmental influences of any and all sorts. Children are irrational and must be civilized into reason; they are prey to their instincts and emotions. All these characteristics allow us to see each child as unique, as being exactly like no other. (Imagine discovering that the "wrong" baby had been brought home from the hospital, and being told that one was very like another.)

Adult actors in the legal system are constructed in a different, more or less opposing fashion. They are treated as independent, autonomous beings, who have a constant "identity" across time. They manipulate the environment; it does not manipulate them. Legal actors are rational beings; emotion is not (openly) appealed to in laws. And they are interchangeable—equal before the law, citizens to whom the law speaks generally.

A legal system set up to acknowledge persons so constructed cannot cope with children of the sort described. In fact, the legal system continues to attempt to modify itself so that it becomes more appropriate for children, or for children's issues. These modifications may, indeed, make for less difficulty. But it is arguable that there will be an irreducible element of difficulty as long as human nature is dichotomized, and childhood is assigned the role of carrier of qualities that we, as adults, do not recognize or value in ourselves.[44]

---

44   There are clear parallels between this dichotomization and the one that used to dominate, and still influences, our understanding of women and men. The group in power will assign "weak" attributes to the others, and, in order to make sure that they stay attached to the powerless, will purport to value these attributes greatly—so greatly, at times, that they simply cannot be ascribed to the unworthy persons of the powerful.

C. ALTERNATIVES TO BEST INTERESTS

1) Joint Custody

If the best interests test is unsatisfactory, how might it be improved or supplanted? One way would be to avoid having to make a judicial decision wherever possible (and thus to avoid using the test). This might be accomplished by a presumption that the regime existing prior to the parents' separation ought to continue after separation. As was seen, the Act makes mother and father equal custodians of their children.[45] This is joint custody in its fullest sense. But the Act does not contain a presumption that this legal state will continue after separation; indeed, it is presumed that after separation only the parent with whom the child resides will have custody rights and responsibilities—or, sole custody, as it is called—unless there is a dispute resolved by a different arrangement.[46]

If there were a presumption that joint custody should continue after separation, it would mean, in effect, that custody would become less of a justiciable issue. Parents would be expected to "work things out for themselves" in much the same way that they had to before separation. Of course, the presumption could be displaced by showing that, in some sense or other, it was inappropriate under the circumstances. One test for inappropriateness might be whether harm to the child would result from continued joint custody. A less stringent test might simply place the onus on either or both of the parents to persuade the court that it was *not* in the best interests of the child that joint custody continue.

It ought to be made clear that joint custody has been given a variety of meanings by courts, experts, and commentators. One fairly clear divide separates those meanings that focus on legal rights from those that emphasize responsibilities and actual care. The former meanings might, for example, describe a post-separation joint custody arrangement in which the children resided with the mother, who had the right (and burden) of day-to-day care and control, and both parents had the right to make major decisions (such as religion, schooling, medical treatment) respecting the child. On the other hand, uses that emphasize responsibility would describe "shared parenting" arrangements, that might, ideally, see the child spending equal amounts of time with each parent, and each parent equally involved in the care and upbringing of the child.

---

45   *CLRA*, above note 3, s. 20(1).
46   *Ibid.*, s. 20(4).

Some experts in child development argue that joint custody after separation—certainly in its shared parenting sense—is generally in children's best interests. And there has been a good deal of lobbying by "fathers' rights" groups aimed at passage of a joint custody presumption. These influences have resulted in the "friendly parent" rule under the *Divorce Act*,[47] and in the legislative clarification that joint custody awards are in fact possible.[48]

Currently, however, no presumption in favour of joint custody exists, and there are serious objections to its implementation. Although it might keep disputes out of the courts, it may do little to resolve them. And it has the capacity to allow a controlling spouse to perpetuate his influence after separation, and as well, where the arrangement is not one of genuinely shared work, to interfere with the authority of the spouse doing the job of child rearing.[49]

In Ontario, at least, courts have generally refused to make orders that impose joint custody where one or both spouses are opposed to it, on the ground that it is not a desirable arrangement except where the parties are able to cooperate to a considerable degree.[50] The somewhat paradoxical result will be that those parties who litigate are *ipso facto* unlikely to be able to achieve the requisite level of cooperation, and so joint custody ought never to be awarded in disputed cases.[51]

Joint custody finds its greatest use in separation agreements, where parties decide to cooperate in the raising of their children. Two difficulties present themselves in this situation, however. There may be a temptation to use joint custody as a way of agreeing without actually resolving

---

47   See section B(1), "The Factors Approach," in this chapter, and note 39 with accompanying text.

48   *CLRA*, above note 3, s. 28: "The court . . . (a) . . . may grant the custody of . . . the child to one or more persons." *DA*, above note 4, s. 16(4): "The court may make an order granting custody of . . . children of the marriage to any one or more persons."

49   Also, a joint custody order might allow a father to pay less child support than would otherwise be the case, and yet might not result in lower costs to the mother.

50   See: *Baker v. Baker* (1979), 23 O.R. (2d) 391 (C.A.); *Kruger v. Kruger* (1979), 25 O.R. (2d) 673 (C.A.), in which there is a strong pro–joint custody dissent by Wilson J.A.; *Goslin v. Goslin* (1986), 4 R.F.L. (3d) 223 (Ont. C.A.), where the opposition is more muted.

51   Not all courts in Ontario have followed the lead of the Court of Appeal. Salhany J. has awarded joint custody over the opposition of one of the parties a number of times; see: *Lewis v. Lewis* (1989), 18 R.F.L. (3d) 97 (Ont. Dist. Ct.); *Alfoldi v. Bard* (1989), 20 R.F.L. (3d) 290 (Ont. Dist. Ct.); *Crawford v. Crawford* (1991), 36 R.F.L. (3d) 337 (Ont. Gen. Div.); *Kaemmle v. Jewson* (1993), 50 R.F.L. (3d) 70 (Ont. Gen. Div.).

difficulties—as a means of postponing issues by simply prolonging the regime that operated before separation. In such cases, and where the exact meaning and consequences of a joint custody choice have not been worked through by the parties, problems may arise later and be difficult, or expensive, to resolve.

As well, there is the problem of how to resolve disputes within a contractually created joint custody regime. There is the danger that courts will regard inability to agree as itself proof of the inappropriateness of joint custody, with the effect that a contract would give rise to no right to joint custody that could be enforced, or, at least, supported by a court. A number of courts, however, have shown themselves willing to maintain agreed-to joint custody arrangements despite difficulties that have arisen.[52] Indeed, some take the position that it is appropriate to start analysis from the assumption that the agreement is "correct" (as would be the case with an original court order) and ought to be displaced only if there has been a material change in circumstances since its making.[53]

2) The Primary Caregiver

Rather than reducing the need to use the best interests test, we might deem it to be satisfied in a way that is based on easily ascertainable facts. In a few jurisdictions[54] this is being done through the use of the primary caregiver presumption. It is presumed that the child's interests are best served by granting custody to that parent who has been the child's primary caregiver. This accords with the value, mentioned above, that is currently placed on continuity of care, and recognizes that, certainly

---

52   See, for example, *Boukema v. Boukema*, [1997] O.J. No. 2903 (Gen. Div.); *Lichter v. Lichter*, [1997] O.J. No. 2558 (Gen. Div.); *Bruce v. Bruce*, [1997] O.J. No. 2031 (Prov. Div.).

53   See, for example, *Boukema v. Boukema, ibid.*; *McAlear v. McAlear*, [1997] O.J. No. 2117 (Prov. Div.).

54   Gary Crippen, "Stumbling beyond Best Interests of the Child: Reexamining Child Custody Standard-Setting in the Wake of Minnesota's Four Year Experiment with the Primary Caretaker Preference" 75 Minn. L. Rev. 427 at 434 (1990):

> Courts in at least sixteen states have identified and showed some favor for the parent who had been the primary caregiver before the couple separated [California, Delaware, Florida, Iowa, Massachusetts, Minnesota, Missouri, Montana, New York, North Dakota, Ohio, Oregon, Pennsylvania, Utah, Vermont, and West Virginia]. Furthermore, courts from at least seven of these states have identified primary caretaking as a significant factor in assessing the child's best interests [California, Delaware, Florida, Massachusetts, Missouri, Montana, and New York]. Courts from five states, although declaring the importance of primary caretaking, have rejected it as a presumptive determinant of custody [Iowa, North Dakota, Pennsylvania, Utah and Vermont].

from a child's perspective, it is the daily acts of caring that are significant and result in an important bond between the caregiver and child. It has the advantage, procedurally, of letting the legal system focus on the past and find facts, and then of using the continuity value to project the past into the future on a simple trajectory.

The presumption also has the consequence of tending to replicate the past on a society-wide scale. Society currently, as it has for a great many years, expects that women will assume the responsibility for childcare; and, although there may be an increasing number of men who are devoting significant amounts of time to this task, overall the job is still gendered, and women in fact perform it most of the time and in most cases. For some women, the facts of their investment in this task and the bond, or relation that results, ought to be acknowledged, respected, and protected by the court. From their vantage point of intense involvement, many, if not most, caregiving women perceive that a child's best interests are served by maintaining the bond with the caregiver, except where the caregiver is unfit.

There is concern, however, that this approach tends to perpetuate the gendered nature of this work and all the political disadvantages that accompany performing one of society's "very valuable" and wholly thankless, unremunerative tasks. It might well be that the way to avoid this (and the other) horn of the "dilemma of difference" is to acknowledge and protect the relationships women form with children for whom they care, and at the same time to ensure that women are given the means—the power—to protect their interests themselves.

D. ACCESS

1) The Nature of Access

When a decision is made that a parent will have sole custody of a child, it is common to order as well that the other parent and the child will have access to each other. There is no authoritative definition of access.[55] The term is simply used to describe forms of contact between an adult and a child that fall short of those associated with the rights and responsibilities of custody. At one end of the spectrum, perhaps, an order for access might provide only that a parent should be provided

---

55   But see *CLRA*, above note 3, s. 20(5): "The entitlement to access to a child includes the right to visit with and be visited by the child and the same right as a parent to make inquiries and to be given information as to the health, education and welfare of the child." This is a presumptive content for access, which can, of course, be altered by agreement or court order: *CLRA*, s. 20(7).

with information about the child on a regular basis.[56] At the other end, access might entail long periods of time during which the child and the parent reside together, and, consequently, during which the access parent will have nearly full authority over the life of the child and whose conduct will likely be indistinguishable from that of a custodial parent.

As the rights and responsibilities of an access parent approach those of a custodial parent, conflicts of authority may develop. The courts are currently attempting without a great deal of success to work out what the respective positions of custodial and access parents ought properly to be.[57] This will be examined to some extent below, in the context of religious education and parental mobility.

2) The Proper Standard

The legislation makes clear that, as with custody, orders respecting access are to be determined with reference only to the best interests of the child.[58] It is important, however, to understand that until fairly recently the non-custodial parent was considered more or less to have a right to access, which would only be refused if there were danger to the child.[59] Gradually, over the past few decades the notion of parental rights has given way to the "child-centred" view that access is a right of the child.[60] However, the Act continues to speak in the language of parental rights and entitlements.[61]

---

56 See *DA*, above note 4, s. 15(5): "Unless the court orders otherwise, a spouse who is granted access to a child of the marriage has the right to make inquiries, and to be given information, as to the health, education and welfare of the child."

57 See, for example, the Supreme Court decisions in *Young* v. *Young*, above note 10 and *Droit de la famille — 1150*, [1993] 4 S.C.R. 141; and see also *M.(B.P.)* v. *M.(B.L.D.E.)* (1992), 97 D.L.R. (4th) 437 (Ont. C.A.), leave to appeal to S.C.C. refused (1993), 48 R.F.L. (3d) 232 (note).

58 See above note 5.

59 *Ader* v. *McLaughlin*, [1964] 2 O.R. 457 at 468 (H.C.), Hughes J.:
    Much has been said and written about the change in the law over the last century and more wherein it is now recognized . . . that in matters of custody and access the paramount consideration is that of the welfare of the children . . . [B]ut through [all the cases] can be discerned a recognition of the fact that although the question of custody is frequently determined by reference to the conduct of the parent, access is never refused except in cases where danger to the children is apprehended.

60 See *Young* v. *Young*, above note 10.

61 See *CLRA*, above note 3, s. 20, where the word "entitlement" is used more than half a dozen times to describe custody or access by an adult. Section 20(4) provides that where parents live separate, unless there is an agreement or order to the contrary, "the right of the [parent with whom the child does not reside] to exercise the entitlement of custody . . . but not the entitlement to access, is suspended."

The earlier rule just referred to was founded on an understanding that a child's welfare required him or her to have contact with both parents. It is fair to say that this view of a child's best interests continues today, and, indeed, is enforced for divorcing parents by the *Divorce Act*'s "friendly parent" rule, which requires, in part, that a child "should have as much contact with each spouse as is consistent with the best interests of the child."[62]

The friendly parent rule would seem to place the burden on the (would be) custodial spouse to persuade the court that it is not in the best interests of the child to have access to the other spouse. But because the rule also requires the court to take into account the willingness of each spouse to facilitate this contact when deciding custody, it operates *in terrorem* to inhibit opposition to access. To seek custody and to oppose access is to risk losing the custody application. An applicant for custody who opposes access may not argue that, as a general matter, there ought to be a demonstration in each case of the benefits to the child from access: the statute precludes this, because maximum contact is of presumptive value to the child. And such an applicant would be wary of arguing an inability in the spouses to cooperate, even though this might be true and could have harmful effects on the child, for fear that the other spouse might take the position that the difficulty is the intransigence of the applicant, and could be mended by giving the respondent custody. This leaves, it would seem, opposition to access based upon undesirable qualities in the other spouse, and leads to mud-slinging, one would think.

Although no such friendly parent rule is found in the Ontario legislation,[63] it would be unreasonable to imagine that the same judges would one day, in divorce court, give effect to the basic understanding about the value of maximum parental contact and the next day, under provincial legislation, require the proposition to be proved, at least in its general form.

---

62 *DA*, above note 4, s. 16(10). See section B(1), "The Factors Approach," in this chapter.

63 Bill 27, *An Act to Amend the Children's Law Reform Act*, 1st Sess., 36th Leg., Ontario, 1995, cl. 3, (a failed private member's bill) would have introduced such a provision, along with various rights for grandparents.

3) Access by Grandparents

There has been a move recently to promote the interests that grandparents have in access to their grandchildren.[64] Nothing in either piece of legislation prevents applications by grandparents for access where the custodial parent is unwilling to grant it.[65] The question of whether grandparents have, by reason of their genetic relationship,[66] a position superior to "strangers" raises broad issues of "belonging" and the willingness of the law to acknowledge relationships beyond those formed in the nuclear family.[67] Analogous questions might be whether a person from an Aboriginal child's first nation, or from his or her religious or ethnic community, for example, should have any advantage thereby in obtaining access to the child.

For the most part, courts have depended upon the existence and quality of a relationship between the child and the grandparents in making the determination. In this respect, grandparents have been treated in the same way as unrelated adults. Some courts, however, have felt it desirable that a child should get to know the extended family, despite the objections of the custodian.[68]

At base, the problem might best be seen as one of custodial authority. It will probably be the case that a child's interests are best served when the custodial parent has effective authority to protect the child and control the child's environment (insofar as this is ever possible for a parent);[69] where grandparents (or others) exercising access to the child do not interfere with this authority too greatly, it could easily be

---

64 Bill 27, *ibid.*, was aimed at giving grandparents rights. It would have provided, among other things, that a custodian "not unreasonably place obstacles to personal relations between the child and the child's grandparents." And the version of the friendly parent rule proposed would have measured possible custodians according to their friendliness respecting grandparents.

65 The *Divorce Act*, above note 4, requires that a person not a spouse obtain leave of the court to apply for access or custody: s. 16(3).

66 A consideration in the Act when determining the best interests of the child is "the relationship by blood" between the child and an applicant: *CLRA*, s. 24(2)(g).

67 See section E, "A Note on the Role of Suprafamilial Groups," in chapter 6, "Adoption."

68 See, for example, *McLellan v. Glidden* (1996), 23 R.F.L. (4th) 106 (Q.B.).

69 See J.Goldstein, A. Freud, & A. Solnit, *Beyond the Best Interests of the Child* (New York: Free Press, 1973) at 38: These authors recommended that the custodial parent be given sole authority to decide who has access to the child, on the ground that a child's proper development requires a parent who is perceived to have (and has) sufficient authority to protect him or her. This recommendation has not been favoured by the courts, needless to say.

assumed that a child would benefit from access to grandparents.[70] But any such benefit might come at too high a cost if access to grandparents undermined or countermanded parental authority.

E. SPECIAL PROBLEMS

1) The Role of the Child

a) The Problem of Standing

Courts are required to consider the "views and preferences of the child" when considering an application with respect to custody and access.[71] But children are not parties to custody or access actions that concern them, and do not have standing before the court to testify or present evidence of their views and preferences.[72] Accordingly, children must operate through adult surrogates.

Courts in Ontario considering custody and access matters, whether under the *CLRA* or the *Divorce Act*, have power to appoint a litigation guardian for the child, or a "legal representative of a minor . . . who is not a party to a proceeding."[73] A litigation guardian is either a party to the litigation or has powers very nearly like those of a party, able particularly to participate at trial, call evidence, and cross-examine wit-

---

70   See, for example, *T.(A.H.)* v. *P.(E.)* (1995), 20 R.F.L. (4th) 115 (Alta. C.A.).

71   *CLRA*, above note 3, s. 64(1), requires the court to take the child's views and preferences into account "where possible" and "to the extent the child is able to express them." See also s. 24(2)(b), which makes the child's views and preferences a circumstance to be considered when determining best interests. Under the *Divorce Act*, above note 4, there is no explicit requirement, but courts will take a child's wishes into account where it is reasonable to do so.

72   *CLRA*, above note 3, s. 63(3), makes the mother and father and various others parties, but does not mention the child. The *Divorce Act*, above note 4, does not address the matter of parties as such.

73   *Courts of Justice Act*, R.S.O. 1990, c. C.43 [as amended in this respect by S.O. 1994, c. 12, s. 37 and c. 27, s. 43(2)], s. 89(3) & (3.1); see also s. 112. Under similar, earlier legislation, the Official Guardian was appointed as litigation guardian. Under the current provisions, the Children's Lawyer may be appointed as litigation guardian. In *Jeffries* v. *Jeffries*, [1997] O.J. No. 3119 (Gen. Div.) the Children's Lawyer was appointed "to represent the interests of the child."

nesses.[74] The litigation guardian then will appoint counsel, who will follow the guardian's instructions. These, of course, must be given in the best interests of the child.

b) Representation (Revisited)

The existence of a power in the court to appoint a litigation guardian or to obtain a legal representative for the child does not mean that it will in all cases be used. In fact, the courts have over the years been sceptical of the independent representation of children in custody actions, certainly as a routine matter;[75] however, this reluctance to provide for representation may be disappearing.[76] In part the opposition appears to stem from the courts' fear that children ought not to be "caught" between their parents, and should be permitted, as it were, to step away from the dispute. And, too, there is a sense that even disputing parents have their children's interests at heart at some level, and can be trusted, with the help of the court, to promote those interests in the course of their dispute.

Even where representation is ordered, there is still a debate in Ontario about the way in which a child ought to be represented. The issue has two aspects, not always separated, or, indeed, capable of separation: the institutional structure that ought to operate to bring about representation; and the role that any selected representative ought to play.

As was seen in chapter 7, the *Child and Family Services Act* accords the child a right to be represented in protection hearings and establishes fairly clearly the child's standing in the matter.[77] This provision gave rise

---

74   The trial court in *Strobridge* v. *Strobridge* (1992), 10 O.R. (3d) 540 at 549 (Gen. Div.), said that the litigation guardian for a child "is a party to the action." The Court of Appeal reversed the judgment in part, at (1994), 18 O.R. (3d) 753 (C.A.), but did not deal with the question of the exact standing of the litigation guardian, except to quote with approval the decision in *Reid* v. *Reid* (1975), 11 O.R. (2d) 622 (Div. Ct.) which gave the litigation guardian significant powers to participate in the trial.

75   See: *Rowe* v. *Rowe* (1976), 26 R.F.L. 91 (Ont. H.C.) expressing general disapproval; *J.* v. *J.*, [1978] 4 R.F.L. (2d) 157 (Man. C.A.) stating that representation as a matter of course is not desirable; *Novic* v. *Novic* (1984), 37 R.F.L. (2d) 333 (Ont. C.A.) approving of representation in this case because of the bitterness of the dispute between the parents.

76   See the trial judgment in *Strobridge* v. *Strobridge*, above note 74 at 544: "For the most part courts no longer have the same misgivings expressed . . . in *Rowe* concerning the desirability of having children represented by their own counsel."

77   R.S.O. 1990, c. C.11 (as amended by S.O. 1994, c. 27, s. 43(2), S.O. 1996, C.2, s. 62), ss. 38(1), 39(4) & (6). See section B, "Statutory Framework," subsection "Role of the Child," in chapter 7, "Child Protection."

to serious questions about the role of counsel so appointed. The Law Society of Upper Canada was of the opinion that if a child could instruct counsel, there should exist a lawyer-client relationship no different, essentially, than that between an adult and a lawyer.[78] This was aimed at, and disapproved of, the view that a lawyer for a child had a duty to act in the child's best interests as the lawyer understood them. But there is no similar right to counsel for a child in a custody or access case,[79] and so it is unlikely that even a child competent to appoint counsel could obtain direct representation in this fashion.[80]

Far more likely, as was seen in the prior section, is that the child will have a litigation guardian appointed, who will instruct counsel. Acting for an adult guardian ought to mean that the lawyer's role is easy: follow instructions. But this merely pushes the question back one degree. What ought the role of the litigation guardian to be, then?

The guardian will act in the best interests of the child, which will often mean ensuring that all the pertinent information is before the court, which may, where relevant, include information about the child's views and preferences.[81] To accomplish this, the counsel retained will have the power to lead evidence and make submissions to the court. Generally, the counsel will act as an advocate and may, where the litigation guardian thinks appropriate, take specific instructions from the child.

c) Learning the Child's Views and Preferences

A variety of means have been used to communicate the child's views and preferences to the court. The open and direct approach is generally not acceptable, however, and children ought not to testify unless they are mature. Nor, it seems, ought counsel to inform the court directly, as though testifying, unless the parties have agreed that this is acceptable.[82] The preferred means would have a person who is not a party or a coun-

---

78   Law Society of Upper Canada, "Report of Sub-Committee on the Legal Representation of Children to the Professional Conduct Committee" (Toronto: The Committee, May 1981).

79   Legislative provision for the representation of children involved in custody disputes has been recommended by the Law Reform Commission of Canada, *The Family Court, Working Paper No. 1* (Ottawa: Information Canada, 1974) at 40–41, and the Ontario Law Reform Commission, *Report on Family Law, Part 3, Children* (Toronto: Department of Justice, 1969) at 124.

80   It is generally not appropriate for one parent in a custody dispute to engage counsel for a child. See *Fiorellino v. Fiorellino* (1995), 132 D.L.R. (4th) 338 (Ont. Gen. Div.).

81   See the appellate decision in *Strobridge v. Strobridge*, above note 74.

82   *Ibid.*

sel for a party interview the children and then testify as to their views and preferences (even though this requires a relaxation of the hearsay rule). Ideally, the selected person will have experience in working with children and will probably be a social worker or a psychologist. This mediating person would typically be selected by counsel for the child or the litigation guardian.

A similar approach is offered by the provisions of section 112 of the *Courts of Justice Act*, which provide for an investigation by the Children's Lawyer in any case "in which a question concerning custody of or access to a child is before the court."[83] The Children's Lawyer may be requested to investigate by the court or "any person," and, indeed, may do so "on his or her own initiative."[84] Of course, if the court has appointed an assessor under the Act,[85] that person will most likely provide the information that the court requires.

It is possible for a judge to interview the child in chambers;[86] however, courts will probably be reluctant to become directly involved in this fashion, particularly as most judges have no special training in interviewing children.

2) Adult Interests and the Child-Centred Approach

a) Parental Mobility

When one parent has custody and the other has a right of access to the child—or when the parents have joint custody—there may be limits on the freedom of a custodial parent to move with the child to a new location.[87] This problem of "parental mobility" has been much litigated

---

83   Above note 73. The legislation provides that this is available whether the matter arises under the *DA*, above note 4, or the *CLRA*, above note 3.

84   *Ibid.*

85   See *CLRA*, above note 3, s. 30, and section B(2), "The Use of Experts," in this chapter.

86   *CLRA*, above note 3, s. 64(2). See *Demeter* v. *Demeter* (1996), 133 D.L.R. (4th) 746 (Ont. Gen. Div.) for a recent example of where a court, with the consent of counsel, interviewed the children; there was an assessment in the case, and as well the children were, at one point at least, represented by the Children's Lawyer.

87   The *Divorce Act*, above note 4, provides specifically in s. 16(7) that courts may require custodians who intend to change the residence of the child to notify any person with access rights. More generally both statutes also enable judges to make any orders that are necessary as an adjunct to custody or access orders, and so enable courts to require that a child's residence not be changed without permission of the access parent, for example. On the issue generally of parental mobility, see M. Bailey & M. Giroux, *Relocation of Custodial Parents: Final Report* (Ottawa: Status of Women Canada, 1998).

recently, and has become, in fact, emblematic of certain troublesome aspects of the law respecting child custody. In particular, as the Supreme Court has re-emphasized in *Gordon* v. *Goertz*, there is no ability within the law to take the interests of the custodial or access parent into account when making custody or access decisions.[88]

Moreover, *Goertz* specifically rejected[89] what had been proposed by the Ontario Court of Appeal in *MacGyver* v. *Richards*,[90] which was that great deference ought to be paid to the "needs of the responsible custodial parent." The child's interests are to be all. And essentially there is to be a weighing of the importance to the child of access to the non-custodial parent against that of maintaining the custodial relationship. Custody is not of a different order of importance than access.

From a broader, policy perspective, it is clearly unrealistic to ignore the fact that adults have interests in the outcomes of custody and access issues. It is unfortunate that there is no means whereby these can be openly acknowledged and taken into account. The bad old days are gone when adult interests were allowed to rule the roost. But the flight all the way to an exclusively child-centred approach—certainly one operated with this degree of purity—goes too far. Yes, the child is not, and should not be allowed to be, a prize to be awarded to a winner in a custody contest; the adult's interest in "having" the child must be subordinated to the child's needs and interests. However, adult interests are not universally so crude or so clearly in opposition to those of the child.

There is an ability, of course, to import adult interests into the deliberations through the child's interests: what makes the custodian happy or materially better off is good for the child. This is not in and of itself inappropriate, for the child and custodian exist in relationship to each other; and only in law's impoverished (but focused) philosophy could we imagine (or speak as if we believe) that a child, *qua* individual, could have interests that are not deeply implicated with the interests of his or her parents—or, for that matter, the rest of us. In fact, it does seem that the importance of the parent-child relation is ultimately the deciding factor

---

88   Above note 26 at 54: "The rights and interests of the parents, except as they impact [*sic*] on the best interests of the child, are irrelevant."

89   *Ibid.* at 60: "[A] legal presumption in favour of the custodial parent must be rejected." The custodial parent's views "are entitled to great respect and the most serious consideration" because the custodian knows the child intimately; thus the custodial parent is transformed into a sort of assessor, and the knowledge of a parent that is useful is the knowledge of an observer rather than that of an empowered decision maker.

90   (1995), 22 O.R. (3d) 481 at 490 (C.A.) [*MacGyver*].

in most cases—even in *Goertz* the mother was permitted to take the child with her to Australia because it turned out to be in the child's best interests to remain with her—and so in that sense adult interests as represented in the person of the custodian are in fact taken into account, as they must be in any rounded view of life, no matter what the rules say.

However, it is one thing to be able to take adult interests into account by hook or by crook, and another to do it directly and with careful explicit thought. Open discussion would likely lead inexorably, as it has in other areas, to the wider and avowedly political context in which these disputes arise and decisions are made. In that context, the likely salient feature is the gendered nature of childcare. Women not only bear but raise our children as well. We expect it to be that way and myriad forces in society reinforce that expectation. Consequently women invest themselves in this task and form strong and deep bonds with their children. To say to such women that these required investments are of no significance when custody is before the court is unjust.

Goertz is technically quite correct that under current legislation the best interests of the child, which were once paramount, are now the sole consideration,[91] and that any regularities established by courts would be errors of law because discretion must not be fettered or anticipated in any way: the very facts of the instant case are the only relevant considerations. If adult interests are to be admitted to the process, the legislation ought properly to be changed.

However, no court ought to operate as though it were in a politics-free zone. Discretion cannot operate in the eye of the political storm, and guides may be given or "indiscretions" permitted that assist in locating the decision in the real world. Each parent, each child is different; but all parents, all children are something alike. This political understanding of what society is like and how it operates must necessarily undergird all court decisions, even those that would direct our attention solely at the facts of the instant case, for judges are not from Mars—or Venus. A child-centred approach must still of necessity entail an adult's view from an imagined child's perspective.

---

91   The court points out (above note 26 at 47 & 48) that in the *Divorce Act*, Parliament has created the presumption in favour of maximum contact between the child and both parents—which operates, of course, against custodial parent mobility—and then goes further to say that in proscribing consideration of an adult's past conduct in s. 16(9) Parliament meant that an adult's reasons or motives for moving are similarly not to be taken into account except insofar as they are relevant to parenting ability. This is a severely ahistorical reading of this provision, and one that ignores the fact that it is directed explicitly at "past conduct." See section B(1), "The Factors Approach," in this chapter.

Nor is it sensible to imagine that the child is best viewed in an apolitical light. Children learn about and exercise power, as they must; they know that their parents and the others around them have interests; and our attempts to insulate them from this aspect of reality is misguided. It may well be that a child needs a superaddition of power when the family is breaking up in order to see that his or her interests are acknowledged appropriately. But it is a long way from proper protection to a solo place in the spotlight, with the rest of the world in obscurity.

The decision of the Ontario Court of Appeal in *MacGyver*[92] made a great deal of sense, adverting as it did to the reality of the lives of the children and their custodians. It is probably inappropriate to allow interference in the child's family on the bases that we now do: the fact of a separation ought not perpetually to subject decisions of the child's custodian to scrutiny at the suit of the access parent, so that when there is a material change in circumstances—and when is there not when children grow up?—all bets are off and the child's custody is in the hands of the court once more. Such insecurity and subordination to public officials is too high a price to be exacted for living apart from the other parent.

b) Religion

The matter of religion has also proved to be difficult, at least for the parents and children in some families. This is understandable, because religious beliefs may be strongly held by adults and, in such cases, are commonly wished to be inculcated in children. Because of religions' tendency to deal in right and wrong, if there are two different religions or sects involved, co-existence may be difficult. Moreover, because the particular practices of a religion are not based in rationality and do not lie in the same matrix as a scientific view of normal, healthy development, courts cannot deal directly with the substance of the dispute (as they might consider, for example, whether a move from one locale to another was a good idea), but must instead work through the issue at a remove. The issue, then, is cast in terms of parental authority, and the debate in the courts is really about the extent of the powers of custodial and access parents.

In the cases of *Young v. Young*[93] and *Droit de la famille — 1150*,[94] released at the same time, the Supreme Court dealt with two very similar cases in which access fathers discussed their Jehovah's Witness beliefs with their children and took them to meetings and canvassing, over the objections of the custodial mothers. Unfortunately, in what might be described

---

92   Above note 90.
93   Above note 10.
94   Above note 57.

as a scattering of opinions, the Court managed to confuse both the *Charter*[95] questions and the issue of a custodial parent's authority. McLachlin J. wrote the majority opinion in the *Young* case (and the dissent in *Droit de la famille—1150*), generally supporting the importance to children of full contact with the access parent, and treating the parents' *Charter* rights as worth arguing about, at least. L'Heureux-Dubé J. wrote the majority opinion in *Droit de la famille—1150* (and the dissent in *Young*) and basically decided that the *Charter* was not an issue in an access dispute and that the custodial parent's authority to decide upon a child's religious training set limits upon any right in the access parent to teach his religious view to the child. A clear majority of justices decided, however, that the *Charter* rights of parents do not outweigh the best interests of their children.

In both cases all judges agreed that the principle to be applied was the best interests of the child, but, as might be imagined, there was disagreement about what that phrase means in practice, particularly insofar as the respective roles of custodial and access parents are concerned. However, *Goertz*[96] would suggest that the view expressed by McLachlin J. has managed, since these cases were decided, to gain support of a clear majority of the court, and that contact between the child and the access parent will be supported by the court (where it is in the best interests of the child) even where it creates distress and runs counter to the wishes or interferes with the authority of the custodial parent.

The proper role of the *Charter* in family disputes—whether it will prove to be a means whereby adult interests may be debated in conjunction with the best interests of the child—is evidently still under examination by the court.

F. ENFORCEMENT OF CUSTODY AND ACCESS ORDERS

Where once a custody order might have been enforced with the assistance of the Ontario Family Support Plan,[97] now both custody and

---

95 *Canadian Charter of Rights and Freedoms*, Part 1 of the *Constitution Act, 1982*, being Schedule B to the *Canada Act 1982* (U.K.), 1982, c. 11 [*Charter*].

96 Above note 26.

97 *Family Support Plan Act*, R.S.O. 1990, c. S.28, repealed by the *Family Responsibility and Support Arrears Enforcement Act, 1996*, S.O. 1996, c. 31, s. 73(1). There is no provision in the new legislation for the enforcement of custody orders; section 6(5), which has not yet been declared in force, will explicitly forbid the Director from enforcing "custody orders made by a Canadian court, even if they were filed with the Director before this section comes into force."

access orders may only be enforced privately. Depending on the nature of the difficulty, there are various ways of approaching enforcement of these orders, none entirely satisfactory, as may be imagined in practical matters where children are involved.

1) Contempt

The power to find a person named in an order in contempt of court for failure to obey the order[98] will probably have the greatest utility in respect of access orders. The courts have shown themselves reluctant to make use of the contempt power to punish,[99] and will more likely use the occasion of an application in this respect to lecture and warn the disobedient parent. One reason for this reluctance ought to be the difficulty facing a custodial parent who suspects the child is being harmed by access: the custodian has the responsibility to protect the child and would be blameworthy if she or he failed to take appropriate steps promptly; yet the custodian must respect the order made by the court.[100]

It is also possible for the court to vary the order in the face of disobedience to provide for more access, and in an extreme case to order that the access parent become the custodial parent.

It is not open to an access parent to withhold child support as a means of compelling the custodian to abide by an order respecting access; and neither is an access parent's failure to pay child support an adequate reason for disobedience of an access order. Access and support are separate matters, and access is a right of the child the benefits of which, in the child's view, are likely independent of the receipt of support.[101]

2) Apprehension

Under section 36 of the Act, when there are reasonable and probable grounds to believe that a child is being unlawfully withheld from an applicant (who may be a custodial or access parent), a court may order

---

98   See also *CLRA*, above note 3, s. 38, giving the Provincial Division of the Ontario Court powers parallel to its powers in respect of contempt to enforce orders through fine or imprisonment.

99   See, for example, *Petryczka* v. *Petryczka*, [1973] 2 O.R. 866 (H.C.), where the court did in fact jail the mother for twenty-four hours.

100 See *M.(B.P.)* v. *M.(B.L.D.E.)* (1992), 97 D.L.R. (4th) 437 (Ont. C.A.), where the mother suspected sexual abuse.

101 See, for example, *C.(L.K.)* v. *C.(M.I.)* (1993), 100 D.L.R. (4th) 68 (B.C.C.A.), and the annotation by J.G. McLeod at (1993), 44 R.F.L. (3d) 229.

that the applicant or another be authorized to apprehend the child. As well, the court may on a similar basis order that a police force "locate, apprehend and deliver the child" to a person named in the order.[102]

In like fashion, a court may order that a child be apprehended where it appears a person is about to remove a child wrongfully from Ontario.[103]

Applications for apprehension may be made *ex parte*.[104]

3) Custody and Enforcement between Jurisdictions

Sometimes, in an attempt to avoid the consequences of local law or orders respecting custody, parents will take children out of the jurisdiction without the consent or knowledge of the other parent. There are two aspects to this problem, one practical and the other legal. The practical problem is that of locating the absconding parent and child, which, indeed, may be difficult even where the abductor has fled within the province. The legal aspect is essentially one of preventing the courts in the jurisdiction to which the absconding parent has fled from becoming engaged with the merits of the particular case. A trial or even a preliminary exploration of the merits might permit the absconding parent to reside with the child in that jurisdiction, frustrating contact with the other parent and causing the child to develop a relationship with the new environment, which might subsequently have to be protected in order to prevent harm to the child.

a) Obtaining Information
The federal government has passed legislation that enables, among others, a person "entitled to have a family provision enforced" to apply to a court for a release (to the court) of certain information held in federal databanks.[105] The information that may be released consists of the addresses of the abductor and the child and the name and address of the employer of either.[106]

---

102   *CLRA*, above note 3, s. 36(2).
103   *Ibid.* See also s. 37, giving the court additional powers in the same situation.
104   *Ibid.*, s. 36(3).
105   *Family Orders and Agreements Enforcement Assistance Act*, R.S.C. 1985, c. 4 (2nd Supp.) (as amended by S.C. 1992, c. 1; S.C. 1993, c. 8; S.C. 1996, c. 11; S.C. 1997, c. 1), s. 7. The databanks are those controlled by the Department of Human Resources Development, the Department of National Revenue, and the Canada Employment Insurance Commission: s. 15.
106   *Ibid.*, s. 16.

Currently, although it is provided for in the federal statute, there is no agreement between the province and the federal government for the sharing of information respecting the enforcement of custody orders.[107] However, section 39 of the *CLRA* empowers a court to order "any person or public body" to provide information about the address of a person if it is needed for the enforcement of an order respecting custody or access.

It is practical, where a child has been wrongfully removed, to consult the police, who have resources at their disposal to locate the child.[108] In many cases it will assist to have a criminal charge laid.

b) Legal Resources

i) The Criminal Code

It is an offence under the *Criminal Code* for a parent to take a child "with the intent to deprive a parent . . . of possession of the child.[109]

Mother and father are equally entitled to custody under the *Children's Law Reform Act*,[110] which provides that either custodian "may exercise the rights . . . of a parent on behalf of them."[111] These "rights" do not include, however, the ability to alter the child's custody unilaterally, particularly where this entails removal of the child from the company or care of the other parent. Access to the parents is a right of the child, and any attempt to curtail this, unless it is done to protect the child, is wrongful behaviour. Not all such wrongful behaviour will be criminal because the *Criminal Code* provision referred to above requires proof of special intent.[112]

---

107   Under Ontario's *Family Responsibility and Support Arrears Enforcement Act*, above note 97, s. 55(1), there is now the ability in the province to make an agreement with the federal government respecting support orders.

108   See A.C. Wilton & J.S. Miyauchi, *Enforcement of Family Law Orders and Agreements: Law and Practice* (Toronto: Carswell, 1989) looseleaf.

109   *Criminal Code of Canada*, R.S.C. 1985, c. C-46 (as amended by S.C. 1993, c. 45, ss. 4 & 5), ss. 282 & 283. It is an offence whether or not there is a custody order in relation to the child, and the offence includes, among other things, taking, concealing, and detaining the child.

110   *CLRA*, above note 3, s. 20(1). This may be changed by court order or agreement, or by a *de facto* giving up of custody by one of them: s. 20(4).

111   *Ibid.*, s. 20(3).

112   It is not necessary that the deprived parent be in possession of the child when the offence is committed: the *mens rea* required by the section exists when there is intent to prevent the other parent from having possession to which he or she would otherwise be entitled. See *R. v. Dawson*, [1996] 3 S.C.R. 783, in which the father, who had custody, committed the offence when he deprived the mother of access to the child to which she was entitled by court order.

It may be desirable to proceed by way of a charge under the *Criminal Code*, especially if locating the child is a problem, because this can result in a nationwide warrant and engage the attention of police forces across the country.

ii) *The* Hague Convention

The *Hague Convention on the Civil Aspects of International Child Abduction* aims at dealing with the problem of abduction of children across international boundaries.[113] At present, the Convention applies between Canada and some forty-one countries. In Ontario the Convention has been made part of the *Children's Law Reform Act*.[114]

Member states are required to establish a Central Authority, of which there are eleven in Canada, one for each province and a federal authority as well. A person seeking the return of a child who has been abducted may apply to the Central Authority in the child's home jurisdiction or in any other jurisdiction, which is obliged to take steps to seek the return of the child,[115] or the person may apply directly to the appropriate decision-making body in the state to which the child has been taken.[116]

The Convention is based on the proposition that a child wrongfully taken from the jurisdiction where he or she is habitually resident must be returned forthwith.[117] The law of the child's habitual residence determines whether the removal to the contracting state was wrongful.[118] There is no definition in the Convention of "habitual residence"; however, the Ontario Act defines it to mean the place where the child resided:

(a) with both parents;
(b) where the parents are living separate and apart, with one parent under a separation agreement or with the consent, implied consent or acquiescence of the other or under a court order; or

---

113 *Hague Convention on the Civil Aspects of International Child Abduction,* 25 October 1980 [Convention], in Hague Conference on Private International Law, Actes et Documents de la Quatorzieme Session, Tome III 413–22 (1982), reprinted in T.I.A.S. No. 11670; 19 I.L.M. 1501.
114 Above note 3, s. 46.
115 *CLRA, ibid.,* s. 46, (Convention) Articles 6–10.
116 *Ibid.,* Article 29.
117 See, example, *W.(V.)* v. *S.(D.),* [1996] 2 S.C.R. 108; *Thomson* v. *Thomson,* [1994] 3 S.C.R. 551.
118 *CLRA,* above note 3, s. 46, (Convention) Article 14.

(c) with a person other than a parent on a permanent basis for a significant period of time;

whichever last occurred.[119]

In order to make it more likely that prompt return will result, the Convention provides that a tribunal "shall not decide on the merits of rights
of custody" unless it is first decided that the child is not to be
returned.[120] It should be noted that the Convention directs itself at the
violation of custody rights and does not protect rights to access.

A few things may prevent return, even where the original removal
was wrongful. First, Article 12 establishes a limitation period of a year,
starting with the date of the wrongful removal or retention. This is
based on the notion that it is important to respect a child's actual relationship with his or her surroundings, and so the limitation period will
not operate to prevent the return unless "it is demonstrated that the
child is now settled in its new environment." Second, according to Article 13, the child will not be returned if this would result in a "grave risk
. . . of physical or psychological harm." As well, return may be refused
where a child of suitable maturity objects to being returned.

iii) Other Statutory Provisions

Where a child is wrongfully taken from one province to another within
Canada (or from a country that is not a member of the Convention to a
province of Canada), provincial laws that mirror the *Hague Convention*
will bring about essentially the same result—that is, the prompt return
of the child to the place of habitual residence. Thus, in Ontario, for
example, the Act provides that where a child has been wrongfully
removed to Ontario, the court is empowered to order the return;[121] and
where there is an order respecting custody or access made by an extra-
provincial tribunal, Ontario courts shall, with some conditions, recognize and enforce the order.[122] Moreover, a court in Ontario may not
exercise jurisdiction to make an order for custody or access unless the

---

119   *Ibid.*, s. 22(2). Note that "[t]he removal or withholding of a child without the
consent of the person having custody of the child does not alter the habitual
residence of the child unless there has been acquiescence or undue delay in
commencing due process by the person from whom the child is removed or
withheld": s. 22(3).

120   *Ibid.*, (Convention) Article 16. See *S.(J.W.)* v. *M.(N.C.)* (1993), 50 R.F.L. (3d) 59
(Alta. C.A.), leave to appeal to the Supreme Court refused (1994), 1 R.F.L. (4th)
60 (note).

121   *CLRA*, above note 3, s. 40.

122   *Ibid.*, s. 41.

child is habitually resident in Ontario,[123] the effect of this being further to discourage abduction to the province and make return more likely, by seeking to prevent the courts from becoming engaged with the best interests of the child.

It should also be remembered in this context that an order respecting custody or access made under the *Divorce Act* has legal effect throughout Canada, and may be enforced in any province, once registered there, in the same way as an order made by a court of that province.[124]

G. OVERLAPPING JURISDICTIONS

The provinces have power to make laws respecting "property and civil rights in the province," from which derives their power to legislate respecting custody and access.[125] Parliament also has jurisdiction to make laws respecting custody and access (and support, as well) ancillary to its power to legislate on divorce.[126] As a consequence, there is overlapping jurisdiction and the potential for conflicts, both between the terms of legislation and between orders made under them. Further, it may be unclear to applicants which is the proper statute to use in a particular circumstance.

However, as a general matter it should be noted that although the Ontario Act contains far more elaborate custody provisions than the *Divorce Act*, the core principle applied is identical in both cases—the best interests of the child. This means that from the perspective of applicants to the courts it will not matter greatly whether relief is sought under one or the other statute.[127]

It is clear that if there is no divorce application pending or granted, there is no jurisdiction to make a custody order under the *Divorce Act*. Equally clearly, there is authority under the language of that legislation

---

123 *Ibid.*, s. 22(1)(a). There are exceptions where there is otherwise the risk of serious harm (s. 23) and where, essentially, the child has a real and substantial connection to the province and there are no extra-provincial orders or applications for custody or access (s. 22(1)(b)). See also s. 25.

124 *DA*, above note 4, s. 20(2) & (3).

125 *Re Adoption Act*, [1938] S.C.R. 396.

126 *Papp v. Papp*, [1970] 1 O.R. 331 (C.A.).

127 See, for example, the Supreme Court decisions (which were released together) of *Young v. Young*, above note 10, and *Droit de la famille — 1150*, above note 57; although the latter arose under Quebec law and the former under the *Divorce Act*, this was not considered relevant by the court, and the same considerations were applied to both because the issue of substance was essentially the same.

to make a custody order respecting a child of the marriage upon or any time after the granting of a divorce.[128] Consequently, it is possible for an applicant to apply under the Ontario Act prior to an application for divorce, and thereafter under the *Divorce Act* (at least, with respect to children of the marriage).

However, this scheme of possible applications probably does not describe the limits of provincial legislative jurisdiction; that is, the ability of Parliament to make laws respecting custody when there is a divorce probably does not mean that the province lacks the ability to make laws respecting custody in such situations. This is certainly the view of the *CLRA* itself, for section 27 provides that an application under the Act that has not been determined is stayed when an action for divorce is begun, "except by leave of the court." "Determined" actions are not stayed, and presumably their rulings are intended to govern until displaced; and leave of the court to continue, presumably to effective judgment, is considered possible.

When, if ever, then, does the doctrine of paramountcy apply in order to suppress provincial law-making authority and the orders issued under provincial law? According to a leading constitutional law authority, "the courts have often disregarded the doctrine of paramountcy and have produced a remarkably inconsistent patchwork of decisions."[129] But some clarity may be possible by thinking in terms of actual orders issued. Given the "express contradiction" test adopted by the Supreme Court as the trigger for the operation of the paramountcy doctrine,[130] it would seem right that an order respecting custody or access made under the *Divorce Act* should render inoperative any order under provincial legislation with which it is inconsistent, which inconsistency is almost certain to be clear on the face of the orders.[131]

---

128   *DA*, above note 4, s. 16, provides for an application by "spouses" and s. 15(1) defines spouse to include a "former spouse." There has been no challenge to the constitutional authority of Parliament to deal with custody of children of divorced spouses after the divorce.

129   P.W. Hogg, *Constitutional Law of Canada* (Scarborough, Ont.: Carswell, 1996) at 654. See also Ontario Law Reform Commission, *Report on Family Law: Part IV, Support Obligations* (Toronto: Department of Justice, 1975) c. 3.

130   *Multiple Access Ltd.* v. *McCutcheon*, [1982] 2 S.C.R. 161 at 191, Dickson J.: "In principle, there would seem to be no good reasons to speak of paramountcy and preclusion except where there is actual conflict in operation as where one enactment says 'yes' and the other says 'no'; 'the same citizens are being told to do inconsistent things'; compliance with one is defiance of the other."

131   Provided, of course, that courts understand that an order by one court for joint custody by the parents, for example, is inconsistent with an order by a second court for sole custody by one of the parents.

The "express contradiction" test would, as suggested earlier, seem to permit the province to make laws respecting custody (and support) applicable to any persons, divorced, divorcing, or otherwise. If both parties were content to seek judgment under provincial legislation, no difficulties would arise. Where, however, divergent applications led to, or had necessarily to result in, inconsistent orders, the application leading to the "federal order" would prevail. This means that, when an order under the *Divorce Act* respecting corollary relief exists or is being sought, there ought to be no reason to apply subsequently under provincial legislation: either the provincial order would be "not inconsistent" and, in which case, otiose, or it would be "inconsistent" and rendered inoperative by the paramountcy doctrine.

Federal law-making jurisdiction, however, is ancillary to its explicit power over divorce; and there are as yet unanswered questions about how long a "divorce" survives, and, so, justifies federal laws respecting custody (and support). The *Divorce Act* simply permits "spouses" and "former spouses" to apply for corollary relief, and the current, reformed provisions evidently provide causes of action, as it were, independent of the core application for the judgment of divorce. But it is a technical view that says two people, once divorced, are forever after a "divorced couple." There will surely come a time, in many if not most cases, when the individuals cease to be "former spouses" and become merely "citizens,"[132] at which time the rationale for granting the federal government legislative jurisdiction will be lost.

FURTHER READINGS

BAILEY, M., & M. GIROUX, *Relocation of Custodial Parents: Final Report* (Ottawa: Status of Women Canada, 1998)

BALA, N., *et al.*, *Spousal Violence in Custody and Access Disputes: Recommendations for Reform* (Ottawa: Status of Women Canada, 1998)

BALA, N., & S. MIKLAS, *Rethinking Decisions about Children: Is "the Best Interests of the Child" Approach Really in the Best Interests of Children?* (Toronto: Policy Research Centre on Children, Youth and Families, 1993)

---

132   See the dissenting judgment of Lamer J. in *Messier v. Delage*, [1983] 2 S.C.R. 401 for similar language used in a different context.

CANADA, DEPARTMENT OF JUSTICE, *Custody and Access: Public Discussion Paper* (Ottawa: Communications and Consultation, Department of Justice, 1993)

GOLDSTEIN, J., *et al.*, *The Best Interests of the Child: The Least Detrimental Alternative* (New York: Free Press, 1996)

LEONOFF, A., & R. MONTAGUE, *Guide to Custody and Access Assessments* (Toronto: Carswell, 1996)

MCLEOD, J.G., *Child Custody Law and Practice* (Toronto: Carswell, 1992) looseleaf service

WILSON, J., *Wilson on Children and the Law* (Toronto: Butterworths, 1994) looseleaf service

CHAPTER 11

FAMILY PROPERTY

A. INTRODUCTION

Part I of Ontario's *Family Law Act*[1] establishes a scheme of deferred sharing of wealth accumulated during marriage.[2] The scheme, in outline at least, is relatively simple, and, perhaps with the exception of its application to pensions, resolves property disputes between most separating spouses without serious problems.

For some, of course, there are difficulties in resolving disputes over property. Wealth is held in a wide variety of complex forms, not all of which lend themselves easily to being accounted for within the terms of the legislation. Then, too, separating couples may choose to fight about money for the reason that there is no other or better way within the legal system for them to express their pain and anger. (And, of course, where there is sufficient wealth to form the ostensible object of a contest, there also will be found the financial means needed to carry on the struggle at law.) As well, because the Act purchases a degree of certainty of outcome

---

1 R.S.O. 1990, c. F.3, as amended by S.O. 1992, c. 32, s. 12; S.O. 1993, c. 27, Sched. [*FLA* or the Act].

2 The scheme applies only to "spouses" as defined in s. 1 of the *FLA*, *ibid.*, which includes married persons and those whose marriages are void or voidable, if the "person asserting a right under this Act" entered into the marriage in good faith. It should also be noted parenthetically that Parliament does not have jurisdiction to make laws affecting property rights, even ancillary to its power over divorce.

at the cost of responsiveness to the circumstances of individual cases, there will be those who try to obtain a more individualized economic justice than is readily available under the main thrust of the scheme.

That main thrust is set out in the purposive subsection of the operative section:

> The purpose of this section is to recognize that child care, household management and financial provision are the joint responsibilities of the spouses and that inherent in the marital relationship there is equal contribution, whether financial or otherwise, by the spouses to the assumption of these responsibilities, entitling each spouse to the equalization of the net family properties, subject only to the equitable considerations set out in subsection (6).[3]

By deeming that in all marriages—"inherent in the marriage relationship"—there is "equal contribution" to the joint responsibilities that make up the enterprise aspect of marriage, the Act seeks to avoid the onerous and dispute-causing task of figuring out who contributed what to the marriage, and how the contributions related to the acquisition of wealth.

The basic structure of the scheme is as follows. Married persons are to share equally the increase in their wealth during marriage. More particularly, upon the functional ending of the marriage, either spouse is entitled to apply for equalization of the net family property. Each spouse calculates the value of all property (with some limited exceptions) he or she owned as of the day the marriage ended; from this is deducted the value of debts and liabilities as of the same date, and also the net value of property brought into marriage (with an exception for any property that turns out to be a matrimonial home). This calculation, essentially, produces a figure for the net family property of each spouse. The two figures are then compared, and the spouse with the greater amount pays half the difference to the spouse with the lesser.

We concern ourselves, then, only with two days: the day marriage began and the day it ended functioning. Marriage essentially becomes, for this purpose, a black box into which we do not see. Property may be acquired, consumed, sold, lost, or otherwise dealt with during marriage; income may be earned, saved, spent; we do not care. With very few exceptions, nothing matters other than that which was there at the beginning and that which survives to the end.

---

3   FLA, ibid., s. 5(7).

Observe that this scheme operates upon a regime of separate property. A spouse may acquire property in his or her own name, or as a co-tenant with the other spouse: the law of property treats spouses by and large as if they were strangers. Thus, during marriage the *FLA* gives one spouse essentially no rights in the property of the other, and each is basically free to dispose of his or her property as if unmarried. Moreover, the equalization scheme in the Act does not directly affect title, but deals instead with value and results in an obligation, an *in personam* right, between spouses.[4] Spouses leave marriage with whatever property they have title to—and a debt owed by one of them to the other.

Finally, the important point ought to be made here that all of the provisions in Part I may be modified by a marriage contract or separation agreement.[5]

B. EQUALIZATION

1) Triggering Events

a) Break-up of the Marriage
Section 5(1) provides that "[w]hen a divorce is granted or a marriage is declared a nullity, or when the spouses are separated and there is not reasonable prospect that they will resume cohabitation" an entitlement arises in the poorer spouse to half the difference between the spouses' net family assets.

Application may be made by either spouse or a former spouse within two years of the judgment of divorce or nullity, or within six years of separation, whichever is the earlier.[6]

b) Death of a Spouse
Where marriage is terminated by the death of one of the spouses and the surviving spouse has the smaller net family property, the survivor is entitled to an equalization payment from the estate of the deceased spouse.[7] Of course, the survivor will be provided for either in a will or,

---

4   *Ibid.*, s. 7(2).
5   *Ibid.*, s. 2(10), says that a domestic contract prevails "unless this Act provides otherwise"; there are no contrary provisions in Part I. A marriage contract, however, that purports to affect a spouse's Part II possessory right in a matrimonial home (see section D, "Possession of a Matrimonial Home," in this chapter) is unenforceable: s. 52(2).
6   *Ibid.*, s. 7(1) & (3).
7   *Ibid.*, s. 5(2).

upon an intestacy, under the *Succession Law Reform Act*[8] and must elect between the entitlement under the will or the *Succession Law Reform Act* on the one hand, and the entitlement under the *FLA* on the other hand.[9] A spouse's will may expressly provide that the survivor shall be entitled both to the gifts under the will and to the entitlements under the Act.[10]

A spouse's election must be made within six months of the death of the other spouse; otherwise he or she will be deemed to have chosen to take the benefits under the will or the *Succession Law Reform Act*.[11]

It is important to note that the survivor's entitlement under the Act has priority over any rights others may have under the will or succession law.[12]

c) Improvident Depletion

Equalization may be also prompted by a spouse where he or she is cohabiting with the other spouse and "there is a serious danger that [the other] spouse may improvidently deplete his or her net family property."[13] The notion here, evidently, is to permit a spouse to protect a portion of the family's assets—essentially what would be his or her share of them were the spouses to separate—from the depredations of the other spouse. Because a spouse may seek equalization upon separation, this provision speaks only to a situation where despite the "improvident depletion" the spouses continue to live together, which means, one supposes, that it will rarely be relied upon.

Clearly, since the Act does not impose a community of property, spouses must be expected to endure the vicissitudes of a life under a regime of separate property within a fairly wide range. The provision would likely apply in situations involving addiction or mental disturbance and diminished capacity; however, it is debatable whether bad

---

8   R.S.O. 1990, c. S.26.

9   *FLA*, above note 1, s. 6(1) & (2). When there is a partial intestacy, the spouse elects between the benefits of the Act and the benefits, combined, of the will and the succession law: s. 6(3).

10   *Ibid.*, s. 6(5).

11   *Ibid.*, s. 6(10) & (11). The time limit may be extended by the court: s. 6(16).

12   *Ibid.*, s. 6(12). There is an exception for gifts under a will made under a contract the deceased entered into for valuable consideration, to the extent of the value of that consideration: s. 6(13).

13   *Ibid.*, s. 5(3). Despite the way in which this provision is worded, spouses do not actually have "net family property" until, in this case, the date of the application under s. 5(3): see the s. 4(1) definitions of "net family property" and "valuation date." It would appear that there are no reported cases dealing with this triggering event.

business judgment, for example, or zealous charity would qualify as "improvidence."

Once a spouse has obtained equalization upon this basis, no further equalization will be possible, even should the spouses later separate.[14]

2) Property

The definition of property in Part I is both broad and unhelpful, boiling down to: "'property' means any interest . . . in . . . property." The definition does make clear that no ordinary variation will take an interest out of the calculation; thus, both real and personal property are included, and all interests whether "present or future, vested or contingent."[15] If any further generalization could be helpful, it might be that the Act seeks to apply in respect of wealth or resources over which a spouse has control sufficient to benefit himself or herself.

It is significant that the definition goes on explicitly to include "the spouse's interest in [a pension] plan including contributions made by other persons." This will often be the largest asset that spouses have, and, because of the variety and complexity of pension schemes, much difficulty has arisen in dealing with this particular kind of contingent future interest.[16]

Canada Pension benefits are "property" within the definition, but the situation is complicated by the fact that the Canada Pension Plan provides for its own division scheme.[17] The solution adopted in practice and by the courts, although not prescribed in the Act, is to exclude CPP benefits from calculations under the Act even so.[18]

There have been a number of attempts to get the courts to characterize "human capital" as property, most typically in the form of professional licences or degrees. Although a few judgments have decided that a future of anticipated earnings may be reduced to or designated as property, most courts have declined to characterize human capital in

---

14 *Ibid.*, s. 5(4). Note that the subsection uses inapt language again in speaking of the court's ordering a "division."

15 *Ibid.*, s. 4(1). The definition of property originates in the scheme that was in place before this one, and there might be difficulties, now that equalization can occur upon the death of a spouse, where the deceased owned a future interest that did not come to fruition. (Note that property is valued as of the day before the death: see section B(3)(a), "Valuation Date," in this chapter.)

16 See section B(3)(c), "Pensions," in this chapter.

17 *Canada Pension Plan Act*, R.S.C. 1985, c. C-8 (as amended by R.S.C. 1985, c. 30 (2nd Supp.), s. 22; 1991, c. 44, s. 6; 1995, c. 33, s. 26) s. 55 ff.

18 *Payne v. Payne* (1988), 16 R.F.L. (3d) 8 (Ont. H.C.).

this way. In *Corless* v. *Corless*[19] a law degree and licence to practice were found to be property, but were also found to have no value because of their lack of marketability. And the finding of the trial judge in *Caratun* v. *Caratun* that the husband's dentistry licence was property was overturned by the Court of Appeal.[20]

At the theoretical level it might make sense to include within the exercise of doing economic justice between the parties the change during marriage in the parties' "value" to the employment market. Such an approach would capitalize everything and would allow a single appropriate sum to be arrived at, the payment of which would satisfy all obligations. From this perspective, it would not matter whether one were dealing with a professional licence, a university degree, or an advancement (or decline) in marketability arrived at in other ways—such as through experience on the job, for example.

However, on a practical level the difficulties with such an approach are evidently too great. First, the future is uncertain in fact. The possession of marketable skills at the present does not mean that the same skills will either exist—illness or injury might intervene, for example—or be marketable tomorrow. Second, an award founded on a particular view of the future might seriously constrain the debtor's freedom to deviate in fact from that future. Third, it is difficult to distinguish between factors that have an influence on marketability and those that do not, and difficult as well to place a value on their impact, particularly where it is an opportunity cost that is to be assessed.[21] Finally, it would often be the case that the value added, so to speak, to a spouse's human capital by the efforts of the other spouse is not returned by the market in fact, and never actually becomes available for payment to the contributing spouse.

---

19   (1987), 58 O.R. (2d) 19 (U.F.C.).

20   (1992), 10 O.R. (3d) 385 (C.A.), leave to appeal to S.C.C. refused [1993] 2 S.C.R. vi, rev'g (1987) 61 O.R. (2d) 359 (H.C.). See also *Linton* v. *Linton* (1988), 64 O.R. (2d) 18 (H.C.), aff'd (1990), 1 O.R. (3d) 1 (C.A.).

21   It is possible, however, to perform similar calculations in respect of persons killed or injured through the fault of another, in order to determine the appropriate measure of damages. It might be that where a defendant can be seen to be blameworthy, we are less concerned about constraining his or her future, and, clearly, more ready to tackle the practical difficulties involved in constructing a future. Of course, in many if not most such tort cases there will be insurance companies standing behind defendants, and so futures might not be so constrained as they would be for a payor spouse.

The fact remains, though, that spouses do contribute to each other's marketablity, and in many cases it would be unjust not to have a significant contribution repaid in some fashion. The Act does in fact provide a way. A distinction is drawn in the statute between capital and income, in the sense that the property provisions intend to deal with accumulated capital and the financial support provisions concern themselves with continuing income for the payee. (Indeed, one of the reasons given for not treating human capital as property under the Act is that to do so would wipe out this legislated line and collapse the two classes into one.)[22] The courts have shown themselves willing, to a degree, at least, to take into account when awarding support the "contribution by the [payee] to the realization of the [payor's] career potential."[23] This approach has the merit of being able to respond to changes in the parties' actual circumstances through time, at least where the award of support is not by way of a lump sum. But because of the vagueness of the rules it would also seem to have the demerit of allowing courts to be lax in acknowledging the extent and worth of women's contributions to men's ability to acquire wealth.[24]

3) Valuation

a) Valuation Date

To arrive at an appropriate equalizing payment, the value of the spouses' property must be determined, and because values may fluctuate over time, the *FLA* fixes a date as of which values are to be calculated.[25] The "valuation date" is the earliest triggering event, whether or not that is the event used as the basis for an equalization claim.[26] Thus, for example, spouses might separate without a reasonable prospect of resumed cohabitation on day 1, but an application for equalization might be made only upon the granting of a divorce on day $1 + n$; valuation day, however, would be the day on which they separated.

---

22 See *Linton v. Linton*, above note 20.
23 *FLA*, above note 1, s. 33(9)(j). See, for example, *Linton v. Linton, ibid.*, and *Ormerod v. Ormerod* (1989), 27 R.F.L. (3d) 225 (Ont. U.F.C.).
24 See generally section C(2)(c)(ii), "Stage Two: Compensatory Support," in chapter 12, "Financial Support."
25 *FLA*, above note 1, s. 4(1): "'Net family property' means the value of all the property . . . that a spouse owns on the valuation date."
26 *Ibid.* See section B(1), "Triggering Events," in this chapter. Note that values are to be calculated as of "close of business on that date": s. 4(4).

In most cases, valuation day will be the date one of the parties dies, because most marriages end by the death of a spouse.[27] The second most common valuation date will be the date of separation, for the reason that separation usually precedes a divorce or nullity application. Separation is a complex human process, and it will often not be easy to fix a date on which the "event" happened—the date on which the "prospect" of reconciliation became too small to be "reasonable," for example—and in disputed cases an element of arbitrariness will likely be present.[28] Where values are relatively steady across the period in question, however, there will be little incentive to worry about the matter, and the spouses will likely be able to agree on a date for the purposes of valuation.

Values may rise or fall significantly between the time of separation and the date of trial or judgment. Where, for example, an asset in the husband's name is worth 100 at the time of separation and 200 at the time of judgment, questions of fairness arise. The Act does not provide an easy means to permit the wife, in the example posed, to share in the rise in the value of the good, even though half of that increase was (presumptively) attributable to value she had put into the common venture, so to speak. Had the equalization been performed promptly upon the end of the marriage, she would have been able to invest her true aliquot portion in whatever way she chose, and thus to participate in the rising market. But because the court has no discretion to determine valuation date in order to achieve substantive aims, such as equity between the parties, valuation date must be the date of separation, and the only value that the court may give the asset is the lower value of 100.

Courts have used a number of means to cope with this difficulty, none entirely satisfactory. It is possible for the court to award pre-judgment interest, but the amount will be set according to the bank rate, which may not compensate for the lost increase in value.[29] And it is possible that an increase in post-valuation date value could constitute

---

27 Note that in this circumstance, the valuation date is "the date before the date on which one of the spouses dies . . .": *FLA, ibid.*, s. 4(1). This has some serious implications, one of which concerns jointly held property: the surviving spouse becomes the sole owner of the asset, by the right of survivorship inherent in the notion of joint tenancy, yet the survivor need only include one-half the value of the asset in his or her family assets because on the day before the death of the other, that was the value of the moiety.

28 See, for example, *Oswell v. Oswell* (1992), 12 O.R. (3d) 95 at 96 (C.A.).

29 *Courts of Justice Act*, R.S.O. 1990, c. C.43, s. 128. See also: *Starkman v. Starkman* (1990), 75 O.R. (2d) 19 (C.A.); S. Grant, "Prejudgment Interest: To Award or Not to Award" (1991) 6 Money and Family Law 41.

"unconscionability" sufficient to license unequal sharing.[30] Finally, the spouse may be found to deserve a share of title to the asset, typically through constructive trust, and so be entitled as an owner to participate in the rise in value of the asset.[31] Because this approach typically involves the use of equity, and constructive trust in particular, it will be considered more fully below, when the role of equity is examined generally.[32]

Where the value of an asset falls between valuation date and trial or judgment, the problem may not be so difficult. The spouse who seeks to take the drop into account is the owning spouse, who had the ability (where the asset was capable of liquidation, certainly) to halt the decline, and may be regarded as the author of his own misfortune. For the same reason, it would typically be unfair to impose a portion of the loss on the non-owning spouse, who lacked the means to deal with the decline. When, however, the loss is attributable to market forces to which the owning spouse was unable to respond effectively, it would be unfair to calculate values as of a date prior to the loss.

b) Fairness

If only because of the *FLA*, ours is a society in which nearly everything must have a value even if it doesn't have a price. Assets come in such variety and such varying degrees of complexity or sophistication that many times it is not easy to fix a value for them. And, of course, the value must be expressed as a number (to two decimal places), so that it can be entered into the arithmetical calculation provided for in the Act: it is not possible simply to say that an asset is probably worth quite a bit, or even somewhere between a hundred and three hundred dollars. Orders of magnitude will not do, but the exactness of dollars and cents cannot ever be wholly justified in the absence of an actual sale. And perhaps not even then, for, as has been pointed out elsewhere, it may be one thing to arrive at a valuation in a commercial context, where each party and his or her advisers need consider only that party's interests, but it is quite another in the family law context where an overarching

---

30   *FLA*, above note 1, s. 5(6). See *obiter* in *Rawluk v. Rawluk* (1987), 61 O.R. (2d) 637 (C.A.), aff'd (but without decision on this point) [1990] 1 S.C.R. 70. See section B(6)(a), "Unconscionability," in this chapter. The Ontario Law Reform Commission has recommended that the Act be amended to permit courts to deviate from equalization where a substantial gain or loss occurred after valuation day and equalization would for that reason be inequitable: Ontario Law Reform Commission, *Report on Family Property Law* (Toronto: The Commission, 1993) at 70–71 [OLRC *Report on Family Property Law*].

31   See *Rawluk v. Rawluk, ibid.*

32   Section E(2), "Under the *Family Law Act*," in this chapter.

concern for fairness and equity is meant to obtain.[33] Indeed, the problem of valuation is one of a number of instances in which ideals that supposedly govern the marketplace run into those that are said to govern families; and spheres of life that are commonly believed to be separate from each other must now interact and be reconciled in some fashion.[34]

The Act does not define value. Courts have most commonly resorted to the relatively familiar concept of fair market value and have attempted to determine what price the asset would fetch in a fair market—that is, one composed of informed, willing purchaser and vendor acting at arm's length and free from compulsion. This notional market is typically operated by having reference to the price that comparable assets actually achieved in a fair market sale.

For there to be a hypothetical sale in the notional market, a great many contingencies may have to be fixed before we can feel confident that the imagined process fairly simulates reality. It may not be at all clear which way this or that vagueness should be clarified, or into what state of certainty this possibility should be collapsed. In short, the whole exercise requires many acts of judgment and means that both expertise and equity are desirable. It has been proposed that the broader term "fair value" most appropriately describes the result of resorting to a notional market in a family property matter.[35]

---

33   This point is made in J. MacDonald & A. Wilton, *MacDonald and Weiler, Family Law Act of Ontario,* Vol. 2, rev. ed. (Toronto: Carswell, 1994) looseleaf service, at v-10 [*MacDonald and Weiler*].

34   See F. Olsen, "The Family and the Market: A Study of Ideology and Legal Reform" (1983) 96 Harv. L. Rev. 1497.

35   See *MacDonald and Weiler,* above note 33, at v-36-7:

> [T]here are many alternative fair values, some of which are listed below: (i) fair market value; (ii) market value; (iii) market price; (iv) value to owner; (v) intrinsic value; (vi) investment value; (vii) liquidation value; (viii) any of the above, with or without the special purchaser premium; (ix) any of the above, with or without a minority discount or premium; (x) any of the above, with or without some other discount or premium for lack of liquidity, lack of marketability, or to accommodate the subjective factors unique to the particular transaction, including the personalities, the intent of the parties, and external financial circumstances. As stated above, there is no one fair value definition or formula that is appropriate to every circumstance. Rather, fair value is to be set at the just and equitable price in the circumstances.

> See also *Menage* v. *Hedges* (1986), 8 R.F.L. (3d) 225 at 245 (Ont. U.F.C.), referring to an article by S. Cole, "Family Law Valuation Comments" in Law Society of Upper Canada Department of Continuing Education, *Valuing Family Property,* 1986.

"Fair value" may also be a more appropriate standard because "fair market value" cannot take into account situations in which the market is constrained or does not exist, or where the personality or special position of the vendor or purchaser has an important impact on value, as it often does in reality. Thus, shares in a closely held corporation, to take a common illustration, do not trade in the ordinary way and might have very little, if any, market value as such, but they may represent a good deal of value to a family member engaged in the operation of an enterprise. Pensions present an even clearer example, perhaps, of where "fair market value" will not work, because there is no market at all in pension benefits due upon retirement, and yet there will probably be a large value in fact to the spouse in belonging to the pension plan.

There is as well the troublesome question of whether the notional costs (such as taxation) of any notional sale should be taken into account, on which point "fair market value" is unhelpful. Is the notional sale to be seen from the purchaser's side, in which case value paid is the measure, or from the vendor's side, in which case value received (after costs) becomes the proper measure? The Act does not offer any direct guidance on the point, and courts have approached the issue in a variety of ways.

The most restrictive view emphasizes the hypothetical nature of notional sales and finds that the contingencies bearing on notional costs are too numerous and difficult to permit sensible estimation and would seem to permit deduction of notional costs only where sale of an asset was proven to be highly likely.[36] The most liberal view yet espoused by an Ontario court would permit the spouses to deduct from the fair market value of their assets the notional tax that each would pay upon a disposition as of valuation date; that is, "[i]n order to equalize value, each spouse's property must be notionally converted to after-tax cash."[37] The Ontario Court of Appeal, rejecting the liberal approach, has said that notional taxes may be deducted only where a sale attracting tax consequences was

---

36 *Dibbley v. Dibbley* (1986), 5 R.F.L. (3d) 381 (Ont. H.C.).
37 *Heon v. Heon* (1989), 69 O.R. (2d) 758 at 775 (H.C). In *Heon* this calculation was seen as part of the fixing of the value of assets. Other courts that have permitted deduction of notional costs have done so under other provisions of the Act: see note 38, below.

probable, and, seemingly, where a sale or liquidation by a payor would be necessary to meet the obligation to make an equalizing payment.[38]

c) Pensions

Pension plans pose a number of difficulties for the scheme under the *FLA*, not the least of which is the determination of a value on the valuation date. The variety of plans is one source of difficulty, but underlying all forms are the problems arising from the "future and contingent nature of pension assets"[39] Before retirement, typically, one is entitled to no benefits under a pension plan, and the amount of benefits one will obtain when the plan begins to pay out will depend upon such things as the choice made about whether to take early retirement or the amount of salary received before retirement.[40]

The difficulties, in fact, are far too many and complex to be aired here, except in brief outline.[41] Indeed, where a pension plan exists, nearly all spouses seeking to deal with property upon breakdown of the marriage will have to obtain the services of an actuary, accountant, or a lawyer in order to calculate what the plan is worth and to determine how to take that value into account generally.

The difficulty with valuation led some courts, when the scheme under the Act was relatively new, to try to finesse the problem by segregating the pension and subjecting it to a separate "if and when" treatment, saying how it would be divided if and when it was ever actually

---

38 *Starkman v. Starkman*, above note 29. It has been pointed out that taking into account the need to make an equalizing payment as part of the process of determining whether such a need exists (i.e., computing net family assets) involves a confusion of categories: see J. McLeod, "Annotation to *Starkman v. Starkman*," *ibid.* See also *McPherson v. McPherson* (1988), 63 O.R. (2d) 641 (C.A.). The court in these cases appeared to treat an admissible notional cost as a "debt" or "liability" to be deducted from the value of an asset in order to produce "net family property." See also *Sengmueller v. Sengmueller* (1994), 17 O.R. (3d) 208 (C.A.), where the court reasoned that it did not matter particularly whether notional costs were treated as a liability or as a factor reducing value.

39 Ontario Law Reform Commission, *Report on Pensions as Family Property: Valuation and Division* (Toronto: OLRC, 1995) at 2 [*Report on Pensions*]. Private sector pensions are governed by the *Pension Benefits Act*, R.S.O. 1990, c. P.8.

40 Valuation difficulties are primarily associated with what are known as defined benefit plans; 91 percent of all pension plan members in Canada belong to this sort of plan: *Report on Pensions, ibid.* at 85 n4.

41 For a full discussion see the *Report on Pensions, ibid.*; L. Coward, *Mercer Handbook of Canadian Pension and Benefit Plans,* 10th ed.(Don Mills, Ont.: CCH Canadian, 1991); and J. Patterson, *Pension Division and Valuation, Family Lawyers' Guide* (Aurora, Ont.: Canada Law Book, 1991).

received.[42] Such an approach, of course, is not correct under the Act, which requires that assets must be valued and permits only net family assets—that is, values—to be equalized, not the actual items of property themselves.

There is, at present, no alternative to the "rough justice"[43] of coming up with an actual value. The probable future income from the pension must be calculated and a present sum is arrived at, which, if invested now, would produce the value of the projected income. The "retirement approach" and the "termination approach" are two methods of calculating the amount of the future income stream.[44] In the former, the court makes the necessary assumptions about retirement, salary increases, and so forth—creates the fictional future, in fact—that will enable a precise value to be determined. The termination method, however, calculates the value on the footing that the employee quits work as of valuation date, and assumptions about income after that date are unimportant (though it remains necessary to make assumptions about other matters, such as retirement date). For the reason of less complexity and because it is felt to be more evidently fair in its exclusion of consideration of post-separation income, courts in Ontario have adopted the termination approach to valuation.[45]

The Ontario Law Reform Commission has made recommendations that the Act be amended to adopt, in regulations, the method for valuing defined benefit pension plans set out in the Canadian Institute of Actuaries Standard of Practice in this respect.[46]

---

42   See *Porter* v. *Porter* (1986), 1 R.F.L. (3d) 12 (Ont. Dist. Ct.); and *Wettlaufer* v. *Wettlaufer* (1988), 12 R.F.L. (3d) 379 (Ont. Dist. Ct.).

43   *Report on Pensions*, above note 39 at 85, quoting E. Roche, "Treatment of Pensions upon Marriage Breakdown in Canada: A Comparative Study" (1986–87) 1 Can. Fam. L. Q. 189 at 215.

44   *Report on Pensions*, above note 39 at 91. There are, of course, various methodological choices to be made even within these approaches. See, for example, *Best* v. *Best* (1997), 35 O.R. (3d) 577 (C.A.), application for leave to appeal to the Supreme Court of Canada granted, S.C.C. Bulletin, 1998, 462, where the termination "value-added" approach was compared to the termination "pro rata" approach.

45   See *Best* v. *Best*, above note 44, and the many cases cited therein. The law in this respect seems sufficiently settled that both parties calculated the pension value using a version of the termination approach.

46   *Report on Pensions*, above note 39 at 268–69; the Actuaries Standard is contained in Appendix B of the Report at 297.

4) Deductions

a) Debts and Liabilities

To arrive at "net family property," the value of property that each spouse owns on valuation date must be reduced by the amount of the "debts and other liabilities" of each spouse on that date.[47] The courts have not required that these debts or liabilities be in connection with any property owned by the spouse.

To some degree, as with the value of property, there may be difficulty in identifying and quantifying debts and liabilities. Where they are the result of commercial dealings or another formal process, as perhaps they most commonly will be, written records will probably clarify the existence and amount of the indebtedness. However, where the arrangement is informal, as it might be among family members, for example, difficulties could arise as to its nature and amount. It is not always easy in such circumstances to distinguish between a gift and a loan; and between spouses, certainly, and between parents and children, there may be a nexus of unclear understandings about transfers of money, goods, or money's worth.[48]

The burden of proof, however, is on the person seeking to establish the debt or liability.[49]

b) Property Brought into Marriage

i) General Scope

The aim of the *FLA* is to ensure that spouses share equally in the increase in wealth during the time of their cohabitation in marriage. Therefore, a spouse's net family property is calculated by deducting not only debts and liabilities on the valuation date but also the net value of property brought into the marriage by the spouse.[50] The assets and debts and liabilities at the time of marriage are valued in current dollars: that is, no attempt has been made by the courts to take inflation into

---

47   *FLA*, above note 1, s. 4(1).

48   It may be relevant in this context that the presumption of advancement from husband to wife has been abolished; except where title is taken in joint names, a presumption of resulting trust applies to transfers between spouses: *FLA, ibid.*, s. 14.

49   *Ibid.*, s. 4(3).

50   *Ibid.*, s. 4(1): Net family property is the value of property owned on the valuation date, after deducting debts and liabilities on that date and: "(b) the value of property, other than a matrimonial home, that the spouse owned on the date of the marriage, after deducting the spouse's debts and other liabilities, calculated as of the date of the marriage."

account. Under the Act spouses are clearly expected to share in the capital gains of assets brought into marriage by each of them, and it may simply be too difficult (and perhaps inapt) to distinguish between increases in value due to inflation alone and those due to other factors.

The only conceptual difficulty raised by this provision has to do with a spouse who enters marriage with more debts than assets: Should the net debt be ignored and the spouse's net value at marriage be treated as nil, or ought the net debt to be treated as a negative deduction, so to speak, and thus as a valuable asset on valuation date. Two reported cases have taken the latter position and have accounted for a spouse's net debt position at the time of marriage.[51]

The Act does not offer any direct guidance on this point. It does say explicitly that a spouse's net family property may not go below zero.[52] This fact, however, can be argued to cut either way: because a spouse's position leaving a marriage cannot be negative, so by analogy the Act must intend that upon entering marriage it cannot be negative;[53] or, because the Act spoke carefully in respect of leaving marriage, it would have done the same in respect of entering marriage if the same result had been intended. The general logic of the Act would argue in favour of treating net debt at marriage as an asset at break-up because, to the extent that the debt is paid during marriage, that repayment will result, in part, from the efforts of the other spouse (diverted to debt repayment from consumption or savings); and to the extent that it survives to break-up, the debt will be treated as a deduction.

ii) The Matrimonial Home

The Act makes an exception of the "matrimonial home." If the asset brought into the marriage is the matrimonial home, it may not be deducted.[54] This provision (and the parallel one respecting excluded property)[55] is unsatisfactory in a number of respects, not the least of which is that it lacks a clear purpose.

---

51   *McDonald* v. *McDonald* (1995), 17 R.F.L. (4th) 258 (Ont. Gen. Div.); *Jackson* v. *Jackson* (1986), 5 R.F.L. (3d) 8 (Ont. H.C.). But see *Menage* v. *Hedges*, above note 35.

52   *FLA*, above note 1, s. 4(5).

53   If the Act, *ibid.*, were not symmetrical in this respect, an odd result might be possible in which a spouse could enter marriage with net debt, and leave with only that "phantom" asset and, consequently, an obligation to make an equalizing payment but no actual means whereby to pay it.

54   *FLA, ibid.*, s. 4(1).

55   See section B(5)(b)(i), "General Scope," in this chapter.

There is no real basis for treating one kind of asset differently from any other kind,[56] and in this case the provision must result in a transfer of wealth from one spouse to another where the transferee can have done nothing to create the wealth (for the reason that it was in existence before the marriage). On the likely assumption that men more often than women will own the matrimonial home, the sole rationale for the exception might be the general desirability of transferring some wealth from men as a class to women as a class, without regard to the equities of particular situations or the evenness of its applications across the groups. But the matrimonial home provision is a crude and haphazard tool indeed to accomplish this, even if such a purpose were regarded as appropriate.[57]

Moreover, the provision operates with seeming arbitrariness—a consequence, in fact, of its unclear purpose. For example, if a matrimonial home worth 100 is brought into marriage, the 100 may not be deducted; but if cash or other property worth 100 is brought into marriage and used the next day to purchase the matrimonial home, a deduction of 100 is possible. In another instance, arbitrariness exists because of the definition of "matrimonial home," which in this context includes only the property occupied by the spouses as their family residence "at the time of separation."[58] Thus, if at the time of separation spouses occupy (in the required fashion) a property brought into the marriage by a spouse, no deduction is possible for that spouse; but if a property brought into the marriage by a spouse is occupied by them (again, in the required fashion) throughout the marriage and is sold (or has its use changed) immediately before separation, it turns out not to have been a matrimonial home that was brought in and so a deduction becomes possible.

The Ontario Law Reform Commission has called for the end to all special treatment for the matrimonial home in Part I of the Act, and,

---

56   The matrimonial home may indeed occupy a special position among assets in that it is the place where the family resided and for that reason has emotional importance to the spouses and the children; but that importance is reflected and dealt with in Part II of the Act, where the right to possession of the matrimonial home is protected. (See section D, "Possession of a Matrimonial Home," in this chapter.) Here, it is "merely" value that is being considered. The 1974 Ontario Law Reform Commission *Report on Family Law, Part IV: Family Property Law* (Toronto: Department of Justice, 1974), upon which the current scheme was ultimately based, recommended automatic joint ownership of the matrimonial home. The Commission's view has now changed: see below note 59 and accompanying text.

57   The broad issue of whether Ontario ought to be a community property regime is not addressed here. In such a regime, however, there is (typically) no "caste" to property, and the matrimonial home is treated like all other assets.

58   *FLA*, above note 1, s. 18(1). (See section D(1), "Definition," in this chapter.)

therefore, to the non-deductibility of that property if brought into the marriage.[59]

iii) Negative Worth

A spouse's net family assets may not go below zero. If the deductions from property would produce a negative sum, the total is deemed to be nil.[60] This is a deviation from the basic theory behind the legislation, in that there is not a complete sharing of the change in value of property during marriage. The rationale for this reluctance, at least as explained by the Ontario Law Reform Commission Report that recommended the current scheme, is that debts may be brought about without any contribution from, or benefit to, the non-debtor spouse, and in circumstances that the non-debtor spouse could not control.[61] Thus, limited sharing was thought appropriate.

It might be appropriate here to make a point about the relevance of ownership under the scheme, because this check on the sharing of debts makes the location of title more important than it might otherwise have been. The point is best made with a few simple examples.

First, assume a situation in which neither spouse has any debts and neither owned any assets or had any debts on the date of marriage. There is one asset worth 100. No matter how that asset is owned, each spouse will walk away from the calculations with 50: if one of them owns the asset, the owner will pay 50 to the non-owning spouse; and if it is jointly owned, each will have net family property of 50 and there will be no equalizing payment.

Now assume that one of the spouses has a debt of 30 on valuation day. If the debtor spouse owns the sole asset worth 100, he or she will pay to the other spouse half of the net family property of 70, leaving each with 35. But if the non-debtor spouse owns the asset of 100, he or she will pay half of that value to the other; and the owner will now leave the calculation with 50. This is so because the non-owning spouse's debt (or other deductions) cannot be shared but can only be used to reduce his or her net family property to zero.

59   *Report on Family Property Law,* above note 30 at 85. Further anomalies resulting from the special treatment of the matrimonial home in Part I of the Act are discussed in this report at 78–81.

60   *FLA,* above note 1, s. 4(5).

61   *Report on Family Law, Part IV: Family Property Law,* above note 56 at 66. See section B(6)(b), "Circumstances," in this chapter, and a qualification to the text above where debts are incurred "for the support of the family."

5) Excluded Property

a) General Scope

In the calculation of net family property, the value of certain property that a spouse owns on valuation date[62] is excluded and, in effect, is not subject to sharing through equalization.[63] Because the value of excluded property does not figure at all in the computation, there is no need, in most cases, to fix a value for it.

Generally speaking, an excluded property may be characterized as being an asset the nature or origin of which takes it out of the theory underlying the duty to share between spouses. Thus, gifts from outside the marriage are windfalls to the donee, value uncaused by either spouse's effort, and, so, nobody's just deserts. Other items—tort damages for certain personal losses, and the proceeds of a life insurance policy—may be seen to be poor surrogates or replacements for lost aspects of the very person of the owning spouse, and for that reason no gains or increase in valuable assets at all. Finally, "[p]roperty that the spouses have agreed by a domestic contract is not to be included in the spouse's net family property"[64] is excluded from the process of sharing values.

Note that the increase in the capital value of excluded property is not to be shared—the *ultimate* value on the valuation date is excluded, not simply the value of the property when first received. It may be thought that although the non-owning spouse could not have contributed to the acquisition of the property and so should not be entitled to a share of the value at the time of acquisition, he or she should share in the increase in value because that could be brought about because of a contribution by the non-owning spouse to the "preservation, maintenance or improvement of the property," to use the language of the Act at another point.[65] Indeed, this is the reasoning behind allowing the

---

62   Strictly speaking there was no need to require that the property to be excluded be owned on the valuation date, because if it was not owned on that date its value would not have been considered in the first place for inclusion into the calculation of net family property. If a portion of excluded property has been dissipated, the value of the surviving portion can be excluded.

63   *FLA*, above note 1, s. 4(1): "'net family property' means the value of all the property, except property described in subsection (2) . . . ." Section 4(2): "The value of the following property that a spouse owns on the valuation date does not form part of the spouse's net family property."

64   *Ibid.*, s. 4(2), para. 6. This provision was unnecessary, given s. 2(10), which provides that "[a] domestic contract . . . prevails unless this Act provides otherwise."

65   *Ibid.*, s. 5(6)(h).

non-owning spouse to share in the increase in capital value of property brought into the marriage by the owning spouse, even though not able to share in the "original" value of the property. It is difficult to justify this divergent treatment of assets,[66] and the Ontario Law Reform Commission has recommended that the Act be amended to provide for the inclusion in the net family property of the owning spouse of the capital gains on excluded property.[67]

b) Gifts

i) General Scope

The value of a spouse's property, other than a matrimonial home, acquired by gift or inheritance from outside the marriage, after the date of the marriage, is excluded from that spouse's net family property. Gifts between spouses are not excluded, although the court may order a payment that is less than equalizing where the donee spouse's net family property is made up so greatly of gifts from the donor spouse that an equalizing payment would be unconscionable.[68]

As implied in the comments in the prior section, the date at which the gift is received is crucial. The value of a gift made before marriage (and brought into marriage) may be deducted from the owning spouse's net family property, but the increase in value during marriage is subject to sharing. Where that same gift is made after marriage, however, the whole value of the gift including capital gain is removed from the sharing process. This element of arbitrariness is not easy to justify.

Further arbitrariness results from the exception made for the value of property that turns out to be a matrimonial home, which may not be excluded from the calculation of net family property. The relevant

---

66   The rationale given in the Legislature was that to permit a sharing of capital gains might compel a donee to sell an heirloom or a gift to which he or she was emotionally attached in order to meet the equalizing obligation. OLRC *Report on Family Property Law*, above note 30 at 74.

67   *Ibid.* at 77. The Commission there points out that this would "effectively end the 'exclusion' of assets from net family property. Rather, all assets will be included in the calculations, but a spouse will be able to deduct from her net family property the value of an asset of the type listed in section 4 (2) at the later of the date of marriage or the date of receipt."

68   *Ibid.*, s. 5(6)(c). But for a different understanding of what was (mistakenly) intended by this provision, see B. Hovius & T.G. Youdan, *The Law of Family Property* (Scarborough, Ont.: Thomson Professional Publishing, 1991) at 402 [Hovius and Youdan].

points are those already made above concerning the special treatment of the matrimonial home in connection with deductions.[69]

ii) Income from Gifts

Although capital gains on gifts made after marriage are not subject to sharing, income from those same gifts is not excluded property unless "the donor or testator has expressly stated that it is to be excluded from the [donee] spouse's net family property."[70] Even if such income is expressly excluded, income on that income is not, and will form part of the owning spouse's net family property. The Ontario Law Reform Commission has recommended that this provision be repealed, with the consequence that income earned on gifts during marriage would always be included.[71] Note that to be excluded (or, for that matter to be included) income must survive as an asset to the valuation date; that is, income spent before that date is ignored by the Act, regardless of whether it was earned on a gift or not.

iii) Added Value

This section (and the one below on tracing)[72] addresses the problems arising from the fact that property may change its form over time. It seems simple enough when a gift is a relatively immutable object—a vase or a painting, for instance—to ascertain that the asset that survived to the valuation date is the same object that was given originally. However, other forms of property are more clearly subject to alteration, whether deliberate or not, over time; and the asset that exists on the valuation date may in some important respects not be the same one that was the subject of the gift.

Where the asset has been subject to degradation or diminution, that portion of the value that survives to the valuation date is excluded, and not the original (*ex hypothesi*) larger value. A gift's value, or a portion of it, may also be lost by being invested in or used as a matrimonial home because excluded property traceable into a matrimonial home may not be excluded.[73]

But what is to be done where the asset has been improved in some fashion and the value thus enhanced? In theory the proper approach is to separate out the value of the improvement from that of the gift with-

---

69   See section B(4)(b)(ii), "The Matrimonial Home," in this chapter.
70   *FLA*, above note 1, s. 4(2) para. 2.
71   *Report on Family Property Law*, above note 30 at 78.
72   Section B(5)(d), "Tracing," in this chapter.
73   *FLA*, above note 1, s. 4(2), para. 5.

out the improvement, and to include the value of the former in the owning spouse's net family assets, excluding only the latter.[74] In practice,
however, it may be difficult indeed to apportion values in this way, particularly where improvement is due to the labour of a spouse or contributions in kind rather than in money. At some point, too, this theory of
apportionment must give way to the legislated policy that the non-owning spouse is not entitled to participate in the capital gains of an
excluded property, even though in fact these may have been in some
sense attributable to the efforts (perhaps indirect) of that spouse.

c) Damages and Insurance Proceeds

Damages (or a right to them) that are personal to a spouse are excluded
from that spouse's net family property. Specifically, the *FLA* identifies
damages for "personal injuries, nervous shock, mental distress or loss
of guidance, care and companionship."[75] Courts have interpreted the
Act to exclude as well payment in hand from a disability pension,[76] but
they have also included Workers' Compensation benefits in hand when
it was decided that they were clearly income replacement payments, and
that the governing provision in the Act goes to general damages for pain
and suffering and not special damages for income lost.[77]

Also excluded from a spouse's net family property are "[p]roceeds
or a right to proceeds of a policy of life insurance, as defined in the
Insurance Act, that are payable on the death of the life insured."[78]

d) Tracing

Property that would be excluded under the *FLA* if it survived to the valuation date may be converted into other forms prior to that time. If it is
possible to trace the excludable property into these new forms, they in
turn may become excluded property.[79] Thus, for instance, a spouse may
receive a gift of money during marriage; if that money, held separate, is
spent to purchase an automobile, which then survives to the valuation
date, the value of that automobile is excluded from the owning spouse's
net family property.

---

74 See: *Oliva v. Oliva* (1988), 12 R.F.L. (3d) 334 (Ont. C.A.); *Andreoli v. Andreoli*
    (1990), 27 R.F.L. (3d) 142 (Ont. Dist. Ct.).

75 *FLA*, above note 1, s. 4(2), para. 3.

76 *Pallister v. Pallister* (1990), 29 R.F.L. (3d) 395 (Ont. Gen. Div.).

77 *Arvelin v. Arvelin* (1996), 20 R.F.L. (4th) 87 (Ont. Gen. Div.).

78 *FLA*, above note 1, s. 4(2), para. 4.

79 *Ibid.*, s. 4(2), para. 5.

6) Unequal Division

a) Unconscionability

Part I of the Act has as its main purpose to recognize the deemed[80] equal contribution of spouses to the assumption of the responsibilities of marriage through equalization of net family properties. This use of a constructed partnership aims at general fairness and the prevention of litigation between spouses. There may, however, be cases where the actual circumstances of the spouses during marriage need to be taken into account in order to prevent serious financial injustice. Courts may "award an amount that is more or less than half the difference between the net family properties" where equalization would be "unconscionable," having regard to any of a number of identified circumstances.[81]

Under the predecessor statute, the term "inequitable" was used to guard an analogous boundary,[82] and the higher standard of unconscionability was brought into the new legislation because of the fear that the relatively greater judicial discretion permitted by "inequitable" would be used to harm the interests of women and reduce their share of net family property.[83] Whether or not that fear was justified, the high threshold has worked to prevent deviation from equalization in all but the exceptional case.[84]

Unconscionability means a situation that shocks the conscience and is so unfair as to "cry out for relief."[85] It is not to be equated with "inequity."[86]

The Ontario Court of Appeal has given section 5(6) an anomalous interpretation in one minor respect that ought to be mentioned here. In a case in which the spouses' net family properties were equal because the wife made a gift to the husband of half of the assets (by making him a joint owner), no equalization payment was required by section 5(1); and, reasoned the court, if there is no equalization payment, then the

---

80   *Ibid.* Section 4(7) speaks of the equal contribution of the spouses as "inherent in the marital relationship."

81   *Ibid.*, s. 4(6).

82   *Family Law Reform Act*, R.S.O. 1980, c. 152, s. 4(4).

83   OLRC *Report on Family Property Law*, above note 30 at 62 n41.

84   See, for example, *Valenti v. Valenti* (1996), 21 R.F.L. (4th) 246 at 255 (Ont. Gen. Div.), Metivier J.: "[I]t is well settled that the court's function does not include a detailed analysis and weighing of the respective contributions of the parties. I agree with Mr. Justice Smith in *Peake v. Peake* (1989), 21 R.F.L. (3d) 364 (Ont. H.C.) that 'unconscionable' is not to be so liberally interpreted as to equate with "inequitable"."

85   *Zabiegalowski v. Zabiegalowski* (1992), 40 R.F.L. (3d) 321 (Ont. U.F.C.).

86   *Valenti v. Valenti*, above note 84.

court does not have the ability under section 5(6) to make that payment more or less than half the difference between the spouses' net family assets.[87] The consequence of this is that in those cases where net family assets are equal, section 5(6) circumstances may not be taken into account even if they amount to an unconscionable situation. The Ontario Law Reform Commission has recommended that the Act be changed to permit an award even where net family properties are equal if the award is necessary to correct an unconscionable situation.[88]

Under the current interpretation of the Court of Appeal, there is no power in the court to do more than give all of the difference between the net family properties to one or other of the spouses.[89]

b) Circumstances

The *FLA* lists seven more or less specific circumstances, and a catch-all set of circumstances, that might make equalization unconscionable.[90] They all appear intended to address or deal with imperfections in, or contraversions of, the assumption of equal contribution upon which the scheme is based. Courts have been concerned to respond, particularly, to those cases in which the identified circumstances are a result of a spouse's bad faith, such as when a spouse incurs debts or disposes of property with the aim of preventing the other spouse from obtaining a proper share of net family property.[91]

---

87 *Berdette v. Berdette* (1991), 3 O.R. (3d) 513 (C.A.), leave to appeal denied (1991), 85 D.L.R. (4th) viii (S.C.C.).

88 *Report on Family Property Law*, above note 30 at 68.

89 *Berdette v. Berdette*, above note 87.

90 They are: (a) a spouse's failure to disclose to the other spouse debts or other liabilities existing at the date of the marriage; (b) the fact that debts or other liabilities claimed in reduction of a spouse's net family property were incurred recklessly or in bad faith; (c) the part of a spouse's net family property that consists of gifts made by the other spouse; (d) a spouse's intentional or reckless depletion of his or her net family property; (e) the fact that the equalization payment would be disproportionately large in relation to a period of cohabitation that is less than five years; (f) the fact that one spouse has incurred a disproportionately larger amount of debts or other liabilities than the other spouse for the support of the family; (g) a written agreement between the spouses that is not a domestic contract; or (h) any other circumstance relating to the acquisition, disposition, preservation, maintenance or improvement of property. These are exhaustive of sorts of circumstances that may be examined for unconscionability: *Berdette v. Berdette*, above note 87.

91 *Ferguson v. Kalupnieks* (1997), 27 R.F.L. (4th) 437 at 441–42 (Ont. Gen. Div.). But see *Filipponi v. Filipponi* (1992), 40 R.F.L. (3d) 296 (Ont. Gen. Div.), where there was no element of bad faith, merely uncontrolled spending.

A relatively recent Court of Appeal decision has made it clear that courts are able to take into account events that occur after separation in deciding whether an equalizing payment would be unconscionable.[92]

7) Distribution

a) Order to Pay

It deserves to be repeated here that the scheme under the *FLA* is not one for the division of property but rather for the division of worth or value. Economic justice between the parties is done with an equalization payment, and, consequently, the appropriate order for the court to make will be an order for the richer spouse to pay the poorer a specified amount.[93] Only unusually will a court go further and order that the debt be satisfied through the transfer of title to property or through the sale of identified property.[94] It is within the court's power to order that security be given for the payment of an equalization order.[95]

b) Instalments

Immediate payment of an order may impose hardship on the payor spouse, particularly where the value of assets has fallen since the valuation date or where they are no longer in existence. Also, many assets may be accorded a value but not in fact be capable of liquidation, such as where, for example, the matrimonial home owned by the payor spouse is the subject of an order for exclusive possession in favour of the non-owning spouse. To avoid hardship the court may order that the equalization payment "be paid in installments during a period not exceeding ten years, or that payment of all or part of the amount be delayed for a period not exceeding ten years."[96]

Two specific circumstances presenting difficulty are examined immediately below.

---

92   *Merklinger* v. *Merklinger* (1996), 30 O.R. (3d) 575 (C.A.).

93   *FLA*, above note 1, s. 9(1)(a).

94   *Ibid.*, s. 9(1)(d). It might be noted that although courts can order transfer of property, they cannot order transfer of debt. A debt is a relationship between a spouse and a third person, and the obligation may not be transferred to the other spouse, in whole or in part, without the agreement of the creditor.

95   *Ibid.*, s. 9(1)(b). Courts may also issue preservation orders to protect a non-owning spouse's interests during pending judgment: s. 12.

96   *Ibid.*, s. 9(1)(c). See also s. 9(3).

c) Pension Plans

Although an interest in a pension plan is clearly "property"[97] to be valued[98] and thus to form part of the basis on which an equalization payment may be ordered, the *FLA* provides no guidance as to how an order to pay might take into account the likely fact that a portion of the payor's assets are inaccessible.[99] A spouse's interest in a plan may, potentially at least, be considerable—indeed, probably the largest item of property owned. Thus, when the value of the plan is anticipated, as it must be under the Act, and a spouse is required to account for that sum to the other, it may be difficult or impossible for the payor spouse to come up with the required sum, even if given the opportunity to make payments over the ten years provided for in the Act.

Courts have developed, and the *Pension Benefits Act* has sanctioned, an "if and when" arrangement, under which a trust is imposed on the plan administrator to pay the appropriate portion of the pension to the non-member spouse, when pension payments in fact begin.[100] The current solution is not wholly satisfactory for reasons that have to do with infelicities in the specific language of the *Pension Benefits Act* (and some inadequacies) rather than with any conceptual difficulty; and the Ontario Law Reform Commission has recommended certain changes.[101]

d) Operating Business or Farm

The *FLA* requires that an order not be made

> so as to require or result in the sale of an operating business or farm or so as to seriously impair its operation, unless there is no reasonable alternative method of satisfying the award.[102]

---

97   *Ibid.*, s. 4(1).

98   See section B(3)(c), "Pensions," in this chapter.

99   The *Pension Benefits Act*, above note 39, makes pension benefits unrealizable until payment out is provided for under the plan.

100 See *Marsham v. Marsham* (1987), 59 O.R. (2d) 609 (H.C.) for an example of an "if and when" trust imposed on the spouse who was the member of the pension plan. Subsequent to this, and similar decisions, the *Pension Benefits Act* was changed in 1988 to permit the imposition of the trust on the plan administrator: now R.S.O. 1990, c. P.8, s. 51. The legislation provides for "if and when" arrangements in a domestic contract as well as in an order.

101 *Report on Pensions*, above note 39 at 45–50, 276–86. "These [concerns] include the lack of security for a non-member spouse, the ongoing interdependency between the spouses, and the failure to provide for an immediate transfer of the pension interest to the non-member spouse at the time of the marriage breakdown. Notwithstanding these inadequacies, the Commission views the general concept of an 'if and when' arrangement as meritorious" (at 45–46).

102 *FLA*, above note 1, s. 11(1).

Instead, the court may order that "one spouse pay to the other a share of the profits from the business or farm" and, where relevant, transfer shares in the business or farm corporation to the payee spouse.[103]

C. AN EXAMPLE OF EQUALIZATION

It may be helpful after the preceding survey to give a simple illustration of the scheme in operation, using the tabular form commonly used by the courts to permit easy calculation.

D. POSSESSION OF A MATRIMONIAL HOME

1) Definition

a) Use
The *FLA* accords special treatment to certain properties identified as "matrimonial homes." In Part I, dealing with equalization of the spouses' net family properties, the value of the matrimonial home is required to be shared because it may not form the basis of a deduction or an exclusion, unless there is a domestic agreement to the contrary.[104] In Part II, the Act creates and protects for the non-owning spouse a possessory right to a matrimonial home, and provides for orders of exclusive possession of such property.

The primary way in which a property becomes a "matrimonial home" is through its use. The section 18(1) definition reads as follows:

> Every property in which a person has an interest[105] and that is or, if the spouses have separated, was at the time of separation ordinarily occupied by the person and his or her spouse as their family residence is their matrimonial home.

---

103   *Ibid.*, s. 11(2).

104   See sections B(4)(b)(ii), "The Matrimonial Home," and B(5)(a), "General Scope," in this chapter. See also the s. 4(1) definition of matrimonial home for the purposes of Part I of the *FLA*, above note 1, which adopts by reference the use-based definition in s. 18. There is no requirement in Part I, or anywhere else in the Act, that a matrimonial home be jointly owned or that title be shared by the spouses.

105   See also *FLA*, above note 1, s. 18(2), which deems ownership of shares in a corporation to be an interest in property, where the shares entitle the owner to occupy a housing unit owned by the corporation.

Net Family Property

	Wife	Husband
1. Sum property owned on the valuation date:	car 3,000 interest in cottage 40,000 RSP 5,000 savings 2,000 furniture 6,000 subtotal: 56,000	interest in cottage 40,000 matrimonial home 140,000 RSP 60,000 furniture 8,000 subtotal: 248,000
2. Deduct debts and liabilities:	Visa balance (1,000) cottage mortgage (13,000) subtotal: (14,000) +56,000 -14,000 42,000	Visa balance (2,000) cottage mortgage (13,000) subtotal: (65,000) +248,000 -65,000 183,000
3. Deduct net value of property at date of marriage:	student loan debt (10,000) jewellery 5,000 subtotal: (5,000)* +42,000 +5,000* 47,000	bonds 12,000 [matrimonial home]** subtotal: 12,000 +183,000 -12,000 171,000
4. Compute difference between net family properties:	(H) 171,000 (W) 47,000 124,000	
5. Divide difference in half and make equalizing payment to poorer:	124,000 / 2 = 62,000 ⟶ wife	

* Note: net debt at marriage becomes an asset included in property
** Note: the matrimonial home cannot be deducted

The definition speaks of "property" rather than of "real property," and includes, therefore, chattels and chattels real (leasehold estates). Thus, mobile homes, boats, and other constructs supporting residence may be matrimonial homes.[106] Spouses may have more than one matrimonial home.[107]

In the context of matrimonial disputes, where the spouses will have separated, it is the "ordinary occupation" as a family residence "at the time of separation" that is important. Thus, a property may have been occupied as a family residence for the whole of the marriage, save for a comparatively short time at the end, and not be a matrimonial home upon separation.[108]

The Act envisages that in some cases the matrimonial home will be only a part of a larger property that is "normally used for a purpose other than residential," in which case "the matrimonial home is only the part of the property that may reasonably be regarded as necessary to the use and enjoyment of the residence."[109] The simplest example might be that of a farm, where only the house and some land around it would be regarded as the matrimonial home.[110]

b) Designation

A second means of influencing whether or not a property is a matrimonial home is designation. The *FLA* permits spouses to designate properties as matrimonial homes and to register the designation. When both spouses designate and register, the designated property becomes (or remains) a matrimonial home, and "any other property that is a matrimonial home under section 18 but is not designated by both spouses

---

106   See *Michalofsky* v. *Michalofsky* (1989), 25 R.F.L. (3d) 316 (Ont. Div. Ct.), aff'd (1992), 39 R.F.L. (3d) 356 (Ont. C.A.).

107   *Da Costa* v. *Da Costa* (1990), 29 R.F.L. (3d) 422 (Ont. Gen. Div.), aff'd in substance (1992), 7 O.R. (3d) 321 (C.A.), amended (1992), 40 R.F.L. (3d) 216n (Ont. C.A.).

108   See, for example, *Folga* v. *Folga* (1986), 2 R.F.L. (3d) 358 (Ont. H.C.), where the house was sold before separation; *Ledrew* v. *Ledrew* (1993), 46 R.F.L. (3d) 11 (Ont. Gen. Div.), where the use changed prior to separation.

109   *FLA*, above note 1, s. 18(3).

110   See, for example, *Leslie* v. *Leslie* (1987), 9 R.F.L. (3d) 82 (Ont. H.C.). It must be remembered that this subdivision is done only for the purpose of arriving at a value or making an order for possession, and not for partition or sale of the property.

ceases to be a matrimonial home."[111] The aims and intricacies of designation, whether by one or both spouses, are better explained within the context of a later section.[112]

2) Possessory Right

When a spouse owns an interest in a matrimonial home, title will be an adequate source of a right to possession. However, if a spouse has no share of title, the *FLA* provides the spouse with a right to possession equal to that of the owner spouse.[113] This right is personal as between spouses, rather than a right *in rem*, and ends "when they cease to be spouses, unless a separation agreement or court order provides otherwise."[114]

The statutory right to possession appears to have three functions. The first is one of reassurance for the non-owning spouse, and placement of the spouses on an equal footing during the marriage, regardless of how title to the matrimonial home is held. A non-owning spouse is not to be a second-class occupant, or a mere licensee of the owning spouse. Second, the right can be seen as the logically necessary starting point that enables a non-owning spouse to apply for an order of exclusive possession, should the spouses be unable or unwilling to cohabit. Finally, the right and its associated protections operate as a clog on title, which may to some degree work to preserve the asset for the Part I equalization process. The last two functions are examined immediately below.

3) Alienation of a Matrimonial Home

A spouse may not "dispose of or encumber an interest in a matrimonial home" unless the other spouse agrees.[115] Where a spouse acts without

---

111 *FLA*, above note 1, s. 20(1) & (4). Designation does not create or define matrimonial homes for the purposes of equalization of net family properties under Part I: s. 4(1) defines matrimonial home within Part I to mean property meeting the requirements of s. 18.

112 See section D(3), "Alienation of a Matrimonial Home," in this chapter.

113 *FLA*, above note 1, s. 19(1). Note that spouses may not contract out of this Part II possessory right and associated protections in a marriage contract: s. 52(2).

114 *Ibid.*, s. 19(2). Because spouses cease to be spouses on the death of one of them, the Act provides that the survivor who has no share of title may continue to occupy the matrimonial home (as against the deceased's estate) rent free for sixty days after the death: s. 26(2).

115 *Ibid.*, s. 21(1). The other spouse may "consent" or show agreement by: "joining in the transaction" (s. 21(1)(a)); by having "released all rights under this Part by a separation agreement" (s. 21(1)(b)); or by having joined in a registered designation of another property as the matrimonial home (s. 21(1)(d)). There is also provision for a court to intervene and authorize the transaction: ss. 21(1)(c) & 23.

the agreement of the other, the transaction may be set aside unless the transferee was a bona fide purchaser for value without notice at the time of acquisition that the property acquired was a matrimonial home.[116] If this were the extent of it, both non-owning spouses and prospective purchasers of property would be unhappy. The former would fear that innocent purchasers might be easy to find, and the latter that actual innocence could be hard to prove and makes too precarious a basis for good title. There are further provisions, however, that seek to meet these concerns.

For prospective purchasers the difficulty is in being able, easily and reliably, to learn whether a property is a matrimonial home. Although a spouse's Part II possessory interest is said to be personal against the other spouse and not a right *in rem*,[117] it nevertheless is given the capacity to affect title in the purchaser's hands. But in most instances this "equity" will not be registrable, and a prospective purchaser could not find it in a title search. Thus, other means must be provided to ensure positively that purchasers can know—that is, get notice of the fact— that the property is *not* a matrimonial home.

The means is supplied by permitting a purchaser to rely on a statement by the vendor "verifying" one of a number of factual circumstances that, if true, would mean the property was not a matrimonial home: such a statement "shall . . . be deemed to be sufficient proof that the property is not a matrimonial home."[118] If, however, the purchaser had "notice to the contrary," the statement will not be sufficient proof, and the transaction may be set aside.[119] The "contrary" here would seem to refer to the specific fact alleged in the statement and not principally to the complex legal fact of the status of the property as a matrimonial home.

None of this protects the non-owning spouse, of course. Indeed, it means that a dishonest owner spouse can fairly easily transfer title to the matrimonial home. The Part II possessory right is protected by the possibility of designation and registration of that designation. Where a property is designated, by one or both spouses, as a matrimonial home, registra-

---

116   *Ibid.*, ss. 21(2) & 23(d). Notice that the transferee does not have to receive a legal (as opposed to an equitable) estate.

117   *Ibid.*, s. 19(2)(a).

118   *Ibid.*, s. 21(3). The statement may "verify" that the vendor is not a spouse, that at the critical time the property was not ordinarily occupied as the family residence, that the other spouse has released Part II rights in a separation agreement, or that another property is designated as a matrimonial home.

119   *Ibid.* The requirement speaks of "notice," which is not restricted to "actual" notice, but encompasses notice in all its forms.

tion of that designation should ensure that any prospective purchaser has notice sufficient to permit a wrongful transaction to be set aside.[120]

The Act draws a distinction between designations by both spouses and those by one spouse alone. The latter is simply provided for, not elaborated on, and must be assumed to work basically as a notice-giving device when registered.[121] A joint designation, however, has the ability to cause the designated property to become a matrimonial home, even if it would not otherwise (under section 18) qualify as one.[122] And, equally important, a registered joint designation suppresses the matrimonial home status of all other properties that would otherwise qualify under the section 18 definition.[123] This means that when there is agreement between the spouses, properties can be freed up to be dealt with by the owner without the need to seek the consent of the other spouse for each transaction.

4) Exclusive Possession

A spouse may apply for an order of exclusive possession of the matrimonial home, which order may persist for any "period that the court directs."[124] The court is to consider certain factors in making the determination, which may be conveniently grouped under three headings.

---

120 See, for example, the *Registry Act*, R.S.O. 1990, c. R.20, s. 74(1), which provides that registration constitutes notice of the instrument registered. Given that a purchaser must avoid "notice" of all forms, this should suffice to oblige a prospective purchaser to make further inquiries or be found to have constructive notice.

121 There is, of course, the risk that a spouse might wrongly designate a house, without the knowledge of the other spouse; a court may cancel the designation in such a case: *FLA*, above note 1, s. 23(e).

122 Oddly, this capacity must be inferred from other provisions, principally from those that say (or must be interpreted to say) that when a designation is cancelled, a designated property loses its status as a matrimonial home unless s. 18, *ibid.*, makes it one: s. 20(6) & (7). Presumably, although spouses may designate "property owned by one or both of them as a matrimonial home," they may designate only property that would be capable of being used as a residence; that is, they could not designate the lawnmower as a matrimonial home. This section is badly drafted in a number of respects.

123 *FLA, ibid.*, s. 20(4). When only one spouse designates a property, there is no comparable suppressive effect: s. 20(5).

124 *Ibid.*, s. 24(1). The order can stay in force even though the named persons have ceased to be spouses, through divorce, for example. Absent such an order (or a provision in a separation agreement), a spouse's possessory right under the Act ends when he or she ceases to be a spouse: s. 19(2)(b).

The first is "the best interests of the children affected," particularly the "possible disruptive effects on the child of a move," and the "child's views and preferences."[125]

Another set of factors has to do with financial or economic matters and is concerned with whether an order for exclusive possession would be practicable and consonant with doing economic justice between the parties. The court must consider the financial circumstances of the spouses, orders respecting equalization of net family property, and the relevant housing market.[126]

The third pertinent matter is "any violence committed by a spouse against the other spouse of the children."[127] The ability of a court to act on this basis may help to protect a spouse or children from an abuser by excluding that person from the matrimonial home.

It is often difficult to make decisions on the issue of exclusive possession because a court is asked, in effect, to compare apples and oranges. For example, there is no guidance in the Act as to how much financial difficulty may be imposed on (typically) the owning spouse in order to meet the children's interests, or how much difficulty children must endure in order to permit the owning spouse to have access to the property for sale or other use.

E. THE ROLE OF COMMON LAW REMEDIES

1) With Respect to Unmarried Persons

a) Unjust Enrichment

The *FLA* does not currently address property rights between unmarried couples.[128] Over the last couple of decades, however, the courts have developed the doctrines of unjust enrichment and constructive trust in such a way as to require sharing of property or wealth in many cases

---

125   *Ibid.*, s. 24(3)(a) & (4).
126   *Ibid.*, s. 24(3)(b), (c), & (e). The court must also consider any written agreement between the parties: para. (d).
127   *Ibid.*, s. 24(3)(f).
128   See note 2, above. The Ontario Law Reform Commission has recommended that the scheme of sharing property values be extended to cohabiting couples: see section D(1), "The Definition and Rights of a Spouse," in chapter 4, "Cohabitation." In its failure to provide property rights to cohabiting couples, the Act may be in violation of their *Charter* rights: *Miron v. Trudel*, [1995] 2 S.C.R. 418; *Canadian Charter of Rights and Freedoms*, Part 1 of the *Constitution Act, 1982*, being Schedule B to the *Canada Act 1982* (U.K.), 1982, c. 11 [*Charter*].

between persons who have cohabited. It is not possible in the context of this book to explore all the issues necessary for a full understanding of the important restitutionary principles and remedies, and what follows will be merely a brief description of the doctrines and some of the difficulties they engender.[129]

The doctrine of unjust enrichment, which is the heart of remedial efforts in this context, may be best described in the words of Dickson J. in *Pettkus* v. *Becker*: "[T]here are three requirements to be satisfied before an unjust enrichment can be said to exist: an enrichment, a corresponding deprivation and absence of any juristic reason for the enrichment."[130] In that case Ms. Becker supported Mr. Pettkus, with whom she was living, for a number of years while he saved money in order to buy a bee-keeping business and farm, and then she worked on the farm for fourteen years without remuneration. At the end of their twenty-year relationship, Ms. Becker was left with no payment and no share of title to the property. The Supreme Court decided that there was unjust enrichment in this case and that Ms. Becker was entitled to a remedial constructive trust in the farm to the extent of half its value.[131]

There have been a great many instances in which this doctrine has been applied in order to do justice between cohabiting persons. In the course of these decisions, a number of problems have been identified and addressed. Some of these will be discussed under two headings: problems associated with the nature of the contribution, and problems associated with the nature of the parties' expectations. The lesson they all teach is that common law remedies are lesser remedies when compared to the scheme provided in the Act for the division of value between married persons.

b) The Nature of the Contribution

i) Directness
As the simple formula from *Pettkus* v. *Becker* makes clear, it is essential that, in effect, something of value passes from the plaintiff to the defendant: the defendant must be enriched, and the plaintiff must undergo a

---

129 For a somewhat fuller description, see OLRC *Report on Family Property Law,* above note 30 at 19–40.

130 [1980] 2 S.C.R. 834 at 848.

131 It should be noted that Ms. Becker never in fact recovered anything whatever from Mr. Pettkus, who resisted successfully the Supreme Court judgment. She died by her own hand, penniless: "Woman's Suicide Ends Fight for Rights" *The Globe and Mail* (12 November 1986) A1; O. Ross, "Ontario Fee System Cited in Woman's Legal Woe" *The Globe and Mail* (13 November 1986) A10.

deprivation that *corresponds* in some way to that enrichment of the plaintiff. This correspondence does not mean that a thing of value must go directly from the plaintiff's pocket into the defendant's pocket; it can find its way there with some indirection, such as when it is invested in an object owned by the defendant, for example, as it was in fact in the case, when the plaintiff's valuable labour was invested in the operations of the business.

There is a problem about how circuitous or indirect the route may be and still have the plaintiff's contribution be recognized as a contribution—as a source of enrichment. This is the problem of directness. In many cases it is solved in a kind of primitive way associated with physical proximity, by assuming that, for example, labour on a site is a direct enrichment of that site or the business located there. The trouble is that because everything is in fact connected to everything else, we cannot easily isolate causes without a frame or a matrix that directs us to ignore certain linkages and pay attention to others.

The courts have not found an entirely satisfactory matrix or set of guiding limitations. The injunction typically is to pay attention only to those contributions that are "sufficiently substantial and direct."[132] More interesting, perhaps, are the references in the cases to the impact of certain acts within the matrix of "a relationship tantamount to spousal"[133] or "a quasi-matrimonial situation."[134] Thus, in this context it becomes clearer, perhaps, that loving childcare is valuable work, and, more important, that its assumption by one spouse frees the other from what would otherwise be his obligation to care for the children, which freedom is valuable and often results in financial gain.[135]

ii) Choice of Remedy

If originally there was some confusion of the notions of unjust enrichment and constructive trust, it is now much clearer that unjust enrichment

---

132   *Pettkus v. Becker*, above note 130 at 852.

133   *Ibid.* at 849.

134   *Peter v. Beblow*, [1993] 1 S.C.R. 980 at 988.

135   See, for example, *Peter v. Beblow*, *ibid.* This last point is related to whether certain behaviour possesses value of the right "sort" to be counted as a contribution. Our courts once took the view that certain conduct by women was the performance of wifely duty rather than a contribution towards enrichment: see, for example, *Murdoch v. Murdoch*, [1975] 1 S.C.R. 423. In the current parlance of unjust enrichment law, there must be no otherwise satisfactory "juristic reason" for the enrichment in order for it to be unjust; thus, the behaviour might be a loan or a gift (but no longer, it seems, the "mere" performance of a marital duty) and not, therefore, count as a contribution.

may be remedied in various ways, only one of which is through the construction of a trust interest in property. Monetary compensation—a species of *quantum meruit* for services rendered—will be the ordinary relief to be given, and only where money would be insufficient will constructive trust be considered.[136] Moreover, for a constructive trust to be created "there must be a link between the services rendered and the property in which the trust is claimed."[137] This is a problem similar to that of directness discussed above.

It appears that, in a family context at least, insufficiency and the linkage may be demonstrated by the (same) circumstance that the spouse's efforts forge or invoke an associative bond between them and a property, as when, in *Peter* v. *Beblow*, home-making and "motherly" activities resulted in a constructive trust in the matrimonial home, or when farm work by a spouse results in a share of the farm.[138]

In theory, it may not matter much to the claimant whether money or property is awarded. However, in practice the way in which the contribution is valued may make the difference important. In *Peter* v. *Beblow*,[139] the majority chose to value the contribution that gave rise to a constructive trust by putting a current value on the property subject to the trust. This is the "value survived" approach. The rejected method, more suitable to valuation where monetary compensation is to be awarded, was the "value received" approach, in which one places a value on the contribution (typically, services) directly. Depending on the vagaries of the market, either may be advantageous to a claimant; however, the contribution is very commonly made in the form of domestic services or labour, and there is the real risk that the court will not place an adequate value on these if considered directly.

iii) Quantum
Whatever the chosen form of remedy, the court must come up with a precise number to value and recompense the deserving spouse. In the commercial context, a buyer and seller fix a price that is exact to two

---

136 *Peter* v. *Beblow, ibid.*

137 *Ibid.* at 997.

138 See *Sorochan* v. *Sorochan*, [1986] 2 S.C.R. 38, where a wife worked on the husband's farm performing farm work and domestic work. In that case, the farm was already owned in full by the husband, so no effort by the wife could be a contribution to its acquisition; however, the court found that her efforts were a contribution to its preservation and maintenance, and entitled her to a constructive trust.

139 Above note 134.

decimal places, but they never have to justify the figure. Here, neither fixing nor justification is easy. Where compensation is to be the remedy, the court can sometimes look at the market price for the value received by the enriched spouse, and fix a sum in that way. But there is no market—no fair market, one might say—for many services performed by spouses within the family.

Where the remedy is to be an interest in property through constructive trust, the extent of that interest must be determined. The theory is that the court should examine those substantial and direct contributions to the property (or in respect of the property, perhaps) and "determine what portion of that property is attributable to the claimant's efforts."[140] It is interesting to note the calculus used by Dickson J. in *Pettkus v. Becker*.[141] He comments on the disparity in the physical size and strength of the parties, observes that both gave the enterprise their all, and concludes therefore that each is entitled to a half share of the bee-keeping farm. This is clearly a way of determining worth that is not reflected in the market, where pay is often if not always a function of how much work a person can perform in a day, rather than the percentage of available effort expended. It may, however, be a more appropriate method for distributing resources within the non-arm's-length economy of a family.

c) The Nature of Expectations

The injustice in unjust enrichment is said to arise

> where one person in a relationship tantamount to spousal prejudices herself in the reasonable expectation of receiving an interest in property and the other person in the relationship freely accepts the benefits conferred by the first person where he knows or ought to have known of that reasonable expectation . . .[142]

The difficulty with this formulation, and those like it,[143] is that it may be impossible to discern what people's expectations are in such relationships. People who live and work together have hazy, unvoiced expectations; they may imagine a life together probably in which a principle of free sharing operates without concern about *meum* and *teum*; they may have clear expectations but fear to raise them with the partner for good

---

140   *Ibid.* at 999.
141   *Pettkus v. Becker*, above note 130.
142   *Ibid.* at 849.
143   "In every case the fundamental concern is the legitimate expectations of the parties." *Peter v. Beblow*, above note 134 at 990.

reasons or bad; or these and other mental states may alternate over time. Whatever is the actual case, the parties will rarely possess and communicate the sharply defined expectations that are associated with transactions in the marketplace, against which, seemingly, family dealings are to be compared.

Courts have shown, however, a fair degree of willingness to substitute the expectations of reasonable persons for those of the parties, even as they state the requirement that there be expectations in fact. Constructed expectations are as necessary to the process of doing justice in a family-like context as constructive trust and other creative remedies, given the inequality in power between men and women that still persists and the continuing social pressure to regard women's efforts as properly located at home, where one is "released" from the "burdens" of worrying about the market's need to put a price on everything.

2) Under the *Family Law Act*

In the case of *Rawluk* v. *Rawluk*, the Supreme Court decided that the scheme under the *FLA* does not prevent a married spouse from seeking a restitutionary remedy under the common law.[144] The facts were that the properties owned by the husband increased dramatically in value after the valuation date, and the Act did not appear to provide a means of permitting the wife to participate in this rise in value.[145] The Supreme Court's solution was to permit the wife to obtain an interest under a constructive trust in the relevant properties, and as an owner claim her share of the current value.

Although it may have been just to permit Mrs. Rawluk to gain a share of the post-valuation date rise in value,[146] it was wrong to do so in this way. Both the Act and the doctrine of unjust enrichment aim to achieve financial or economic justice between cohabiting persons; where the Act is available to a claimant, there is no need to make another set of remedies available as well, particularly when these differ in substantial ways from the scheme enacted by the legislature. The court, however, was able to reconcile the two bodies of remedial law, and found that the Act actually contemplated the use of the remedial

---

144 [1990] 1 S.C.R. 70.
145 See section B(3)(a), "Valuation Date," in this chapter.
146 For one reason, because she did not receive her equalizing payment promptly upon separation from her husband, and so was unable to profit from the investment of these assets; and, perhaps, for another, because the Act does not go far enough to institute a community of property regime.

constructive trust.[147] The Ontario Law Reform Commission has recommended that the Act be amended to preclude a spouse from applying for common law relief of the sort just discussed.[148]

The way in which the court analysed the problem resulted in their finding that a spouse might invoke the remedy of constructive trust at the point in the equalization scheme where the value of property owned is calculated. That is, it saw constructive trust as part of the equitable property law used to determine title. This does not mean, however, that all spouses are compelled to do a restitutionary analysis before undergoing the analysis required by the Act. There will be a limited number of circumstances, apart from a post-valuation date rise in value, where the two bodies of law can sensibly intersect.

There are few occasions when ownership is important under the Act in the determination of the equalization payment.[149] In the ordinary course of events, all property is valued and taken into account, such that if one spouse is accorded title the other will receive half the value of the asset. However, there may be cases in which it would benefit a spouse to keep an asset (or as much of it as possible) out of the ownership of the other spouse because of the deductions available to that other spouse. Because net family property cannot go below zero, the other spouse can gain by taking property to place it in his or her "column," where the other spouse's debt or other deductions cannot be set off against it (or against other sharable property).[150]

Another circumstance where ownership becomes important is where the property in question would otherwise be excluded property and not taken into account at all. If a spouse without original title to the excluded property were able to show that he or she had acquired an interest in it, the value of that portion, at least, would be subject to sharing.

---

147   It found, for example, that the Preamble to the Act, which speaks of "the orderly and equitable settlement of the affairs of spouses" and the fact that marriage is "a form of partnership," recognizes and accommodates the remedial constructive trust because "[t]hese fundamental objectives are furthered by the use of the constructive trust remedy in appropriate circumstances."

148   *Report on Family Property Law*, above note 30 at 150.

149   It may be, of course, that ownership will be important to a spouse for non-monetary reasons.

150   See section B(4)(b)(iii), "Negative Worth," in this chapter.

FURTHER READINGS

FREEDMAN, A., & S. COLE, *Property Valuation and Income Tax Implications of Marital Dissolution* (Toronto: Carswell, 1991) looseleaf service

HOVIUS, B., & T.G. YOUDAN, *The Law of Family Property* (Scarborough, Ont.: Thomson Professional Publishing, 1991)

MACDONALD, J., & A. WILTON, *MacDonald and Weiler, Family Law Act of Ontario*, Vol. 2, rev. ed. (Toronto: Carswell, 1994) looseleaf service

ONTARIO LAW REFORM COMMISSION, *Report on Family Property Law* (Toronto: The Commission, 1993)

ONTARIO LAW REFORM COMMISSION, *Report on Pensions as Family Property: Valuation and Division* (Toronto: The Commission, 1995)

CHAPTER 12

FINANCIAL SUPPORT

A. INTRODUCTION

When a family member is in need, there may be an obligation upon a spouse or a parent[1] to provide financial support.[2] It is likely the case that while the family is intact, and while family members are residing together, needed support will be forthcoming without resort to law.[3] However, when families break up, it will commonly be necessary to provide formally for the payment of support, often as part of a more com-

---

1   As well, to the extent they are able, adult children are obliged to support their parents who are in need, where in the past the parent "has cared for or provided support for the child": s. 32, *Family Law Act* R.S.O. 1990, c. F.3, as amended by S.O. 1992, c. 32, s. 12; S.O. 1993, c. 27, Sched., S.O. 1997, c. 20 [*FLA*]. Actions under this section are very rare, but see: *Skrzypacz* v. *Skrzypacz* (1996), 22 R.F.L. (4th) 450 (Ont. Prov. Div.); *Godwin* v. *Bolsco* (1993), 45 R.F.L. (3d) 310 (Ont. Prov. Div.), aff'd (1995), 16 R.F.L. (4th) 419 (Ont. C.A.).

2   The terms "maintenance" and "alimony" are no longer used to describe transfer payments between family members.

3   Nothing in the *FLA*, above note 1, appears to prevent a spouse or a child from suing for support while residing with the payor. The *Divorce Act*, S.C. 1986, c. 4, as amended by S.C. 1990, c. 18, ss. 1 & 2; S.C. 1992, c. 51, s. 46; S.C. 1993, c. 8, ss.1–5; S.C. 1993, c. 28, s. 78; S.C. 1997, c. 1, ss. 1–15 [*DA*], the other source of legal obligation, contemplates a divorce as a precondition to any support obligation; and while divorced persons may live together, it seems unlikely that they would.

prehensive reorganization of affairs. Too, it may be necessary to resort to law to obtain or formalize support for a child in situations where the parents have never lived together.

Although support and property obligations are conceptually distinct, they may overlap in practice a good deal. Matrimonial property law looks to the proper redistribution of assets between spouses in the light of past behaviour—transfers of title, expectations aroused, and effort expended in relation to goods or land. Support law, by contrast, seeks to deal with circumstances as they exist now or in the near future, and has traditionally been seen as a coping mechanism rather than as a means for doing economic justice between the parties.

Yet financial support obligations between spouses are coming to depend more and more on an ethic of deservingness that is rooted in the parties' past; and support is used with increasing frequency to remedy economic injustice resulting from cohabitation, especially where there are insufficient assets available to do the job upon break-up. Moreover, from the perspective of the payee, it may not matter much how the transfer of wealth is justified conceptually, so long as the payment is made.

Child support and spousal support obligations are founded on different bases, and so the courts treat these duties and the payments under them as being separate;[4] that is, there is no general "family" support obligation. But it is not easy to disentangle a child's circumstances and needs from those of the custodial spouse to arrive at the separate budgets necessary to justify two orders for two precise sums. Again, from the point of view of the custodial parent receiving support, the practical fact is that the money usually goes into a common fund or budget whatever its label.

With child support, there is little if any debate about the existence of the obligation: it is understood that parents are expected to support their children. The discussion is about the amount of any order, particularly in relation to the payor's means. New child support guidelines will now redirect that debate into the specific terms of the legislation, which will be examined below.

There is debate, however, about when spousal support is owed. Historically, spousal support was simply a duty of marriage and not required to have an independent justification. The right and corresponding obligation arose concretely where the payor had been guilty of a matrimonial offence and the payee was blameless and thus entitled

---

4   The *DA*, *ibid.*, as recently amended, now requires that child support and spousal support be treated distinctly as well: s. 2(1).

to live separately, when a support payment would be needed. After the move away from fault as a basis or pretext for legal action, the notion was retained that support was an obligation arising out of marriage (or marriage-like relationships), and, in a formulation found in Ontario's legislation today, the duty was made simply to turn on need and the ability of the other spouse to meet that need.

However, courts and legislatures have increasingly found it necessary to justify imposing support obligations on spouses; the simple fact that one was married to a person is no longer felt sufficient, in every case certainly, to explain why or to what degree one is required to support that person. The various theories that are in contention will be explored below.

There is, too, a problem that arises from the fact that, as with child custody, both the federal Parliament and the provincial legislatures have constitutional jurisdiction to make laws respecting support. Ontario law respecting child support, however, has been changed to correspond closely to the federal law.[5] The situation is less drastic with respect to spousal support, and although there are differences in language between the two relevant statutes, the courts appear to be treating them as raising the same issues of principle. This matter will be examined in more detail below.

Finally, it should be noted that there have been severe and persistent problems concerning the compliance with and enforcement of support orders. A great many orders are seriously in arrears, and recent cutbacks by the Ontario government to the scheme put in place for the enforcement of orders have made the situation worse. Legislative changes at both the federal and provincial levels aim to provide support enforcement agencies with greater access to information concerning defaulters and with greater legal powers to exact compliance.[6] The enforcement of orders will not be examined further in this book.[7]

---

5   *FLA*, above note 1, as amended by S.O. 1997, c. 20, s. 1.

6   See: *Family Orders and Agreements Enforcement Assistance Act*, R.S.C. 1985, c. 4 (2nd Supp.), as amended by S.C. 1992, c. 1, s. 66; S.C. 1993, c. 8, ss. 6–9, 10(1)–(5), 11, 12, 14–18(1)–(3); S.C. 1996, c. 11, ss. 95, 97, 99; S.C. 1997, c. 1, ss. 16–23; and *Family Responsibility and Support Arrears Enforcement Act*, 1996, S.O. 1996, c. 31.

7   For enforcement of orders, see A.C. Wilton & J.S. Miyauchi, *Enforcement of Family Law Orders and Agreements: Law and Practice* (Toronto: Carswell, 1989) looseleaf service.

B. CHILD SUPPORT

1) Sources of Law

a) The *Divorce Act*

i) *The Obligation*

Spouses have a joint obligation to support their children "in accordance with their relative abilities to contribute to the performance of that obligation."[8] Note that "spouse" includes "former spouse," meaning that the obligation to support children under the *Divorce Act* is not fixed only at the time of divorce and is not lost upon divorce.[9] A court may make an order requiring a spouse to fulfil this obligation—that is, to pay child support—on the application of either or both spouses.[10] The order is to be made "in accordance with the applicable guidelines."[11]

The use of guidelines is new and represents a departure from the traditional Canadian approach in which judicial discretion was used to do what was right and reasonable in the particular case. Under the *Federal Child Support Guidelines*[12] a spouse's obligation is supposed to be (by and large) fixed mechanically according to a table, on the bases of his or her annual income and the number of children for whom support is owed. This approach aims, in the words of the Guidelines:

(a) to establish a fair standard of support for children that ensures that they continue to benefit from the financial means of both spouses after separation;

(b) to reduce conflict and tension between spouses by making the calculation of child support orders more objective;

(c) to improve the efficiency of the legal process by giving courts and spouses guidance in setting the levels of child support orders and encouraging settlement; and

---

8   *DA*, above note 3, s. 26.1(2).

9   *Ibid.*, s. 15. It also makes clear that more than two adults may wind up being obliged to support a child under the *Divorce Act*—a custodial spouse, her current spouse, and her former spouse, for example—though perhaps only in subsequent actions.

10 *Ibid.*, s. 15.1(1). Both spouses would apply when there is an agreement and they seek a consent order: see section B(2)(d)(i), "Agreement and Consent Orders," in this chapter.

11 *Ibid.*, s. 15(3).

12 SOR/97-175 [Guidelines].

(d) to ensure consistent treatment of spouses and children who are in similar circumstances.[13]

The tables, which are the heart of the Guidelines, prescribe amounts that are based on studies of what parents in families at different economic levels actually spend on children.[14] The amount payable by the non-custodial spouse is independent of the income of the custodial spouse, on the theory that children are to benefit from the income of both spouses as they would if the spouses were living together. By basing the tables on amounts that a parent at a particular income level would be likely to spend on his or her children within an intact family, the Guidelines seek to minimize the financial effects of family breakdown on children.

The *Divorce Act* provides that the federal Guidelines are to be used, unless the province in which both spouses reside at the time of application has passed its own set of comparable guidelines.[15]

A number of factors set out in the Guidelines can affect whether the court may order an amount that is more or less than the normal amount, which is essentially that prescribed in the appropriate table together with an amount for some special expenses. These factors will be considered below. Taken as a whole, the qualifications and exceptions describe a scheme of considerable complexity, and the important issue will be whether they have so compromised the basic rule that the main aims of objectivity and predictability have been lost.

ii) Children of the Marriage

The obligation on spouses is to support "children of the marriage," defined to turn on combinations of three circumstances: the child's age, independence, and relation to the payor spouse.[16]

Where the child in question is under the age of majority, as determined by the province of ordinary residence,[17] support must be pro-

---

13 *Ibid.*, s. 1. See also Federal/Provincial/Territorial Family Law Committee, *Report and Recommendations on Child Support* (Ottawa: Communications and Consultations Branch, Department of Justice, 1995) [*Report on Child Support*].

14 There is a table for each province and territory; the amounts in them vary "because of differences in provincial income tax rates": Guidelines, above note 12, Schedule I, note 4.

15 *DA*, above note 3, s. 2(1) & (5). The *DA* provides that before provincial guidelines may be used under the *Divorce Act*, the Governor in Council must "designate" the province.

16 *Ibid.*, s. 2(1) & (2).

17 In Ontario this is eighteen: *Age of Majority and Accountability Act*, R.S.O. 1990, c. A.7, s. 1.

vided unless the child has "withdrawn from [the spouses'] charge." Where the child is at or over the age of majority, support must still be provided if he or she is "unable, by reason of illness, disability, pursuit of reasonable education or other cause, to withdraw from their charge or to obtain the necessaries of life."[18]

This particular formulation of the definition is new. Under the prior version, all children under sixteen were "children of the marriage," and the requirement of being under the spouses' charge arose only with respect to older children, where, as now, inability to withdraw was focused on a defined set of reasons.

Being under parents' charge appears to depend on a number of factors, although the courts have never been entirely clear on the matter.[19] The child must be in need and dependent on the parent to meet that need. The purely financial aspect of this factor has rarely been a problem, particularly because children's needs are perceived by the courts to be elastic: they need the sort of support their parents' incomes enable them to have. This is all the more true under the new Guidelines scheme, where the amount of support is a direct function of parental income.

What has been occasionally problematic is the aspect of need that involves the child's ability to provide for himself or herself. The *Divorce Act*, as just seen, draws a line in this regard between minor children and those at the age of majority. It seems fairly clear that minor children will rarely be seen as able to meet their own needs and thus, for that reason alone, as withdrawn from the spouses' charge. Older children, however, are presumed to be able to provide for themselves unless they have a good reason of the kind identified by the statute.[20] Courts must examine, for example, whether, in the words of the revised Act, the child's educational plans are "reasonable."

In addition to need, there is the factor of parental control. Classically this has been dealt with through the proxy of residence: a needy child is under the parents' control (and, so, within their charge) if he or

---

18   *DA*, above note 3, s. 2(1).
19   See *Cole* v. *Cole* (1995), 15 R.F.L. (4th) 399 (N.S. Fam. Ct.), where some sixteen considerations are extracted from the case law.
20   See, for example, *Eyjolfson* v. *Eyjolfson*, [1997] O.J. No. 2155 (Gen. Div.), where illness was one of the factors affecting the life of a dependent eighteen-year-old. See also *Anderson* v. *Anderson* (1997), 27 R.F.L. (4th) 323 (B.C.S.C.), where the court includes among the relevant circumstances: the nature of the plan of study, the availability of loans or bursaries, the child's career plans and their relation to the course of study, the appropriateness of part-time employment, the child's age, the child's academic performance, parental plans for the child's education (particularly those made during cohabitation).

she lives with either of them.[21] However, exception has been made for children who live away from the parents in order to attend university,[22] where illness is involved,[23] or where the parent has been responsible for the child's leaving home.[24] If the matter of control cannot be glossed in this way, however, it can become difficult. Take the factor of age, for example. Younger children might be expected to submit to greater parental authority than older children. Yet, where younger children exhibit serious opposition to parental control, we are reluctant to "discipline" them by withholding needed support, given their lack of realistic financial alternatives. Where older children make their own decisions, we are pleased, perhaps, but then uncertain about how far into adulthood they should be supported, and about what an adult's being in a parent's charge might look like, apart from purely financial aspects.[25]

A child who is in need and not emancipated must also have a particular relation to the payor spouse in order to be a "child of the marriage" and, so, eligible for support. Where the spouse is the genetic or adoptive parent of the child, there is no difficulty. The *Divorce Act* extends the definition of "child of the marriage" to include a child for whom either spouse "stands in the place of a parent." This aspect of the provision is examined in chapter 5.[26]

---

21   The *obiter* concerning residence in *Tapson* v. *Tapson*, [1970] 1 O.R. 521 (C.A.) was adopted as establishing a principle. This issue arose, of course, only with respect to children over sixteen. There are no precedents under the *Divorce Act* respecting younger children.

22   *Coakwell* v. *Baker* (1994), 4 R.F.L. (4th) 345 (Ont. Gen. Div.). But see *Van Wynsberghe* v. *Van Wynsberghe*, [1997] O.J. No. 2566 (Gen. Div.), where the court was of the opinion that the new Guidelines might require a reaffirmation of the residency requirement.

23   See, for example, *James* v. *James* (1995), 18 R.F.L. (4th) 463 (B.C.S.C.), where the child's psychological and emotional difficulties explained the fact that she did not live at home.

24   *C.(J.J.D.)* v. *C.(S.L.)* (1996), 25 R.F.L. (4th) 288 (Ont. Gen. Div.).

25   See *Anderson* v. *Anderson*, above note 20, where the court required a child of nineteen to "[expend] the effort to maintain the reciprocal bonds of respect and affection natural between father and daughter." See also *Law* v. *Law* (1986), 2 R.F.L. (3d) 458 (Ont. H.C.).

26   See section D(2), "Under the *Divorce Act*," in chapter 5, "Parentage,"

b) The *Family Law Act*

i) *The Obligation*

The *Divorce Act* invited the provinces to pass their own guidelines for use when their residents divorce.[27] Ontario accepted the invitation in December 1997, amending the *Family Law Act* to make its child support provisions essentially the same as those under the *Divorce Act*, relying also on presumptive guidelines.[28]

In stating the general obligation, the provincial legislation provides that

> [e]very parent has an obligation to provide support for his or her unmarried child who is a minor or is enrolled in a full time program of education, to the extent that the parent is capable of doing so.[29]

The obligation (under provincial law) does not extend to children of sixteen and older who have withdrawn from parental control.[30] The use of the child support guidelines is made mandatory in section 33(11).[31] The use of the guidelines will be discussed in the context of the federal law, immediately below.

ii) *Relevant Persons*

The word "parent" receives an extended definition in the *Family Law Act*, including, along with genetic and adoptive parents, anyone "who has demonstrated a settled intention to treat the child as a child of his or her family."[32] Thus, more than two persons may be required to support a child under provincial law. The respondent in a suit for support may apply to have added as a party "another person who may have an obligation to provide support to the same dependant."[33]

A child may apply for support directly under Ontario's statute, or the child's parent may apply on his or her behalf,[34] whereas, by contrast, only a spouse may initiate an application for child support under the *Divorce Act*.

---

27   See above note 15.

28   *FLA*, above note 1, as amended by S.O. 1997, c. 20.

29   *FLA*, above note 1, s. 31(1), as amended by S.O. 1997, c. 20, s. 2.

30   *Ibid.*, s. 31(2). The issue of parental control is essentially the same as that under the *Divorce Act*, where the language is "withdraw from [the spouses'] charge": see section B(1)(a)(ii), "Children of the Marriage," in this chapter.

31   *Ibid.*, as amended by S.O. 1997, c. 20, s. 3. See also s. 12 of the amendments, providing for the making of guidelines as regulations.

32   *Ibid.*, s. 1(1). See section D(1), "Under the *Family Law Act*," in chapter 5, "Parentage."

33   *Ibid.*, s. 33(5) & (6).

34   *Ibid.*, s. 33(2). As well, certain social agencies may apply for support on behalf of a dependant when they are providing benefits to the dependant: s. 33(3).

2) The Federal Child Support Guidelines

a) The Simple Case

In the most straightforward of cases, when a custodial spouse applies for child support from the non-custodial spouse, the monthly[35] amount owed, if any, is "the amount set out in the applicable table, according to the number of children . . . to whom the order relates and the income of the spouse against whom the order is sought."[36] The tables for various provinces deal with incomes of between $6,700 and $150,000 a year, and with one to six children per family. Income is set out in increments of $1,000 with a basic amount of support prescribed for each incremental interval, and there is a simple formula for fixing exact amounts, depending on how much the actual income exceeds the incremental level.

For example, if an order were sought against a man whose income was $54,000 a year for the support of three minor children in Ontario, the currently applicable table would be that for Ontario in the Federal Child Support Guidelines, and the amount owed per month would be calculated pursuant to that table as $982. If the payor's income was $54,500, however, the basic amount of $982 would have added to it another $7.70 to account (at a rate given in the table for that level of 1.54 percent) for the $500 by which the actual income exceeds the basic interval amount in the table.

The other spouse's income is irrelevant in these calculations, and, thus, in the determination of the amount of child support in the simple case.

A number of circumstances may complicate a case, however, and require that it be given special or different treatment under the *Divorce Act* or the Guidelines. A consideration of these follows.

b) Determining Annual Income

The spouse's annual income (for the purpose of use in the tables) is essentially his or her "'Total income' in the T1 General form issued by Revenue Canada" after making certain adjustments described in Schedule III of the Guidelines.[37] The adjustments involve deducting certain

---

35   Support is customarily paid periodically, and the period is most commonly a month. However, the court may order—and parties may agree to—lump sum payments or regular payments of any period, and a combination of these: The Guidelines, above note 12, s. 11.

36   *Ibid.*, s. 3(1)(a).

37   *Ibid.*, ss. 15(1) & 16.

employment expenses,[38] amounts received for support,[39] and various other amounts described in some dozen sections.

The Guidelines permit the court some leeway in determining income. Thus, the court may consider a pattern of income over three years to fix an income that most fairly represents what is available to pay child support.[40] If the payor spouse is a shareholder, director, or officer of a corporation,

> and the court is of the opinion that the spouse's annual income as determined [in the manner described in the prior paragraph] does not fairly reflect all the money available to the spouse for the payment of child support,

the court may make appropriate adjustments.[41] And the court may impute to a spouse such amount of income as it considers appropriate in the circumstances; for instance, where it finds that the spouse is intentionally underemployed or unemployed (unless there is a good reason for it), where the spouse is exempt from paying tax, where income has been diverted, or where the spouse has failed to provide required information about his or her income.[42]

Clearly, in order to make the kinds of precise determinations envisaged by the Guidelines, applicants and courts require detailed information concerning the payor spouse's financial situation. Accordingly, the Guidelines provide that a respondent spouse must, within 30 days of an application, provide both applicant and court with, among other things:

(a) a copy of every personal income tax return filed by the spouse for each of the three most recent taxation years;

(b) a copy of every notice of assessment or re-assessment issued to the spouse for each of the three most recent taxation years;

(c) where the spouse is an employee, the most recent statement of earnings indicating the total earnings paid in the year to date, including overtime or, where such a statement is not provided by the employer, a letter from the spouse's employer setting out that information including the spouse's rate of annual salary or remuneration;

(d) where the spouse is self-employed, for the three most recent taxation years

---

38   *Ibid.*, Schedule III, s. 1: Those described in section 8 (1) (c)–(q) (excluding paras. h.1 and k) of the *Income Tax Act*, R.S.C. 1985, (5th Supp.), c. 1, as amended.

39   *Ibid.*, Schedule III, ss. 2 & 3.

40   *Ibid.*, s. 17.

41   *Ibid.*, s. 18.

42   *Ibid.*, s. 19. Other specific circumstances are identified in this section as well.

(i)   the financial statements of the spouse's business or professional practice, other than a partnership, and

(ii) a statement showing a breakdown of all salaries, wages, management fees or other payments or benefits paid to, or on
behalf of, persons or corporations with whom the spouse
does not deal at arm's length . . .[43]

It should be noted that the Guidelines permit the spouses to agree
in writing as to the annual income of a spouse, and where "the court
thinks that the amount is reasonable having regard to the income information provided" pursuant to the Guidelines' requirements, the court
may adopt that agreed-upon amount for the purposes of the tables or
other aspects of the Guidelines.[44]

Finally, it must be noted that the Guidelines require a spouse
against whom a child support order has been made to provide information every year in the form just described, should the payee spouse
request it.[45]

c) Special or Extraordinary Expenses

The Guidelines provide that the court may award amounts in addition
to the table amounts for certain identified expenses that, presumably,
were not at all or inadequately accounted for in the calculations that
produced the table amounts.[46] The expenses identified are:

(a)   child care expenses incurred as a result of the custodial parent's
employment, illness, disability or education or training for
employment;

---

43   *Ibid.*, s. 21(1). The following also must be produced:

(e)   where the spouse is a partner in a partnership, confirmation of the spouse's
income and draw from, and capital in, the partnership for its three most
recent taxation years;

(f)   where the spouse controls a corporation, for its three most recent taxation years

(i)   the financial statements of the corporation and its subsidiaries, and

(ii) a statement showing a breakdown of all salaries, wages, management
fees or other payments or benefits paid to, or on behalf of, persons or
corporations with whom the corporation, and every related
corporation, does not deal at arm's length; and

(g)   where the spouse is a beneficiary under a trust, a copy of the trust settlement
agreement and copies of the trust's three most recent financial statements.

44   *Ibid.*, s. 15(2).

45   *Ibid.*, s. 25. Note that in cases where the payee spouse's annual income is relevant
to the amount of support, that spouse is obliged to provide the same detailed
documentation: ss. 21(1) & 25(3).

46   *Ibid.*, s. 3(1)(b).

(b) that portion of the medical and dental insurance premiums attributable to the child;

(c) health-related expenses that exceed insurance reimbursement by at least $100 annually per illness or event, including orthodontic treatment, professional counselling provided by a psychologist, social worker, psychiatrist or any other person, physiotherapy, occupational therapy, speech therapy and prescription drugs, hearing aids, glasses and contact lenses;

(d) extraordinary expenses for primary or secondary school education or for any educational programs that meet the child's particular needs;

(e) expenses for post-secondary education; and

(f) extraordinary expenses for extracurricular activities.[47]

The court "may" (not "must") add an amount for these expenses to the table amount after taking into account

> the necessity of the expense in relation to the child's best interests and the reasonableness of the expense, having regard to the means of the spouses and those of the child and to the family's spending pattern prior to the separation.[48]

And the "guiding principle" for the court's determination is said to be that the spouses share the approved expenses "in proportion to their respective incomes."[49]

Some aspects apart, this provision represents a major retreat from the philosophy that lay behind the adoption of this kind of guideline. That is, the Guidelines are of the sort known as the Percentage of Income Model, the principal aim of which is to achieve adequate levels of child support within a system that makes payable amounts "objectively determinable, consistent and predictable."[50] There is concern that this provision will act to undermine the aim of predictability and permit spouses to argue regularly about the appropriateness of table amounts, thus delaying agreement and promoting litigation.[51]

---

47 *Ibid.*, s. 7(1).

48 *Ibid.*

49 *Ibid.*, s. 7(2).

50 *Report on Child Support*, above note 13.

51 In the words of one commentator: "What we have now is a 'mishmash', combining a fixed percentage system with various add-ons which in effect accomplish few of the objectives of the fixed percentage system and continue the disadvantages of the cost sharing system." T. Bastedo, "Add-Ons" in *Child Support Guidelines: The Mysteries Unravelled* (Toronto: Canadian Bar Association (Ontario), Law Society of Upper Canada, 1996).

The courts may still save the system if they make it clear that ordering payment for these expenses will be an unusual event. It helps in this respect that the ability of the court to add an amount under this provision is discretionary. It perhaps helps, too, that certain of the identified expenses are clearly labelled as "extraordinary," although the absence of that label from the majority clearly invites the conclusion that they were intended to refer to routine or ordinary events in family life.

d) Factors Affecting Departure from Guideline Amounts

i) *Agreement and Consent Orders*
The court may award on consent "an amount that is different from the amount that would be determined in accordance with the applicable guidelines" where the parties have made "reasonable arrangements" for the support of the child.[52] These arrangements will typically be reduced to terms in a separation agreement or minutes of settlement. In judging whether arrangements are reasonable, the court must "have regard to the applicable guidelines" but must treat them as advisory only.[53]

Agreements between the spouses that bear upon child support are also relevant to the provision discussed immediately below.

ii) *Special Provisions for Child*
Where "special provisions" have already been made for the child and the application of the Guidelines would then "result in an amount of child support that is inequitable," the court may award an amount different from that required by the Guidelines.[54] These special provisions may be found within a court order or a written agreement and must be such as to "directly or indirectly benefit a child" in question. It is this provision that will enable spouses to argue that child support arrangements put into place before the Guidelines are appropriate to be continued. The deviation from the Guidelines may be based on arrangements that indirectly benefit the child, such as where they provide for the custodial parent to have exclusive possession of the matrimonial home. It is not clear what, if anything, must be "special" about the provisions made in respect of the child.

---

52 *DA*, above note 3, s. 15.1(7).

53 *Ibid.*, s. 15.1(8). See also section D(2), "Maintenance Arrangements for Children," in chapter 9, "Divorce," respecting the related bar to divorce. It ought to be the case that the onus is on the spouses to demonstrate convincingly that the Guideline amounts are inappropriate.

54 *Ibid.*, s. 15.1(5).

iii) Age of Child

Spouses are required to support "children of the marriage" who are over the age of majority and unable to withdraw from the spouses' charge for approved reasons.[55] Orders in respect of such children are to be in the amounts prescribed by the Guidelines unless, having regard to the circumstance of the child and the "financial ability of each spouse to contribute to the support of the child," the court considers a different amount to be "appropriate."[56] Given that there is no upper limit placed on the age of children entitled to support, it seems sensible that the court be given latitude (here as well as when deciding the question of whether an adult remains "a child of the marriage") to respond to the unpredictable variety that adult lives display.

iv) Relation to Child

Spouses who are not genetic or adoptive parents but parents of intention[57]—that is, who stand "in the place of a parent"—are not necessarily required to provide support to children of the marriage in Guideline amounts but only in such amounts "as the court considers appropriate, having regard to these Guidelines and any other parent's legal duty to support the child."[58] In other words, the court will consider the duty of support of the child's other genetic or adoptive parent, and, presumably, that as well of any parent of intention under the *Family Law Act*.[59] It is likely, however, that this provision does not license the court to consider the duty owed by the custodial parent, given that the *Divorce Act* and the Guidelines operate basically without regard to that parent's financial ability, on the theory that custodial parents spend maximum amounts on their children regardless of what the other spouse contributes. There appears to be no reason to require that another parent's duty be reduced to an order or agreement before it can be considered.

This provision establishes a somewhat secondary role for parents of intention. There is no comparable provision permitting genetic or adoptive parents to point to others who are or might be obliged to contribute to the support of the child, even though there is a clear financial relevance to such obligations.

---

55   See section B(1)(a)(ii), "Children of the Marriage," in this chapter.
56   The Guidelines, above note 12, s. 3(2).
57   See section D(2), "Under the *Divorce Act*," in chapter 5, "Parentage."
58   The Guidelines, above note 12, s. 5.
59   See section D(1), "Under the *Family Law Act*," in chapter 5, "Parentage."

v) Size of Income

The Guidelines do not apply to a spouse whose income is at or below a certain threshold, currently $6,700 for Ontario.[60] For annual incomes over $150,000, the amount payable is either that provided by the Guidelines or, "if the court considers that amount to be inappropriate," the base amount for $150,000 required by the table, plus an "appropriate" amount, determined by considering the child's circumstances and the "financial ability of each spouse to contribute to the support of the children."[61]

vi) Custody Arrangements

In two circumstances, the custody arrangements between the spouses may affect the amount of support payable. First, in the words of section 8 of the Guidelines:

> [w]here each spouse has custody of one or more children, the amount of a child support order is the difference between the amount that each spouse would otherwise pay if a child support order were sought against each of the spouses.

The set-off in cases of split custody, as this relatively rare arrangement is known, would appear to produce no greater difficulties than the need to apply the Guidelines to both spouses.

The second circumstance, however, is not so straightforward. In certain cases of shared custody, the ordinary Guidelines approach must be put aside and support determined by taking into account:

(a) the amounts set out in the applicable tables for each of the spouses;[62]

(b) the increased costs of shared custody arrangements; and

---

60   The Guidelines, above note 12, s. 2(1), Schedule I, table for Ontario.

61   *Ibid.*, s. 4. The tables do not chart increments of annual income over $150,000 but provide a formula for calculating a monthly payment. Thus, currently in Ontario, a high-income spouse with one child would be required by the table to pay the base amount of $1,108 plus 0.67 percent of income over $150,000. See *Francis* v. *Baker* (1998), 157 D.L.R. (4th) 1 (C.A.): even where the payor's income is over $150,000, table amounts can only be reduced when the child is the age of majority or older, when the paying spouse is not the child's parent, when there is split or shared custody, or in cases of undue hardship; otherwise the presumptive table amounts can only be added to.

62   It might have been more appropriate to identify one-half the table amount for each spouse; given that something like half the child's time is spent with the spouse, half the table amount would be spent on the child while resident, the other half representing the remaining obligation. The difference between the spouses' "halves" might represent an appropriate transfer payment.

(c) the conditions, means, needs and other circumstances of each
spouse and of any child for whom support is sought.[63]

Note that the court is obliged to take into account the table amounts and
not the amounts the Guidelines would otherwise have produced. Under
section 3(1), the normal approach is to adopt table amounts plus special
and extraordinary expenses (determined under section 7); but the reference here is simply to the first of these, that is, the table amounts, with
the implication that section 7 special and extraordinary expenses are
not to be considered *per se* in cases of shared custody.

The net effect of this would appear to be that support is to be calculated very much in the old way, involving a budget of needs for each
child and a discretionary judgment about the relative abilities of each
parent to meet those needs, the only distinction being the advisory
assistance that reference to table amounts may provide. It might have
been better if a formulaic approach had been taken, involving the transfer of some predictable amount from the spouse with the higher income
to the spouse with the lower income.

This special approach is to be applied "[w]here a spouse exercises a
right of access to, or has physical custody of, a child for not less than 40
per cent of the time over the course of a year."

The Guidelines are for the most part premised on the assumption that
the one spouse will be custodian and the other spouse will not. Accordingly, the non-custodial spouse may be required to reduce his obligation of
support to a particular sum and then to transfer that sum to the custodian,
where, practically speaking, it can best be used to benefit the children. The
custodial spouse also has a duty of child support, of course, but the practi-
calities of the situation—the shared daily lives of custodian and children—
see that duty fulfilled without the need to identify a separate sum.

When, however, the spouses share the responsibility for day-to-day
care more or less equally, the original assumption no longer holds. We
cannot use the custody arrangement, then, to identify the payor spouse.
Why require any transfer payment in such situations? The rationale
must be that children should be able to benefit from the means and
assets of both parents as much of the time as is possible and not have to
alternate between high and low standards of living.[64]

---

63 The Guidelines, above note 12, s. 9. Note that the provision says the amount of
child support "must" be determined in this way.

64 When the spouses have means that are more or less the same, there will likely be
little if any support ordered, and the near equality of custodial time will ensure
near equality of contribution and evenness of benefit for the children.

It is unclear how the "40 percent" of the year requirement is to be calculated. In cases where there are precise custody orders or agreements that have been followed in practice, there may be little difficulty; as where, for example, the parties are to have equal amounts of time with the children, or a specific number of days or weeks is identified for access or custody. Where arrangements are more loosely described, however, or where actual practice diverges from the prescribed arrangements, there will be difficulty.

More troubling than the practical difficulty of calculation, perhaps, is the likelihood that this provision, taken as a whole, will encourage spouses to press for shared custody for the financial advantages that it may appear to offer, and thus endanger the best interests of the children concerned.[65] Objectivity and predictability are absent, and the uncertainty alone will promote disagreement and litigation.

vii) Undue Hardship

A court may deviate from the Guideline amount if it finds that awarding that sum would cause "undue hardship" to "the child in respect of whom the request is made"[66] or to the spouse who seeks the deviation.[67] The use of this particular phrase means that some hardship must be accepted as a result of the use of the Guidelines. The key term is not exhaustively defined in the Guidelines, though section 10(2) provides that "[c]ircumstances that may cause a spouse or child to suffer undue hardship include the following:"

(a) the spouse has responsibility for an unusually high level of debts reasonably incurred to support the spouses and their children prior to the separation or to earn a living;

(b) the spouse has unusually high expenses in relation to exercising access to a child;

---

65 See chapter 10, "Custody and Access," generally, and section C(1), "Joint Custody," and section D(2), "The Proper Standard," specifically, concerning the issues of custody and the desirability of a child's having contact with both parents.

66 This child may, of course, be the "child of the marriage" for whom the support order is sought. But it seems fairly clear that it may also be any child appropriately involved by the remainder of the provision, which would include, for example, any other child whom the spouse is obliged to support. The complications entailed in dealing with even a small-scale political economy of two families are considerable, and a three-family problem is not really unlikely. The Gordian knot of relation should have been cut more neatly by the scheme.

67 The Guidelines, above note 12, s. 10(1). Such deviation is said to be possible where otherwise the amount would be determined under ss. 3–5, 8, & 9; that is, for the ordinary circumstance, the adult child, a high-income payor, a parent of intention, and split or shared custody, respectively.

(c) the spouse has a legal duty under a judgment, order or written separation agreement to support any person;

(d) the spouse has a legal duty to support a child, other than a child of the marriage [who is either a minor or unable for good reason to obtain the necessaries of life]; and

(e) the spouse has a legal duty to support any person who is unable to obtain the necessaries of life due to an illness or disability.

These would seem to be categories of expenses or obligations that were not taken into account when the table amounts were calculated because they are not common enough to affect all children. Any other argued-for circumstances ought to be of the same kind; that is, not merely circumstances of financial difficulty facing the individuals in a case, but circumstances of a kind unusual enough not to have been accommodated already in the process that produced the table amounts.

Before any finding of undue hardship can lead to deviation from the Guidelines, the court must compare the standards of living at the two households. The comparison is made using the assumption that the Guideline amount is ordered; and if, on this assumption, the spouse pleading undue hardship, would (already) have a higher household standard of living, the application for deviation must be denied. The comparatively well-off may not be made even more well-off by pointing to the fact of undue hardship.[68] The court may use the "comparison of household standards of living test" provided in the Guidelines.[69]

Any court that does deviate from the Guidelines under this provision "must record its reasons for doing so."[70] This requirement is aimed at enabling the spouses to know when, if ever, the specific circumstances that gave rise to the special amount of child support are no longer in existence or no longer have any force.[71]

---

68   The actual language of s. 10(3) of the Guidelines, *ibid.*, is as follows:
    Despite a determination of undue hardship under subsection (1), an application under that subsection must be denied by the court if it is of the opinion that the household of the spouse who claims undue hardship would, after determining the amount of child support under any of sections 3 to 5, 8 or 9, have a higher standard of living than the household of the other spouse.

69   *Ibid.*, s. 10(4), Schedule II. This is a six-step process that is too detailed to explore in this context.

70   *Ibid.*, s. 10(6).

71   Thus, the court may specify a "reasonable time for the satisfaction of any obligation arising from circumstances that cause undue hardship": *Ibid.*, s. 10(5).

e) Orders and Agreements in Existence Prior to the Guidelines

A court order for child support that was made before the Guidelines came into force remains in effect. Either spouse may apply for a variation, however, for the reason that the very coming into force of the Guidelines is deemed to be a "change in circumstances" of the sort necessary to license variation.[72] Spouses will have to do the calculations to determine whether the change in the law would make an application for variation worthwhile.[73]

No special treatment is accorded to a prior agreement. A court may decide to take jurisdiction despite the agreement and to make an order for an amount different from that the spouses had agreed to. The principles governing such decisions are discussed below.[74]

3) Relationship to Spousal Support

Before the passage of the Guidelines, it was possible, though unusual, for a court to make a single, combined order for the support of a spouse and children together. Now this will not be possible, given that the *Divorce Act* separates out child support and spousal support orders, and makes them payable on quite different bases. Where an old combined order is brought today for variation, the court must rescind the old order and treat the application as a pair of new applications for child support and spousal support.[75]

As between them, child support is to be given priority over spousal support.[76] If this means that less spousal support is ordered than would otherwise have been appropriate, the court is to record this fact and its reasons; and any subsequent reduction in child support is, by statute, to constitute a change of circumstances enabling the disappointed spouse to apply for a variation of the original, insufficient order.[77]

These provisions do not apply to support sought under the provincial Act, however. The *Family Law Act* permits a court to make an order for the support of a person's dependants, a term that embraces spouses

---

72   *DA*, above note 3, s. 17(4), and the Guidelines, above note 12, s. 14(c). This affects agreements made before 1 May 1997.

73   In addition to the obvious factors that would go into the determination of amount, and the attendant legal costs, there will be the income tax consequences of variation, as to which see section B(4), "Taxation," in this chapter.

74   See section E, "The Role of Contract," in this chapter.

75   *DA*, above note 3, s. 34(1.1).

76   *Ibid.*, s. 15.3(1).

77   *Ibid.*, s. 15.3(2) & (3).

and children, and so allows a single, combined order.[78] Even so, this is a practice to be discouraged.

4) Taxation

Until recently, a person who paid child support under an agreement or court order was able to deduct that sum from his or her income and so reduce the amount of income tax payable. The sum was added to the income of the custodial parent in receipt of the payment, who then paid tax on it. This deduction permitted "income splitting" and so resulted in a significant overall loss of tax revenue, and a corresponding gain to separated families, resulting from the fact that many payor spouses paid tax at a higher marginal rate than their payee spouses. But in any given case there might be no gain or the gain might not be equitably shared.

This fact led to a challenge that the deduction was contrary to the *Charter*, ultimately unsuccessful at the Supreme Court.[79] Subsequently, however, the *Income Tax Act* was changed and the deduction removed in respect of child support orders or agreements made after the change.[80]

The old regime continues to apply, however, in respect of orders and agreements made prior to the change in the tax law, until they are varied in any respect whatever, whereupon, the new law applies and the amount of support is no longer deductible from the income of the payor.[81]

C. SPOUSAL SUPPORT

1) Sources of Law

a) The *Divorce Act*

The *Divorce Act* provides no single basis for awarding spousal support. Instead, it sets out four objectives for such an order, which should

(a) recognize any economic advantages or disadvantages to the spouses arising from the marriage or its breakdown;

(b) apportion between the spouses any financial consequences arising from the care of any child of the marriage over and above any obligation for the support of any child of the marriage;

---

78   *FLA*, above note 1, s. 33(1).

79   *Canadian Charter of Rights and Freedoms*, Part 1 of the *Constitution Act, 1982*, being Schedule B to the *Canada Act 1982*, c. 11 [*Charter*]. See *Thibaudeau v. Canada (M.N.R.)*, [1995] 2 S.C.R. 627.

80   S.C. 1997, c. 25, s. 8(1), amending s. 56(1)(b) of the *Income Tax Act*, above note 38.

81   *Income Tax Act*, above note 38.

(c) relieve any economic hardship of the spouses arising from the breakdown of the marriage; and

(d) in so far as practicable, promote the economic self-sufficiency of each spouse within a reasonable period of time.[82]

Courts have taken the position that these various objectives bespeak a number of rationales for requiring one spouse to support another, which rationales will not necessarily be capable of integration under one philosophy or principle. The various principles currently in contention will be discussed below.

When deliberating, the court must consider "the condition, means, needs and other circumstances of each spouse," and in particular should look at the length of cohabitation, the "functions performed by each spouse during cohabitation," and any existing agreement or order for support.[83] The court may not, however, take into account "any misconduct of a spouse in relation to the marriage."[84]

The court may order periodic payments, a lump sum payment, or a combination of these; as well, it may order the payor spouse "to secure or pay, or to secure and pay" the required sum.[85]

b) The *Family Law Act*

By contrast to the *Divorce Act*, the Ontario statute pins the obligation of support to the primary principle that "[e]very spouse has an obligation to provide support for himself or herself and for the other spouse, in accordance with need, to the extent that he or she is capable of doing so."[86] Although this might have been originally intended to establish a simple duty and to banish all difficulty to the realm of mere computation, it has not worked out that way. Because the extended definition of spouse brings unmarried persons within the duty of support,[87] it became clear that some feature other than formal marriage must be the moral or

---

82 *DA*, above note 3, s. 15.2(6). The power to make orders is found in s. 15.2(1).

83 *Ibid.*, s. 15.2(4).

84 *Ibid.*, s. 15.2(5).

85 *Ibid.*, s. 15.2(1).

86 *FLA*, above note 1, s. 30. The explicit obligation of self-support appears simply to be a means of understanding that there are limitations on a spouse's capacity to support the other spouse. Compare this language with Marx's statement: "From each according to his abilities, to each according to his needs." (C.P. Dutt, ed. *Critique of the Gotha Program; with appendices by Marx, Engels and Lenin; a revised translation* (New York: International Publishers, 1966)). There is more than one echo of socialism in the law's approach to economic justice within the family: see, for example, section E(1)(b)(iii), "Quantum," in chapter 11, "Family Property."

87 See section B(2), "The *Family Law Act*," in chapter 4, "Cohabitation."

motivating factor behind the obligation, which in turn meant that the obligation need not be seen as automatically flowing from a legal status.

To assist courts, the legislation was amended to set out four objectives for a support order, from which those under the *Divorce Act* were essentially copied.[88] There are as well some seventeen "circumstances" or factors that a court is to consider when determining the amount of spousal support; but, because these are merely phrases and not sentences containing clear thoughts, they are of limited utility, and, in any event, have not served to refine or delimit the principled basis on which spousal support is to be ordered. Instead, they reveal the profusion, not to say confusion, of competing rationales.

Whereas courts operating under the *Divorce Act* are not to consider spousal misconduct at all, courts making orders under the *Family Law Act* may, in unusual circumstances, take spousal conduct into account in respect of quantum.[89] This provision was rarely ever used and has now almost completely fallen out of favour.[90]

Courts may make a wide variety of orders for the satisfaction of an obligation to support, requiring that amounts be paid periodically, that lump sums be paid or held in trust, that any property be transferred or held in trust, and so forth.[91]

2) Principles under Development

The current legislation would appear to support three basic principled approaches to the awarding of spousal support, none of which is easy to rationalize with the others. To an extent, they describe the historical development in the courts of the rationale behind spousal support, but succeeding bases are added to the previous ones and do not entirely replace them. Essentially the development has been one of widening the context in which decisions are made, so as to bring into the calculation

---

88 The four objectives are very similar but not identical. They require a spousal support order to:

  (a) recognize the spouse's contribution to the relationship and the economic consequences of the relationship for the spouse; (b) share the economic burden of child support equitably; (c) make fair provision to assist the spouse to become able to contribute to his or her own support; and (d) relieve financial hardship, if this has not been done by orders under Parts I (Family Property) and II (Matrimonial Home). (*FLA*, above note 1, s. 33(8))

89 *Ibid.*, s. 33(10): the court "may have regard to a course of conduct that is so unconscionable as to constitute an obvious and gross repudiation of the relationship."

90 But see *Krigstin v. Krigstin* (1992), 43 R.F.L. (3d) 334 (Ont. Gen. Div.).

91 *FLA*, above note 1, s. 34(1).

ever more complex understandings of the financial situation in which spouses find themselves. The process of sophistication does not appear to have stopped; however, it seems clear that at some point the limits of family law will be reached, and any further development will have to tackle the broad social and economic issues that address the financial fate of us all.

a) Obligation out of Status (Caring)

The first approach began as a function of status: a spouse was entitled to be supported because spousal support was a concomitant right and obligation of legal marriage. It was part of what it meant to be (or to have been) married. There were reasons for the institution of marriage to have developed in this way, of course, but those reasons rarely if ever needed to be adverted to in specific cases: it is, after all, one of the functions of a status approach to relegate (or to try to, at least) issues of principle to parliamentary and other non-judicial debates. When courts have sought to ascribe a deeper rationale, it has typically been one of marriage as agreement, or, more expansively, of supporting reasonable expectations.

It would be unusual today to find a court willing to impose a spousal support obligation solely on the basis that the parties had legally married—a month of marriage no longer entitles a spouse to a lifetime of support.[92] Yet it is clear from the legislation that a spousal support order may legitimately aim to "relieve any economic hardship of the spouses arising from the breakdown of the marriage."[93] There is an ethic of care here—together, perhaps, with a lingering sense that status gives rise to obligation—that can still be used to justify support orders. How else can we explain decisions to require the support of a spouse who is in need because of illness or disability?[94]

---

92   "It is now uncontentious in our law . . . that marriage per se does not automatically entitle a spouse to support." *Moge* v. *Moge*, [1992] 3 S.C.R. 813 at 864, L'Heureux-Dubé J.

93   *DA*, above note 3, s. 15.2(6). "Arising from the breakdown of the marriage" may, of course, mean a number of things; but the sense taken here is that of hardship arising immediately following marriage breakdown, that is, upon the cessation of the sharing that ordinarily occurs during ongoing marriage. See also *FLA*, above note 1, s. 33(8)(d). As well, the *FLA* simply makes need and means the primary considerations in whether there is an obligation: s. 30.

94   See, for example, *Smith* v. *Smith* (1987), 63 O.R. (2d) 146 at 151 (H.C.), decided under the *DA*: "If a wife becomes seriously ill while happily married her husband is responsible for her support and the expenses resulting from her illness. He does not avoid this continuing responsibility by obtaining a divorce. This is so even if there is no causal connection between the illness of the spouse and the marriage." And see *Fisher* v. *Fisher* (1989), 70 O.R. (2d) 336 (Div. Ct.), leave to appeal to Ont. C.A. refused (1989), 70 O.R. (2d) 336n, decided under the *FLA*. Most courts, however, have ruled against a support obligation under the *DA* where need is based on illness uncaused by the marriage. See, for example, *Willms* v. *Willms* (1988), 65 O.R. (2d) 151 (C.A.).

b) Obligation to Rehabilitate

Perhaps in reaction to the liberality of the needs-means-status approach, the courts began in the late seventies to promote the value of spousal independence.[95] In the dissenting judgment in the Supreme Court decision in *Messier v. Delage*,[96] the idea was forcefully expressed that there must come a moment when a divorced person ceases to be a "former spouse" and becomes instead (simply) a citizen, who must look to society generally for the satisfaction of unmet needs. Gradually this idea took hold, under various labels and with various emphases. Orders for support became instrumental in this view, aimed at "rehabilitation," the fulfilment of an obligation to assist the needy spouse to become self-supporting.[97]

The force of this approach, of course, depends upon the ease with which courts are prepared to declare that a spouse has achieved independence or economic self-sufficiency. It is difficult to know what a person "needs." There are no agreed-upon means of distinguishing between needs and wants in our society, so that it is a matter of opinion whether true "rehabilitation" has occurred. However, it is fair to say that many decisions that were justified or explained by reference to the value of spousal independence left one spouse—almost always the woman—with a standard of living well below that of the other. Women, it seemed, had fewer needs than men.

The impatience to "deem" the woman self-sufficient[98] is partly explained by what is known as the "clean break theory," in which it is held to be of value to the parties to become unconnected from continuing legal obligations and thus, presumably, more able to achieve full psychological or emotional satisfaction in their lives.[99]

---

95   The *Family Law Reform Act*, 1978, S.O. 1978, c. 2, predecessor to the *FLA*, for the first time imposed on spouses the obligation to be self-supporting that is now found in the *FLA*, above note 1, s. 30.

96   [1983] 2 S.C.R. 401.

97   This rehabilitative function survives today in *DA*, above note 3, s. 15.2(6)(d), which states that one of the objectives of spousal support is, "in so far as practicable, [to] promote the economic self-sufficiency of each spouse within a reasonable period of time." See also: *FLA*, above note 1, s. 33(8)(c).

98   L'Heureux-Dubé J. labelled this approach the "deemed self-sufficiency model" in *Moge v. Moge*, above note 92 at 853.

99   See *Pelech v. Pelech*, [1987] 1 S.C.R. 801 at 849.

c) Obligation out of Cause

i) Stage One: The "Causal Connection" Principle

In a trio of cases, the Supreme Court laid the groundwork for the doctrine that one spouse should be obliged to support another only to the extent that there was a causal connection between the relationship and the need of the applicant spouse.[100] In all three cases, which were applications under the previous *Divorce Act*, the spouses had reached agreement as to spousal support, and this fact played a dominant role in the decisions. However, Wilson J., writing the majority judgments, made statements that clearly applied to spousal support obligations generally, and from which the requirement of "causal connection" was drawn by the courts.

This was always one of the views capable of being supported by aspects of the *Family Law Act*, particularly by certain of those "circumstances" to be considered by the court when "determining the amount . . ., if any, of support in relation to need."[101] The courts elected by and large, however, to treat the "causal connection" test as inapplicable to applications under the provincial statute, certainly where there was no agreement under consideration.[102]

One clear merit of the test was that it provided for the first time a principled basis for decisions that could actually assist courts. No other rationale existed that usefully answered the questions that were felt to be difficult, such as how long support obligations ought to continue, and what upper limits might be placed on budgets of need, or when a spouse should be required to support a former spouse disabled by illness.

ii) Stage Two: Compensatory Support

The "causal connection" test, as applied to spousal support generally, met a great deal of opposition.[103] The difficulty, essentially, lay not in the

---

100   *Pelech* v. *Pelech*, *ibid.*; *Caron* v. *Caron*, [1987] 1 S.C.R. 892; *Richardson* v. *Richardson*, [1987] 1 S.C.R. 857.

101   See, for example, *FLA*, above note 1, s. 33(9), paras. (j) ("a contribution by the dependant to the realization of the respondent's career potential" and (l)(ii) ("the effect on the spouse's earning capacity of the responsibilities assumed during cohabitation").

102   *Fisher* v. *Fisher*, above note 94, decided the test was inapplicable to the *FLA*; leave to appeal to the Court of Appeal was refused. But see *Willms* v. *Willms*, above note 94, in which the Court of Appeal seems to say the test can apply in the right circumstances.

103   See, for example, B.J. Cossman, "A Matter of Difference: Domestic Contracts and Gender Equality" (1990) 28 O.H.L.J. 303; C.J. Rogerson, "The Causal Connection Test in Spousal Support Law" (1989) 8 Can. J. Fam. L. 95.

principle itself but in the manner of its application. It is correct that, in most cases certainly, there ought to be a rational connection between the obligation imposed on a spouse and the conduct of the spouses within the relationship—and the "reason" is most conveniently seen as "causal." The real problem comes in deciding how to construct lines of cause and effect, how widely or narrowly one will look for responsibility and explanation.

In the trio of Supreme Court cases that gave rise to this development, the court adopted a very restricted context, one that largely ignored systemic inequality between men and women and that failed to take into account the impact that this inequality would have on the applicant spouses.[104] As a consequence, the decisions were unfair, when looked at from certain broader perspectives.

The corrective came with *Moge* v. *Moge*, a 1992 decision of the Supreme Court.[105] L'Heureux-Dubé J., writing the majority opinion, opened out the context within which support decisions are made so as to include the gender inequality that flows from the roles assumed by men and women within marriage.[106] Where, as commonly happens, women leave or fail to enter the job market in order to devote themselves to childcare or other domestic work, the cost to the women of such decisions can be considerable, and may include income forgone and prospects narrowed because of lost seniority or the deterioration of marketable skills. L'Heureux-Dubé J. pointed out that the overall impact of gendered roles in society has been the "feminization of poverty."

To the extent that these opportunity costs correspond to advantages conferred on the other spouse that have resulted in economic gain, equalization of net family properties may compensate the woman to

---

104 Wilson J. apparently made a choice to ignore the wider context. She says, when considering whether courts should be prepared to examine spousal agreements on a case by case basis, that taking systemic factors into account in individual cases this way "will ultimately reinforce the very bias [one] seeks to counteract." She ignores difference when rule making for fear of perpetuating it. *Pelech* v. *Pelech*, above note 99 at 849.

105 Above note 92. Note that compensatory support was ordered in a number of cases decided under the *FLA* well before the *Moge* decision: see, especially, *Keast* v. *Keast* (1986), 1 R.F.L. (3d) 401 (Ont. Dist. Ct.).

106 She also avoided *Pelech*, above note 99, and the other cases in the trio by expressing the view that "[a] careful reading of the trilogy in general and *Pelech* in particular indicates that the Court has not espoused a new model of support under the Act. Rather, the Court has shown respect for the wishes of persons who, in the presence of the statutory safeguards, decided to forego litigation and settled their affairs by agreement under the 1970 Divorce Act." *Moge* v. *Moge*, above note 92 at 836.

some degree. However, as the court in *Moge* recognized, not all couples have property sufficient to accomplish this, and it can be the job of support law to bring about the compensation:

> [T]he absence of accumulated assets may require that one spouse pay support to the other in order to effect an equitable distribution of resources . . . Fair distribution . . . involves the development of parameters with which to assess the respective advantages and disadvantages of the spouses as a result of their roles in the marriage, as the starting point in determining the degree of support to be awarded. This, in my view, is what the Act requires.[107]

Various limits, however, attend the compensatory principle. First, it may not be easy to calculate the costs incurred by the disadvantaged spouse. L'Heureux-Dubé J. acknowledges this difficulty but finds that the court ought not to proceed only where there is expert evidence available, but as "the paramount goal is to render justice to the parties"[108] courts should struggle as best they can. Second, there are limits as to what family law can accomplish in the move to correct injustices arising from the gendered nature of our society; employment policies and practices, for instance, are evidently important but beyond the control, in any conventional sense, certainly, of the courts deciding spousal disputes. The wider social context invoked in *Moge* permits a broader responsibility for support to be placed on men, but at the same time reveals that relations within marriage are not the sole cause of economic injustice to women.[109]

Limits arise, too, from the legislation. In both the *Divorce Act* and the *Family Law Act*, as was seen above,[110] there are four objectives of a spousal support order. L'Heureux-Dubé J. has said that these four, taken together, "can be viewed as an attempt to achieve an equitable sharing of the economic consequences of marriage or marriage breakdown";[111] however, two of them point rather more clearly to other goals, namely that of relieving "any economic hardship . . . arising from the breakdown

---

107   *Ibid.* at 849.

108   *Ibid.* at 874.

109   There are limits, as well, on what a spouse may be able to do to recompense another. This reflects the fact that opportunity costs borne by one spouse may not be paralleled by advantages conferred on the other spouse, and, thus, there may be inadequate means to compensate the former upon marriage breakdown. See, for example, *Elliot v. Elliot* (1993), 15 O.R. (3d) 265 (Ont. C.A.), leave to appeal to S.C.C. refused (1994) 18 O.R. (3d) xvi.

110   Above notes 82 and 88, and accompanying text.

111   *Moge v. Moge*, above note 92 at 866.

of the marriage" and of promoting "the economic self-sufficiency of each spouse."[112] The view expressed in the concurring opinion of McLachlin J. is that

> [n]either a "compensation model" nor a "self-sufficiency model" captures the full content of the section, though both may be relevant to the judge's decision. The judge must base her decision on a number of factors: compensation; child-care; post-separation need; and the goal, in so far as practicable, of promoting self-sufficiency.[113]

To the extent that this view is adopted despite the unifying gloss placed on the legislation by L'Heureux-Dubé J., the difficulty will remain that the three surviving rationales—status (or "need"), rehabilitation (or "self-sufficiency"), and caused need (or "compensation")—are not contained within any comprehensive theory capable of deciding when and to what extent each is appropriate to govern the situation. That is, our law of spousal support will remain incoherent.

As a final matter it should be noted that spousal support is in fact awarded in a small minority of cases that come before the courts.

3) Taxation

When a person pays spousal support pursuant to an agreement or a court order, the payor is entitled to deduct the amount paid from his or her income, thus reducing the income tax paid. The recipient of spousal support so paid and deducted must treat it as income and is liable to pay income tax on it.[114] When income is moved in this way from the spouse who pays tax at a higher marginal rate to the spouse who pays tax at a lower marginal rate, an overall gain to the parties will result from tax saved. It is a matter of concern that any such potential saving be recognized by spouses who are negotiating a settlement or by courts making support orders, in order that it may be distributed between the parties appropriately.[115]

It should be noted that recent changes to the *Income Tax Act* treat child support differently in this respect.[116]

---

112   *DA*, above note 3, s. 15.2(6)(c) & (d). See also *FLA*, above note 1, s. 33(8)(c) & (d).
113   *Moge v. Moge*, above note 92 at 879.
114   *Income Tax Act*, above note 38, s. 60(b), as amended by S.C. 1997, c. 25, s. 10(1).
115   See *Thibaudeau v. Canada (M.N.R.)*, above note 79.
116   See section B(4), "Taxation," in this chapter.

D. VARIATION

1) Child Support Orders

a) Under the *Divorce Act*

When the order is for child support under the *Divorce Act*, either party may apply for a variation if there has been a "change of circumstances as provided for in the applicable guidelines" since the making of the order or the last variation.[117] According to the Guidelines: where a table was involved in determining the amount, a change in circumstances means any change "that would result in a different child support order or any provision thereof"; and where no table was involved in determining the amount, "any change in the conditions, means, needs or other circumstances of either spouse or of any child who is entitled to support" is a change in circumstances.[118] Any variation must be made "in accordance with the applicable guidelines."[119]

Essentially, this will mean that in straightforward, simple cases, variation will be possible where the payor's income has changed, or where the number of children of the marriage changes. In more complex cases involving tables, the likelihood of variation may be clear if the original amount was based in part on a discernible fact that has changed. This may be so, for example, where an order was made on the basis of "undue hardship"; when such orders are made the court must "record its reasons" for making the order,[120] and it may be possible to see that things have changed such that the reasons no longer obtain. Or, where there were amounts originally ordered for special expenses such as extracurricular activities, variation would be possible when these activities cease.[121]

It is important to note that the recent amendment of the *Divorce Act* is itself deemed to be a change of circumstances with respect to orders made before 1 May 1997.[122] This means that either spouse may successfully obtain variation of a child support order made before the imposition of the Guidelines simply by asking for it, and, thus, the application of the Guidelines to the situation of the children of the marriage.

---

117   *DA*, above note 3, s. 17(4). A party may apply for "variation" simply in order to have the new guidelines apply.

118   The Guidelines, above note 12, s. 14(a) & (b).

119   *DA*, above note 3, s. 17(6.1).

120   The Guidelines, above note 12, s. 10(6). See section B(2)(d)(vii), "Undue Hardship," in this chapter.

121   See section B(2)(c), "Special or Extraordinary Expenses," in this chapter.

122   The Guidelines, above note 12, s. 14(c).

b) Under the *Family Law Act*

Under the Ontario legislation, variation of child support orders is possible "if the court is satisfied that there has been a change in circumstances within the meaning of the child support guidelines or that evidence not available on the previous hearing has become available."[123]

For variation of an order of spousal support, there must have been "a material change in circumstances" or evidence must become available that was "not available on the previous hearing."[124] Thus, an applicant for variation must, in effect, persuade the court that the original order would have been different if the changed circumstances had then obtained or the fresh evidence had then been before the court. The possibility of variation does not, however, imply a full relitigation of the issue; the original order is presumed correct, on the evidence as it was then presented.

No application for variation may be brought within six months of the making of the order sought to be varied, unless the court gives leave.[125]

Spousal support orders under the *Family Law Act* may be indexed such that they increase annually by the percentage change in the Consumer Price Index for Canada.[126]

2) Spousal Support Orders

a) Under the *Divorce Act*

Before varying an order for spousal support, "the court shall satisfy itself that a change in the condition, means, needs or other circumstances of either former spouse has occurred" since the order sought to be varied, and "in making the variation order, the court shall take that change into consideration."[127] Presumably, the latter provision means that the change must be a relevant or material change, one that would in fact make a difference to the amount of an order.

As was noted above, application for variation is not an opportunity to appeal the original order: the order sought to be varied is presumed to be correct. There must be an attempt, therefore, to acquaint the second

---

123   *FLA*, above note 1, s. 37(2.1).
124   *Ibid.*, s. 37(2). The court is explicitly given power under this provision to vary the order prospectively or retroactively, including the power to dispense with any arrears.
125   *Ibid.*, s. 37(3).
126   *Ibid.*, s. 34(5) & (6). Orders not originally indexed may be later indexed (for the prior year and thereafter) if the court considers this appropriate: s. 38(2) & (3).
127   *DA*, above note 3, s. 17(4.1).

court with the position occupied by the first court and the parties before it. What was then known becomes the starting point, such that a fact known when the original order was made cannot be subsequently relied upon as a changed circumstance, for instance. If the first court had (or might reasonably have) anticipated the changed circumstance relied upon and already taken it into account when making the original order, variation should not be permitted.

b) Under the *Family Law Act*

See section D(1)(b), "Under the *Family Law Act*," in this chapter for the principles governing variation under the Ontario legislation.

E. THE ROLE OF CONTRACT

Spouses and parents may seek to keep the settlement of their affairs within their own hands and, among other things, to provide for support payments, or the waiver of the right to support, through the mechanism of separation agreements.[128] However, agreements have a limited ability to control rights and obligations concerning support.

Spouses cannot by their agreement oust the jurisdiction of the court to make support orders under the *Divorce Act*.[129] The *DA* makes clear, indeed, that an agreement respecting support is one factor among others to be considered by a court when making an order for spousal support.[130] However, the Supreme Court in three important cases (decided under the 1968 *Divorce Act*, but after it had been replaced by a version of the current statute) ruled that considerable deference ought to be given to spouses' contracts when these were made in final settlement of their affairs. It held that before a court takes jurisdiction and substitutes its opinion for that of the parties as to the amount of support, there must be a radical unforeseen change of circumstances since the making of the agreement and as well "some causal connection between the changed circumstances and the marriage."[131]

The rule of deference applied whether the application was for an original order for spousal support in spite of a previous agreement,[132] or

---

128   See chapter 13 for a general discussion of separation agreements.
129   *Hyman* v. *Hyman*, [1929] A.C. 601 (H.L.); *Pelech* v. *Pelech*, above note 99.
130   *DA*, above note 3, s. 15.2(4)(c).
131   *Pelech* v. *Pelech*, above note 99 at 850 & 851; see also *Richardson* v. *Richardson*, *Caron* v. *Caron*, above note 100.
132   As, for instance, in *Richardson* v. *Richardson*, above note 100.

whether it was for a variation of an order incorporating an agreement between the parties.[133]

This *Pelech* standard, which was higher than the previous "material change" threshold, has since been doubted, and replaced in some provinces.[134] The majority judgment of the Supreme Court in *Moge* deliberately declined to rule on whether the *Pelech* test continued to apply when there was a final agreement, but the basic thrust of that judgment appeared to cast doubt on its continued validity.[135] More explicitly, in *B.(G.)* v. *G.(L.)* in the minority judgment, L'Heureux-Dubé J. said the test no longer applied[136] and that

> such agreements are only one factor . . . which must be considered in the exercise of the judge's discretionary power . . . The weight to be given to agreements will depend, first, on the extent to which the agreement reflects the principles and objectives stated in s. 17 of the 1985 Act and, second, on the scope and nature of the change which has occurred, taking into account all the circumstances of the parties.[137]

The majority, however, held it unnecessary in that case to "review the application of the trilogy . . . to the support provisions of the 1985 *Divorce Act.*"

Courts in Ontario have generally continued to use the *Pelech* test.[138] In *Santosuosso* v. *Santosuosso* the Divisional Court held that

> the analysis undertaken by Wilson J. in the trilogy strikes a proper balance between respect for final informed agreements and recognition of economic dependencies resulting from the nature of the marriage relationship. This balance is not in conflict with the objectives of the Divorce Act 1985 as articulated in *Moge*.[139]

---

133 As was the case in *Caron* v. *Caron*, above note 100. See also *Santosuosso* v. *Santosuosso* (1997), 32 O.R. (3d) 143 at 153 (Div. Ct.).

134 See: *Stroud* v. *Stroud* (1996), 20 R.F.L. (4th) 392 (B.C.C.A.); *Ginn* v. *Ginn* (1995), 11 R.F.L. (4th) 377 (Alta. Q.B.).

135 *Moge* v. *Moge*, above note 92 at 839, L'Heureux-Dubé: "I leave for another day the question of causal connection under the Act which was discussed in the trilogy in the particular context of a final settlement under the [1968] Divorce Act."

136 [1995] 3 S.C.R. 370 at 393: "The specific point at issue is whether the criteria set out in the trilogy should continue to be applied under the 1985 [Divorce] Act. In my opinion, the answer must be no."

137 *Ibid.* at 398.

138 See J. McLeod, Annotation of *Kilpatrick* v. *Kilpatrick* (1997), 27 R.F.L. (4th) 296 (B.C.S.C.).

139 Above note 133 at 153, Corbett J.

Child support, however, is a different matter. In *Richardson* v. *Richardson* the Supreme Court made clear that "a spouse cannot barter away his or her child's right to support in a settlement agreement. The court is always free to intervene and determine the appropriate level of support for the child."[140] In a later decision the Court observed that an agreement between spouses operates as "strong evidence that at the time each accepted its terms as adequately providing for the needs of the children."[141]

Now, under the revised *DA* and accompanying Guidelines, it would seem that contracts between parents will play an even more limited role upon applications for child support. A spouse is free to apply for child support even when there is an agreement; the amount of any order is to be determined through the use of the Guidelines, and, presumptively, will be the table amount plus extraordinary expenses.[142] But a court may award an amount that is different from the Guideline amount "on the consent of both spouses if it is satisfied that reasonable arrangements have been made for the support of the child to whom the order relates."[143] In considering this, the court must "have regard to the applicable guidelines." Thus, parties can give some effect to an agreement regarding child support to the extent that they are able to persuade a court to make a consent order on their terms.[144]

Under the *Family Law Act*, domestic contracts may be filed with the Ontario Court (Provincial Division) and a provision for spousal support therein "may be varied . . . as if it were an order of the court."[145] As was seen above, this means that if there has been a "material change in circumstances" the filed agreement will be varied. As well, it should be noted that the *FLA* provides that a court disregard any provision of a domestic contract affecting a child if it would be in the best interests of the child to do so.[146]

---

140   Above note 100 at 869–70.

141   *Willick* v. *Willick*, [1994] 3 S.C.R. 670 at 687, Sopinka J.

142   See section B(1)(a)(i), "The Obligation," in this chapter.

143   *DA*, above note 3, s. 15.1(7).

144   See also B(2)(d)(ii), "Special Provisions for Child," in this chapter.

145   *FLA*, above note 1, s. 35(1) & (2). This applies unless there is an agreement to the contrary: s. 35(4). Note that the section speaks of "a provision for support" and does not expressly include the waiver of a right to support, as, for example, s. 33(4)(a) does in a different context.

146   *Ibid.*, s. 56(1).

F. THE PROBLEM OF OVERLAPPING JURISDICTION (REVISITED)

Both the federal and provincial governments have power to make laws respecting support (and custody). This matter of overlapping jurisdictions was discussed in some detail in respect of custody and will only be addressed here briefly.[147]

As was the case with respect to custody, the Ontario legislation seeks to direct traffic, so to speak, in some aspects of the matter, providing that the commencement of proceedings under the *Divorce Act* stays any uncompleted application under the *Family Law Act*, unless the court orders otherwise; and if the divorce court does not adjudicate the issue of support, any earlier provincial order continues in force.[148] The implication of this provision is that where an order for support is made under the *Divorce Act*, any earlier provincial order is no longer in force. A further implication, though less clear, is that when an order for support is made under the *Divorce Act*, no subsequent order may be made under the provincial act.

Provincial legislation cannot, of course, determine its own constitutional authority. But it would seem that the scheme described fairly accurately captures the courts' view of the constitutional situation.

Potential conflicts are governed by the paramountcy doctrine, which renders inoperative provincial legislation or orders made under it, when there is an "express contradiction" between provisions or orders under the competing pieces of legislation. There may be a problem in knowing when two orders for support are in conflict because of the arithmetical nature of the orders: an order that the defendant pay $1,000 is compatible with an order that he or she pay $500 in that a payment of the larger amount will include necessarily payment of the lesser. (Some have suggested that there is no conflict because both can be complied with by paying their sum—$1,500.) The only sensible view is that a support order means "pay this amount and no less and no more," and, so, orders in different amounts are in conflict.

---

147 See section G, "Overlapping Jurisdictions," in chapter 10, "Custody and Access."
148 *FLA*, above note 1, s. 36(1) & (3).

FURTHER READINGS

MacDonald, J.C., *et al.*, *Law and Practice under the* Family Law Act *of Ontario*, rev. ed. (Toronto: Carswell, 1994) looseleaf service, Part III

MacDonald, J.C., & A.C. Wilton, *Child Support Guidelines in Divorce Proceedings: A Manual* (Scarborough, Ont.: Carswell, 1997)

Finnie, R., *Good Idea, Bad Execution: The Government's Child Support Package* (Ottawa: The Caledon Institute of Social Policy, 1996)

Davies, C., "The Emergence of Judicial Child Support Guidelines" (1995–1996) 13 C.F.L.Q. 89

Wilson, J., *Wilson on Children and the Law* (Toronto: Butterworths, 1994) looseleaf service, c. 4

CHAPTER 13

SEPARATION AGREEMENTS

A. INTRODUCTION

Contracts do not play much of a role in the functioning of happy families. The wealthy have for a considerable period of time made use of pre-nuptial contracts concerning property, of course. But in modern times, certainly, the largest role for contracts has been when families break up and amicable accord is replaced by conflict and dispute; it is then that contract, in the form of the separation agreement, proves especially useful.

The law of contracts was developed and has its greatest use in the commercial context, and there is some difficulty in knowing how properly to apply it or modify it to suit the needs of broken families.[1] In the last few decades the provincial legislatures have provided some direction in this respect; but, even so, a good many issues still remain unclear about the applicability of the general law of contract in this context.

In Ontario, the *Family Law Act* establishes a class of "domestic contracts" that includes a "separation agreement,"[2] the device that separated couples typically use to resolve their disputes over custody, property, and

---

1 See, for example, *Stark* v. *Stark* (1990) 71 D.L.R. (4th) 446 (B.C.C.A.), leave to appeal to S.C.C. refused (1991), 53 B.C.L.R. (2d) xxxi (note), 77 D.L.R. (4th) vii (note).
2 R.S.O. 1990, c. F.3, as amended by S.O. 1992, c. 32, s. 12; S.O. 1993, c. 27, Sched., s. 51. [*FLA* or the Act]. The *FLA* provides in s. 2(10) that a domestic contract "prevails" over any provision of the Act "unless this Act provides otherwise."

support. It is not clear whether the Act intends to capture for itself the whole field of agreements between separating couples, and thus exclude the general law of contracts, or only to provide special benefits to those agreements that meet the definition and other strictures of the statute, although the latter view seems the one most likely to find favour with the courts.

Parties do not need to be married in order to make a separation agreement, but it is required, perhaps logically, that they must first have cohabited[3] and then be living separate and apart[4] at the time they enter into the separation agreement.[5] Only heterosexual couples may make a separation agreement, at least according to the language of the Act.[6]

Unlike marriage contracts and cohabitation agreements, separation agreements under the Act are essentially unfettered as to scope. The parties may agree respecting property, spousal and child support, custody of and access to their children, and, indeed, "any other matter in the settlement of their affairs."[7] As just suggested, the Act imposes some requirements on separation agreements in order for them to be valid and enforceable, aiming essentially to strike a balance between the supposed market values of freedom and certainty in commitment, on the one hand, and those values said to operate in the family context such as fairness and caring, on the other hand.

---

3   "Cohabit" is defined in the *FLA, ibid.,* to mean "live together in a conjugal relationship, whether within or outside marriage": s. 1(1). See also section B(2)(b), "Persons Who Cohabit," in chapter 4, "Cohabitation."

4   The Act, *ibid.,* does not define the phrase "separate and apart"; it is used under the *Divorce Act,* S.C. 1986, c. 4, where it has received some considerable judicial consideration: see section B(3), "By Reason of Living Separate and Apart," in chapter 9, "Divorce."

5   *FLA,* above note 2, s. 54. See chapter 3 concerning marriage contracts and cohabitation agreements. As to cohabitation outside marriage generally, see chapter 4.

6   "A man and a woman . . ." *Ibid.,* s. 54. This same phrase has been held to be in violation of the *Canadian Charter of Rights and Freedoms,* Part 1 of the *Constitution Act, 1982,* being Schedule B to the *Canada Act 1982* (U.K.), 1982, c. 11 [*Charter*], when used in s. 29 of the Act to define "spouse" for the purposes of support obligations: see section B(2)(a), "A Man and a Woman," in chapter 4, "Cohabitation." See also the discussion of whether same-sex couples may enter into cohabitation agreements, another form of "domestic contract" under the Act: section B(1), "A Man and a Woman," in chapter 3, "Cohabitation Agreements."

7   *Ibid.* For restrictions on the scope of cohabitation agreements and marriage contracts, see section C, "Scope of the Agreement," in chapter 3, "Cohabitation Agreements." It may be important to point out especially that, unlike couples entering a marriage contract, separated couples who are married are free to contract respecting a spouse's Part II rights in a matrimonial home: see *FLA,* above note 2, s. 52(2).

In most cases separation agreements take considerable time to become fully executed, commonly providing for periodic payment of support and regular access to children of the relationship across a period of months or years. As well, many separated couples find it difficult to be friendly until a long time after the break-up of their relationship, and some even find mere civility a burden. For both these reasons separation agreements are a special breed of contract, imposing special burdens on the parties and their advisers to negotiate to clear and full agreement, despite a situation that may well be characterized by pain and anger.

Furthermore, because separation agreements typically have long lives, their makers must anticipate how the circumstances of the parties will change, if the agreements are to remain useful in fact. Foresight is limited, even in the most acute of parties and their advisers, and therefore provision might well be made in the contract for adjusting the terms of the agreement when required, either according to a prescribed formula or plan, or pursuant to the direction of some arbitrator, for example. Of course, different contracting parties will differ as to whether and how changed circumstances ought to be accommodated by changes in their agreements, some preferring more fixity, others greater flexibility.

It can also be helpful to anticipate difficulties of interpretation during the life of a separation agreement, and to provide from the outset in the contract for means of resolving such disagreements through arbitration or mediation, for example. Resort to the courts is always possible to settle differences of interpretation, of course, but this is likely to be more expensive and stressful than the use of alternative means of dispute resolution.

B. LIMITS ON CONTRACT[8]

1) Validity

a) General Scope

A contract must be valid for it to have any effect, or, indeed, even to exist as such. Section 56 of the *FLA* addresses validity[9] and provides in

---

8   The basic three-stage structure of the analysis that follows is taken from the work of Professor James G. McLeod: see Annotation to *Grant-Hose* v. *Grant-Hose* (1991), 32 R.F.L. (3d) 26 (Ont. U.F.C.).

9   See *Grant-Hose* v. *Grant-Hose, ibid.*, treating s. 56 as going to validity, and not merely enforceability or the ability of the court to override the agreement. The provisions of s. 56(4) as to validity cannot be contracted out of: s. 56(7).

subsection (4)(c) that a court may "set aside a domestic contract or a provision in it[10] . . . in accordance with the law of contract." Contracts may be declared void or nullified on various bases, such as duress, mistake, *non est factum*, fraud, material misrepresentation, undue influence, unconscionability, inequality in bargaining power—all typically going to defects in the formation of the agreement.[11]

Courts have generally taken the position that, absent proof of invalidity, a separation agreement ought to be regarded as valid and, subject to other considerations raised in the following material, enforced according to its terms.[12] Thus, the onus is typically placed upon the party seeking to upset the agreement to show that it is invalid. Where, however, a contract is "unconscionable and improvident on its face," the onus shifts to the party relying on it to persuade the court that the bargain was not arrived at through fraud, undue influence, or other unconscionable conduct.[13]

b) Unfair Advantage

Perhaps the most frequently used common law basis on which it is sought to set aside a separation agreement is that described in the case of *Mundinger* v. *Mundinger*.[14] The Ontario Court of Appeal stated that equity was concerned to protect the weaker party, not against his or her own foolishness, but against the stronger party's taking advantage of the weaker, and it adopted a commentator's analysis that

> [i]f the bargain is fair the fact that the parties were not equally vigilant of their interest is immaterial. Likewise if one was not preyed upon by the other, an improvident or even grossly inadequate consideration is no ground upon which to set aside a contract freely entered into. It is the combination of inequality and improvidence which alone may invoke this jurisdiction. Then the onus is placed upon the party seeking to uphold the contract to show that his conduct throughout was scrupulously considerate of the other's interests.[15]

---

10   The issue of severability becomes important in this respect.

11   See *The Canadian Encyclopedic Digest (Ontario)*, 3rd ed., Vol. 5, Title 32, Part VII, for a general statement of validity in the law of contract.

12   See, for example, *Dal Santo* v. *Dal Santo* (1975), 21 R.F.L. 117 (B.C.S.C.).

13   *Mundinger* v. *Mundinger*, [1969] 1 O.R. 606 (C.A.), aff'd (1970), 14 D.L.R. (3d) 256 (S.C.C.).

14   *Ibid.*

15   *Ibid.* at 609–10, quoting B. Crawford (1966) 44 Can. Bar Rev. 142 at 143.

Inequality in bargaining power may result from any of various aspects of the parties' circumstances such as "abuse or intimidation or . . . learning or other disability . . . anxiety or stress or a nervous break-down or indulgence in drugs or alcohol."[16] The inequality must lead to a bargain that is seriously improvident, something that may not always be easy to determine. Quite apart from the fact that reasonable people may differ as to when the improvidence becomes too great, a separation agreement is not simply a linear matter, in which one value must increase or decrease in regular increments; it is rather the resolution of various issues, the importance of some of which may only be weighed on the idiosyncratic scales of the parties.

c) Failure to Disclose

The *FLA* gives the court the power to set aside a contract or a term of it "if a party failed to disclose to the other significant assets, or significant debts or other liabilities, existing when the domestic contract was made."[17] Although the explicit reference is to assets, debts, and liabilities, a court has held that the duty extends to changes in income.[18] It would seem that the duty imposed by the Act is to provide information upon request or when circumstances are such that a request for information can reasonably be inferred.[19] There need not be a formal disclosure of information: the provision aims at ensuring the parties have the knowledge needed to reach an appropriate agreement; thus, where the court is satisfied that a party was aware of the other's financial situation, the agreement will not be invalid.[20]

---

16 *Rosen* v. *Rosen* (1994), 18 O.R. (3d) 641 at 645, 646 (C.A.), application for leave to appeal dismissed (16 February 1995), S.C.C. Bulletin, 1995, p. 340. There may be still a species of equitable wrong known as "undue influence" that means to describe advantage accruing from "a longstanding relationship of control and dominance": see J. McLeod, Annotation to *Sartor* v. *Sartor* (1993), 45 R.F.L. (3d) 250 at 251; see also J. McLeod, Annotation to *Zegil* v. *Zegil* (1992), 41 R.F.L. (3d) 49 at 53: "[I]t is questionable whether any difference between undue influence and unconscionability exists today. Interestingly, the courts seem to be moving toward a general duty to bargain in good faith." For a recent instance of undue influence, said to be a defect going to the sufficiency of consent, see *S.M.B.* v. *K.R.B.*, [1997] O.J. No. 3199 (Gen. Div.).

17 *FLA*, above note 2, s. 56(4)(a).

18 *Underwood* v. *Underwood* (1995), 11 R.F.L. (4th) 361 (Ont. Div. Ct.), deciding that the right to an income stream is an asset, at least for this purpose, and ought to have been disclosed when the change occurred during negotiation of a settlement.

19 See *Farquar* v. *Farquar* (1983), 43 O.R. (2d) 423 (C.A.).

20 See: *Lecot* v. *Lecot* (1995), 19 R.F.L. (4th) 14 (Ont. Gen. Div.); *Brosseau* v. *Shemilt* (1995), 16 R.F.L. (4th) 129 (Ont. Gen. Div.).

There are other sources of a duty to disclose information that would typically be relevant when negotiating a separation agreement. Section 8 of the Act requires that each party to an application respecting equalization of net family property provide the other with a sworn statement "disclosing particulars of . . . the party's property and debts and other liabilities." When child support is claimed under the *Divorce Act*, the respondent must provide the custodial parent with extensive financial information, and, indeed, income tax returns for the three previous years.[21]

Duties to disclose relate to fairness, of course, in that the possession of information may give one party a superior bargaining position and, so, an ability to exact an unfair bargain. The broader question is how far the courts are prepared to go in seeking to ensure that parties to a domestic contract are evenly matched in power. It is generally assumed that domestic contracts are not contracts *uberrimae fidei* (utmost good faith),[22] in which full disclosure of all facts, requested or not, is a positive duty, but the situation is not entirely clear.[23]

d) Lack of Understanding

A domestic contract may be set aside, pursuant to section 56(4)(b), if "a party did not understand the nature or consequences" of the agreement. In a fundamental sense, understanding is central to the very notion of contract: there ought to be informed consent to an arrangement, which is what, after all, gives contract its moral legitimacy as a legal tool. More elaborately, full understanding relates to the possibility of striking a bargain that is fair, a special anxiety in the family law context, as has been seen.

Because a separation agreement typically deals with very important and complex issues, entailing an appreciation of difficult family laws, the understanding required by this provision is best obtained by ensuring that each party to the contract has competent, independent legal

---

21   *Federal Child Support Guidelines*, SOR/97-175, s. 21(2).

22   See *Stern v. Sheps*, [1968] S.C.R. 834, where the court said that not all pre-nuptial agreements were to be regarded as *uberrimae fidei* but failed to opine which ought to be so regarded. See also *Murray v. Murray* (1994), 10 R.F.L. (4th) (C.A.), which points out the problems that would result if domestic contracts were treated as *uberrimae fidei*.

23   See: *Underwood v. Underwood* (1994), 113 D.L.R. (4th) 571 (Ont. Gen. Div.), holding that separation agreements are *uberrimae fidei*; aff'd in part (1995), 11 R.F.L. (4th) 361 (Ont. Div. Ct.), deciding that full financial disclosure is necessary; *Stutt v. Stutt*, [1993] O.J. No. 2149 (Prov. Ct.), deciding that a contract for child support was invalid because of the wife's failure to disclose that the husband was not the biological father of the child. See also *Kristoff v. Kristoff* (1987), 59 O.R. (2d) 464 (Ont. Dist. Ct.).

advice. Legal advice is not a requirement, however.[24] Nor is it an obligation of one party to ensure that the other has legal advice;[25] it is enough
that it is available to the other.[26] Thus, even though the court was of the
opinion that "had [the wife] consulted a reasonably competent lawyer
for advice at the time of signing he or she would have advised against
signing, not because of oppression by the husband but because it was
not a good bargain for the wife," the contract was not invalid because
she had chosen foolishly not to obtain legal advice.[27]

2) Enforceability

a) Formality Requirements
Domestic contracts must be "in writing, signed by the parties and witnessed, if they are to be enforceable.[28] However, the courts have held
that minutes of settlement of litigation may be less formal than this and
still be capable of enforcement, a view that supports the "established
policy of encouraging the settlement of disputed claims and recognizing
and preserving the validity of settlements freely and properly entered
into under advice."[29]

A court considering whether to uphold informal minutes of settlement might ask the following questions:

1. Were either of the parties represented by legal counsel or the beneficiary of legal advice?
2. Was either party otherwise disadvantaged at any time during the
   course of the negotiations?
3. Can the written material the parties prepared, or the oral representations, that are being relied upon support a prima facie conclusion
   that either constitutes a settlement agreement?

---

24 See *Kristoff* v. *Kristoff*, *ibid*.
25 *Ablaka* v. *Ablaka* (1991), 32 R.F.L. (3d) 369 (Ont. U.F.C.).
26 *Settle-Beyrouty* v. *Beyrouty* (1996), 24 R.F.L. (4th) 318 (Ont. Gen. Div.).
27 *Rosen* v. *Rosen*, above note 16; the Ontario Court of Appeal was considering both s.
    56(4) of the Act and unconscionability generally, and (at 645) quoted B. Crawford
    to the effect that "even grossly inadequate consideration is no ground upon which
    to set aside a contract freely entered into."
28 *FLA*, above note 2, s. 55.
29 *Geropoulos* v. *Geropoulos* (1982), 35 O.R. (2d) 763 at 769 (C.A.); see also *Harris* v.
    Harris, [1996] O.J. No. 2430 (Gen. Div.); but see *Thornton* v. *Thornton* (1983), 33
    R.F.L. (2d) 266 (C.A.), where the settlement was not upheld because the client had
    not properly authorized it.

4. Does the evidence demonstrate that the parties intended that the written or oral representations or negotiations are to be binding on them?

5. Was there an intention that some final act or determination be made before the settlement was to be final and binding?

6. Does the enforcement or non-enforcement of the negotiated resolution result in an injustice to either of the parties?

7. Does enforcement encourage negotiated settlement and discourage litigation and does it support the overall purpose and intent of the principles of the Family Law Act?[30]

Despite the language of section 55, which appears to invite no exercise of discretion, courts have held that a separation agreement need not be witnessed to be enforceable.[31] The argument in favour of enforceability in such cases seems to depend upon a finding that the parties intended to produce the result argued for, which is not particularly responsive to the specific formality requirement.

b) Requirement to Be Chaste

At one time it was common for husbands to stipulate in separation agreements that support would be provided as long as a wife remained chaste. Any such *dum casta* provision (as the clause was known) is nowadays unenforceable.[32] It is, however, permissible to create a contingency on marriage or cohabitation with another person.

c) Utility of Unenforceable Agreements

A valid contract that is unenforceable might nevertheless have some utility. The classic view is that a party may not obtain the assistance of the court to give effect to rights acquired under such a contract. This may mean that acts performed pursuant to an unenforceable separation agreement, such as the transfer of title to property, may be legally effective and incapable of being undone when the contract is found to be unenforceable. It seems unlikely that the remedy of self-help to obtain rights under an unenforceable separation agreement will be of much use to parties, and, indeed, would probably be frowned on by the courts.

---

30 *Harris* v. *Harris, ibid.* at para. 10. Many of the concerns expressed in these questions are shared by courts considering unconscionability and undue influence.

31 *Lecot* v. *Lecot*, above note 20, deciding to give effect to a homemade separation agreement that was written and signed, but not witnessed. See also *Hyldtoft* v. *Hyldtoft* (1991), 33 R.F.L. (3d) 99 (Ont. Gen. Div.).

32 *FLA*, above note 2, s. 56(2).

More useful, perhaps, would be the effect of a valid but unenforceable agreement in the context of an application for a support order under the *Divorce Act*. There, presumably, the court could follow the doctrine established in *Pelech* v. *Pelech*[33] and decline to substitute a court order for the terms agreed to by the parties, since nowhere in the *Divorce Act* or in the *Pelech* doctrine is the formality of the agreement made important.

It might also be worth noting that a court may have regard to "a written agreement between the spouses that is not a domestic contract" when considering whether to deviate from an equalizing share of the net family property;[34] it seems probable that a contract that is unenforceable as a domestic contract for want of formality might nevertheless be "a written agreement" for this purpose.

3) Power to Override

a) General Scope
There are a number of instances when a court has the power to override a valid, enforceable separation agreement, in order, typically, to substitute a ruling of its own for the term in the contract. Ordinarily, parties to a separation agreement will agree to give up any rights they may have against the other under statute or common law in return for the rights created in the agreement. Such agreements can clearly prevail respecting property matters generally.[35] But public policy prevents the parties from irretrievably bargaining away certain other rights.

b) Respecting Children
Parents are not permitted to agree authoritatively as to the rights of their children. Thus, section 56(1) of the *FLA* provides that

> [i]n the determination of a matter respecting the support, education, moral training or custody of or access to a child, the court may disregard any provision of a domestic contract pertaining to the matter where, in the opinion of the court, to do so is in the best interests of the child.

---

33 [1987] 1 S.C.R. 801. See section C(2)(c)(i), "Stage One: The "Causal Connection" Principle," in chapter 12, "Financial Support."

34 *FLA*, above note 2, s. 5(6)(g).

35 *FLA*, above note 2, s. 2(10), provides that contract prevails over the Act unless the Act provides otherwise, which it does not, where Part I rights are concerned, or where Part II rights are concerned, once the parties have separated and contract in the form of a separation agreement.

The party who seeks to upset the provision in the agreement has the onus of persuading the court as to the interests of the child.

Although there is no such provision under the *Divorce Act*, it is clear that an agreement may not oust the jurisdiction of the court to make an order for corollary relief (which includes child support, custody, or access) under that statute where the court thinks it appropriate.[36] It would seem that if either party can persuade the court that the interests of the child require it, a term of an agreement will be ignored and an order substituted for it.[37]

c) Respecting Spousal Support

As has just been seen, no contract can oust the jurisdiction of the court to make an order for corollary relief under the *Divorce Act*. However, in a trio of cases the Supreme Court decided that as a general matter separation agreements should be respected by the courts, and the jurisdiction to make an order for support under the *Divorce Act* ought not to be exercised unless, since the making of the contract, there had been a radical, unforeseen change in circumstances causally connected to the marriage.[38] Although this high threshold has since been doubted, and indeed altered by some courts, it apparently remains the law in Ontario.[39]

Under the *Family Law Act*, a number of provisions make it possible for the court to override the terms of a separation agreement respecting spousal support. Pursuant to section 33(4) the court may "set aside"[40] a provision for or the waiver of a right to support, despite any provision to the contrary in the contract where the provision would result in "unconscionable circumstances," or the applicant for support is qualified for public welfare assistance, or the payor under the agreement is in default when the application for support is made. In determining whether "unconscionable circumstances" have resulted from a contractual provision respecting support, courts have considered a wide range of matters, including facts surrounding the creation of the agreement,

---

36   See: *Pelech* v. *Pelech*, above note 33; *Caron* v. *Caron*, [1987] 1 S.C.R. 892; *Richardson* v. *Richardson*, [1987] 1 S.C.R. 857.

37   See *Richardson* v. *Richardson*, *ibid.* at 869–70.

38   Above note 36. See section E, "The Role of Contract," in chapter 12, "Financial Support."

39   *Ibid.*

40   It may be more accurate to regard this as enabling a court to invalidate a support provision, rather than permitting a valid term to be overridden, although little may hang on the distinction. Presumably, however, the terms of an agreement may be construed to be sufficiently interdependent that an invalid support provision cannot be severed from the rest and so brings the whole contract down.

the effect that the provision respecting support had on the financial circumstances of the parties (and, so, other factors affecting their financial circumstances, such as the parties' behaviour), and the current and likely future circumstances of the parties.[41] It may be that the policy behind *Pelech* and the other cases under the *Divorce Act* of respecting settlements will affect a court's willingness to exercise its discretion to find that an agreement should be set aside as resulting in unconscionable circumstances.[42]

The *FLA* permits a party to a domestic contract to file that contract with the Ontario Court (Provincial Division) and to have "a provision for support or maintenance" in that agreement enforced or varied "as if it were an order of the court."[43] However, contracting parties are permitted to provide in a separation agreement that variation in this way will not be possible.[44] Variation of a support order under the Act is permitted where the court is satisfied that either evidence exists that was not available at the previous hearing, which in this context presumably means at the time of the making of the agreement, or there has been a "material change" in the circumstances of either of the parties since the last order (viz, agreement) was made.[45]

---

41 See, for example, *Newby* v. *Newby* (1986), 56 O.R. (2d) 483 (H.C.); *Lecot* v. *Lecot*, above note 20; *Farn* v. *Lewis*, [1994] O.J. No. 1692 (Prov. Div.). It has been held that the limitation period in s. 50 of the Act (two years from separation or from default under a contract providing for support on separation) applies to applications for order of support even when combined with a claim of unconscionable circumstances: *Bell* v. *Bell*, [1997] O.J. No. 2584 (Gen. Div.).

42 See *Hartwick* v. *Hartwick-Buchanan*, [1996] O.J. No. 2208 (Prov. Div.), where the court found that because "the intent of the parties to this agreement could not be clearer . . . [i]n order for this court to exercise its discretion to override that intent, the degree of unconscionability must be very, very high indeed."

43 *FLA*, above note 2, s. 35(1) & (2).

44 *Ibid.*, s. 35(4). The Act explicitly provides that filing and enforcement of agreements as orders cannot be prevented by contract. The omission of variation clearly licenses contracting out of this possibility. See *O'Connor* v. *O'Connor*, [1990] O.J. No. 2693 (Prov. Ct.). The Act provides in s. 35(3), however, that the ability to set aside in unconscionable circumstances, etc., still applies to filed contracts, and thus it would be possible to set aside a term that purports to prevent a court from varying a filed agreement.

45 *FLA*, above note 2, s. 37(2). See section D(1)(b), "Under the *Family Law Act*," in chapter 12, "Financial Support." It has been held that the limitation period under s. 50 for bringing an application for support does not apply to variation of the term in a contract in this way: *Santosuosso* v. *Santosuosso*, [1992] O.J. No. 2982 (Prov. Div.).

FURTHER READINGS

MacDonald, J.C., *et al.*, *Law and Practice under the* Family Law Act *of Ontario*, rev. ed. (Toronto: Carswell, 1994) looseleaf service, Part IV

CHAPTER 14

CONCLUSION

Change is the constant element in family law at the present time. Few would be bold enough to predict the destination to which current forces for change will take us, but it may be less challenging to identify the shape of these forces as they now appear.

Although the word "family" is not a term of art in law, it is the word that best summarizes the catalogue of legal relations between adults, and between adults and children, that has been explored in this book. The first observation, then, is that the legal meaning of family continues to expand. As we have seen, cohabitants may be obliged to support each other, may acquire the legal rights and obligations of parents, and may contract for property and other rights. The Ontario Law Reform Commission has recommended that same-sex couples be accorded many of the rights and obligations traditionally restricted to married persons; and the courts have begun to require it. Indeed, the former, in proposing the "registered domestic partnership," comes close to redefining family as any consensual association.

Another way to say this is to observe that marriage itself declines in legal importance, and, together with divorce, now forms slender parentheses surrounding the "real" legal issues of substance: custody, support, and property. Law is, as it were, getting out of the business of marriage and divorce.

It would appear that intimacy *per se* is a value now, one that increasingly finds recognition in *Charter*[1] protections and legal rights and

---

1   *Canadian Charter of Rights and Freedoms*, Part 1 of the *Constitution Act, 1982*, being Schedule B to the *Canada Act 1982* (U.K.), 1982, c. 11 [*Charter*].

duties. This is the movement from perceived form—rites and ceremonies—to perceived substance, a completing, perhaps, of the law's long slow turn from status to contract. Intimacy is also the terrain of morals, mores, and religion, some of which are at odds with this sanctioning by law of ever more sorts of relation. Yet, law's movement away from the formalities permits other institutions to assume responsibility for them: particular rites or customs may now become important for their practitioners in a way they could not be before, when the state was truly and not merely perfunctorily interested in marriage and divorce.

It is clear that Canada is not a homogeneous society in the way that it was once thought to be. Immigrant groups and Aboriginal peoples present their cultures as being important and worthy of recognition within our mainstream legal structure. Family matters—the forms of intimacy—are among the most important aspects of a culture, and family law will continue to confront the matter of diversity and difference across a wide range of issues. Already, as we have seen, our law acknowledges in a relatively unclear way the importance of heritage to an Aboriginal child; it attempts to confront the problem that the voluntary nature of the Jewish *get* can pose for some spouses; and it worries over child-rearing practices that differ from those of the middle-class mainstream. Such issues are likely to increase in number and importance.

We have seen that family law functions in part as a means whereby those who have been traditionally excluded from the market may make their claim on a share of society's resources: the family functions as an important distributive mechanism within the capitalist system. But a claim by a woman to participate in the wealth or income of her spouse causes us to examine the broad issues of who must and who may work, what counts as work, and which work is done for love and which for money. As a consequence, we are changing the perceived relationship of family and the economy, such that in law we less and less see them as separate spheres of activity. Whether the reality is changing as well as our perception remains to be seen. But it seems clear that the issue of equality will continue to be debated in this context.

In all of this, family law turns often to other professions. Social work, psychology, economics, accounting, medicine, and many others are increasingly integrated with law, as we come to see that the institution of the family is not tractable to legal understanding alone. The limits of this cooperation have not yet been tested. There is a tendency, perhaps decreasing, for the legal profession (along with the rest of society) to expect clear "objective" answers from experts to questions that do not admit of such answers other than through difficult political choice among competing values. It will require increasing sophistication on the part of judges, lawyers, and legislation to enable the legal system to take as much help as can be had from the other professions without abdicating that system's responsibility to make these political choices in an open, advertant way.

One of the most fruitful cooperative ventures at the present is that between lawyers and the social work and other helping professions aimed at modifying the very way in which legal disputes are resolved. Alternative dispute resolution (ADR), as it is known, has grown from small beginnings within family law to a widespread practice in law generally. As has been suggested a number of times in this book, the nature of an institution such as law will be changed when it takes seriously the concerns of another and differently constituted institution, such as the family. Its form is "informed." The move to ADR is a part of this continuing change.

However, this change is not without danger. The movement away from a rights-based approach towards a consensus approach tends to favour those who have power; that is, rights are one important means whereby people who lack it may gain and use power. It is possible, in family law, to see conciliation and mediation as essentially the perpetuation of the informal play of power that resolved disputes within the family before the dispute went public, and resolved them to the disadvantage of the relatively powerless. Once again to treat law and the family as more or less separate institutions, we could say that critics of ADR in family law worry that the law is becoming too much like the family—it may be "informed" too well, and could lose its protective, adjudicative purpose.

Perhaps contrarily we can also see in some areas an increase in rule at the expense of discretion—what might better be called a retreat from discretion. For many years family law has been characterized by rules that devolve a good deal of discretion onto decision makers: as we have seen, for instance, parties to a marriage must have the capacity to "understand" the nature of a marriage; a couple may be statutory spouses if they lived together in a "conjugal" relationship, or, better, one of "some permanence"; support is owed a spouse if that spouse has "need"; custody is decided according to the "best interests of the child." These and other broad standards permit decisions to be tailored to the contours of the very disputants. But they also permit the varying attitudes of judges to play a large role, offer little guidance to disputing parties, and allow allegations of unfairness as cases thought to be alike are treated differently.

Two decades ago, the law of matrimonial property shifted from the uncertainties of equity to a rule-bound system that now offers considerable certainty, if at the cost of fine-grained fairness. The move took place over many years and required that we become clear about the values and principles underlying the particular area of law. Very recently we have jumped from a child support law that said little more than that each child should have what he or she needs, according to the respective means of the parents, to a very elaborate system of guidelines and charts that seeks to provide clarity and better decisions for children. It seems possible that the next discretionary area to be recaptured for rule will be the law of custody and access. The best interests test has long been castigated as hopelessly vague, and the uncertainty in the courts recently has shown clearly that the standard lacks any power to guide judges in the resolution of some of the serious current problems, such as mobility rights or access by grandparents, for instance.

Finally, it might be observed that any change in the direction of detailed rules in family law has the power to shift the forum of the debate from courts to legislatures, with the consequence that the political nature of family law can be clearly seen and acted upon.

TABLE OF CASES

INDEX

ABOUT THE AUTHOR

Simon Fodden is Associate Dean of Osgoode Hall Law School at York University where he has taught family law for thirty years. Professor Fodden has written and lectured extensively on family law, welfare law and property law.